FIVE FACES OF MODERNITY

FIVE FACES OF MODERNITY

───

Modernism   Avant-Garde   Decadence

Kitsch   Postmodernism

MATEI CALINESCU

DUKE UNIVERSITY PRESS   DURHAM   1987

Seventh printing in paperback, 1999

Faces of Modernity was originally published by
Indiana University Press in 1977.

Library of Congress Cataloging-in-Publication Data
Calinescu, Matei.
Five faces of modernity.
Rev. ed. of: Faces of modernity/Matei Calinescu.
c 1977.
Bibliography. Includes index.
1. Modernism (Aesthetics) 2. Avant-garde (Aesthetics)
3. Kitsch. 4. Decadence in literature. I. Calinescu,
Matei. Faces of Modernity. II. Title.
BH301.M54C34 1987 111'.85 86-32756
ISBN 0-8223-0726-X
ISBN 0-8223-0767-7 (pbk.)

For Adriana and Irina

Now, there is an urgent need for experiment in criticism of a new kind, which will consist largely in a logical and dialectical study of the terms used. . . . In literary criticism we are constantly using terms which we cannot define, and defining other things by them. We are constantly using terms which have an *in*tension and an *ex*tension which do not quite fit: theoretically they ought to be made to fit; but if they cannot, then some other way must be found of dealing with them so that we may know at every moment what we mean.

T. S. ELIOT, "Experiment in
Criticism" (1929)

CONTENTS

THE IDEA OF MODERNITY

THE IDEA OF THE AVANT-GARDE

THE IDEA OF DECADENCE

KITSCH

ON POSTMODERNISM (1986)

PREFACE TO THE SECOND EDITION

This second edition of *Faces of Modernity* differs from the first mainly in that it contains an extensive new chapter, "On Postmodernism," written in 1986. Hence the altered title, *Five Faces of Modernity: Modernism, Avant-Garde, Decadence, Kitsch, Postmodernism.*

The single most significant change affecting the vocabulary of modernity since 1977, the year my book appeared, has been the emergence of an international concept of postmodernism. In 1977 postmodernism was still a comparatively rare and fuzzy term, used almost exclusively in America, and I felt I could deal with it appropriately in a rather brief section of the chapter "The Idea of the Avant-Garde." Today a volume on modernity lacking a more substantive treatment of postmodernism would hardly be credible.

The addition of "On Postmodernism" is by itself a major retroactive revision of the entire work. In a sense, this revision illustrates obliquely the "strategy of retraction" or "palinode," which, as I suggest in "On Postmodernism," springs from an essential quality of the postmodernist spirit.

Writing the new revisionary chapter has helped me to resist the temptation of altering the text of the first four essays in any major or minor way. However, even without changes in the earlier chapters, I feel that the sequence of thought in the present version reflects the development of my views on modernity, a modernity now revealing the latest of its intriguing faces, postmodernism.

Of course I have corrected the occasional typos or infelicities—when I spotted them. The "Selected Critical Bibliography" has been revised and updated. The major change has been, again, the addition of a new separate section devoted entirely to postmodernism. Omitted from this edition is the "Epilogue," rendered superfluous by the new final chapter.

Over the years I have published several independent essays on diverse issues of postmodernism, ranging from such general ones as the pluralist renaissance in contemporary thought to such particular ones as the status of postmodernism in the language of historical periodization.[1] Since 1977 I also have dealt at more length with aspects or themes of modernity only briefly touched upon in *Faces of Modernity*, such as, among others, the question of modernism and ideology (including politics), the philosophical metaphor of "the death of man," so widely debated, particularly on the Continent, during the 1960s and 1970s, and, in literary criticism, the conflict between poetics and new versions of hermeneutics.[2] Such outgrowths of my study were too extensive to permit even partial incorporation in the new edition. One day I will perhaps consider assimilating them into a separate volume.

I wish to acknowledge for their suggestions, insights, and animating spirit of friendship Ihab Hassan, Virgil Nemoianu, Mihai Spariosu, Marjorie Perloff, Douwe Fokkema, Ricardo Quinones, and, last but not least, Willis Barnstone, who also insisted that I undertake this new edition. My deep thanks go to my editor, Reynolds Smith of Duke University Press, for his especially warm and affirming role.

1. See items listed under my name in the "Postmodernism" section of the "Selected Critical Bibliography."
2. See items listed under my name in the "Modernity/Modernism" section of the "Selected Critical Bibliography."

ACKNOWLEDGMENTS

The possibility for undertaking and completing this book I owe mainly to the John Simon Guggenheim Memorial Foundation, which awarded me a Fellowship for the academic year 1975–76.

Part of the chapter "The Idea of the Avant-Garde" has appeared in somewhat different form as " 'Avant-Garde': Some Terminological Considerations" in the *Yearbook for Comparative and General Literature* 23 (1974). Another part of the same chapter, originally presented as a talk at the University of Chicago in the fall of 1973, has been published under the title "Avant-Garde, Neo-Avant-Garde, Postmodernism: The Culture of Crisis" in *Clio* IV, 3 (1975). An earlier and shorter version of the chapter on "Kitsch" has appeared as "The Benevolent Monster: Reflections on *Kitsch* As an Aesthetic Concept" in *Clio* VI, 1 (1976). I wish to express here my thanks to the editors of these two journals, by whose permission the above mentioned texts appear in fresh incarnations in this volume.

Other parts of the book were drafted or tried out as lectures or talks at various universities, among which I would like to acknowledge Harvard, the Claremont Colleges, the University of California at Riverside, Stanford, and the University of Massachusetts.

The manuscript has been read wholly or in part by numerous colleagues and friends who have offered valuable suggestions. At various stages of my work, Professor René Wellek's encouragement and observations have been extremely helpful. Burton Feldman has read part of the manuscript and made a number of challenging remarks, from which the whole book has benefited in more ways than I can acknowledge here. Among my colleagues at Indiana University I am particularly grateful to Willis Barnstone (who chastened my English with a friendly ferocity of which, I am afraid, even more would have been needed), Alvin H. Rosenfeld, Kenneth Johnston, James Jensen, and Timothy Wiles. My discussions on modernity with André Reszler, who now teaches at the Institut d'Etudes Européennes in Geneva, have been highly stimulating, and I hope that our older project of a collaborative study of the aesthetics of modernism will materialize one day.

Indiana University, Bloomington
January 1977

FIVE FACES OF MODERNITY

INTRODUCTION

During the last one hundred and fifty years or so, such terms as "modern," "modernity," and more recently "modernism," as well as a number of related notions, have been used in artistic or literary contexts to convey an increasingly sharp sense of historical relativism. This relativism is in itself a form of criticism of tradition. From the point of view of modernity, an artist—whether he likes it or not—is cut off from the normative past with its fixed criteria, and tradition has no legitimate claim to offer him examples to imitate or directions to follow. At best, he invents a private and essentially modifiable past. His own awareness of the present, seized in its immediacy and irresistible transitoriness, appears as his main source of inspiration and creativity. In this sense it may be said that for the modern artist the past imitates the present far more than the present imitates the past. What we have to deal with here is a major cultural shift from a time-honored aesthetics of permanence, based on a belief in an unchanging and transcendent ideal of beauty, to an aesthetics of transitoriness and immanence, whose central values are change and novelty.

Even during the late seventeenth and eighteenth centuries, most of the "moderns" involved in the famous *Querelle des Anciens et des Modernes,* or in its English counterpart, the *Battle of the Books,* continued to consider beauty as a transcendental, eternal model, and if they thought themselves superior to the ancients, they did so only insofar as they believed they had gained a better, more rational understanding of its laws. But since the late eighteenth and early nineteenth centuries or, more specifically, since aesthetic modernity under the guise of "romanticism" first defined its historical legitimacy as a reaction *against* the basic assumptions of classicism, the concept of a universally intelligible and timeless beauty has undergone a process of steady erosion. This process first became self-conscious in France.

For a student of terminology, Stendhal's clear-cut and polemical dichotomy between *"le beau idéal antique"* and *"le beau idéal moderne,"* which occurs in his *Histoire de la peinture en Italie* (1817), and especially his relativistic definition of romanticism, as formulated in his *Racine et Shakespeare* (1823), constitute highly significant events. Stendhal believed that *"romanticisme,"* a word he borrowed from the Italian, was simply "the art of presenting to the peoples literary works which, in view of the present-day state of their customs and beliefs, afford them the utmost possible pleasure." Earlier theorists of the "gothic," the "characteristic," the "interesting," the "sentimental" (Schiller), or even the "romantic" (the Schlegel brothers, Madame de Staël) as opposed to the "classical" were, on the whole, much less militant in their defense of modernity, and some of them even had nostalgic feelings about the lost ancient ideal of beauty. Nothing of that sort in Stendhal. His notion of "romanticism" carries not only a definite sense of commitment to an aesthetic program, but also a sense of presentness and immediacy that would certainly not have been shared by most of his predecessors, who saw in romanticism nothing less than an artistic expression of the whole of Christianity as opposed to the world-view of pagan antiquity.

With the breakup of traditional aesthetic authority, time, change, and the self-consciousness of the present have tended increasingly to become sources of value in what Lionel Trilling once called, with a felicitous phrase, the "adversary culture" of modernism. Historically, Baudelaire, one of the first artists to oppose aesthetic modernity not only to tradition but also to the practical modernity of bourgeois civilization, illustrates the intriguing moment when the old notion of universal beauty had shrunk enough to reach a delicate equilibrium with its modern counterconcept, the beauty of transitoriness. In a famous passage, which will be analyzed later, the author of *Les Fleurs du Mal* writes: "Modernity is the transitory, the fugitive, the contingent, the half of art, of which the other half is the eternal and the immutable. . . ."

After Baudelaire, the fleeting, ever-changing consciousness of modernity as a source of beauty succeeds in prevailing over, and finally in eliminating, the "other half" of art. Tradition is rejected with increasing violence and the artistic imagination starts priding itself on exploring and mapping the realm of the "not yet." Modernity has opened the path to the rebellious *avant-gardes*. At the same time, modernity turns against itself and, by regarding itself as *decadence*, dramatizes its own deep sense of crisis. The apparently contradictory notions of avant-garde and decadence become almost synonymous and, under certain circumstances, can even be used interchangeably.

Modernity in the broadest sense, as it has asserted itself historically, is reflected in the irreconcilable opposition between the sets of values corresponding to (1) the objectified, socially measurable time of capitalist civilization (time as a more or less precious commodity, bought and sold on the market), and (2) the personal, subjective, imaginative *durée*, the private time created by the unfolding of the "self." The latter identity of *time* and *self* constitutes the foundation of modernist culture. Seen from this vantage point, aesthetic modernity uncovers some of the reasons for its profound sense of crisis and for its alienation from the other modernity, which, for all its objectivity and rationality, has lacked, after the demise of religion, any compelling moral or metaphysical justification. But, being produced by the isolated self, partly as a reaction against the desacralized—and therefore dehumanized—time of social activity, the time consciousness reflected in modernist culture also lacks such justifications. The end result of both modernities seems to be the same unbounded relativism.

The clash between the two modernities, renewed with increasing intensity over the last one hundred and fifty years or so, appears to have led to a near-exhaustion of both, at least insofar as they function as intellectual myths. After the Second World War, and especially since the 1950s, the concept of a *postmodern* age has been advanced by a variety of thinkers and scholars, including a philosopher of history and culture such as Arnold Toynbee (who coined the term); a number of literary and art critics such as Harry Levin, Irving Howe, Leslie Fiedler, George Steiner (according to whom we are living in *post-culture*), and Ihab Hassan; and certain proponents of radical atheistic theologies. Naturally, sociologists have not been long in joining a debate that was triggered, among other things, by sociological theories and notions such as "mass society" (as defined by David Riesman in his influential 1960 book, *The Lonely Crowd*), "consumer's society," "mass" or "popular culture," "post-industrial society," etc. It should not, therefore, be surprising that one of the broadest and most perceptive discussions of the culture of modernism/postmodernism is found in the work of a sociologist—Daniel Bell's recent book *The Cultural Contradictions of Capitalism.*

According to Bell, the exhaustion of antibourgeois modernist culture is to be explained through its wide acceptance and subsequent banalization. During the last few decades the antinomian and deliberately deviant patterns of modernist imagination have not only won out culturally but have been adopted practically and translated into the life style of an increasingly large intellectual minority. Parallel to this process, the traditional ideal of bourgeois life, with its concerns for sobriety and rationality, has lost its cultural champions and has reached the point where it simply can no longer be taken seriously. The contemporary scene presents some of the signs of a possible revolution. Bell writes:

> What we have today is a radical disjunction of culture and social structure, and it is such disjunctions which historically have paved the way for more direct social revolutions. In two fundamental ways the new revolution has already begun. First, the autonomy of culture, achieved in art, now begins to pass over into the arena of life. The post-modernist temper demands that what was previously played out in fantasy and imagination must be acted in life as well. There is no distinction between art and life. Anything permitted in art is permitted in life as well. Second, the life-style once practiced by a

small *cénacle*... is now copied by the "many"... and dominates the cultural scene. [New York: Basic Books, 1976, pp. 53–54]

However, on a much larger social plane, today's "pop hedonism," cult of instant joy, fun morality, and the generalized confusion between self-realization and simple self-gratification, has its origin not in the culture of modernism but in capitalism as a system that, born from the Protestant work ethic, could develop only by encouraging consumption, social mobility, and status seeking, that is, by negating its own transcendental moral justification. The "abandonment of Puritanism and the Protestant ethic," Bell writes, "... emphasizes not only the disjunction between the norms of culture and the norms of social structure, but also an extraordinary contradiction within the social structure itself. On the one hand, the business corporation wants an individual to work hard, pursue a career, accept delayed gratification—to be, in the crudest sense, an organization man. And yet, in its products and its advertisements, the corporation promotes pleasure, instant joy, relaxing and letting go. One is to be 'straight' by day and a 'swinger' by night" (pp. 71–72).

The phenomenon of compulsive consumption, the fear of boredom, and the need for escape, combined with the widespread view of art as both play and display, are among the factors that in various degrees and fashions have contributed to the growth of what is called *kitsch*. Kitsch is one of the most typical products of modernity. However, this alone would not be sufficient reason for discussing kitsch along with the ideas of modernity, the avant-garde, and decadence, which, on the one hand, are so closely related through the common theme of time, and on the other, are so much wider in scope. What justifies the inclusion of kitsch among the central concepts of modernity analyzed in the book is the fact that in kitsch the two bitterly conflicting modernities are confronted, as it were, with their own caricature. Grossly exaggerated, their contradictions and secret implications suddenly become obvious.

Thus, the temporal relativism implied by the aesthetic concept of modernity, and specifically the view that no tradition is by itself more valid than any other, while serving as a justification of the overall antitraditionalism of modernism and the total freedom of individual artists to choose their ancestors at their own discretion, may also be seen as a precondition for the all-embracing and blandly tolerant eclecticism of kitsch as a style. More important, modernity's concern with the *present* may be said to have found its unwittingly parodic counterpart in the "instant" beauty of kitsch. Modernism's negation of aesthetic transcendence and of the ideal of permanence—a negation that inspires certain extreme avant-garde tendencies, such as those represented by Tinguely's mechanical self-destructive "sculptures"—has its rather grotesque parallel in the built-in commercial obsolescence of so many kitsch objects and in the general notion of "expendable art," as advanced by certain theorists of the pop movement.

But kitsch is in no way a direct consequence of the rise of aesthetic modernity. Historically, the appearance and growth of kitsch are the results of the intrusion of the other modernity—capitalist technology and business interest—in the domain of the arts. Kitsch was brought into being by the industrial revolution, at first as one of its marginal products. In time, with the sweeping social and psychological transformations brought about by industrial development, the "culture industry" has steadily grown, to the point where now, in the predominantly service-oriented postindustrial society, with its stress on affluence and consumption, kitsch has become one of the central factors of *modern civilized* life, the kind of art that normally and inescapably surrounds us.

In the postmodern age, kitsch represents the triumph of the principle of immediacy—immediacy of access, immediacy of effect, instant beauty. The great paradox of kitsch, as I see it, is that being produced by an extremely time-conscious civilization, which is nevertheless patently unable to attach any broader values to time, it appears as designed both to "save" and to "kill" time. To save time, in the sense that its enjoyment is effortless and instantaneous; to kill time, in the sense that, like a drug, it frees man temporarily from his disturbed time consciousness, justifying "aesthetically," and making bearable an otherwise empty, meaningless present.

To go now into further detail concerning the relationships between modernity, the avant-garde, decadence, and kitsch, would be to anticipate questions, arguments, and opinions that are discussed at length in the following chapters. The purpose of these brief introductory remarks has been simply to point out that the concepts under scrutiny, for all their heterogenous origins and diversity of meaning, share one major characteristic: they reflect intellectual attitudes that are directly related to the problem of *time*. Clearly, this is not the metaphysical or epistemological time of the philosophers, nor the scientific construct dealt with by physicists, but the *human time* and sense of history as experienced and valued culturally.

My concern with modernity and the other notions analyzed in this book is primarily *cultural* (in the traditionally restricted sense of artistic and literary culture), but it obviously would have been impossible to explain such complex terms if the wide variety of nonaesthetic contexts in which they are used had been ignored. However, the ultimate reason for grouping together modernity, the avant-garde, decadence, and kitsch is aesthetic. It is only from such an aesthetic perspective that these concepts reveal their more subtle and puzzling interconnections, which, in all probability, would escape the attention of an intellectual historian with a predominantly philosophical or scientific orientation.

Both as term and concept, modernity has a long and very intricate history. Being in the first place interested in aesthetic modernity—and specifically in those of its lines of development that led to what today we agree to call "modernism"—I felt that my study could start somewhere around the mid-nineteenth century. However, it should not be difficult to realize that certain issues raised by modernity even in this restricted sense cannot be conveniently dealt with if earlier stages in the evolution of the concept of modernity are ignored. But to account even briefly for the diverse intellectual responses to the problem of modernity, or for the forms of time consciousness involved in this notion, would have required a close examination of trends in philosophy, religion, and science over many centuries. A more detailed history of modernity would have taken me too far from the aesthetic concerns of this study. The stages through which the idea of modernity passed before the mid-nineteenth century clearly form the matter of another book that remains to be written.

The first subchapters of the opening essay should therefore be regarded as nothing more than a very general and inevitably sketchy introduction. For purposes of expository clarity, I took into account only those developments that had an explicit relationship to the centuries-old and ever-renewed "Quarrel between the Ancients and the Moderns." Further, I have chosen to refer mostly to texts in which the term "modern" was actually used or at least directly implied. Of course, I am fully aware that such a limitation is artificial and that the "consciousness of modernity" is not tied down to the use of a specific word or of a set of phrases, similes, or metaphors that obviously derive from it. In spite of its numerous lacunae, I am hopeful that the broad historical outline attempted in the first thirty pages or so is sound enough to serve as a working hypothesis. This hypothesis is meant to prepare the reader to follow the main argument of the book: aesthetic modernity should be understood as a crisis concept involved in a threefold dialectical opposition to tradition, to the modernity of bourgeois civilization (with its ideals of rationality, utility, progress), and, finally, to itself, insofar as it perceives itself as a new tradition or form of authority.

THE IDEA OF MODERNITY

MODERN DWARFS

ON THE SHOULDERS OF ANCIENT GIANTS

It is always hard to date with precision the appearance of a concept, and all the more so when the concept under scrutiny has been throughout its history as controversial and complex as "modernity." It is clear, however, that the idea of modernity could be conceived only within the framework of a specific time awareness, namely, that of *historical time*, linear and irreversible, flowing irresistibly onwards. Modernity as a notion would be utterly meaningless in a society that has no use for the temporal-sequential concept of history and organizes its time categories according to a mythical and recurrent model, like the one described by Mircea Eliade in his *Myth of the Eternal Return*.[1] Although the idea of modernity has come to be associated almost automatically with secularism, its main constitutive element is simply a sense of *unrepeatable time*, and this element is by no means incompatible with such a religious Weltanschauung as the one implied by the Judeo-Christian eschatological view of history. That is why, while conspicuously absent from the world of pagan antiquity, the idea of modernity was born during the Christian Middle Ages. The direct and indirect relationships between modernity and Christianity will be discussed at more length later on; for the moment, it suffices to note that the hypothesis of modernity's medieval origin is confirmed linguistically. It was during the Middle Ages that the word *modernus*, an adjective and noun, was coined from the adverb *modo* (meaning "recently, just now"), in the same fashion as *hodiernus* had been derived from *hodie* ("today"). Modernus signified, according to *Thesaurus Linguae Latinae*, "*qui nunc, nostro tempore est, novellus, praesentaneus. . . .*" Its major antonyms were, as the same dictionary lists them, "*antiquus, vetus, priscus. . . .*"[2]

It is remarkable that older Latin could do without the opposition "modern/ancient." This may be explained by the disinterest of the classical Latin mind in diachronical relationships. The term "classic" itself offers a significant example. The first literary use of "classic" (*classicus*) occurs in the second century, in Aulus Gellius's *Noctes Atticae* (19,8,15). The classic writers, we are told, are to be found among the ancient orators or poets (*"cohors antiquior vel oratorum vel poetarum"*), but the meaning of *classicus*, with its strongly positive connotations, is determined in the first place by the social reference to the "first class" of Roman citizens. The aristocratic analogy is underscored by the explicit opposition between *scriptor classicus* and (*scriptor*) *proletarius*—the antonym of "classic" is "vulgar," instead of "new" or "recent," as we might have expected.

The need for a word for "modern" must have been felt, however, at least since the time when Cicero adopted the Greek term νεώτερος, which was later acclimatized in Latin as *neotericus*. As Ernst Robert Curtius points out in his *European Literature and the Latin Middle Ages*, "The older Antiquity became, the more a word for 'modern' was needed. But the word 'modernus' was not yet available. The gap was filled by 'neotericus.' . . . Not until the sixth century does the new and happy formation *modernus* . . . appear, and now Cassiodorus can celebrate an author in rolling rhyme as '*antiquorum diligentissimus imitator, modernorum nobilissimus institutor*' (*Variae*, IV, 51). The word 'modern' . . . is one of the legacies of late Latin to the modern world."[3]

Modernus was widely used in medieval Latin throughout Europe starting not with the sixth century, as Curtius believed, but with the late fifth century.[4] Such terms as *modernitas* ("modern times") and *moderni* ("men of today") also became frequent, especially after the tenth century. The distinction between *antiquus* and *modernus* seems to have always implied a polemic significance, or a principle of conflict. The reader of today is nonetheless surprised to learn that the Quarrel between the Ancients and the Moderns actually began as early as the Middle Ages and that it involved ideas and attitudes that few people outside the circles of medieval scholars would care to look for in the "Dark Ages." The facts, however, are there, and one can safely say that during the twelfth century a full-fledged row about the moderns was raging among poets who all wrote in Latin but were sharply divided on issues of aesthetics. After 1170, as Curtius relates, there were "two hostile factions: the humanistically minded disciples of antique poetry, and the *moderni*. The latter... represent a 'new' poetics. They are masters of a virtuoso style formed in the practice of dialectics, and hence consider themselves superior to the 'ancients.'"[5] It is even more interesting to note that, beyond matters of style, broader philosophical questions were raised.

Historians of the idea of progress have established that the famous maxim about the dwarf standing on the shoulders of a giant and being thus able to see farther than the giant himself can be traced back to Bernard of Chartres, who died in 1126. Bernard's saying is reported for the first time in John of Salisbury's *Metalogicon*, which was completed in 1159 and is rightfully regarded as one of the major documents of what scholars have come to call the Twelfth Century "Renaissance." Here is the passage that interests us:

> We frequently know more, not because we have moved ahead by our own natural ability, but because we are supported by the mental strength of others, and possess riches that we have inherited from our forefathers. Bernard of Chartres used to compare us to puny dwarfs perched on the shoulders of giants. He pointed out that we see more and farther than our predecessors, not because we have keener vision or greater height, but because we are lifted up and borne aloft on their gigantic stature.[6]

Bernard's simile is vivid and easy to visualize, which explains its immediate imaginative appeal; and its subtle ambiguity succeeds in reconciling some of the basic claims of the *moderni* (namely, that they occupy a more advanced position in comparison to the ancients) with the requirements of an age for which tradition was still the only reliable source of value (the relation of modernity to antiquity is consequently characterized as analogous to that of dwarfs to giants). It was certainly the ambiguity, by which one enjoyed the freedom to stress only one of the two meanings combined in the metaphor, that made Bernard's dictum into a widely circulating formula and, eventually, into a rhetorical commonplace.[7] A striking fact about this comparison is that it represents an equally significant stage both in the history of the idea of progress and in that of the idea of decadence. Seen from this vantage point, progress and decadence appear indeed to be intimately linked: the men of a new age are more advanced but at the same time less deserving than their predecessors; they know more in absolute terms, by virtue of the cumulative effect of learning, but in relative terms their own contribution to learning is so small that they may justly be compared to pygmies.

A few instances of later uses of the medieval analogy can illustrate its semantic flexibility. Late in the sixteenth century, when the self-confidence of the Renaissance was being replaced by the baroque consciousness of universal illusion and mutability, the old image was revived by Michel de Montaigne. The contrasting figures of the giants and the dwarfs were eliminated, but the essential idea of succeeding generations symbolized by human bodies sitting on the shoulders of each other was kept and developed. The moderns, Montaigne suggests, may be more advanced than the ancients, but they should not on this count be honored, for they have done nothing heroic to get where they are; their high position on the scale of progress is a consequence of natural law rather than of personal endeavor and merit. Montaigne's view of progress is not without a touch of melancholy—a welcome reminder that recognition of progress does not automatically lead to optimistic exultation. "Our opinions," Montaigne writes, "are grafted one upon the other. The first serves as a stock to the second, the second to the third. Thus, we mount stairwise from step to step. So it comes about that he who has mounted highest has often more honour than he deserves, for on the shoulders of the last but one he is only one barleycorn higher."[8]

At the beginning of the seventeenth century, Robert Burton makes use of the figure in the introductory part of his *Anatomy of Melancholy* (1621), "Democritus to the Reader." By then, we may assume, the old simile had become a more or less conventional device by which an author would try to justify his undertaking in the field of learning. Burton cites as his source a rather obscure Spanish author and mystic, Diego de Estella (1524–1578), but the whole passage, with its air of quaint erudition, can be taken as hardly more than a rhetorical exercise. Both the praise of the predecessors and the self-demeaning implication of the dwarf as a symbol for the author himself have no real force: "Though there were giants of old in physics and philosophy, yet I say with Didacus Stella, 'A dwarf standing on the shoulders of a giant may see farther than the giant himself'; I may likely add, alter, and see farther than my predecessors."[9]

During the second half of the same century, Isaac Newton employs the figure in an important letter to Robert Hooke. But even in this case the metaphor seems intended not so much to convey a philosophy of progress as to give expression to feelings of personal modesty, gratitude, and admiration for earlier thinkers and scientists. "But in the mean time," Newton wrote to Hooke on February 5, 1675/76, "you defer too much to my ability in searching into this subject. What Descartes did was a good step. You have added much in several ways. . . . If I have seen farther, it is by standing on the shoulders of giants."[10] With the omission of any explicit reference to the "dwarfs," Newton's "giants" is meant merely as a laudatory hyperbole.

One of the most significant metamorphoses of the medieval analogy is to be found, toward the middle of the seventeenth century, in Pascal's *Preface to the Treatise on Vacuum* (1647?). Published posthumously, this early piece is perhaps Pascal's most Cartesian writing. Like Descartes, Pascal is a staunch defender of the moderns' freedom of research and criticism against the unwarranted authority of the ancients. Antiquity has become the object of a cult carried to the point "that oracles are made of all its thoughts and mysteries, even of its obscurities."[11] But unlike Descartes, Pascal does not think that the new science and philosophy are to start from scratch. There is no real rupture in the continuity of the human effort to know, and the contribution of the ancients has made it easier for the moderns to understand aspects of nature that in antiquity would have been impossible to grasp. It is our duty, therefore, to acknowledge our indebtedness. Pascal says:

> It is in this manner that we may at the present day adopt different sentiments and new opinions, without despising the ancients and without ingratitude, since the first knowledge which they have given us served as a stepping-stone to our own, and since in these advantages we are indebted to them for our ascendency over them; because by being raised by their aid to a certain degree, the slightest effort causes us to mount still higher, and with less pain and less glory we find ourselves above them. Thence it is that we are enabled to discover things which it was impossible for them to perceive. Our view is more extended, and although they knew as well as we all that they could observe in nature, they did not, nevertheless, know it so well, and we see more than they.[12]

There is little doubt that Pascal had in mind the old simile when writing the passage. He probably found it still suggestive, despite the rather grotesque contrast between dwarfs and giants, which might have appeared to his taste—educated by an epoch of demanding intellectual refinement—as both too crude and too childishly fabulous. But beyond such hypothetical considerations it is certain that the young Pascal, at the time when he wrote the *Preface to the Treatise on Vacuum*, did not think of his contemporaries as pygmies. Pascal uses a series of elements taken from the original metaphor, the most striking one being the reference to the higher position and consequently to the more extended view of the moderns, but giants and dwarfs are left out. If the medieval figure contained an antimodern bias, in Pascal's treatment it has totally vanished.

THE PROBLEM OF TIME:

THREE ERAS OF WESTERN HISTORY

The opposition "modern/ancient" took on particularly dramatic aspects in the consciousness of the Renaissance with its sharply contradictory awareness of time in both historical and psychological terms. During the Middle Ages time was conceived along essentially theological lines, as tangible proof of the transient character of human life and as a permanent reminder of death and what lay beyond. This thinking was illustrated by the recurrence of such major themes and motifs as *memento mori, fortuna labilis* (the instability of fate), the ultimate vanity of all things, and the destructiveness of time. One of the most significant *topoi* of the Middle Ages, the idea of a *theatrum mundi*, drew an analogy between this world and a stage, on which humans are actors who unwittingly play the roles assigned to them by the divine Providence. Such conceptions were natural in an economically and culturally static society dominated by the ideal of stability and even quiescence—a society wary of change, in which secular values were considered from an entirely theocentric view of human life. There were also practical reasons for the rather loose and blurred time consciousness of the medieval individual. We must remind ourselves, for instance, that no accurate measurement of time was possible before the invention of the mechanical clock in the late thirteenth century.[13] For all these combined causes, as a recent student of the Renaissance discovery of time has pointed out, the medieval mind "could exist in an attitude of temporal ease. Neither time nor change appear[ed] to be critical, and hence there [was] no great worry about controlling the future."[14]

The situation changed dramatically in the Renaissance. The theological concept of time did not disappear suddenly, but from then on it had to coexist in a state of growing tension with a new awareness of the preciousness of practical time—the time of action, creation, discovery, and transformation. To cite again Ricardo Quinones's study of *The Renaissance Discovery of Time,* "Dante, Petrarch and Boccaccio share their society's sense of energy and rejuvenation, as well as its most practical concerns with time. In them we find aroused energy and love of variety. They themselves were something of pioneers and acutely conscious of living in a new time, a time of poetic revival. But they also could regard time as a precious commodity, an object worthy of scrupulous attention."[15]

It has been convincingly demonstrated that the division of Western history into three eras—antiquity, Middle Ages, and modernity—dates from the early Renaissance. More interesting than this periodization *per se* are the value judgments passed on each of these three eras, expressed by the metaphors of light and darkness, day and night, wakefulness and sleep. Classical antiquity came to be associated with resplendent light, the Middle Ages became the nocturnal and oblivious "Dark Ages," while modernity was conceived of as a time of emergence from darkness, a time of awakening and "renascence," heralding a luminous future.

The Renaissance approach to history is illustrated in the fourteenth century by the father of humanism—Petrarch. Theodor E. Mommsen has pointed out that Petrarch introduced the notion of the "Dark Ages" in the periodization of history. Summing up the results of his research, Mommsen writes: "The fact that we are able to associate this conception of the 'Dark Ages' with Petrarch means more than merely the fixation of a date. For the whole idea of the Italian 'rinascita' is inescapably connected with the notion of the preceding era as an age of obscurity. The people living in that 'renascence' thought of it as a time of revolution. They wanted to break away from traditions and they were convinced that they had effected such a break."[16]

But Petrarch's dream of ancient Rome's glory and of its impending restoration at the end of a long period of forgetfulness was not without the realization that he himself had been doomed to live "amid varied and confusing storms," and that he was still the son of the hated age of darkness. His message, as expressed in *Africa*, the poem in Latin which he considered his highest achievement, was certainly one of optimism and heroic hope. We should, however, be aware that this hope vied with the poet's deep feeling of personal frustration, as shown in his own words: "My fate is to live amid varied and confusing storms. But for you perhaps, if as I hope and wish you will live after me, there will follow a better age. This sleep of forgetfulness will not last for ever. When the darkness has been dispersed, our descendants can come again in the former pure radiance."[17]

Clearly, Petrarch had a divided self. He has often been described in terms of his conflicting allegiances to the classical and the Christian value systems as a personality embodying the whole spiritual drama of an age of transition. What has been perhaps less noticed is that Petrarch tended to extend his and his age's contradictions to the concept of world history. To Petrarch and then to the next generation of humanists, history no longer appeared as a continuum but rather as a succession of sharply distinct ages, black and white, dark and bright. History seemed to proceed by dramatic ruptures, alternating periods of enlightened grandeur with dark periods of decay and chaos. Here we are faced with an obvious paradox, namely, that the Renaissance's much discussed activist optimism and cult of energy emanate from a vision of world history that is essentially catastrophic.

To speak of the immediate past—the past that naturally structures the present—as "dark" and at the same time posit the certainty of a "luminous" future—even if it be the revival of a previous Golden Age—involves a *revolutionary* way of thinking, for which we would try in vain to find coherent precedents before the Renaissance. Is it necessary to stress that revolution is more than, and qualitatively distinct from, a simple expression of dissatisfaction or rebellion? Revolution is distinguished from any form of spontaneous or even conscious rebellion because it implies, besides the essential moment of negation or rejection, a specific consciousness of time and an alliance with it. Here again etymology is revealing. "Revolution," in its original and still primary meaning, is a progressive movement around an orbit, and also the time necessary for the completion of one such movement. Most historical revolutions have conceived of themselves as returns to a purer initial state, and any consistent theory of revolution implies a cyclical view of history—whether successive cycles are seen as alternating (light, darkness) or as forming a symbolic ascending spiral, in accordance with a more systematic doctrine of progress.

Insofar as the Renaissance was self-conscious and saw itself as the beginning of a new cycle in history, it accomplished an ideologically revolutionary alliance with time. Its whole philosophy of time was based on the conviction that history had a specific direction, expressive not of a transcendental, predetermined pattern, but of the necessary interaction of immanent forces. Man was therefore to participate consciously in the creation of the future: a high premium was put on being with one's time (and not against it), and on becoming an agent of change in an incessantly dynamic world.

Here again Petrarch's case offers a good illustration. For him, the *moderni* were still men of the Dark Ages, but with an important difference: they knew the future would restore the "pure radiance" of antiquity. Petrarch himself, in spite of his conflicting allegiances, was stimulated by his belief in the future. This prevented him from ever becoming a passive admirer of the ancients' grandeur. On the contrary, his cult of antiquity—far from being mere antiquarianism—was a form of activism. He was convinced that the passionate study of antiquity could and should kindle a sense of emulation. It was because he wanted so much to *revive* the spirit of antiquity that he was conscious of the dangers of an exclusive and single-minded cult of the past for its own sake, and so outspoken in his opposition to those who despised anything modern, *contra laudatores veterum semper presentia contemnentes.*

IT IS WE WHO ARE THE ANCIENTS

The late seventeenth-century Quarrel between the Ancients and the Moderns (or, as it is known in England, after the title of Swift's famous satire, *The Battle of the Books*) was a direct consequence of the erosion of Tradition's authority in matters of knowledge and eventually—as was unavoidable—in matters of taste. The process of erosion was started by a momentous revision of the values and doctrines that formed the legacy of the Middle Ages. But the Renaissance itself was unable to go beyond replacing the authority of the church with the authority of antiquity. We may even say— insofar as the Middle Ages themselves had recognized the authority of Greek and Roman antiquity in nontheological matters—that the Renaissance was in certain respects less free from medieval traditions than it actually believed. Indirectly, though, the Renaissance created a set of *rational* and *critical* arguments for breaking away from not just one but all forms of intellectual authority; and its fight against certain medieval cultural patterns made it discover and perfect ideological weapons that could well be—and in fact later would be—used against those same ancients whom they were supposed to vindicate.

The *Querelle des Anciens et des Modernes* in its aesthetic aspects was rooted in much of the philosophic and scientific discussion of the sixteenth and seventeenth centuries, which resulted in the liberation of reason not only from the tyranny of medieval Scholasticism but also from the equally restricting fetters imposed on it by the Renaissance idolatry of classical antiquity. Montaigne's *Essays* (1580), Francis Bacon's *Advancement of Learning* (1605) and *Novum Organum* (1620), Descartes's *Discours de la méthode* (1634) are some of the important landmarks in the history of modernity's self-assertion. In one form or another, most of these authors and their followers blame antiquity—or rather the blind veneration of antiquity—for the prevailing sterility of thought and the general lack of adequate methods in the sciences.

Terminologically, it is interesting to note that the word "modern"—and the concept as well—had acquired predominantly negative connotations in the general usage, and all the more so when it occurred, implicitly or explicitly, in contrast with "ancient." In Shakespeare, for instance, "modern" was a synonym for "common-place, trite" (Alexander Schmidt, *Shakespeare Lexicon*, 3d ed., N.Y., 1968, p. 732), as can be seen in the following passage from *All's Well That Ends Well* (II, 3, 2), where Lafew says: "They say miracles are past, and we have our philosophical persons, to make modern and familiar, things supernatural and causeless." As far as the relation between antiquity and modernity was concerned, the general feeling was that the moderns were still dwarfs in comparison with the ancient giants. This may explain why some of the more advanced minds of the time, philosophers and scientists, reacted with such intensity against the cult of antiquity. This may also explain, at a more specialized level, the highly interesting terminological strategy adopted by the defenders of modernity.

Francis Bacon is, most probably, the originator of a new and powerful simile illustrating his and his generation's view of the rapport between antiquity and the modern age. Whereas in the old dwarf/giant metaphor of Bernard de Chartres and John of Salisbury the idea of progress had been translated into a spatial-visual relationship, in Bacon's version a temporal-psychological contrast is called upon to convey a sense of progressive development by which modernity is completely vindicated. Bacon constructs a paradox involving the inexperience of boyhood and the wisdom of old age. From the vantage point proposed by the philosopher there is little doubt that it is we, the moderns, who are the real ancients, the ancients having been, when they lived, young and "modern." For those whom we call ancients are only with respect to ourselves ancient and elder, being clearly younger than we with respect to the world. There are several statements of this paradox in Bacon's writings. In the *Advancement of Learning*:

> And to speak truly, *Antiquitas saeculi juventus mundi*. These times are the ancient times, when the world is ancient, and not those which

we account ancient *ordine retrogrado,* by a computation backwards
from ourselves.[18]

In the Preface to *Instauratio Magna*:

> And for its value and utility it must be plainly avowed that the wis-
> dom which we have derived principally from the Greeks is but like
> the boyhood of knowledge, and has the characteristic property of
> boys: it can talk, but it cannot generate; for it is fruitful of controver-
> sies but barren of works.[19]

Or in *Novum Organum*:

> As for antiquity, the opinion touching it which men entertain is quite
> a negligent one, and scarcely consonant with the word itself. For the
> old age of the world is to be accounted the true antiquity; and this is
> the attribute of our own times, not of the earlier age of the world in
> which the ancients lived; and which, though in respect to us it was
> elder, yet in respect to the world it was younger. And truly as we look
> for greater knowledge of human things and a riper judgment in the
> old man than in the young, because of his experience and the number
> and variety of things which he has seen and heard and thought of; so
> in like manner from our age, if we but knew its own strength and
> chose to essay and exert it, much more might fairly be expected than
> from the ancient times, inasmuch as it is a more advanced age of the
> world, and stored and stocked with infinite experiments and observa-
> tion.[20]

Bacon's reasoning appealed to the defenders of modernity, and
one should not be surprised to discover that his comparison was
reformulated and developed throughout the seventeenth century
and then passed on to the eighteenth. In France, where the
Querelle (which had actually begun much earlier) was to be formally
started in the 1680s by Perrault and Fontenelle, Descartes closely
followed Bacon when he said *"C'est nous qui sommes les anciens,"*
not without implying that the praise given to the ancients should
rightfully go to the real ancients—the moderns. Other French authors, including Pascal (in the already mentioned *Preface to the
Treatise on Vacuum*), used the paradoxical figure before Fontenelle

introduced it in his *Digression sur les Anciens et les Modernes* (1688).[21]

If Bacon's paradox was new, the implied parallelism between the life of mankind and that of a human individual had a long tradition. It has been suggested that "the earliest use of the simile in terms similar to those of Bacon is probably to be found in Saint Augustine's *City of God* (X, 14)."[22] Augustine's text, in which the education of the human race is compared to that of an individual passing through certain stages or ages, has nevertheless a strong theological sense that makes it quite different from Bacon's purely secular paradox about modernity's ancientness. The "progress" that Saint Augustine speaks of is in fact an ascension from earth to heaven, a passage from time to eternity.[23] There is an entirely new quality of time involved in Bacon's view of the advancement of learning and in his implicit rejection of an authority whose prestigious oldness is but the effect of an optical illusion.

COMPARING THE MODERNS TO THE ANCIENTS

The Italian Renaissance is largely responsible for the idea of comparing on a more or less systematic basis the achievements of the moderns with those of the ancients. At the beginning of the fifteenth century, the title of one of Leonardo Bruni's dialogues synthesizes a broader trend: *De modernis quibusdam scriptoribus in comparatione ad antiquos.*[24] Such parallels were not unknown to the Middle Ages, but the concept of antiquity was then quite different from what it came to mean after the Renaissance. Curtius calls our attention to this crucial distinction: "This view may seem strange to the modern reader. When we speak of the 'Ancients', we mean the pagan writers. In our view Paganism and Christianity are two separate realms, for which there is no common denominator. The Middle Ages think differently. 'Veteres' is applied to both the Christian and pagan authors of the past."[25]

The old and lingering quarrel between the ancients and the moderns did not gain momentum until rationalism and the doctrine of progress won the battle against authority in philosophy and the sciences. The *Querelle* proper started when some modern-minded French authors, led by Charles Perrault, thought fit to apply the *scientific* concept of progress to literature and art. It is significant that neither scientists nor philosophers suggested the conspicuously fallacious line of reasoning that gave the moderns the feeling that they were entitled to transfer their scientific superiority over antiquity into an artistic one. Let me also note that those who sided with the moderns in the notorious row were comparatively minor figures, in both France and England. This is certainly why what has remained alive from the whole controversy in England, in terms of the interests of today's nonscholarly reader, is Swift's devastating irony against the forgotten Wottons and Bentleys of the time.

The story of the *Querelle* has been told repeatedly since the appearance of the first comprehensive and still authoritative study, Hippolyte Rigault's *Histoire de la Querelle des Anciens et des Modernes* (1856). Apart from a host of erudite articles, we can say that almost all the relevant facts have been collected and set in perspective in a number of comprehensive studies, from Hubert Gillot's *La Querelle des Anciens et des Modernes en France* (1914) to Hans Robert Jauss's recent study "Aestetische Normen und geschichtlische Reflexion in der 'Querelle des Anciens et des Modernes'" (1964);[26] and, in English, Anne Elizabeth Burlingame's *The Battle of the Books in Its Historical Setting* (1920) and Richard Foster Jones's *Ancients and Moderns: A Study of the Background of the 'Battle of the Books'* (1936). It will suffice here to recall a few more or less familiar facts that have direct bearing on the evolution of modernity as a concept, with the intention of giving a systematic rather than an historical account of the dispute and its results.

The moderns subjected antiquity and its defenders to a variety of criticisms, which may be divided into three broad categories. Clearly, we are concerned here with the arguments of the moderns that have some kind of relevance to aesthetics, and not with what they had to say about modernity's scientific and technological superiority (that superiority, for obvious tactical reasons, was often brought up by most of the "modernists").

A. *The argument of reason.* French neoclassicism was certainly subservient to antiquity, but a close study of the aesthetics of the period shows that imitation of the ancients was rarely recommended dogmatically after 1630—indeed, it was criticized as a fallacy. The famous neoclassical rules had been introduced and developed throughout the seventeenth century as an attempt to rationalize the indiscriminate Renaissance cult of antiquity and, moreover, to found a perfectly rational theory of beauty. As René Bray pointed out in his book *La Formation de la doctrine classique en France* (first published in 1927), the discussion about rules that started in the early seventeenth century has to be considered in the larger context of the dominance of rationalism in philosophy and the growing influence of Cartesianism. The elaboration and formulation of the rules of beauty were the expression of the triumph of rationality over authority in poetics, and they definitely paved the way for the moderns' later claims of superiority.

By nearly unanimous consent, the most general rule is that of pleasing, and the first norm of artistic gratification—so the neoclassical argument goes—is verisimilitude in harmony with the requirements of beauty. All the other rules, from the most comprehensive to the most specific, are derived *more geometrico* from these principles, and they are to be used as guidelines for the production (by natural genius) of any work of genuine merit. Left by itself, poetic genius is doomed—if not to fail completely, then to err and give much less gratification than it would have been able to provide if it had known and observed the rules. In his *Parallèle des Anciens et des Modernes* (1688–97), Charles Perrault tries to demonstrate the superiority of the moderns by carrying such a line of thinking to its extreme. The larger the number of rules, the moderns' champion seems to suggest, the more advanced the age and its representative artists. A new Virgil, born in the century of Louis le Grand, would write a better version of the *Aeneid* because—granted his genius was the same—he could benefit from the more numerous and sophisticated rules at his disposal. Perrault writes:

> So when I have made clear that Homer and Virgil made countless mistakes which the moderns no longer make, I think I have proved that the ancients did not have all our rules, since the natural effect of rules is to prevent one from making mistakes. So that if today heaven were disposed to bring forth a man who had a genius of the magnitude of Virgil's, it is certain that he would write a more beautiful poem than the *Aeneid* because he would have, in accordance with my supposition, as much genius as Virgil and at the same time a larger amount of precepts to guide him.[27]

If we take into account Perrault's view of the development of reason and of general progress, we should not be surprised to find that the oldest of Greek poets, Homer, is by far the most frequently attacked for his errors and scientific inaccuracies. For instance, how on earth could the author of the *Odyssey* say that Ulysses was recognized by his dog, which he had not seen for twenty years, when Pliny makes it quite clear that a dog cannot live for more than fifteen years?[28] Such censures may seem utterly petty, but in the French seventeenth century such matters were taken seriously, as is shown by Boileau, who, in his *Réflexions critiques sur Longin* (1694; 1710), defended Homer from Perrault's accusation by citing the case of one of the king's dogs, which was known to have lived for twenty-two years! In England, Swift was much better aware of the absurdity of such a "scientific" approach to the poetry of the ancients, and turned into ridicule the excesses of Perrault and Fontenelle:

> But, besides these Omissions in Homer, already mentioned, the curious Reader will also observe several Defects in that Author's Writings for which he is not altogether accountable. For whereas every Branch of Knowledge has received such wonderful Acquirements since his Age, especially within the last three Years or there-

abouts; it is almost impossible, he could be so perfect in Modern Discoveries as his Advocates pretend. We freely acknowledge Him to be the inventor of the Compass, of Gunpowder, and the Circulation of the Blood: but I challenge any of his Admirers to show me in all his Writings, a complete Account of the Spleen. Does he not also leave us wholly to seek in the Art of Political Wagering? What can be more defective and unsatisfactory than his long Dissertation upon Tea?[29]

B. *The argument of taste.* Taste, the seventeenth-century moderns believed, developed along with other aspects of civilization, becoming more demanding and refined. The concept of progress is explicitly applied to the area of civility, mores, and cultural conventions. Antiquity was therefore more primitive than modern times and, worse, it went so far as to tolerate the reflection in poetry of rude and barbaric customs, which cannot help offending the taste of the civilized reader. In the third volume of Perrault's *Parallèle*, the *abbé*, who is the spokesman of the author, expresses his deep shock at hearing Achilles insult Agamemnon by calling him "drunkard," "wine-bag," and "dog-face." Kings and great heroes, Perrault goes on to say, could never have used such a brutal language, and even if they did, "such customs are too indecent to be represented in a Poem, where things ought to be shown not as they can but as they should happen, so they may instruct and please."[30] Such a bluntly normative attitude was an exaggeration of the typically neoclassical urge toward the combination in poetry of usefulness and pleasure—Horace's *utile dulci*—which for the French poets of the second half of the seventeenth century was directly subjected to the imperative of decorum, or the tyrannical "bienséance." Considered from this vantage point, the moderns were clearly not revolutionary in matters of taste or in any way more "advanced" and daring than their contemporaries. On the contrary, the basic neoclassicism of the moderns was rather more intolerant than that of the ancients' admirers, whose aesthetic concepts were certainly not more relativistic, but more flexible and comprehensive.

Perrault's vocal nonconformism was in fact little more than a disguise of deep conformism and consciousness of fashion. We should not forget that the *Querelle* was indeed highly fashionable, and the court of Louis XIV and the salons passionately participated in it, with a natural majority favoring the moderns (the epithet "natural" is justified if we realize that the aesthetic traditionalism of the "anciens" had little to attract a wider public of *mondains*). So the famous battle was no real battle, and the moderns were hardly heroes. Today's reader of Perrault cannot help being struck by the narrow theoretical orthodoxy of this author who had been so controversial in his time. Actually all the arguments brought forth by Perrault to demonstrate the superiority of the moderns over the ancients are purely neoclassical. Throughout the whole dispute there were practically no *theoretical disagreements* among the participants. Perrault was certainly criticized during the debate, and sometimes quite bitterly, but none of his adversaries could find fault with the principles themselves, in the name of which the ancients were being attacked. Roughly speaking, Perrault was scolded for two main reasons, a moral one (it was petty, ungrateful, and self-serving to denigrate the ancients in order to underscore one's own merits), and a technical one (the defects attributed to the ancients were in fact attributable only to their unfaithful and ungifted translators, whom the moderns were referring to simply because they knew neither Greek nor Latin). In a debate that had so much to do with intellectual history, both factions show a complete lack of historical sense, and both agree that the values involved in their discussion are absolute and changeless.

The rationalist concept of progress is by no means incompatible with the belief in the universal and timeless character of values. During the seventeenth and the eighteenth centuries even the most single-minded progressivist doctrinaires had no doubts about the absolute validity of their value system and value judgments. What makes Perrault and his followers no less neoclassic than their enemies, beyond the questions at issue, is their common belief in a *transcendent and unique model of beauty*. The merit of each particular artist is measured by how closely his works approximate this pure and incorruptible ideal. Beauty, like all the other fundamental values, has nothing to do with time, but exists objectively and eternally. The progressivists think that the advancement of learning, the development of civilization, and the enlightening influence of reason contribute to a better, more effective understanding of those perennial and universal values, which were no less real in older times but only less clearly discerned. So Perrault and the moderns did not think that antiquity's ideal of beauty could have been different from their own. What they prided themselves on was only their ability to be more faithful to an ideal that the ancients had pursued less successfully.

This is an essential point in our discussion. In their claim of superiority over the ancients, the late seventeenth- and eighteenth-century moderns did not challenge any of the fundamental criteria of beauty recognized and promoted by their opponents. So we could say that Perrault and his party were fighting the ancients with aesthetic arguments borrowed from those who had imposed the cult of antiquity. The moderns did not negate the ancients. We might label their approach "a criticism of imperfections," in the sense that they tried to point out where and how the ancients had failed to live up to the demands of timeless perfection. In typically neoclassical fashion, the concept of perfection itself was never questioned.

C. *The religious argument.* During the seventeenth century and even later, the opposition between authority and reason was not automatically extended to religious matters, and one could well be in favor of rationalism and the doctrine of progress in all areas concerned with the study of nature, while readily accepting the principle of authority in theology. Pascal's *Preface to the Treatise on Vacuum* offers once again a clear illustration. Authority

   ... has the principal weight in theology, because there she is inseparable from truth, and we know it only through her; ... since [theology's] principles are superior to nature and reason, and since, the mind of man being too weak to attain them by its own efforts, he cannot reach these lofty conceptions if he is not carried thither by an omnipotent and superhuman power. [Obviously,] it is not the same with subjects that fall under the senses and under reasoning; authority here is useless; it belongs to reason alone to know them.[31]

Although determined by the growing prestige of reason as a *critical* faculty and by the revolutionary discoveries of science, the self-consciousness of modernity as a distinct and superior period in the history of mankind was not free from all association with religion. On the contrary, such associations were, during certain periods, numerous and very close, and it is only by bringing them into focus that we can become fully aware of one of the structural ambiguities of modernity's idea, an ambiguity that accounts for the fact that at the beginning of the nineteenth century the romantic irrationalists could still, while rejecting the progressivism and philosophical optimism of the Enlightenment, be committed to a broadly conceived modern ideal. Keeping in mind Pascal's distinction between rational truth (whose gradual discovery in time reflects the law of progress) and the supernatural truth of religion, we may remark that the moderns could claim a double advantage over the ancients: First, they were older than the ancients, intellectually more mature; and second, they were in possession of the revealed truth of Christ, which had been inaccessible to the ancients. The only thing that the ancients still had on their side—this as a result of the work of the Renaissance humanists—was beauty. Speaking of the ambivalent appraisal of antiquity's heritage by the sternly religious Jansenists, Sainte-Beuve cites in his history of Port Royal an aphorism by Joubert (1754–1824), which suggestively sums up the attitude of the religious-minded classicists of the seventeenth and eighteenth centuries: "God," Joubert said, "unable to reveal the truth to the Greeks, gave them the genius for poetry instead." But such a clear-cut statement would not have gone unchallenged even in the French seventeenth century, the neoclassical century *par excellence*.

Several questions, although not asked explicitly as early as the seventeenth century, were somehow implied in the critical battle that started in France and had as an object the legitimacy of the Christian epic. Is beauty an exclusively heathen invention and concept? Or are there two fundamental types of beauty, one pagan, the other Christian? And if so, which type is superior? Epic poems, imitating by and large the classical models of the genre, but in which God, the hierarchies of angels, and Satan with his legions of devils had replaced the gods of Greek and Latin mythology, had been popular in France and other Western countries since the mid-sixteenth century. The acknowledged masters of epic poetry being Homer and Virgil, the authors of such poems sometimes felt the need to justify their use of Christian heroes and themes instead of the classical "machines" of heathenism (cf. Tasso in his *Discorsi del Poema Eroico*, 1594). But the existence of this genre was never actually threatened before Boileau's bitter attack in his *Art poétique* (1674). If we keep in mind that Boileau was shortly to become the leader of the *"anciens"* in their quarrel with the moderns, we can understand the strong antimodern implications of the passage from *L'Art poétique*:

> In vain have our mistaken authors tried
> To lay these ancient ornaments aside,
> Thinking our God, and prophets that he sent,
> Might act like those the poets did invent,
> To fright poor readers in each line with hell,
> And talk of Satan, Ashtaroth, and Bell.
> The mysteries which Christians must believe
> Disdain such shifting pageants to receive....[32]

When he wrote these lines Boileau was thinking, among others, of Desmarets de Saint-Sorlin, the author of the Christian epic *Clovis* (1657), who also composed a series of critical writings, including a treatise, *Traité pour juger les poètes grecs, latins et français* (1670) and a *Discours pour prouver que les sujets chrétiens sont seuls propres à la poésie héroique* (1673). Besides praising his own poem in hyperbolic terms, Desmarets voiced ideas totally opposed to the narrow neoclassical stance represented by Boileau's circle. His point was that he had written a poem on a noble and true subject, the "true religion fighting and conquering the false one."[33] The superiority of the moderns over the ancients is a religious one this time. Is it an exaggeration to think that Desmarets and other minor religious poets of his time contributed to the enlargement of the idea of modernity, and perhaps even to a greater extent than some of those directly and notoriously involved in the *Querelle?* The fact is that the religious definition of modernity, or, to put it differently, the recognition of the essential connection between Christianity and modernity, was to become one of the major themes of romanticism. But the religious argument was not used openly during the heyday of the *Querelle* and did not become a significant factor in the reshaping of the modern idea before the emergence of romanticism.

What were the main results of the *Querelle?* The most important one was probably the enrichment of the term "modern" with a number of sharply polemical connotations. Not in France or in England or in the other countries reached by the echoes of the controversy could the moderns have won more than a reputation for gallantry and, perhaps, for iconoclasm. No distinctly new values were promoted or suggested. But it is interesting to note that the terminological opposition, "modern/ancient," was transformed into a framework for aesthetic partisanship. In this way, the pattern of literary and artistic development through negation of the established models of taste was created.

FROM MODERN TO GOTHIC TO ROMANTIC

TO MODERN

Since the mid-eighteenth century the "ancient/modern" opposition has generated countless broadly historical and eventually typological antitheses, without which the whole evolution of the modern critical consciousness would be incomprehensible. It is not too difficult to demonstrate that such terminological pairs of opposites as "classic/modern," "classic/gothic," "naïve/sentimental" or "sentimentive" (Schiller), "classic/romantic," and, in the more recent critical idiom, "classic/baroque," "classic/ mannerist," etc., can be traced to the cardinal distinction "ancient/modern." It should be observed, however, that such a development at the level of terminology would have been impossible without a more profound change in taste and in the very conception of beauty.

It was during the eighteenth century that the idea of beauty began to undergo the process through which it lost its aspects of transcendence and finally became a purely historical category. The romantics were already thinking in terms of a relative and historically immanent beauty and felt that to make valid judgments of taste one was supposed to derive one's criteria from historical experience—not from a "utopian," universal, and timeless concept of beauty. The opposition between ancient and modern played the role of a shaping influence in this process.

The Quarrel offered the pattern for a broader distinction between two autonomous world views and scales of value, both of them equally legitimate *historically:* the genius of antiquity and the modern genius. Of a great many examples available, there is one that clearly anticipates the late eighteenth-century distinction between classic and romantic; I am referring to the "classic/gothic" antinomy as it occurs in English criticism, and more precisely in Richard Hurd's *Letters on Chivalry and Romance* (1762). Hurd speaks of *classic* and *gothic* as two perfectly autonomous worlds, neither of which can be considered superior to the other. Quite naturally, one who approaches the gothic with classical criteria will be unable to discover in it anything except irregularity and ugliness. But this, obviously, does not mean that the gothic has no rules or goals of its own by which its achievements should be judged. "When an architect examines a Gothic structure by Grecian rules," Hurd writes, "he finds nothing but deformity. But the Gothic architecture has its own rules, by which when it comes to be examined, it is seen to have its merit, as well as the Grecian."[34] Hurd, who tries to defend the use of "gothic" fictions in poets like Spenser and Tasso against neoclassical rationalistic attacks, argues that a poem like *The Faerie Queene* must be read and criticized according to the idea of a gothic, not of a classical poem, in order to be adequately understood: "And on these principles, it would not be difficult to unfold its merit in another way than has been hitherto attempted."[35]

Going beyond the scope of a mere defense, Hurd's discussion of Tasso concludes with the typically romantic pronouncement that gothic customs and fictions are superior to classical ones insofar as poetry and "poetic truth" are concerned. Such ideas are consistent with Hurd's endorsement of the cult of imagination (as opposed to the neoclassical doctrine of imitation), and with his belief that, above and beyond nature, the poet has "a supernatural world to range in." Interestingly, Hurd uses the "classic/gothic" distinction almost interchangeably with "ancient/modern" or "classic/modern," "modern" designating here the whole culture of Christianity as distinct from that of the heathen world. Hurd says: ". . . The fancies of our modern bards are not only more gallant, but . . . more sublime, more terrible, more alarming, than those of the classic fablers. In a word, you will find that the manners they paint, and the *superstitions* they adopt, are more poetical for being Gothic."[36]

Such theories, critical of the major assumptions of neoclassicism, enjoyed an increasing popularity in England and in Germany, and contributed directly to the emergence of romanticism at the turn of the century. The term "romantic" was not adopted immediately in England, but it circulated widely in Germany, from the Schlegel brothers to Hegel; in France, from Madame de Staël's *De l'Allemagne* (1813) to Victor Hugo; and in other European countries, being used in an incomparably wider sense than the one that prevailed later in the language of literary and art history. At the beginning of the nineteenth century, the word "romantic," a synonym for "modern" in the broadest acceptation, designated all the aesthetically relevant aspects of Christian civilization, seen as a distinct period in world history. According to that notion, romanticism was essentially an expression of the *Genius of Christianity*, to use the title of Chateaubriand's famous book, in which a new parallel between the ancients and the moderns was drawn, and in which the superiority of the latter was seen as resulting from their practice of not only the truest but also the most poetical of all religions. The medieval legends, epics, and romances, the poetry of the troubadours, Dante, Petrarch, Ariosto, Shakespeare, Tasso, Milton, etc., were all included in the sphere of romanticism thus understood. It was only later that the meaning of the term was narrowed down to designate primarily the literary and artistic schools that reacted against the neoclassical system of values during the first decades of the nineteenth century.

For the romantics (in the limited historical sense of our contemporary notion) the aspiration toward universality, the desire to make the work of art resemble as closely as possible the transcendent model of beauty, belonged to the classical past. The new type of beauty was based on the "characteristic," on the various possibilities offered by the synthesis of the "grotesque" and the "sublime," on the "interesting," and on other such related categories that had replaced the ideal of classical perfection. The pursuit of perfection came to be regarded as an attempt to escape history and the shortest way toward "academicism." Especially in France, where the young and rebellious romantics had been confronted with the most stubborn and narrow-minded neoclassical prejudices, the partisans of the new movement were forced to use as unambiguously as possible the argument of historical relativism. To be of one's own time, to try to respond to its problems became more than an aesthetic—it became almost a moral obligation.

This significant stage in the development of the consciousness of modernity is illustrated in the famous definition of romanticism that Stendhal formulated almost a decade after having worked out a preparatory opposition between *"le beau idéal antique"* and *"le beau idéal moderne"* in his *Histoire de la peinture en Italie* (1817).[37] Stendhal is probably the first major European writer to term himself a romantic and to understand by romanticism not a particular period (longer or shorter), nor a specific style, but an awareness of contemporary life, of *modernity* in its immediate sense. His definition of romanticism is more than a piece of paradoxical commonsense; it is, one may say, by its implied synonymity between "romantic" and "modern," and by the sharp sense of temporality it conveys throughout, a kind of first draft of Baudelaire's theory of modernity, which I shall examine later. Here is what the author of *Racine et Shakespeare* (1823) had to say about "romanticisme" as opposed to "classicisme":

> *Romanticism* is the art of presenting to the peoples literary works which, in view of the present-day state of their customs and beliefs, affords them the utmost possible pleasure. *Classicism*, on the contrary, presents them with the literature that used to give the utmost pleasure to their great-grandfathers.... To imitate Sophocles and Euripides today, and to pretend that these imitations will not cause the nineteenth-century Frenchman to yawn, is to be classicist.[38]

Stendhal does not hesitate to say that Sophocles and Euripides were romantic in their day. So was Racine—his particular kind of romanticism consisting in his faithfulness to the taste of the court of Louis XIV, a taste characterized mainly by the "extreme dignity" that was then fashionable, and that made "a Duke of 1670, even when overwhelmed with paternal affection, never fail to call his son: Monsieur." In another piece of criticism, Stendhal quotes Goethe to underscore the equation between *goût* (taste) and *mode* (fashion): Taste is the ability of pleasing today.[39] Taste is fashion. Set in historical perspective, such statements are rich in polemical implications. By his overt praise of fashion, for instance, does not Stendhal make fun of the neoclassical view that the artist should try to approximate as closely as possible *the* universal and atemporal model of beauty?

The paradox, of which Stendhal is an illustration, is that the modern-minded writer often finds that the present is unprepared to accept the very things that it most needs. So, the relevance of the artist's intuitions is to be confirmed by the future. The relations between the early nineteenth-century romantic and his time turn out to be quite strained. When referring to the contemporary situation, Stendhal speaks of the writer as a fighter rather than a pleaser: "One needs courage to be a romantic... a writer needs almost as much courage as a soldier (*guerrier*)."[40] This military analogy and the whole context in which it appears suggest the concept of the avant-garde, itself derived from a military metaphor. In contrast to the boldness of the romantic, the classicist is cautious to the point of cowardice. And the contemporary public protects him because it is terrorized by the great reputations of the past. This explains why the present does not dare ask for what it needs. People are unwittingly victims of the despotic power of habit, and it is one of the writer's major tasks to try to eliminate its inhibiting and almost paralyzing effects in matters of imagination.[41] Stendhal is aware that to be consistently modern (romantic, in his terminology) one has to take the risk of shocking the public, at least insofar as its taste is influenced by official academicism and a host of deep-rooted prejudices, for which an inadequate understanding of tradition is responsible.

In brief, for Stendhal the concept of romanticism embodies the notions of change, relativity, and, above all, presentness, which make its meaning coincide to a large extent with what Baudelaire would call four decades later "*la modernité.*" Romanticism, simply put, is the sense of the present conveyed artistically. Its sphere is thus much restricted, but at the same time its identity becomes essentially fleeting, extremely difficult to grasp because it cannot be defined in terms of past traditions (Christian or otherwise), and very provisional because it stakes its survival on the confirmation of the future. It is known that Stendhal himself, throughout a literary career that went almost unnoticed by his contemporaries, took comfort in the thought that the future would do him justice. There is much more to Stendhal's preoccupation with the future than the mere compensatory dream of someone suffering from lack of recognition. His personality is structurally that of a self-willed and entirely self-conscious *precursor*, although he clearly does not approve the vague rhetoric of futurity in which other romantics indulged (his known dislike of Victor Hugo's prophetic attitudes is significant). Stendhal was a "romantic" in his own sense of the word, and this is why, even in *Racine et Shakespeare*, written before his major works, he could sometimes be blatantly antiromantic, and consistent with his lifelong literary creed that was later termed "realist." In Stendhal, some of the distinctive paradoxes involved in the idea of literary modernity are already present. The most striking one is that, liberated from the constraints of tradition, the writer should strive to give his contemporaries a pleasure that they seem unprepared to enjoy and perhaps do not even deserve.

THE TWO MODERNITIES

It is impossible to say precisely when one can begin to speak of the existence of two distinct and bitterly conflicting modernities. What is certain is that at some point during the first half of the nineteenth century an irreversible split occurred between modernity as a stage in the history of Western civilization—a product of scientific and technological progress, of the industrial revolution, of the sweeping economic and social changes brought about by capitalism—and modernity as an aesthetic concept. Since then, the relations between the two modernities have been irreducibly hostile, but not without allowing and even stimulating a variety of mutual influences in their rage for each other's destruction.

With regard to the first, bourgeois idea of modernity, we may say that it has by and large continued the outstanding traditions of earlier periods in the history of the modern idea. The doctrine of progress, the confidence in the beneficial possibilities of science and technology, the concern with time (a *measurable* time, a time that can be bought and sold and therefore has, like any other commodity, a calculable equivalent in money), the cult of reason, and the ideal of freedom defined within the framework of an abstract humanism, but also the orientation toward pragmatism and the cult of action and success—all have been associated in various degrees with the battle for the modern and were kept alive and promoted as key values in the triumphant civilization established by the middle class.

By contrast, the other modernity, the one that was to bring into being the avant-gardes, was from its romantic beginnings inclined toward radical antibourgeois attitudes. It was disgusted with the middle-class scale of values and expressed its disgust through the most diverse means, ranging from rebellion, anarchy, and apocalypticism to aristocratic self-exile. So, more than its positive aspirations (which often have very little in common), what defines cultural modernity is its outright rejection of bourgeois modernity, its consuming negative passion.

Before referring more specifically to the origins of the split between the two modernities it is useful to focus on the term "modernity" itself.[42] In view of Baudelaire's cardinal importance as a theorist of aesthetic modernity, it should be pointed out that the word, a recent neologism in mid-nineteenth-century France, had circulated in English at least since the seventeenth century. The OED records the first occurrence of "modernity" (meaning "present times") in 1627. It also cites Horace Walpole, who in a letter of 1782 spoke of Chatterton's poems in terms of "the modernity of [their] modulation," which "nobody [that has an ear] can get over."[43] Horace Walpole's use of "modernity" as an argument in the famous controversy about the *Rowley Poems* (1777) of Thomas Chatterton—a poet whose work and tragic myth were to become so popular with the next, fully romantic generation—implies a subtle sense of *aesthetic* modernity. "Modernity" appears to be close to both the idea of personal "fashion" ("the *fashion* of the poems was Chatterton's own") and to what Walpole terms "the recent cast of the ideas and phraseology," but one should not confuse it with either. Its actual sense, in Walpole's view, was one of sound and "modulation," and we can best comprehend it musically.

As for France, the corresponding term, "*modernité*," was not used before the middle of the nineteenth century. Littré identifies it in an article by Théophile Gautier published in 1867.[44] The more recent and comprehensive Robert Dictionary discovers its first occurrence in Chateaubriand's *Mémoires d'outre-tombe,* which appeared in 1849. Neither Littré nor Robert mentions Baudelaire's use of *"modernité"* in his article on Constantin Guys, written in 1859 and published in 1863.

To appreciate the oustandingly original and seminal quality of Baudelaire's concept of "modernity" it will be instructive to consider here the way Chateaubriand employed the term about two decades earlier. In the 1833 diary notes taken during his trip from Paris to Prague and included as such in *Mémoires d'outre-tombe,* Chateaubriand uses *"modernité"* to refer disparagingly to the meanness and banality of everyday "modern life" as opposed to the eternal sublimity of nature and the grandeur of a legendary medieval past. The triteness of "modernity" comes out quite unequivocally: "The vulgarity, the modernity of the customs building and the passport," Chateaubriand writes, "were in contrast to the storm, the Gothic gates, the sound of the horn and the noise of the torrent."[45] I might add that the pejorative meaning of "modernity" has coexisted with the opposite, approbative sense in a fluctuating relationship that reflects the larger conflict between the two modernities.

The history of the alienation of the modern writer starts with the romantic movement. In an early phase, the object of hatred and ridicule is *philistinism,* a typical form of middle-class hypocrisy. The best example is preromantic and romantic Germany, where the critique of philistine mentality (with all its heavy and stupid pretensions, crass prosaism, and false, totally inadequate praise of intellectual values to disguise an obsessive preoccupation with material ones) played an essential role in the overall picture of cultural life. The satirical portrait of the philistine is frequently encountered in German romantic prose—we have only to recall E.T.A. Hoffmann's tales of the supernatural, and the typically Hoffmannesque antithesis between the creative powers of imagination (symbolized by, among others, the unforgettable Anselmus in *Der Goldene Topf)* and the utterly platitudinous character of the bourgeois world, with its solemn and empty earnestness. As a result, the term "philistine," negative and insulting as it was, acquired a definite social meaning, first in Germany, then in all Western cultures.

The significance of this semantic shift may be better understood when we compare the philistine to the laughingstock of the preceding neoclassical period, namely, the pedant. The pedant is a purely intellectual type and, as such, his social background is immaterial to the satirist who wants to portray him. The philistine is, on the contrary, defined mainly by his class background, all his intellectual attitudes being nothing but disguises of practical interests and social concerns.

The romantic critique of philistinism in Germany was taken over by young radical groups in the 1830s and 1840s, and worked out into a clear-cut opposition between two types: *the revolutionary* and *the philistine.* This is obviously the source of one of the most stubborn clichés in the Marxist criticism of Goethe, namely, that the great poet had a double nature, that he was both a rebel and a philistine, as Engels saw him in 1847: "Goethe's relation to the German society of his time in his works is of two kinds. At one time he is hostile to it, . . . he rebels against it as Gotz, Prometheus, Faust. . . . At another time he is friendly to it, 'accommodates' to it. . . . Thus Goethe is at one time colossal, at another petty; sometimes a defiant, scornful genius full of contempt for the world, other times a cautious, contented, narrow Philistine."[46] Interestingly, the notion of philistinism, which was originally a form of aesthetic protest against bourgeois mentality, was transformed in Germany into an instrument of ideological and political criticism.

In postrevolutionary France the opposite trend prevailed: various kinds of antibourgeois political radicalism (with both leftist and rightist implications, mixed in the most diverse proportions) underwent a process of aestheticization, so that we should not be surprised to discover that movements characterized by their extreme aestheticism, such as the loosely defined *l'art pour l'art*, or the later *décadentisme* and *symbolisme*, can best be understood when regarded as intensely polemical reactions against the expanding modernity of the middle class, with its *terre-à-terre* outlook, utilitarian preconceptions, mediocre conformity, and baseness of taste.

The idea of art's autonomy was by no means a novelty in the 1830s, when the battlecry of Art for Art's Sake became popular in France among circles of young Bohemian poets and painters. The view of art as an autonomous activity had been defended half a century earlier by Kant, who, in his *Critique of Judgment* (1790), had formulated his paradoxical concept of art's "purposiveness without a purpose" and thus affirmed art's fundamental disinterestedness. But *l'art pour l'art* as it was conceived by Théophile Gautier and his followers was not so much a full-fledged aesthetic theory as a rallying cry for artists who had become weary of empty romantic humanitarianism and felt the need to express their hatred of bourgeois mercantilism and vulgar utilitarianism. The central statement of Gautier in his preface to *Mademoiselle de Maupin* (1835) is characteristically negative, a definition of beauty in terms of its total uselessness: "*Il n'y a de vraiment beau que ce qui ne peut servir à rien; tout ce qui est utile est laid.*" In contrast to the views defended by Kant and his disciples in Germany, the partisans of *l'art pour l'art* promote a primarily polemical concept of beauty, derived not so much from an ideal of disinterestedness as from an aggressive assertion of art's total gratuitousness. This concept of beauty is perfectly summed up by the famous formula—*épater le bourgeois*. Art for Art's Sake is the first product of aesthetic modernity's rebellion against the modernity of the philistine.

Given that modern civilization is ugly, Théophile Gautier's attitude toward it is in fact more complex and ambivalent than his youthful preface to *Mademoiselle de Maupin* tends to suggest. In an article published in 1848 and entitled "Plastique et civilisation—Du beau antique et du beau moderne," Gautier argues that the ugliness of modern industrial life can be transformed. The result would be a *modern kind of beauty,* different from the canonic beauty of antiquity. Obviously, this can be achieved only on the basis of an acceptance of modernity as it is. Gautier writes specifically:

> It goes without saying that we accept civilization as it is, with its railroads, steamboats, English scientific research, central heating, factory chimneys and all its technical equipment, which have been considered impervious to the picturesque.[47]

Like Baudelaire—whose concept of the "heroism of modern life" he seems to echo here—Gautier is aware that the straight rejection of modern civilization as irredeemably ugly can be as much of a philistine attitude as the superficial praise of it. At the same time, he seems to realize that the aesthetic promotion of modernity can be turned against both the spirit of academicism and the escapist tendencies nurtured by romantic clichés. Gautier did not explore all the consequences of this viewpoint, but he was one of the first to suggest that certain images of modern life could become significant elements in the general strategy of artistic modernity, with its compelling aim of *épater le bourgeois.*

BAUDELAIRE AND THE PARADOXES OF
AESTHETIC MODERNITY

Baudelaire's preoccupation with modernity dates from his youth—I am thinking of his first comprehensive definition of romanticism in "The Salon of 1846," a definition that, interestingly, follows Stendhal's: "For me, romanticism is the most recent, the most contemporary expression of beauty."[48] And Baudelaire goes on to say that "there are as many kinds of beauty as there are habitual ways of seeking happiness"—the association of beauty with happiness coming again from Stendhal, specifically from the latter's aphorism in which beauty is defined as a promise of happiness (*"Le Beau n'est que la promesse du bonheur"*). The argument of change, on which the defense of contemporary taste is based, may also be Stendhalian, but Baudelaire's explicit identification of romanticism with *modern art* puts a new and radical emphasis on the idea of modernity and on the value of novelty.

> . . . Just as there have been as many ideals as there have been ways in which people understand morality, love, religion, etc., so romanticism will not consist in perfect execution, but in a conception analogous to the morality of the period. . . . Thus, above all it is necessary to know those aspects of nature and those situations of man which were disdained or unknown to the artists of the past. To speak of romanticism is to speak of modern art—that is, of intimacy, spirituality, color, aspiration toward the infinite, expressed by all means available to the arts.[49]

Romanticism is, in Baudelaire's view, not only the "most recent, the most contemporary form of the beautiful," but also—and this point deserves to be stressed—it is substantially different from *everything* that has been done in the past. The awareness of this dissimilarity is actually the starting point in the search for *novelty*, another cardinal concept of Baudelaire's poetics ("what has been disdained or unknown to the artists of the past" should become a subject of active meditation for the modern artist). The conclusion of the above-quoted passage is paradoxical and deeply revealing at the same time: "Hence," Baudelaire writes, "it follows that there is an obvious contradiction between romanticism and the works of its principal adherents. . . ." Today, we might speak of the romanticism Baudelaire had in mind as largely "antiromantic," or "modern," if we consider "modern" as an antonym for "romantic," according to a more recent terminological opposition for which Baudelaire's critical influence is directly responsible.

To give a more specific insight into Baudelaire's concept of romanticism, let us examine an instance in which it is applied more concretely. In the same "Salon of 1846," when discussing the paintings of Eugène Delacroix, Baudelaire expresses his impatience with the comparison between Delacroix and Victor Hugo, a comparison so popular among critics of the time as to become part of "the banal realm of accepted ideas." For, Baudelaire argues, to compare Delacroix to Hugo is just "sophomoric nonsense" ("*naiseries de rhétoricien*"): ". . . for if my definition of romanticism (intimacy, spirituality, etc.) places Delacroix at the head of this movement, it naturally excludes Victor Hugo."[50] The qualities by which Delacroix is distinguished from Victor Hugo are highly significant for Baudelaire's conception of romanticism (or modernity): inventiveness, the naïveté of genius, adventurous *imagination* as opposed to dexterity, adroitness, craftsmanship (the latter being characteristic of the gift for imitation).

The "Salon of 1846" deals at length with modernity, both directly (the chapter entitled "On the Heroism of Modern Life") and indirectly (the definition of romanticism), and there are many scattered remarks on it in other critical writings of Baudelaire, but there is little doubt that his most complete and pregnant treatment of modernity is to be found in his article on Constantin Guys, "The Painter of Modern Life" (1863). In this essay, modernity's most striking feature is its tendency toward some sort of immediacy, its attempt to identify with a sensuous present grasped in its very transitoriness and opposed, by its spontaneous nature, to a past hardened in frozen traditions and suggestive of lifeless quiescence:

> Modernity is the transitory, the fugitive, the contingent, the half of art, of which the other half is the eternal and the immutable. . . . As for this transitory, fleeting element whose metamorphoses are so frequent, you have no right either to scorn it or to ignore it. By suppressing it, you are bound to fall into the emptiness of an abstract and undefinable beauty, like that of the one woman before the first sin. . . . In a word, if a particular modernity is to be worthy to become antiquity, it is necessary to extract from it the mysterious beauty that human life involuntarily gives it. . . . Woe unto him who seeks in antiquity anything other than pure art, logic, and general method. By plunging too deeply into the past, he loses sight of the present; he renounces the values and privileges provided by circumstances; for almost all our originality comes from the stamp that *time* imprints upon our feelings.[51]

Baudelaire's *modernité*, both as defined theoretically and as applied practically to the works of Constantin Guys, embodies the paradoxes of a time awareness so strikingly new—by comparison with all the previous stages of the discussion of the modern—and so rich and refined, that it can be judged a qualitative turning point in the history of modernity as an idea. For Baudelaire "modernity" to a large extent has lost its usual *descriptive* function, that is, it can no longer serve as a criterion for cutting out from the historical process a segment that might be convincingly designated as *the present* and, in that capacity, be compared to *the past* either wholly or in certain specific respects. Baudelaire's approach to modernity renders impossible a systematic comparison between the moderns and the ancients, and in this sense it may be said to bring to a close an intellectual dispute whose origins go back to the late Middle Ages and whose history seems to be almost one with the development of the modern idea itself.

But why can modernity not be compared to anything in the past? Baudelaire thinks that what has survived (aesthetically) from the past is nothing but the expression of a variety of successive modernities, each one of them being unique and, as such, having its unique artistic expression. There is no link between these individual entities and, therefore, no comparison is actually possible. That is why an artist cannot learn from the past. The successful expression of a past modernity in a masterpiece can be useful to someone who is interested in studying the "general method" of art, but it does not contain anything that might help the contemporary artist discern *"le caractère de la beauté présente."* An artist needs creative imagination to give expression to modernity, and the proper functioning of imagination seems to imply for Baudelaire a forgetful immersion in the "now," the real source of "all our originality." Taken as models, the masterpieces of the past can only hinder the imaginative search for modernity.

Because of its newly discovered but deep hostility to the past, modernity can no longer be used as a periodizing label. With characteristic logical rigor, Baudelaire means by modernity the present in its "presentness," in its purely instantaneous quality. Modernity, then, can be defined as the paradoxical possibility of going beyond the flow of history through the consciousness of historicity in its most concrete immediacy, in its presentness. Aesthetically speaking, the "eternal half of beauty" (consisting of the most general laws of art) can be brought to a fleeting life (or afterlife) only through the experience of modern beauty. In its turn, modern beauty is included in the transhistorical realm of values—it becomes "antiquity"—but only at the price of renouncing any claim to serve as a model or an example to future artists. Separated from tradition (in the sense of a body of works and procedures to be imitated), artistic creation becomes an adventure and a drama in which the artist has no ally except his imagination.

Before going into the questions raised by the "drama of modernity," one more general observation concerning Baudelaire's use of the concept needs to be made. Deprived of its previously descriptive function, "modernity" becomes an emphatically normative concept. One may even speak of an imperative: art *ought* to be modern. With Baudelaire modernity ceases to be a given condition and the idea that, for better or worse, the moderns have no choice and cannot help being moderns is no longer valid. On the contrary, to be modern *is* a choice, and a heroic one, because the path of modernity is full of risks and difficulties.

Some of the inner conflicts of modern aesthetic consciousness as illustrated by Baudelaire form the central theme of the important essay "Literary History and Literary Modernity" by Paul de Man,[52] whose arguments and conclusions deserve to be considered at some length. Significantly, de Man starts his discussion of literary modernity by choosing among the possible opposites of "modernity" the one that he deems the most fruitful, namely "history." To exemplify the sense in which this opposition should be taken, he cites Nietzsche's second *Unzeitgemässe Betrachtung*, the polemical essay "Vom Nutzen und Nachteil der Historie für das Leben" ("Of the Use and Misuse of History for Life"), in which the philosopher establishes a far-reaching antithesis between "history" and "life," the latter conceived in both biological and temporal terms. "History" (memory) is shown as an irreducible enemy of "life" (spontaneous action) and, in de Man's words, "Nietzsche's ruthless forgetting, the blindness with which he throws himself into an action lightened of all previous experience, captures the authentic spirit of modernity,"[53] even though the word "modernity" is not used in Nietzsche's essay.* Modernity in this sense, de Man further argues, has always been an essential urge of literature, because "literature has a constitutive affinity with action, with the unmediated, free act that knows no past."[54] On the other hand, the distinctive character of literature being "its inability to escape from a condition that is felt to be unbearable," or simply its "inability to be modern," modernity, "which is fundamentally a falling away from literature and a rejection of history, also acts as the principle that gives literature duration and historical existence."[55]

Although the best part of de Man's essay consists of a sensitive and subtle analysis of Baudelaire's article on Constantin Guys, the author is obviously interested in reaching more general conclusions regarding the essence of literature: "As soon as Baudelaire has to replace the single instant of invention, conceived as an act, by a successive movement that involves at least two distinct moments, he enters into a world that assumes the depths and complications of an articulated time, an interdependence between past and future that prevents any present from ever coming into being."[56] I do not wish to argue here with de Man's view that all literature embodies in some fashion the "unsolvable paradox" of modernity. My own opinion is that modernity in general, and literary modernity in particular, are aspects of a time consciousness that has not remained the same throughout history, and that Baudelaire's theory of modernity cannot be enlarged to account for the whole of literature, simply because modernity is a rather recent invention that has little to say

---

*But de Man disregards the important fact that the term "modernity" ("*Modernität*") is frequently used in the later works of Nietzsche. For Nietzsche the notion of modernity is overwhelmingly negative—see below, "Nietzsche on 'Decadence' and 'Modernity,' " pp. 178–95.

about varieties of aesthetic experience unconcerned with time. Paul
de Man's impatience with positivistic history goes so far as to demand "a revision of the notion of history, and, beyond that, a revision of the notion of time on which our idea of history is based." He
also speaks, quite sweepingly, of "abandoning the preassumed concept of history as a generative process, . . . as a temporal hierarchy
that resembles a parental structure in which the past is like an
ancestor begetting, in a moment of unmediated presence, a future
capable of repeating in its turn the same generative process."[57] Such
criticisms of our historical terminology are useful, but the solution
he offers remains all too vague: instead of practicing a history based
naïvely on "empirical facts" and parental metaphors, we are told, we
should strive to become aware that the real (how real?) sources of
our historical knowledge are "written texts, even if these texts masquerade in the guise of wars and revolutions." So all the problems of
history are transferred to the plane of language and *écriture*, with
the only apparent result that they become much more intricate,
while remaining as metaphorical as ever. Leaving aside such
generalizations, whose discussion would carry us too far beyond the
purposes of this study, I retain from de Man's article both his excellent analysis of "Le Peintre de la vie moderne" and the suggested
opposition between *modernity* and *historical time*. Both are actually
very helpful for the understanding of a specific stage in the development of modernity's concept, if not of the essence of literature
or history, and my own account of Baudelaire's *modernité*, even
though I set it in a diachronical or evolutionary perspective, has
benefitted substantially from de Man's insight.

There is indeed a conflict between modernity and history, but
this conflict itself has a history. As far as literature and the arts are
concerned, one may even point to an approximate date: Baudelaire's
poetics of modernity can be taken as an early illustration of the
revolt of the present against the past—of the fleeting instant against
the steadiness of memory, of difference against repetition. Returning now to Baudelaire himself, this account of his treatment of

modernity would remain incomplete and onesided if it disregarded (as Paul de Man seems to disregard) another highly significant aspect of the poet's conception of beauty, namely, his dualistic vision of an "eternal beauty" and a "modern beauty." Such dualism is by no means the result of a whimsical association; on the contrary, it is basic to Baudelaire's way of thinking and entire creative activity. This deep-rooted belief in duality cannot fail to direct attention toward the poet's essentially and dramatically Christian frame of mind. It is almost a truism to say that there are few moderns in whose world outlook Christian dichotomies (God/Satan, heaven/ hell, soul/body, supernatural virtue/natural sinfulness, eternity/ time, etc.) play such a vast and complexly dialectical role as they do in Baudelaire's. A brief examination of the spiritual element in the poet's thought will open up a new perspective on his concept of modernity and, more generally, on the relationship between modernity and a Christianity that has ceased to be a religious guide and norm of life, and has instead become a means to attain and dramatize a lingering consciousness of crisis. (The broader theme of modern Christianity as a religion of despair and existential crisis will be treated in another chapter.)

To begin with, let me recall the often quoted passage from the posthumous *Mon coeur mis à nu*, in which Baudelaire speaks of the simultaneous existence in man of two contradictory urges—one toward God, the other toward Satan ("*Il y a dans tout homme, à toute heure, deux postulations simultanées, l'une vers Dieu, l'autre vers Satan*"[58]). This has to be related to the poet's most complete statement on beauty, which occurs in the also posthumous *Fusées:* "I have found the definition of Beauty—of my Beauty. It is something ardent and sad, something a little vague, allowing for conjecture. . . ."[59] Interestingly, the passage contains once again a quite unequivocal pledge of allegiance to *modernity in aesthetics:* Beauty, Baudelaire says, conveys a sense of strangeness, of *mystery,* and "finally (so as to admit courageously how modern I feel in matters of aesthetics), a sense of *unhappiness.*" The conclusion of this remarkable passage brings in, significantly, the figure of Satan: ". . . the most perfect type of masculine beauty is Satan—as Milton saw him."[60]

Modernity, from this point of view, appears as a spiritual adventure: the poet sets out to explore the forbidden realm of *evil*, whose most recent *flowers*, dangerously beautiful, he is supposed to discover and pluck. The task of the artist is akin to the alchemical one of extracting gold from mud or—if we translate this typically Baudelairean metaphor—to reveal the poetry hidden behind the most horrifying contrasts of social modernity: Baudelaire is quite explicit in this respect when he characterizes the "heroism of modern life" by, among other things, "the spectacle of fashionable life and of thousands of roaming existences—criminals and kept women—drifting about in the undergrounds of a great city."[61] *Les Fleurs du mal* and the prose poems of *Le Spleen de Paris* carry out both the program of a poetry of urban modernity and the most general project of a beauty, infernal and divine, whose being is the paradoxical place where opposites coincide—as in the famous "Hymne à la Beauté":[62]

> Did you spring out of heaven or the abyss,
> Beauty? Your gaze infernal, yet divine,
> Spreads infamy and glory, grief and bliss,
> And therefore you can be compared to wine.
> . . . .
> You trample men to death, and mock their clamour,
> Amongst your gauds pale Horror gleams and glances,
> And Murder, not the least of them in glamour,
> On your proud belly amorously dances.
>
> The dazzled insect seeks your candle-rays,
> Crackles, and burns, and seems to bless his doom.

It is important to stress that for Baudelaire "modernity" is not a "reality" to be copied by the artist but, ultimately, a work of his imagination by which he penetrates beyond the banality of observable appearances into a world of "correspondences," where ephemerality and eternity are one. Since Baudelaire, the aesthetics of

modernity has been consistently an aesthetics of imagination, opposed to any kind of realism (it is noteworthy that Baudelaire himself angrily rejected the recently coined term "realism,"[63] although
its inventor happened to be one of his close friends, Champfleury).
In light of this both implicit and explicit antirealism, it should be
stressed that Baudelaire's *modernité* is *not* cut off from the other,
historical and bourgeois, modernity, as has already been suggested.

A defender of modernity in aesthetics, Baudelaire is at the same
time an almost perfect example of the modern artist's alienation
from the society and official culture of his age. The poet's aristocratic
creed in a time of egalitarianism, his exaltation of individualism, and
his religion of *art* extended to a cult of the *artificial* (the dandy
becomes a hero and a saint, makeup is praised as "a sublime defor-
mation of nature," etc.) qualify his bitter hostility toward a prevailing
middle-class civilization, in which the only unchallenged standards
are utilitarian and mercantile. Baudelaire's portrait of Edgar Allan
Poe, seen as a victim of American democracy and as a martyr in the
catalogue of modern artistic alienation, sums up his main arguments
against bourgeois modernity. In "Edgar Poe, His Life and Works"
(1852) we read, for instance:

> All the documents that I have read lead to the conviction that for Poe
> the United States was nothing more than a vast prison which he
> traversed with the feverish agitation of a being made to breathe a
> sweeter air—nothing more than a gas-lighted nightmare—and that
> his inner, spiritual life . . . was nothing but a perpetual effort to escape
> the influence of this unfriendly atmosphere. In democratic societies
> public opinion is a pitiless dictator. . . . It could be said that from the
> impious love of liberty a new tyranny has been born, the tyranny of
> animals, or zoocracy, which in its ferocious insensibility resembles
> the Juggernaut. . . . Time and money have such a great value there.
> Material activity, disproportionately emphasized to the point of being
> a national mania, leaves little room in their minds for things which are
> not of this world. Poe, who . . . maintained that the great misfortune
> of his country was the lack of an aristocracy of birth, since, among a
> people without an aristocracy the cult of the Beautiful could only
> become corrupt, diminish and disappear—who charged fellow citi-
> zens, in their costly and pretentious luxury, with all the symptoms of

bad taste characteristic of upstarts—who considered Progress, the *great modern idea* [italics mine], as the fatuous dream of simpletons... —Poe was an exceptionally solitary mind.[64]

The general thrust of Baudelaire's criticism of America is reminiscent of de Tocqueville's analysis of American democracy (1835–40), especially with regard to the idea of the dictatorship of the majority and its effects on the development of the arts. What is important for us, however, is Baudelaire's view of America as a paradigm of bourgeois modernity, not inhibited, as it still was in the Old World, by any traditions, and thus revealing unashamedly its latent savagery. Baudelaire the "modernist" sounds like a staunch defender of the ancien régime in politics when he writes, in "New Notes on Edgar Poe" (1857):

> For every intellect of the old world, a political state has a center of movement which is its brain and its sun, old and glorious memories, long poetic and military annals, an aristocracy... ; but That! that mob of buyers and sellers, the nameless creature, that headless monster... you call that a State.[65]

When he has such a context in mind, Baudelaire does not hesitate to use the word "modern" in a downright pejorative sense, as when he expresses his admiration for Poe as a "prankster," as an artist who, besides his "noble conceptions," has ironically attempted "to delight the stupidity of his contemporaries," and "has very ingeniously fabricated hoaxes flattering to the pride of modern man."[66]

It is my view that Baudelaire's entire critique of sociopolitical modernity hinges on the idea that modern times favor the increasingly unrestricted manifestation of man's natural instincts—which the author regards as all-hateful and horrible. Rejecting "the eighteenth century's false conception of morality" (namely, that man is naturally good), Baudelaire writes in a famous passage (in "The Painter of Modern Life"):

> Examine, analyze everything that is natural, all the actions and desires of the purely natural man; you will find nothing but the horrible. Everything that is beautiful and noble is the result of reason and

thought. Crime, for which the human animal acquires a taste in his mother's womb, is of natural origin. Virtue, on the contrary, is artificial and supernatural.... Evil is done without effort, naturally, inevitably; good is always the product of an art.[67]

Modern democracy—as seen in its purest state, in America—is nothing but the triumph of that which is both most natural and worst in man (self-interest, aggressiveness, herd instinct, etc.).

This condemnation is a moral (and aesthetic) one. It does not imply either an irrationalistic stance or an inimical attitude toward science. As a matter of fact, in Baudelaire's case, the opposite appears to be true. Consistently with his antinaturalism (in the sense indicated above), the poet rejects both the romantic idea of a "natural genius" (analogous to a force of nature) and the already well-established and rich tradition of the organic concept of art. He stresses (not without clearly distinguishable polemic undertones) the conscious and willful element in the process of artistic creation—"inspiration" becomes a question of method and will ("Inspiration always comes when one wills it but does not go away at will"[68]). Although its pursuit is not that of truth in a logical or scientific sense, the poet's mind has to be as disciplined as that of a scientist. Poetry and mathematics are inherently related—a belief that Baudelaire shares with Novalis and other German romantics and, obviously, with Edgar Allan Poe, but not with most of the French romanticists, who advocated the aesthetic heresy of *la poésie du coeur*. Impatient with the way many romantics described art objects in terms of organic processes, our poet has a clear and highly significant bias in favor of *mechanical metaphors*. The functioning of a machine becomes, by implication, more beautiful than the growth of a plant (we should also recall here Baudelaire's phobia for the world of plants[69]). Separated from its utilitarian goal, a machine can become an object of aesthetic contemplation, and a work of art is not downgraded when it is compared to a machine. "There is no chance in art as there is no chance in mechanics," the author of "The Salon of 1846" remarks. And he goes on to say that "a painting is a machine whose systems are all intelligible for an experienced eye; in which everything has its reason to be where it is, if the painting is good; in which every single tone is meant to help bring forth another one. . . ."[70] If we take into account all these aspects we are entitled to say that one can distinguish in Baudelaire some of the first unmistakable traces of what would become later, with the emergence of various modernisms and avant-gardes, a full-fledged "mechanical-scientific myth," as described by Renato Poggioli.[71] Adding to all this the consideration of Baudelaire's genuine fascination with urban modernity (another facet of his highly consequential rejection of Rousseauian "nature"), one has to reach the conclusion that the author of *Le Spleen de Paris* was not opposed to the idea of civilization but rather to the new wave of barbarism, which, disguised as "progressive modernity," was threatening the foundations of human creativeness. But was not this very threat a cause of intensified awareness of that creativeness in the modern, heroically alienated artist?

Baudelaire's aesthetic seems caught up in a major contradiction. On the one hand, he calls for a rejection of the normative past, or at least for a recognition of tradition's irrelevancy to the specific creative tasks the modern artist is faced with; on the other hand, he nostalgically evokes the loss of an aristocratic past and deplores the encroachment of a vulgar, materialistic middle-class present. His program of modernity appears as an attempt to solve this conflict by rendering it fully and inescapably conscious. Once such consciousness is attained, the fleeting present can become truly creative and invent its own beauty, the beauty of transitoriness.

MODERNITY, THE DEATH OF GOD,

AND UTOPIA

At first sight, nothing seems farther removed from religion than the idea of modernity. Is not "modern man" an unbeliever and a "free thinker" *par excellence*? The association between modernity and a secular view of the world has become almost automatic. But as soon as we try to set modernity in an historical perspective, we realize that this association is not only relatively recent but also of minor significance when compared to the relationship between modernity and Christianity. In regard to this relationship we can distinguish four main phases.

The first is characterized by the medieval use of *modernus* as opposed to *antiquus*. *Modernus* designated a man of the day, a newcomer, while *antiquus* referred to anyone whose name had come down from the past surrounded by veneration, irrespective of whether he had lived before or after Christ or whether he had been a Christian or not. *Antiquitas* conveyed the sense of the essential *oneness* of tradition, whose continuity had not been interrupted by the coming of Christ, at least insofar as the distinction between antiquity and modernity was concerned. This was so perhaps because *modernus* (coined after *hodiernus*) was used in its narrow etymological meaning by men whose time consciousness was not yet assailed by any of the forthcoming dilemmas and paradoxes of unrepeatable time.

The second phase, starting with the Renaissance and extending through the Enlightenment, is characterized by a gradual separation of modernity from Christianity. At the beginning, the idea of modernity asserted itself only in nonreligious matters—the philosophy of nature, science, poetics. As a result of the Renaissance such notions as "antiquity" or the "ancients," while preserving their strongly positive connotations, underwent a significant semantic change: they no longer designated an undifferentiated past but rather a privileged and exemplary portion of it—the pagan classical times and authors of Greece and Rome. The moderns were supposed to imitate the ancients, then to emulate them, until some of the moderns proclaimed themselves superior to the ancients. During most of this period the principle of authority was challenged directly only outside religion, and tradition remained the cornerstone of theology, although even there the modern critical spirit was responsible for renewed attempts to distinguish between apocryphal, distorted, or false and genuine traditions, and was behind the dramatically different and unorthodox *interpretations* given to otherwise widely accepted traditions of Christianity. But the argument of modernity was too relativistically temporal to be used in religious disputes. Conversely, even the good Christians among the committed moderns of the late seventeenth and eighteenth centuries felt that the religious argument was too atemporal for their purpose, and confined themselves to using secular concepts derived from the philosophy of reason and progress. Toward the end of the rationalist and empiricist period of the Enlightenment the idea of modernity had lost much of its previous neutrality. Its conflict with religion finally came out into the open, and to be modern became almost equivalent to being a "free thinker."

The third phase covers the romantic period. The late eighteenth-century religious revival in literature, the new emphasis laid on sentiment and intuition, the cult of originality and imagination, combined with a widespread craze for the gothic and for the whole civilization of the Middle Ages, are part of a larger and sometimes confusingly complex reaction against the dry intellectualism of the *siècle des lumières* and its counterpart in aesthetics, neoclassicism. One of the most interesting results of the early romantic debate in Germany and then in other European countries is the enlargment of modernity's concept to cover the whole romantic, i.e., Christian era in Western history. The idea of a Christian poetry as distinct from and superior to that of antiquity was not absolutely new; as we have seen, it had been expressed (not very consequentially) by Christian authors of the sixteenth and seventeenth centuries, only to be abandoned during the neoclassical age by both the "ancients" and the "moderns." The romantic identification of the *modern genius* with the *genius of Christianity* and the view that, separated by an unbridgeable gap, there are *two* perfectly autonomous types of beauty, the first pagan, the second Christian, constitute a truly revolutionary moment in the history of aesthetic modernity. The cautiously relativistic Enlightenment philosophy of beauty is now replaced by a fatalistic historicism, which stresses the idea of total discontinuity between cultural cycles. Historical periods are analogous to living individuals, whose existence is ended by death. If the metaphor is older, the use the romantics make of it is new. Let us think of their consciousness—which has proved historically correct—of living toward the end of the Christian cycle, in a modernity both vast and narrow, exalting and tragic. It is this new feeling of modernity, derived from the notion of a dying Christianity, that explains why the romantics were the first to conceive the death of God and to incorporate in their works this essentially modern theme, long before Nietzsche gave it a central place in Zarathustra's prophetic doctrine.

The paradoxical implications of the romantic myth of God's death have been pointed out with remarkable insight by Octavio Paz in his recent book on modern poetry, entitled *Children of the Mire*. One of the essay's basic ideas is that modernity is an "exclusively Western concept" and that it cannot be dissociated from Christianity because "it could appear only within this conception of irreversible time; and it could appear only as a criticism of Christian eternity."[72] The myth of the death of God is in effect nothing but a result of Christianity's negation of cyclical time in favor of a linear and irreversible time—the axis of history—that leads to eternity. Octavio Paz writes:

> The death of God is a romantic theme. It is not philosophical, but religious: as far as the reason is concerned, God either exists or does not exist. If He exists, He cannot die; if not, how can someone who has never existed die? But this reasoning is only valid from the point of view of monotheism and the rectilinear and irreversible time of the West. The ancients knew that gods were mortal; they were manifestations of cyclical time and as such would come to life again and die again. . . . But Christ came to earth only once, for each event in the sacred history of Christianity is unique and will not be repeated. If someone says "God is dead," he is announcing an unrepeatable fact: God is dead forever. Within the concept of time as a linear and irreversible progression, the death of God is unthinkable, for the death of God opens the gates of contingency and unreason. There is a double reply to this: irony, humor, intellectual paradox; and also the poetic paradox, the image. Both appear in all the Romantics. . . .

)

> Although the source of each of these attitudes is religious, it is a strange and contradictory sort of religion since it consists of the awareness that religion is hollow. Romantic religiosity is irreligious, ironic: Romantic irreligion is religious, anguished.[73]

To continue our broad survey of the relationships between the idea of modernity and Christianity, one may speak of a new phase, the fourth, starting some time toward the middle of the nineteenth century. This phase reaffirms the death of God—until the expression becomes in our century a sort of cliché—but it is mainly concerned with exploring the consequences of God's unthinkable yet already banal demise. This time, the separation between modernity and Christianity seems to be complete, but once again this turns out to be an illusion if we think that a large number of the most prominent authors whom we label as "modern" either are incomprehensible outside the Judeo-Christian tradition (which they continue to represent, no matter how deviantly), or practice a passionate atheism about whose religious inspiration and motives there is little doubt. So, the death of God appears to have opened a new era of religious quest—a quest, it is true, that often is no longer measured or valued by its results but by its sheer intensity, a quest that is on its way to becoming an end in itself. In the questing phase, the consciousness of modernity takes the intellectual and poetic paradox of God's death for granted, so that, not surprisingly, even theologians dispense with the name of God (Paul Tillich prefers to speak of the "fundament of our existence") and include in the curriculum of more advanced divinity schools the new discipline of Death of God Theology, or Theothanatology. The crisis of religion gives birth to a religion of crisis, in which—as in Kierkegaard's extraordinarily anticipatory philosophy—all the unsolvable contradictions of the Judeo-Christian tradition are brought up simultaneously to unsettle every single certainty and induce existential despair and anguish.

On the whole, then, modernity, even if it attempted to do so, did not succeed in suppressing man's religious need and imagination; and by diverting them from their traditional course it may even have intensified them in the guise of an untold flourishing of heterodoxies—in religion proper, in morals, in social and political thinking, and in aesthetics. Directly linked to the decline of traditional Christianity's role is the powerful emergence of utopianism, perhaps the single most important event in the modern intellectual history of the West. In hindsight, although man was certainly a utopian dreamer long before, this appears to have been the eighteenth century's most significant legacy to our modernity, obsessed as it is with the idea and myth of Revolution. Indeed the rage for utopia—either directly and positively or by way of reaction and polemicism—pervades the whole intellectual spectrum of modernity from political philosophy to poetry and the arts.

The concept of utopia was originally based on a spatial association (*topos*—place, *u*—no, *utopia*—nowhere), but today its temporal implications far outweigh whatever it may have preserved of its strict etymology. A history of the term "utopia" would certainly be able to document in suggestive detail its progressive enrichment with temporal elements since the day when in 1516 Thomas More published his *De optimo reipublicae statu deque nova insula Utopia.* As a parenthesis, the genre of utopian fiction (including its parody, dystopia), a genre whose appearance should be connected to the powerful impact on imagination of the great Renaissance geographic discoveries, has for more than a century abandoned its traditional spatial setting—a faraway island or unexplored land—to convey directly the sense of futurity. (The last significant spatial utopia was probably Samuel Butler's *Erewhon*, published in 1872.)

Utopian imagination as it has developed since the eighteenth century is one more proof of the modern devaluation of the past and the growing importance of the future. Utopianism, however, would hardly be conceivable outside the specific time consciousness of the West, as it was shaped by Christianity and subsequently by reason's appropriation of the concept of irreversible time. The religious nature of utopianism is recognized by both its adversaries and advocates. A conservative thinker and defender of orthodox Roman Catholicism like Thomas Molnar, for instance, establishes a close connection between *heresy* and *utopia*, and discovers the latter's structural traits in the millennialism of medieval chiliastic movements and, more specifically, in the sharply dualistic (Manichean) premises of gnosticism. The gnostics upheld the belief that the world, essentially evil as it is, could not have been created by God, but only by His evil opposite, the Demiurge or the devil; thus, the task of man's soul is to find its way toward its original divine source by a total rejection of the body as part of the irredeemably corrupt material world (the orthodox view would be that life in its entirety, soul *and* body, mind *and* matter, is God's creation and as such should be thought of in relationship to Him).[74] Like heresy, then, utopia springs from a radical impatience with the imperfection of the world as it is, and claims that no matter how difficult to attain, perfection *is* accessible to man as a social being. The orthodox stance, according to Molnar, would consist of the recognition not only of man's imperfect nature but also of the diversity of *positive* values attached to this imperfection, which can only be irretrievably lost in the onesidedness of utopian thinking. The difficulty of this position comes from its implicit advocacy of a *status quo* that repels modern man's imagination of change. Finally, Molnar's conservative approach, for all its merits, is no less "utopian" than the "heresies" he condemns (imperfection becomes an ideal, it is associated with and redeemed by a vision of resourceful variety and inexhaustible richness).

Even more difficult to defend convincingly in a pluralistic age like ours is the idea of an orthodoxy by whose standards we could decide whether this or that tendency is heretical or not. Our specific time consciousness, which has brought about the loss of transcendence, is also responsible for the present-day conceptual emptiness of the opposition between orthodoxy and heresy. The term "orthodoxy" itself has acquired definitely pejorative connotations in a world in which "orthodoxies" can only define themselves in the most blindly sectarian fashion. When they are successful, their incoherence and arbitrariness become even more obvious, blown up, as it were, by the rule of terror that characterizes all totalitarianisms, right or left.

In contrast to the conservative view of utopia as a modern disguise of "eternal heresy" is the radical approach of a social and religious philosopher like Ernst Bloch. For him, since his early book on *The Spirit of Utopia* (*Geist der Utopie*, 1918), utopia is not only authentically religious in nature but also the sole legitimate heir of religion after the death of God. It is impossible here to go into the intricacies of his phenomenology of hope, which combines a messianic Marxism with insights borrowed from Freud's psychoanalysis and Jung's theory of archetypes, not to speak of the numerous themes coming from Jewish mysticism; nor can we consider the ideas it shares with existential ontology and other contemporary directions in philosophy. What in Bloch's thought is most relevant to our present concern is modern man's task of filling "the place into which Gods were imagined," a place that the philosopher defines in terms of an open-ended futurity, as the "not-yet" that never grows old because, as he puts it in *A Philosophy of the Future* when he paraphrases a famous dictum by Schiller, "Only that which has never yet come to pass never grows old."[75] The major thrust of Bloch's philosophy is well summed up in Jürgen Habermas's article, "Ernst Bloch—A Marxist Romantic": "God is dead, but his locus has survived him. The place into which mankind has imagined God and the gods, after the decay of these hypotheses, remains a hollow space. The measurements-in-depth of this vacuum, indeed atheism finally understood, sketch out the blueprint of a future kingdom of freedom."[76] Once again, atheism is regarded not as a neutral but as a highly and directly religious concept.

It is interesting that this defense of utopia comes from a Marxist. We know that Marx himself, while assimilating critically the heritage of the utopian socialism of Saint-Simon, Fourier, and Robert Owen, was openly opposed to any survivals ("petty-bourgeois" or other) of utopian thinking in a time when his own "scientific" doctrine of socialism was there to dispel such "naïve" daydreaming. Ironically, what some of today's Western neo-Marxists find outdated in Marx has to do precisely with what he himself considered emphatically *scientific* in his work. The essentiality of modernity's utopian dimension is verified—to scandalize Eastern "orthodox" Marxists—in the broad trend within contemporary Marxism that stresses the hidden utopian core of Marx's thought and thus gives his philosophy utopian dignity. This trend is represented, among others, by Herbert Marcuse and his followers in the now largely moribund New Left.

To account for modernity's complex and dramatically contradictory time consciousness, however, the concept of utopia has to be broadened to comprise its own negation. Born as a criticism of both Christian eternity and the present (insofar as the present is the product of the past, which it attempts to prolong), the utopian drive involves modern man in the adventure of the future. But, postulating the accessibility of a perfect state, the modern utopian spirit gets tangled in a dilemma that is at least as compelling as those posed by Christianity. On the one hand, the future is the only way out of the "nightmare of history," which in the eyes of the utopist makes the present essentially rotten and intolerable; but on the other hand, the future—the begetter of change and *difference*—is suppressed in the very attainment of perfection, which by definition cannot but repeat itself *ad infinitum*, negating the irreversible concept of time on which the whole of Western culture has been built. If we think that modernity came about as a commitment to otherness and change, and that its entire strategy was shaped by an "antitraditional tradition" based on the idea of *difference*, it should not be difficult to realize why it balks when it is confronted with the perspective of infinite *repetition* and the "boredom of utopia." Modernity and the critique of repetition are synonymous notions. That is why we can speak of the "modern tradition" only in a paradoxical way, as Octavio Paz does when he characterizes it as "A Tradition Against Itself," or when he stresses that

> The modern age is a separation.... The modern age is a breaking away from Christian society. Faithful to its origins, it is a continual breaking away, a ceaseless splitting apart.... As if it were one of those tortures imagined by Dante (but which is for us a stroke of luck: our reward for living in history), we search for ourselves in otherness,

find ourselves there, and as soon as we become one with this other whom we invent and who is our reflection, we cut ourselves from this phantom being, and run again in search of ourselves, chasing our own shadow.[77]

Not surprisingly, arguments previously used against Christian eternity are now turned against the secular eternity envisioned by utopianism. This and other aporias attached to the utopian mentality are responsible for the sweeping antiutopian drive that is equally characteristic of cultural modernity (and, needless to say, much wider than certain antiutopian fictions from Zamiatin to Huxley to Orwell might indicate). The real question at issue, simply put, is that of the *meaning of fulfillment*—in both general and individual terms. Even enthusiastic defenders of utopia like Ernst Bloch speak of the "melancholy of fulfillment" and stress the importance of the "not-yet" in the vision of the future. But to what extent is a consistent philosophy of the "not-yet" possible nowadays? Unfortunately, the modern utopist cannot afford to follow Lessing, who in his famous apologue imagined himself choosing, at God's invitation, between all Truth and just the active search for Truth (with the condition of never finding it). It was not too difficult for Lessing to make up his mind and, without hesitating, take the active, though endless, search—for "absolute truth belongs to Thee alone," he told God. Lessing's way of putting the problem would hardly make sense in a world where God—even as an abstraction or working hypothesis—is dead and everybody knows it. The heroic optimism of infinite search justified by the sheer greatness of a transcendent goal has been lost by modernity. The goals of the modern utopist are supposedly immanent and within reach, and to postpone attaining them would be irresponsible, despite the "melancholy of fulfillment."

Modern artistic creation illustrates in diverse ways the utopian/antiutopian relationship with time. It has become almost a truism to describe the modern artist as torn between his urge to cut himself off from the past—to become completely "modern"—and his dream to found a new *tradition*, recognizable as such by the future. Modernity, rendered possible by the consciousness of an irreversible time (which critical reason has purified of all transcendent or sacred meaning), engenders the utopia of a radiant instant of invention that can suppress time by repeating itself endlessly—as the central element of a new and final tradition (no matter how antitraditionally conceived). In principle, if not in practice, the modern artist is both aesthetically and morally obliged to be aware of his contradictory position, of the fact that his achievement of modernity is bound not only to be limited and relative (circumscribed by what Beckett calls the "order of the feasible"), but also to perpetuate the past that it tries to negate and to oppose the very notion of the future that it tries to promote. Some of the nihilistic statements of modern and avant-garde artists seem to be made in direct response to such a disturbing awareness of being snarled in a knot of incompatibilities. The clash between the utopian criticism of the present and the antiutopian criticism of the future resolves itself into a variety of nihilisms that will be discussed at more length in the chapter dealing with the concept of decadence.

LITERARY AND OTHER MODERNISMS

The history of the word "modernism" shows that it was not used, in Europe or elsewhere, before the Quarrel between the Ancients and the Moderns had reached its climax, that is, before the first decades of the eighteenth century. It is not difficult to understand why, at the height of the Battle of the Books, the suffix *ism*—indicative, among other things, of irrational adherence to the principles of a cult—was added to the term *modern* not by the moderns themselves but by their adversaries. The defenders of classical tradition were thus able to suggest that the attitude of the moderns was biased, that their claim of being superior to the ancients contained an element of dubious and finally disqualifying partisanship. An expression of intellectual contempt, "modernism" was little more than a terminological weapon in the hands of the antimoderns. In his *Dictionary of the English Language* (1755), Samuel Johnson, who lists the word as a neologism invented by Swift, quotes the following passage from a letter to Pope: "Scribblers send us over their trash in prose and verse, with abominable curtailments and quaint modernisms."[78] In Swift's eye, modernism was nothing but a self-evident example of the corruption of English by those derogatorily referred to as "modernists" in *The Tale of a Tub* (1704).[79]

To come across conscious attempts to rehabilitate "modernism" or at least neutralize its polemical connotations we have to wait until the last decades of the nineteenth century. But, as we shall see, even after such attempts were made, the lingering pejorative meaning of the word could be brought to the surface again, as in the condemnation of the heresy of "modernism" by the Catholic church in 1907. With occasional lapses into the semantics of disparagement, the notion gained wider acceptance and legitimacy only after the 1920s. Within the highly controversial terminological "constellation" of the "modern," "modernism" was not only a latecomer but certainly the concept with the most deep-rooted polemical connotations. That is why it took such considerable time for it to be vindicated.

The first to use the label of "modernism" approvingly to designate a larger contemporary movement of aesthetic renovation was Rubén Darío, the acknowledged founder of *el modernismo* in the early 1890s. There is nearly unanimous consent among literary historians of the Hispanic world that the birth of the *movimiento modernista* in Latin America has, among other things, the significance of a declaration of cultural independence of South America. The spirit of Darío's modernism clearly implied a downright rejection of Spain's cultural authority. The refreshing, "modernizing" French influence (combining the major postromantic trends, parnassian, decadent, and symbolist) was consciously and fruitfully played off against the old rhetorical clichés that prevailed in the Spanish literature of the time. The new movement, which achieved full self-awareness in Darío, went quite quickly through its first tentative stages. Its representatives, perfect contemporaries of the French "decadents," flirted for a short while with the notion of decadence, then took on the label of "symbolism" (which had become popular in France after Moréas's 1886 Symbolist Manifesto), then, finally, in the early 1890s, chose to call themselves *modernistas*. The choice of *modernismo* was a felicitous one because it made it possible for the adherents of the new poetic movement to go beyond the rather parochial squabbles that were characteristic of the contemporaneous French literary scene. Although Hispanic modernism is often regarded as a variant of French *symbolisme*, it would be much more correct to say that it constitutes a *synthesis* of all the major innovative tendencies that manifested themselves in late nineteenth-century France. The fact is that the French literary life of the period was divided up into a variety of conflicting schools, movements, or even sects (*"Parnasse," "décadisme," "symbolisme," "école romane,"* etc.) which, in their efforts to assert themselves as separate entities, failed to realize what they actually had in common. It was much less difficult to perceive this common element from a foreign perspective, and this was exactly what the *modernistas* succeeded in doing. As foreigners, even though some of them spent long periods in France, they were detached from the climate of group rivalries and petty polemics that prevailed in the Parisian intellectual life of the moment, and they were able to penetrate beyond the mere appearances of difference to grasp the underlying spirit of radical renovation, which they promoted under the name *modernismo*.

It is interesting to note here that French literary history itself, fascinated with the detail of late nineteenth-century aesthetic polemics, has been unable or unwilling to develop an historical-theoretical concept comparable to the Hispanic *modernismo*. This fascination with detail and minimal issues was perhaps the result of the belated triumph of positivism in French literary scholarship.[80] Suspicious of theory and theoretical constructs, positivism in historical disciplines has invariably led to the kind of historical "atomism" that has characterized the bulk of France's *critique universitaire* for more than a half century. It is true that during the last two decades a strong reaction against this type of aconceptual criticism has manifested itself under the label of *"la nouvelle critique."* But this new criticism, mostly structuralist and, as such, uninterested in history, has done practically nothing to replace the atomistic outlook of positivist criticism with broader and more fruitful *historical* hypotheses.

Rubén Darío spoke of *modernismo* as early as 1888, when, in an article published in the Chilean *Revista de Arte y Letras*, he praised the modernist quality of style of the Mexican writer Ricardo Contreras (*"el absoluto modernismo en la expresión"*).[81] His first description of *modernismo* as a movement (represented by "a small but triumphant and proud group of writers and poets from Spanish America") dates from 1890. It occurs in an article entitled *"Fotograbado,"* apparently written in Guatemala, and recounting Darío's encounter in Lima with Ricardo Palma (1833–1919). Palma was not a *modernista*, but his open-mindedness and catholicity of taste, which Darío highly commends, permitted him to understand the *espíritu nuevo* (new spirit) that modernism was consistently promoting both in prose and poetry.[82] Three years later Darío once again employs the term *modernismo* in the preface to Jesús Hernández Somoza's book *Historia de tres años del Gobierno Sacasa* (1893). Here the author of *Azul* recalls that Modesto Barrios, the Nicaraguan writer, had been one of the initiators of modernism with his translations from Théophile Gautier (*"traducía a Gautier y daba las primeras nociones del modernismo"*). But even before Barrios, Darío goes on to say, "a great writer, Ricardo Contreras, had brought us the good tidings, preaching the gospel of French letters."[83]

In 1894, in a review of Gómez Carrillo's *Sensaciones de arte*, Darío Herrera conveys his perception of *el modernismo*, stressing the importance, indeed the essentiality, of the French example. Gómez Carrillo, we are told, "like Rubén Darío, like Gutiérrez Nájera, like Soto Hall, like all those who drink from the French fountain, has been able to add to the sonorous music of the Spanish the concision, grace, coloring, the brilliant turns of phrase and the artis-

tic and exotic rarities which abound in modern Gallic literature."[84]
Modernism is nothing but the assimilation by Castilian poetry and
prose of the exacting refinements that characterize the best in
modern French writing.

"*Modernismo,*" used with increasing frequency in its positive
sense, was not long in revealing its latent negative connotations—a
situation the traditionalists quickly turned to their own advantage.
The term became their most potent weapon against the
modernistas, a strategy so effective that after 1894 Darío himself
avoided the word. In the preface to *El canto errante* (1907), for
instance, he spoke, without qualifying it, of the *movimiento* that he
had largely contributed to initiate in "las flamantes letras es-
pañolas."[85] In the meantime, reflecting the powerful reaction
against modernism, the 1899 edition of the *Diccionario de la lengua
española* published by the Spanish Academy defined the term
modernismo as follows: ". . . excessive affection for the modern and
contempt for the ancient, especially in art and literature."[86]

Neither the cause fought for under the banner of modernism nor
the notion itself was abandoned, however. In the chapter devoted to
the term *modernismo* ("*Historia de un nombre*") in his important
book *Breve historia del modernismo* (1954), Max Henríquez Ureña
cites two highly significant modernist professions of faith during the
very heyday of the antimodernist reaction. The first one comes from
the Latin American José Enrique Rodó, who in his study on *Rubén
Darío* (1899) declared: "*Yo soy un modernista también. . . .*" The
second one, dating from 1902, involves one of the greatest names of
continental Spanish literature, Ramón del Valle-Inclán.[87] Valle-
Inclán's testimony is interesting because it anticipates a later tendency to consider modernism not just as a literary school or movement but as a larger phenomenon, the expression of the spiritual
needs of a whole epoch. The Spanish writer perceives modernism as
a deeply liberating influence: "I have preferred to struggle to create
for myself a personal style instead of looking for a ready-made one
by imitating the writers of the seventeenth century. . . . This is how

I became a professed modernist: Looking for me in myself and not in others.... If in literature there exists something which could be called modernism, it is certainly a strong desire for personal originality [*personalidad*]."[88]

The term *modernismo* went on being used by Spanish-speaking writers and critics, and by the middle of the next decade it had become less controversial but at the same time less precise, so that in *La guerra literaria, 1898–1914* Manuel Machado could complain: "A word of purely common origin, created out of the astonishment of the majority for the latest novelties, modernism means something different to each person who utters it."[89] This lack of an accepted definition prompted the same author to note that modernism, "far from being a school, is the complete and utter end of all schools."[90] As demonstrated by the subsequent development of the concept in Hispanic criticism, it was precisely the impossibility of identifying modernism with a particular school or narrowly defined movement that constituted its basic quality, namely, that of offering the opportunity to account for a diversity of schools and individual initiatives by means of a unitary yet flexible critical category.

Since the early 1920s, *modernismo* has established itself as a major period term in Hispanic criticism. I do not intend here to follow in any detail the history of this concept in South American and Spanish criticism. The problem has been dealt with by, among others, Ned J. Davison, whose book *The Concept of Modernism in Hispanic Criticism* (1966) offers a useful review of scholarship on the subject (although I disagree with certain aspects of his analysis). After trying to delineate the area of essential critical "Consensus," Davison groups the various and sometimes sharply contradictory interpretations of Hispanic modernism into two broad categories under the headings: "Modernism as Aestheticism" and "The Epochal View." This distinction presents major difficulties (is not aestheticism an epochal phenomenon?), but it is acceptable as a working hypothesis in a study that, like Davison's, has primarily didactic and expository purposes. One may, however, reproach Davison with having reduced the aestheticist interpretation of modernism to a single author, Juan Marinello, and moreover to one who, as a quasi-Marxist, is totally opposed to the "fetishism of form," which, according to him, constitutes the essence of modernism; even more surprising is Davison's failure to point out the ideological reasons for Marinello's polemical attitude toward modernism. Probably the chapter on "Modernism as Aestheticism" should have centered around the various efforts to find convincing criteria for differentiating between the Latin American *modernismo* (characterized, according to Pedro Salinas, by "aestheticism and the search for beauty"[91] and the Spanish Generation of 1898 (which assigned itself broader ethical and philosophical goals).

Pedro Salinas's view, expressed in his important article *"El problema del modernismo en España, o un conflicto entre dos espíritus"* (1941), implies both a narrowing down and a rejection of modernism because of its cosmopolitan aestheticism. Considered largely as a fashion, the spirit of modernism had nothing in common with the seriousness of the will to change and the complex intellectual pathos of the Generation of 1898. To make his point as clear as possible, Salinas approvingly quotes Unamuno's indictment of *modernismo* (included in the 1912 volume of polemical essays *Contra esto y aquello*): "Eternalism [*eternismo*] and not modernism is what I stand for; not modernism, which will be antiquated and grotesque in ten years, when the fashion is gone."[92] But can we actually reduce modernism to a passing fad, as its adversaries at the beginning of the century attempted to do? Or, on the contrary, should we try to set modernism in a broader perspective and, instead of regarding it as a Spanish American or even Hispanic phenomenon, discover in it, apart from the numerous distinctive features, the elements by which it is related to other Western cultures similarly engaged in the adventure of modernity?

If we consider the evolution of the concept of modernism during the last three or four decades, it is clear that the second alternative has proven more fruitful. Salinas's approach has found some defenders (for instance, Guillermo Diaz Plaja in his *Modernismo frente a noventa y ocho*, 1951) and there are still literary historians who for ideological or other reasons prefer to deal with a strictly limited version of *modernismo*. The opposite trend, however, seems to be prevailing. The most famous defender of the broad interpretation was without doubt Juan Ramón Jiménez, whose notes for the course on *modernismo* held at the University of Puerto Rico in 1953 were published in 1962.[93] This orientation is also represented, among others, by Federico de Onís and by Jiménez's editor and commentator, Ricardo Gullón (*Direcciones del Modernismo*, 1963, reprinted in an enlarged edition in 1971).[94] After all, there is a choice between a more or less parochial view of *modernismo* (an Hispanic variant of French *symbolisme*, both notions taken in a positivistically restricted sense) and a view according to which there would be no substantial differences between *modernismo* and what Anglo-American criticism understands by "modernism."

The latter view appears as no novelty if we think that, back in 1920, Isaac Goldberg was arguing in his *Studies in Spanish American Literature* that modernism "is not a phenomenon restricted to Castilian and Ibero-American writers of the late nineteenth and early twentieth century, but rather an aspect of a spirit that inundated the world of Western thought during that era." And the same author goes on to say that modernism could not be characterized as a "school." Likewise, he points out that the word "movement" would be inadequate because "it does not convey the dynamic conception at the bottom of modernism, which . . . is the synthesis of several movements. In the latter sense modernism, far from having run its course, has entered upon a continental phase which promises to bear fruitful and significant results."[95]

From the point of view defended by Jiménez, Onís, or Gullón, the Spanish American *modernismo* and the so-called Generation of Ninety-Eight are related phenomena, and Unamuno, who was horrified by the term, appears as one of the most typically modernist spirits in the Hispanic world. This does not mean that these critics ignore the differences between modernism in Latin America and Spain. Onís does not fail to stress them in his essay *"Sobre el concepto del Modernismo"* (1949):

> When during the decade 1890–1900 the first great representatives of modernism—Benavente, Unamuno, Ganivet, Valle-Inclán, *Azorín*— emerge in Spain belatedly as compared to America and Europe, the literature they produce has an autochthonous and original character, and is independent from previous American examples. However, American and Spanish literature coincide in tendency and spirit, despite the differences that will always exist between Spain and America. Individualism is stronger in Spain and cosmopolitanism weaker; the attitude toward the nineteenth century more negative; and the problem of closing the gap between Spain and Europe takes on the dimensions of a national tragedy. But deeply there is an essential correspondence between modernism in Spain and America.[96]

Hispanic modernism, Onís contended in 1934, in the introduction to his anthology of modernist poetry, was nothing but the "Hispanic form of the universal literary and spiritual crisis started around 1885 . . . and manifesting itself in art, science, religion, politics and, gradually, in all other aspects of life. . . ."[97] But the "epochal" theory of modernism became both more consistent and more complex only as a reaction to the view plausibly and pregnantly expressed by Salinas in *"El problema del modernismo."* Ironically, Salinas rendered a great service to the very cause he opposed: he gave his potential adversaries a fertile topic for debate, aroused their self-consciousness, and furnished them with what they had been missing—the opportunity for rallying. In other words, he made an issue out of modernism. As Gullón has suggested, Jiménez became a theorist of modernism by way of reaction to Salinas and to those others who had developed Salinas's distinction between *modernismo* and the Generation of Ninety-Eight into a downright opposition.[98]

In his massive *Antología de la poesía española e hispanoamericana* (1882–1932), Federico de Onís offers perhaps the best example of how *modernismo* can be applied as a broad period concept. A glance at the anthology's table of contents is sufficient to give us an idea of what Onís understands by *modernismo*. The book is divided into six parts: "The Transition from Romanticism to Modernism: 1882–1896," which offers selections from the poetry of such authors as Manuel Gutiérrez Nájera, José Martí, José Asunción Silva, etc.; a section devoted entirely to Rubén Darío; "The Triumph of Modernism: 1896–1905," which consists of three sections, the first two being devoted respectively to *Poetas españoles* (Miguel de Unamuno, Francisco Villaespesa, Manuel Machado, Antonio Machado, Eduardo Marquina, Ramón Pérez de Ayala, and Ramón del Valle-Inclán) and *Poetas Americanos* (Guillermo Valencia, Ricardo Jaimes Freyre, Leopoldo Lugones, Amado Nervo, etc.); a section devoted entirely to Juan Ramón Jiménez; "Postmodernismo: 1905–1914"—postmodernism, according to the author, being "a conservative reaction within modernism itself, when the latter settles down and becomes rhetorical like any literary revolution that has won out";[99] and "Ultramodernismo: 1914–1932," which consists of two sections, each one of them observing the dichotomy between American and Spanish poets: (1) "The Transition from Modernism to *Ultraísmo*" and (2) "*Ultraísmo*." Among the Spanish ultraists we come across such important names as Pedro Salinas, Jorge Guillén, Federico García Lorca, Rafael Alberti. The representatives of American ultraism are Vicente Huidobro, César Vallejo, Jorge Luis Borges, Pablo Neruda, etc. As we can see, the restricted sense of *modernismo* is not negated but, being introduced in a larger historical context, it is actually enlarged and renewed on the very basis of its original meaning. Clearly, ultramodernism is different from (and in almost every respect more extreme than) *modernismo*, but this does not preclude the possibility of seeing them both as manifestations of the same interest in *modernity*, a modernity which is certainly changing—to the point that change constitutes its essence—and which is in any one of its major aspects in radical contrast to the stability of tradition. In this sense, Onís is perfectly entitled to argue that it is an error to disregard the indissoluble link between modernism and modernity: "Our error is,"

Onís confesses, "in the implication that there is a difference between 'Modernism' and 'modernity,' because Modernism is essentially, as those who gave it the name realized, the search for modernity."[100] As we have seen earlier, modernity always implies the sense of an "antitraditional tradition," and this accounts for, among other things, modernism's renewed capability of denying itself—its various historical "traditions"—without losing its identity. Modernity—and modernism—is a "tradition against itself," to repeat once again Octavio Paz's previously quoted formula.

Students of the concept of modernism in Hispanic criticism, and in particular those who defend the broad "epochal" approach to it, have consistently stressed the parallelism between the emergence of *modernismo* in literature and the sweeping theological debate on "modernism" that marks the turn of the century in the history of the Roman Catholic church. The term "modernism" first acquired a clearly international—though largely negative—status when it was used in connection with the modernizing tendency that appeared within the Catholic world, manifesting itself most significantly in France, Germany, and Italy. This tendency, which challenged some of the basic tenets of Catholicism (probably the most organically traditional of all Christian churches), had been tolerated if not encouraged during the liberal pontificate of Leo XIII, but was actively opposed and officially suppressed by Leo's conservative successor, Pius X. In hindsight, it is not too difficult to understand why such figures as the Abbé Alfred Loisy, Friedrich von Hügel, Ernesto Buonaiuti, George Tyrell, and others, who believed in the possibility of a synthesis of Catholicism and modernity and tried to reconcile Catholic tradition with the conclusions of positive science and historical criticism, were bound to come under official attack. Their ideas had a Reformation ring about them, insofar as they implied a thorough revision of the concepts of supernatural authority and unquestionable historical legitimacy, on which the whole of Catholic doctrine was based. So, the harsh condemnation of "modernism" in the encyclical letter *Pascendi dominici gregis* (issued in September

1907) should not be considered an exception to the Vatican's philosophy; the exception had occurred in the earlier official toleration of what was going to be called "modernism."

Loisy was certainly right when he claimed that *il y a autant de modernismes que de modernistes* (a statement, incidentally, that applies perfectly to literary modernism as well). It is quite clear that the Pope's encyclical letter was less than fair when it attempted to create the notion that there was such a thing as a "unitary" modernist doctrine that the faithful should reject globally. In theory, however, the encyclical was justified in pointing out the incompatibility between Catholic tradition and modernity; and if it is true that "there are as many modernisms as there are modernists," it is equally true that modernism, excluding any predetermined unity of views among its adherents, has, nevertheless, an identity, albeit an entirely negative one. This identity is based on a rejection of or, as is the case with the Catholic modernists, at least a questioning of authority in both its theoretical and practical aspects.

We are not interested here in either the exact history of the controversy or the validity of one or the other side's arguments, but strictly in the terminological strategy adopted by the church. By defending the *spiritual* (and atemporal) concept of religion against the broadly and variedly *temporal* and critical-historical concerns of the "modernists," the Pope and his advisers were able to exploit the still very strong polemical connotations of the word "modernism." Interestingly, the term had not been employed before (except very sporadically in 1904 and 1905) in the official language of the Roman Catholic church.[101]

Is it because of the influence of the church that in Italy "*modernismo*" has retained a largely pejorative meaning? Or should we look for the explanation of this remarkable fact elsewhere—in the association of the term with certain superficial and boisterous avant-garde manifestations? For, when applied to literature, the Italian notion of "*modernismo*" clearly tends to suggest the rather cheap and verbose "modernolatry" of people like Marinetti and some other futurists. It is probably with such an association in mind that Renato Poggioli in his *Theory of the Avant-Garde* tries to work out a clear-cut opposition between "modernity" and what appears to be its grotesque parody, "modernism":

> Both modernity and modernism go back etymologically to the concept of *la mode* [this etymology, suggestive as it may be, is erroneous]; but only the second agrees with the spirit and the letter of it. It is not in fact the modern which is destined to die... but the modernistic.... The avant-garde... is characterized not only by its own modernity but also by the particular type of modernism which is opposed to it.... Modernism leads up to, and beyond the extreme limits, of everything in the modern spirit which is most vain, frivolous, fleeting, and ephemeral. The honest-to-goodness nemesis of modernity, it cheapens and vulgarizes modernity into what Marinetti called, encomiastically, *modernolatry*: nothing but a blind adoration of the idols and fetishes of our time.[102]

Poggioli's view of "modernism" as an "involuntary caricature" of modernity may appear surprising to today's Anglo-American student of literature, for whom "modernism" is a scholarly label as legitimate as, say, "baroque" or "romanticism" (amusingly, when Poggioli's book was published in translation in the United States, reviewers disregarded the author's distaste for the notion "modernism" and proposed that the reader simply understand "modernism" whenever he comes across the term "avant-garde").

When was "modernism" used in the English-speaking world in anything close to its present-day literary meaning? It is difficult to set even an approximate date. The OED turns out not to be very helpful. With the exception of Swift's already mentioned "Letter to Pope," all the examples found under the heading of "modernism" are drawn from works written during the nineteenth century, and in most of them the word is used as a synonym for "modernity" in a very general sense (this becomes clear when we consider such phrases as "the modernism of its language"—with reference to *The Anglo-Saxon Chronicle*—or "illustrating... the spirit of modernism"—with reference to the American Republic). More recent and more specialized dictionaries or literary encyclopedias—such as Joseph T. Shipley's *Dictionary of World Literary Terms*[103]—list the word and sometimes offer useful definitions, but they all seem uninterested in the question of when and how "modernism" became a specifically literary or artistic notion. This is so perhaps because the use of "modernism" in the language of criticism is quite recent, and nothing is more difficult to deal with than recent history. Under the circumstances it seems safe to assume that in the English-speaking countries the term "modernism" acquired a distinctive literary significance during the first two decades of our century.

For the historian of the notion of modernism in an artistic-literary sense it may be noteworthy that a short-lived little magazine, calling itself *The Modernist: A Monthly Magazine of Modern Arts and Letters,* was published in 1919. The first issue (I, 1, November 1919) lists among the contributors such names as George Bernard Shaw, Theodore Dreiser, Hart Crane, and Georges Duhamel, but the reader is soon disappointed to realize that none of these authors had offered the magazine anything previously unpublished. The foreword to the first issue makes it clear that *The Modernist,* after all, is more concerned with politics than with literature or the arts. In the aftermath of World War I, the program of the magazine is committed to the cause of progress, revolutionary change, and socialism. "In the crucible of this awful conflict," the editor, James Waldo Fawcett, writes, "every tradition, every inherited standard, has been tested; many laws have been destroyed, many pretences have been abandoned. . . . In the sky of Russia a new star has appeared, a star progressing westward, watched now by the poor and downtrodden of every land with shining, eager eyes. . . . The very atmosphere is electric with impending revolution, revision and reconstruction in all the affairs of life. The past is dead. Only the present is reality. We dream of the future, but we may not see it yet as it will truly be."

Much more interesting for the specifically literary use of the term modernism is John Crowe Ransom's statement on "The Future of Poetry," made in *The Fugitive* in 1924 (*The Fugitive: A Journal of Poetry*, Vol. III, No. 1, February 1924, pp. 2–4). John Crowe Ransom, who later on was to create the label of "New Criticism" and to become one of the major representatives of this movement, did not attempt to define modernism, but some of the points he made can help us see how modernism was viewed in the early 1920s by an outstanding member of an advanced literary group. Ransom writes in "The Future of Poetry," which may well be considered a poetic manifesto:

> The arts generally have had to recognize Modernism—how should poetry escape? And yet what is Modernism? It is undefined.... In poetry the Imagists, in our time and place, made a valiant effort to formulate their program. Their modernist manifestoes were exciting, their practice was crude.... They announced at least two notable principles.
>
> In the first place, they declared for honesty of theme and accuracy of expression.... They conceived the first duty of the Moderns as being to disembarrass poetry of its terrible incubus of piety, in the full classical sense of that term, and they rendered the service.
>
> Their second principle followed. Emphasizing the newness of the matter, ... they were obliged to make their meters more elastic to accommodate their novelties.... Their free verse was no form at all, yet it made history.

Quite predictably, as John Crowe Ransom goes on to point out, against the formlessness involved by the second of these principles there came a "sweeping reaction." The problem was to take account of the dual role of words in poetry, and "to conduct a logical sequence with their meanings on the one hand, and to realize an objective pattern with their sounds on the other." Ransom was conscious of the fact that the difficulties posed by such a strict poetics were insurmountable and were bound to lead to a situation of crisis. Although the word "crisis" does not occur in his article, this notion is clearly implied, and it is probably more important for the understanding of Ransom's concept of modernism than the actual terms in which he formulates the modern poet's predicament:

But we moderns are impatient and destructive [my italics]. We forget entirely the enormous technical difficulty of the poetic art, and we examine the meanings of poems with a more and more microscopic analysis: we examine them in fact just as strictly as we examine the meanings of a prose which was composed without any handicap of metrical restrictions; and we do not obtain so readily as our fathers the ecstasy which is the total effect of poetry, the sense of miracle before the union of inner meaning and objective form. Our souls are not, in fact, in the enjoyment of full good health. For no art and no religion is possible until we make allowances. . . . Modern poets are their own severest critics; their own documents, on second reading, have been known to induce in poets a fatal paralysis of the writing digit. . . .

The future of poetry is immense? One is not so sure in these days, since it has felt *the fatal irritant of Modernism* [my italics]. Too much is demanded by the critic, attempted by the poet. . . . The intelligent poet of today is very painfully perched in a position which he cannot indefinitely occupy: vulgarly, he is straddling the fence, and cannot with safety land on either side.

By 1927, when Laura Riding and Robert Graves publish their collaborative *Survey of Modernist Poetry,* the term must have established itself as a meaningful—though still largely controversial— literary category. Characteristically, Riding and Graves define "modernist" poetry (as distinct from "modern" poetry in the neutral chronological sense) by its willful deviation from accepted poetic tradition, by the attempt to "free the *poem* of many of the traditional habits which prevented it from achieving its full significance."[104] Seen from this point of view, the most outstanding feature of "modernist" poetry is the difficulty it presents to the average reader. Their survey is to a large extent an attempt to explain the "unpopularity of modernist poetry with the plain reader" (the title of the fourth chapter) and to point out the specifically aesthetic reasons for "the divorce of *advanced contemporary* poetry [italics mine] from the common-sense standards of ordinary intelligence."[105]

Concerning the term "modernism" itself, Riding and Graves seem to take it for granted and as a result do not try to offer an even remotely systematic definition. The main elements for such a definition are there, however, and the reader can bring them together and work out a fairly consistent concept of modernism. The basic opposition between traditional poetry/modernist poetry is stated from the outset. Modernist poetry is also characterized as *advanced* ("the sophistications of advanced modern poetry," "advanced contemporary poetry"[106]). Modernist poets like e. e. cummings, we are told, are supported by "the pressure of more advanced critical opinion."[107] The seventh chapter of the book, "Modernist Poetry and Civilization," brings new and helpful terminological clarifications. The authors distinguish between "genuine modernism" and the "vulgar meaning of modernism... [which] is modern-ness, a keeping-up in poetry with the pace of civilization and intellectual history."[108] In its "perverted sense," modernism can become a sort of antitraditional "tyranny, increasing contemporary mannerisms in poetry."[109] The sense of modernism can be further perverted, the authors go on to say, by the existence of the middle class— representing "the intelligent plain-man point of view." "This middle population... is the prop and advocate of civilization; and the idea of civilization as a steady human progress does not exclude the idea of a modernist, *historically* forward poetry. A possible rapprochement exists, therefore, between this middle population, to whom poetry is just one of the many instruments of progress, and that type of contemporary poetical writing which advertises itself by its historical progressiveness."[110]

But surely this is false modernism. True modernism is not *historically* but only *aesthetically* forward. False modernism, then, is reducible to "faith in history," while genuine modernism is nothing more than "faith in the immediate, the *new* doings of poems (or poets or poetry) as not necessarily derived from history."[111] But why call such a poetry "modernist"? Riding and Graves fail to give a satisfactory answer to this important question. The fact that the representatives of "new poetry" are called (and call themselves) modernists is more than just a matter of arbitrary preference. Is not the cult of novelty a specific product of the history of modernity? Is not the "purist" creed of some outstanding modernists an *attitude* toward history and specifically toward modernity? Is not modernism's antitraditionalism an aesthetic manifestation of the characteristically modern urge for *change* (an urge that has been historically served by the myth of progress but that can exist outside and sometimes even in direct opposition to that myth)? The argument of modernism's neutrality with regard to history is unconvincing, as is the opinion of Riding and Graves that the term "modernism" as applied to the innovative trends in the poetry of the 1920s is justified by little more than a subjective preference: "There is, indeed, a genuine modernism which is not a part of a 'modernist' programme but a natural and personal manner and attitude in the poet to his work, and which accepts the denomination 'modernist' because it prefers it to other denominations."[112]

A *Survey of Modernist Poetry* was published at a time when the spirit of modernism was asserting itself with full force in English and American literature. Modernism had already produced a highly significant body of works in both poetry and prose, although its creativity was to continue at the same level of intensity and richness for another two decades or more. It was, however, too early for a more comprehensive critical synthesis or for a critical assessment of the concept of modernism. The student of terminology should also consider another aspect of historical semantics that may explain why the development of an independent notion of "modernism" was rather slow in England and the United States. This comparative slowness was partially due to the evolution of "modern" as both an adjective and a noun. When "modern" ceased to be a synonym for "contemporary," it became capable of performing the basic semantic functions of "modernism," unimpeded by the potentially pejorative or vulgar associations from which the latter term had freed itself only very recently. Thus, a large number of aesthetic theories, insights, and choices, which today we would not hesitate to describe as "modernist," went on being formulated within the broader framework of the idea of "the modern."

COMPARING THE MODERNS TO THE

CONTEMPORARIES

During the last century there has been such an enormous increase in the use of the terms "modern," "modernity," and "modernism" (the latter designating a conscious commitment to modernity, whose normative character is thus openly recognized), that in the domain of aesthetics alone it would probably take a study of forbidding proportions to follow in any detail the terminological history of the modern idea. But even before such extensive research is undertaken and its conclusions known, there are a few crucial points that no student of the concept of modernity should ignore.

From a broader perspective, the most important recent event seems to be the desynonymization of "modern" and "contemporary." Such a development would have been difficult to predict, even as recently as the time of Baudelaire. The author of the "Salons" went on using the two words interchangeably, although not without showing a clear preference for "modern," with all its implicit ambiguities. As I have tried to suggest, "modern" was for Baudelaire a privileged semantic space, a locus where opposites coincided and where, for a fleeting instant, the poetic alchemy was rendered possible by which mud is changed into something rich and strange. Baudelaire was undoubtedly attracted by the lack of neutrality of "modern" as a notion, which sometimes he could use derogatorily, at other times positively, and which he was finally able to cast into the more comprehensive and highly original mold of *modernité*. Thus to be "modern" became the central norm of an aesthetics that might be described as a dialectic of temporality (hinging on the notions of permanence and impermanence) applied to the arts. But Baudelaire did not establish a clear-cut distinction between "modern" and "contemporary." When was this distinction first used? We are unable to fix a date, but it seems reasonable to assume that "modern" and "contemporary" were not felt to be crucially different before the early twentieth century, when the movement that we call modernism had become fully self-conscious.

It is not surprising that "modern" and "contemporary" came to be desynonymized. The process that is accountable for this differentiation is not without some striking precedents if we think of the evolution of other major concepts of criticism. Despite unavoidable exceptions, there seems to be a general rule applying to literary and artistic terms that are employed, at some point or other in their semantic career, for the purposes of periodization (Wellek and Warren call them "period terms" and discuss some of the logical difficulties implied in their usage[113]). The genetic rule I have in mind is based on the demonstrable fact that each one of these terms has three fundamental aspects of meaning, which are formed in a corresponding number of broadly defined stages. The triple semantic structure of most "period terms" is quite easy to indicate: they always imply a *value* judgment, positive or negative (for instance, we may like or dislike "baroque" art or, more generally, things that strike us as "baroque"); they refer with more or less specificity to a particular segment of *history*, depending very much on the context and the concerns of the user; they also describe a *"type,"* which may have been more frequent in a certain historical period, but can have been illustrated in other periods as well (can we not attribute a "romantic" frame of mind to a contemporary artist? and can we not discuss the "modernity" of the seventeenth-century "metaphysical poets"?). Considering now the question of how these meanings were generated (different in each individual case, but similar when conceived in a broader historical outline), let us briefly examine each of the three phases, by means of which it may be possible to impose some order on this tremendously intricate matter.

(1) To begin with, we note that the most important period terms in use today come from the common language, and, with respect to their origins, they seem to be and actually are almost hopelessly heterogeneous: some of them were assimilated from classical Latin

(*classicus*), some come from medieval Latin ("romantic" was derived from *romanice*, designating the vernacular languages spoken by Western European peoples, as distinguished from Latin), some others were borrowed from modern languages ("baroque" originated from the Portuguese *barrueco*, originally used in the technical jargon of jewelers to designate a pearl of irregular shape), etc. The only common feature of such terms, at this early stage of their rich semantic careers, appears to have been their capacity for lending themselves to figurative uses, combined with a strong value statement—"classic" was originally a good word, applied to things that deserved to be admired; "baroque," in seventeenth-century France, a definitely bad word, referring to a certain kind of ugliness due to irregularity and exaggeration; etc.

(2) During the second phase of their evolution, period terms undergo a process of "historicization." They are used increasingly as periodizing instruments, but without losing their original function of expressing choices of taste. In France, for instance, the term "*classique*," as applied to the neoclassical authors of the seventeenth and eighteenth centuries, and to their followers, became strongly pejorative in the language of the young romantics; at the same time, in academic circles, "*romantique*" came to be equated with "decadent" and was regarded as an insulting label.

(3) In time, the polemical potential of such terms becomes eroded, and with this erosion a more relativistic approach becomes possible. In this phase, the meaning of already well-established period terms undergoes a process of conceptual "systematization," in the sense that the distinctive features of the various historical styles are projected structurally, and thus taken out from the linear and irreversible flow of historical time. That is why we can speak of a "romantic," or "baroque," or, in our case, "modern" type that can be encountered in both chronologically remote and chronologically contiguous periods of history. This possibility accounts for the emergence (especially in Germany, where Nietzsche's theory of the Apollonian-Dionysian conflict was so influential) of a global view of cultural history as a process explainable through continually renewed clashes between two recurrent and opposing types. It is

interesting, from our point of view, that the propounders of such dual evolutionary schemes of cultural history often make use of terms previously employed in the language of periodization— Wölfflin identifies the two principles at work throughout cultural history as "baroque" and "classicism"; Curtius and his disciples speak of "mannerism" and "classicism" (along these lines the view of G. R. Hocke that the modernist movement is just the most recent variant of "mannerism" is noteworthy).[114]

Returning to our account of the modern concept's historical metamorphoses, let us now consider the opposition between "modern" and "contemporary" as it is exemplified in a significant critical text written by a participant in the modernist adventure— Stephen Spender's *Struggle of the Modern* (1963):

> Modern art is that in which the artist reflects awareness of an unprecedented modern situation in its form and idiom. The quality which I call modern shows in the realized sensibility of style and form more than in subject matter. Thus, early in the scientific and industrial era, the age of Progress, I would not call Tennyson, Ruskin, Carlyle moderns because although they were aware of the effects of science, and most contemporary in their interest, they remained within the tradition of rationalism, unshaken in the powers of what Lawrence called the "conscious ego." They had the Voltairean "I".... The Voltairean "I" of Shaw, Wells, and the others, acts upon events. The "modern" "I" of Rimbaud, Joyce, Proust, Eliot's *Prufrock* is acted upon by them. The Voltairean "I" has the characteristics— rationalism, progressive politics, etc.—of the world the writer attempts to influence, whereas the modern "I" through receptiveness, suffering, passivity, transforms the world to which it is exposed.... The Voltairean egoists are contemporaries without being, from an aesthetic or literary point of view, moderns. What they write is rationalist, sociological, political and responsible. The writing of the moderns is the art of observers conscious of the action of the conditions observed upon their sensibility. Their critical awareness includes ironic self-criticism.[115]

Spender goes on to say that while the contemporary accepts (not uncritically) "the forces moving through the modern world, its values of science and progress," the modern "tends to see life as a whole and hence in modern conditions to condemn it as a whole."[116]

Although he accuses the contemporaries of having "partisan" attitudes (they are even likely to be "revolutionary"), Spender's own approach to modernity (through the concept of "wholeness" as opposed to contemporary "fragmentation") is hardly an example of impartiality. But in spite of his subjectivity, Spender's effort—not just in the quoted passages but throughout the entire book—is directed toward a structural rather than a merely historical definition of the modern. We need not agree with his particular conclusions to realize that his approach is fruitful, at least insofar as it tries to solve terminologically the inner tensions that went on growing within the concept of modernity since the romantic movement. It is not difficult to notice that what Spender means by "contemporary" specifically refers to the *other* modernity (and its effects on the literary mind), to the modernity of reason and progress, to the bourgeois modernity, whose principles can be turned even against the bourgeoisie (as happens in most contemporary revolutionary doctrines), to the modernity that produced the notion of "realism" and against which *aesthetic modernity* has reacted with increasing intensity ever since the first decades of the nineteenth century. It is, however, questionable whether aesthetic modernity has ever been capable of totally separating itself from its "contemporary" counterpart. Is not the polemicism of aesthetic modernity—even in its most implicit forms (not to mention the obvious ones, charged as they are with a sense of frustration and outrage)—a kind of dependence? And, on the other hand, has not the hated bourgeois modernity, at least during the last half century, tried to assimilate and promote artistic modernity to the extent that today the heritage of modernism and even the most extreme manifestations of the avant-garde have gained "official" recognition?

These and other similar questions will be raised again and again in this study, especially in the chapters devoted to the concepts of the "avant-garde" and "postmodernism," where they will receive closer attention. For the moment I shall limit myself to adding a few more general observations in connection with the remarkable phenomenon of the taming of the aesthetic and subversive modernity

by the "contemporary" spirit (in Spender's sense). This taming is
nowhere so evident and so effective as in the teaching of modern
literature.

The incompatibilities involved in the position in which the self-
conscious professor of modern literature finds himself have been
discussed in "On the Teaching of Modern Literature,"[117] the
thought-provoking essay by Lionel Trilling, included in his volume
Beyond Culture (1961). In the introductory part of the essay, Trilling recalls the highly interesting sense given to the term "modern"
by Matthew Arnold in the inaugural lecture held at Oxford in 1857
and published in 1867 in *Macmillan's Magazine* under the title "On
the Modern Element in Literature." It might be instructive to think
of the two perfectly contrasting uses made of the word "modern" by
two perfect contemporaries: Matthew Arnold and Baudelaire. A
cultural traditionalist, for whom the role of religion was to be taken
over by culture, Matthew Arnold enlarged the scope of modernity's
concept to comprise whatever was rationally valid and relevant in
the whole cultural heritage of mankind. We may add that he was, in
light of his understanding of modernity as a period of universal
syntheses of values, a follower of Goethe's particular kind of cultural
utopianism expressed in the idea of *Weltliteratur*—World Literature. If we take into account Arnold's loftily idealistic frame of reference, it is not hard to understand why he could, as Trilling puts it,
"use the word modern in a wholly honorific sense. So much so,
indeed, that he seems to dismiss all temporal ideas from the word
and makes it signify certain timeless intellectual and civic virtues. A
society, he said, is a modern society when it maintains a condition of
repose, confidence, free activity of the mind, and tolerance of diver-
gent views. . . ."[118] Clearly, Arnold's ideal of the modern has nothing to do with our sense of modernity as a culture of rupture. However, in a way—and Trilling should perhaps have made this point
more explicit—the professor of modern literature is put in the ironic
position of "Arnoldizing" ideas and experiences that would have
horrified Arnold. Is he not supposed to establish, within the context
of the modern, validities, preferences, and, finally, hierarchies of

value? In the final analysis, he is there to serve the "contemporary" spirit, which believes in progress, education, perfectibility, etc.; and he serves it even if he does not want to, because the bare fact of lecturing on modernity implies an "honorific" and dignified use of the term "modern." The professor of modern literature, however, has a right to feel anguished when he discerns in his students' response, as Trilling puts it, "the socialization of the anti-social, the acculturation of the anti-cultural, the legitimization of the subversive."

In sum, the *Querelle des anciens et des modernes* has been replaced by a Quarrel between the moderns and the contemporaries.[119] This unexpected situation is another suggestive illustration of modernity as a "tradition against itself." When modernity comes to oppose concepts without which it would have been inconceivable—concepts such as those included by Spender in his definition of the "contemporary" (reason, progress, science)—it is simply pursuing its deepest vocation, its constitutive sense of creation through rupture and crisis.

THE IDEA OF THE AVANT-GARDE

FROM MODERNITY TO THE AVANT-GARDE

Insofar as the idea of modernity implies both a radical criticism of the past and a definite commitment to change and the values of the future, it is not difficult to understand why, especially during the last two centuries, the moderns favored the application of the agonistic metaphor of the "avant-garde" (or "advance guard," or "vanguard")[1] to various domains, including literature, the arts, and politics. The obvious military implications of the concept point quite aptly toward some attitudes and trends for which the avant-garde is directly indebted to the broader consciousness of modernity—a sharp sense of militancy, praise of nonconformism, courageous precursory exploration, and, on a more general plane, confidence in the final victory of *time* and immanence over traditions that try to appear as eternal, immutable, and transcendentally determined. It was modernity's own alliance with time and long-lasting reliance on the concept of progress that made possible the myth of a self-conscious and heroic avant-garde in the struggle for futurity. Historically, the avant-garde started by dramatizing certain constitutive elements of the idea of modernity and making them into cornerstones of a revolutionary ethos. Thus, during the first half of the nineteenth century and even later, the concept of the avant-garde—both politically and culturally—was little more than a radicalized and strongly utopianized version of modernity.

From the point of view of a doctrinaire revolutionary (who cannot help considering himself a member of the avant-garde) the arbitrary past is automatically doomed, because justice is bound to triumph in the long run; but, as the oppressive influence of tradition can extend itself over a long period of time, it is important to act against it immediately and suppress it as soon as possible—by urgently joining the avant-garde. Although nothing can save it in the broad perspective of history's evolution, the past and what the revolutionist assumes to be its perverse forms of survival take on an obsessive, diabolically threatening power. And so, hypnotized by his enemy—of whom he makes an infinitely cunning and terrifying monster—the avant-gardist often ends up forgetting about the future. The future, he seems to imply, can take care of itself when the demons of the past are exorcised. As we are primarily interested in aesthetics, let us note that the avant-garde's theoretical futurism is frequently little more than a mere justification for the most radical varieties of polemicism and for the widespread use of subversive or openly disruptive artistic techniques. The overwhelming importance of the negative element in the actual programs of diverse artistic avant-gardes shows that ultimately they are committed to an all-encompassing nihilism, whose unavoidable consequence is self-destruction (here dadaism with its suicidal aesthetics of "antiart for antiart's sake" is an example in point).

Originating from romantic utopianism with its messianic fervors, the avant-garde follows a course of development essentially similar to that of the older and more comprehensive idea of modernity. This parallelism is certainly due to the fact that both rest originally on the same linear and irreversible concept of time and, as a consequence, are faced with all the insoluble dilemmas and incompatibilities involved in such a time concept. There is probably no single trait of the avant-garde in any of its historical metamorphoses that is not implied or even prefigured in the broader scope of modernity. There are, however, significant differences between the two movements. The avant-garde is in every respect more radical than modernity. Less flexible and less tolerant of nuances, it is naturally more dogmatic—both in the sense of self-assertion and, conversely, in the sense of self-destruction. The avant-garde borrows practically all its elements from the modern tradition but at the same time blows them up, exaggerates them, and places them in the most unexpected contexts, often making them almost completely unrecognizable. It is quite clear that the avant-garde would have been

hardly conceivable in the absence of a c
consciousness of modernity; however,
does not warrant the confusion of moderr
avant-garde, a confusion that frequently
criticism and that this terminological anal

THE "AVANT-GARDE" METAPHOR

IN THE RENAISSANCE: A RHETORICAL FIGURE

The word *"avant-garde"* (fore-guard) has an old history in French.
As a term of warfare it dates back to the Middle Ages, and it developed a figurative meaning at least as early as the Renaissance.
However, the metaphor of the avant-garde—expressing a self-
consciously advanced position in politics, literature and art, religion, etc.—was not employed with any consistency before the
nineteenth century. Among other things, this fact accounts for the
indelibly modern appearance of the label "avant-garde." Poggioli's
earliest example of the cultural use of the term is from a little-known
pamphlet published in 1845 by Gabriel Désiré Laverdant, a follower of Charles Fourier.[2] I was convinced, with Donald Drew
Egbert, that the cultural notion of the avant-garde had been introduced at least two decades earlier, in 1825, and that the utopian
philosophy of Saint-Simon had been responsible for this specific
application of the term.[3] Actually, the avant-garde metaphor was
applied to poetry almost three centuries earlier, as I found out
looking up the word "avant-garde" in the recent and excellent *Trésor de la langue française* (Paris: Editions du CNRS, 1974, vol. 3,
pp. 1056–57). During the second half of the sixteenth century, in a
period that anticipates certain themes of the later Quarrel between

nts and the Moderns, the French humanist lawyer and
an Etienne Pasquier (1529–1615) wrote in his *Recherches de*
rance:

> A glorious war was then being waged against ignorance, a war in
> which, I would say, Scève, Bèze, and Pelletier constituted the
> avant-garde; or, if you prefer, they were the fore-runners of the other
> poets. After them, Pierre de Ronsard of Vendôme and Joachim du
> Bellay of Anjou, both gentlemen of noblest ancestry, joined the
> ranks. The two of them fought valiantly, and Ronsard in the first
> place, so that several others entered the battle under their banners.[4]

This interesting passage occurs in chapter XXXVIII of the Feugère edition of *Recherches* (1849), "*De la grande flotte des poëtes*
que produisit le regne du roi Henri deuxième, et de la nouvelle forme
de poésie par eux introduite." The chapter is part of a larger tableau
of the overall development of French poetry, one of the first such
attempts, in any European country, at national literary history in
the modern sense (contemporary with Claude Fauchet's erudite
study of medieval French poetry, *Recueil de l'origine de la langue et*
poésie française..., which appeared in 1581). Pasquier employs an
evolutionary concept of history when he discusses the rise of poetry
in the vernacular in terms of *progress*—his own word (cf. "*De l'an-*
cienneté et progrès de notre poésie française"[5]). Without rejecting
the notion of imitation of antiquity (a notion that had been strongly
promoted by the representatives of the *Pléiade,* whom he admires),
Pasquier is on the side of the moderns ("*Que nos poëtes français,*
imitant les latins, les ont souvent égalés et quelque fois surmontés")
and may be considered one of the *direct* forerunners of the *Querelle*
that was to break out a century later. The whole chapter XLII of *Re-*
cherches is devoted to a comparison of selected passages from
French poets (mainly Ronsard) and from their Latin models (Catul-
lus, Ovid, Virgil). Guarding against the exaggerated and often
superstitious respect for antiquity—"*un respect que parfois avec*
trop de superstition nous portons à l'ancienneté"[6]—Pasquier is obviously delighted to point out when and how modern French poets
are superior to their ancient masters.

Pasquier's *modern* attitude is illustrated not only by the general conclusion of his comparison but also by certain extremely suggestive stylistic details that could explain, among other things, his use of the avant-garde analogy. Thus, after admiringly quoting one of Ronsard's poems, Pasquier feels like challenging antiquity to come up with equally impressive poetic achievements: *"Je defie toute l'ancienneté de nous faire part d'une pièce mieux relevée, et de plus belle etoffe que celle-ci."*[7] The same pugnacious mood reveals itself in the later statement that Ronsard's works at their best *"font contrecarre à l'antiquité."*[8] The noun *"contrecarre"* comes from the verb *"contrecarrer"*—meaning "to oppose, to contradict, to run counter"—and is plainly suggestive of antagonism. But the moderns as Pasquier saw them did not really oppose the aesthetic ideal of antiquity and, finally, their apparent fight against the ancients, observing the rules laid down by the latter, was hardly more than a heightened form of emulation. Even so, Pasquier's idea of a *competition* for aesthetic supremacy between the moderns and the ancients remains very interesting for the time when it was expressed.

In view of Pasquier's general conception of literary evolution, his metaphorical use of the term "avant-garde" appears less than surprising. The author of *Recherches* had a marked predilection for agonistic analogies. As we remember, the whole passage in which the word "avant-garde" occurs is nothing but an extended military simile. Besides the "war against ignorance" and "avant-garde" itself, we encounter the significant expression by which the role of Ronsard and du Bellay is characterized: *"se mirent sur les rangs,"* meaning literally "they entered the battle" (*"rang"* in a military sense is "rank," and the phrase *"se mettre sur les rangs"* originally signified "to enter the battle or tournament"—whence its current French usage, "to be or become a competitor"). We also find the phrase *"sous leurs enseignes plusieurs se firent enrôler"* ("several others enrolled to fight under their banner").

In spite of the "modernity" of his outlook, Pasquier had a long and respectable tradition behind him when he drew upon the analogical resources of war imagery. In fact, his "war against ignorance" sounds almost like a cliché, and as such it fits very well into the age-old codified symbolism of war. Does not every war— mythological or historical—concern the struggle of light, life, and knowledge against darkness and evil? Pasquier, in trying to chronicle the growth of his country's poetry, felt entitled to transfer certain notions of the language of history (a language directly connected with the central reality of war, from which it derives much of its narrative structure and dramatic quality) to the language of an early and still very tentative kind of *literary history*. As a result, the metaphor of the avant-garde was coined. But the avant-garde analogy as used by Pasquier is just one among several elements that *together* form what might be called a rhetorical "constellation." No one of these elements is particularly emphasized in the context, and the reader is offered no criteria by which any one of them could be singled out.

THE ROMANTIC "AVANT-GARDE":

FROM POLITICS TO THE POLITICS OF CULTURE

For Pasquier, "avant-garde" was simply a suggestive figure of style, which, together with other similar rhetorical devices, conveyed his sense of change and evolution in literature. Significantly, he never implied that those whom he ranged in the "vanguard" had been in any way *conscious* of their role. And, as we shall soon see, self-consciousness—or the illusion of self-consciousness—is absolutely crucial to the definition of the more recent avant-garde.

Although it is encountered in the language of warfare, the modern notion of "avant-garde" has a lot more to do with the language, theory, and practice of a comparatively recent kind of warfare, the revolutionary civil war. In this sense, it is safe to say that the actual career of the term avant-garde was started in the aftermath of the French Revolution, when it acquired undisputed political overtones. The first periodical to bear this specific word in its title was, to be sure, a military one, but it left little doubt as to its revolutionary political stance. I am referring to *L'Avant-garde de l'armée des Pyrenées orientales*, a journal that appeared in 1794 and whose watchword—engraved on the blade of an emblematic sword—was: *"La liberté ou la mort."* This journal was committed to the defense of Jacobin ideas and was intended to reach, beyond military circles, a broader audience of "patriots."[9] We can therefore take the 1790s as a starting point for the subsequent career of the concept of avant-garde in radical political thought. In hindsight, considering the analogical potentialities of the military notion, it is not difficult to explain the appeal of the metaphor for various kinds of revolutionary, and therefore future-oriented, philosophies: their representatives certainly liked the idea of being, at least intellectually, closer to Utopia than the rest of mankind, which was to follow their paths.

It is, therefore, not by chance that the romantic use of avant-garde in a literary-artistic context was directly derived from the language of revolutionary politics. This occurred in 1825, when the term avant-garde was applied to the arts in a dialogue written by one of the closest friends and disciples of Saint-Simon, namely, Olinde Rodrigues. Rodrigues's dialogue, *"L'Artiste, le savant et l'industriel,"* was published in a volume entitled *Opinions littéraires, philosophiques et industrielles*, which appeared in 1825, the year of Saint-Simon's death. Although generally attributed to Saint-Simon, it is known that this unsigned volume was, in fact, the result of a collaboration, which, beside the work of the master, included those of his disciples: Léon Halévy, Rodrigues, Duvergier, and Bailly.[10] This occurrence of avant-garde was discussed at some length by Donald Drew Egbert but, curiously, the author—who seems only to have consulted the 1825 edition of *Opinions . . .* —attributes the use of the term avant-garde to Saint-Simon and does not mention the

name of Rodrigues, who, even if inspired by Saint-Simon's socialism, actually wrote the dialogue between the artist, the scientist,
and the industrialist.

Certainly, in order to understand Rodrigues's text we have to
define the place it occupies in the larger framework of Saint-Simon's
late political philosophy, although the idea that artists constitute the
"vanguard" in the moral history of mankind was, to a large extent,
the result of a more general romantic and messianic belief. Toward
the end of his life, Saint-Simon regarded artists, along with scientists and industrialists, as naturally destined to be part of the trini-
tarian ruling elite in the ideal state. This principle of social organization—which made the artists prominent elements in the leadership of a new kind of society—had already been formulated by
Saint-Simon, and elaborated upon by him and his disciples in the
early 1820s. The idea was unequivocally expressed, for instance, in
the *Lettres de H. de Saint-Simon à Messieurs les Jurés* (1820), where
Saint-Simon declared: "New meditations have proved to me that
things should move ahead with the artists in the lead, followed by
the scientists, and that the industrialists should come after these two
classes."[11] As we can easily see, the artist was assigned a specifically
"avant-garde" role, although the term itself was not employed in
this context. To Saint-Simon, the artist is the "man of imagination"
and, as such, he is capable not only of foreseeing the future but also
of creating it. His grandiose task is to take the "Golden Age" of the
past and project its magic glow into the future. In *De l'organisation
sociale* (1825), Saint-Simon envisions the artists as opening the
"march," the triumphant march toward the well-being and happiness of all mankind:

> . . . in this great undertaking the artists, the men of imagination will
> open the march: they will take the Golden Age from the past and offer
> it as a gift to future generations; they will make society pursue
> passionately the rise of its well-being, and they will do this by pre-
> senting the picture of new prosperity, by making each member of
> society aware that everyone will soon have a share in enjoyments
> which up to now have been the privilege of an extremely small class;

they will sing the blessings of civilization, and for the attainment of
their goal they will use all the means of the arts, eloquence, poetry,
painting, music; in a word, they will develop the poetic aspect of the
new system.[12]

The paradox of this approach to the problem of the artist is not
difficult to perceive: on the one hand, the artist enjoys the honor of
being in the forefront of the movement toward social prosperity; on
the other, he is no longer free but, on the contrary, given—by the
same political philosopher who so generously proclaimed him a
leader—a whole program to fulfill, and a completely didactic one, at
that. All of this definitely reminds us of the theory of "socialist
realism" in our century. This didactic-utilitarian conception, which
assigns to the artist an avant-garde role only to make of him a disciplined soldier or militant, is even less ambiguously affirmed in Rodrigues's dialogue. If artists have previously performed only a secondary role in social life—Rodrigues argues—that was due to their lack
of a "common impulsion" and a "general idea." This "general idea"
will be, of course, that of the Saint-Simonian, highly centralized
type of socialism, which the artists are called upon to popularize.
Rodrigues writes:

> It is we, artists, that will serve as your avant-garde; the power of the
> arts is indeed the most immediate and the fastest. We have weapons
> of all sorts: when we want to spread new ideas among people, we
> carve them in marble or paint them on canvas; we popularize them by
> means of poetry and music; by turns, we resort to the lyre or the
> flute, the ode or the song, history or the novel; the theatre stage is
> open to us, and it is mostly from there that our influence exerts itself
> electrically, victoriously. We address ourselves to the imagination
> and feelings of people: we are therefore supposed to achieve the most
> vivid and decisive kind of action; and if today we seem to play no role
> or at best a very secondary one, that has been the result of the arts'
> lacking a common drive and a general idea, which are essential to
> their energy and success.[13]

Interested as we are in the avant-garde as a concept of criticism,
we cannot overlook the fact that its early nineteenth-century use in

an artistic context—by a political thinker—still had very strongly military connotations. That is why in the quoted passages we find such military or quasi-military notions as: "march," "power," "arms," "victorious," "decisive action," etc.

However, if we compare what Rodrigues has to say about the avant-garde mission of the artist with the rather narrow significance of Pasquier's stylistic figure, it becomes clear that a very important shift has occurred in the function of the avant-garde metaphor as well as in that of related military analogies. The major change consists in the implication that the avant-garde is—or should be— *conscious* of being in advance of its own time. This consciousness not only imposes a sense of mission on the representatives of the avant-garde but confers upon them the privileges and responsibilities of leadership. To be a member of the avant-garde is to be part of an elite—although this elite, unlike the ruling classes or groups of the past, is committed to a totally antielitist program, whose final utopian aim is the equal sharing by all people of all the benefits of life. This basically elitist-antielitist approach to the problem of the avant-garde has been preserved, as we shall see, in the Marxist-Leninist theory of the party as the revolutionary avant-garde of the proletariat. As for the late nineteenth- and twentieth-century *artistic avant-garde*, the same paradox, although interpreted from an aesthetic angle, offers the key to most of its strikingly contradictory pronouncements and actions. This may be illustrated by, among other things, Lautréamont's famous anarchist dictum, later included in the credo of the surrealists: "Poetry should be made not by one but by all." The main difference between the political and the artistic avant-gardes of the last one hundred years consists in the latter's insistence on the *independently* revolutionary potential of art, while the former tend to justify the opposite idea, namely, that art should submit itself to the requirements and needs of the political revolutionists. But both start from the same premise: life should be radically changed. And the goal of both is the same utopian anarchy (even Marx was an anarchist at heart, and when he polemicized against Bakunin and his followers he disagreed not with their goal—the destruction of the state—but only with the practical means they recommended for its attainment).

If we dwell upon Saint-Simon's and Rodrigues's ideas concerning the mission of the artist, we cannot fail to recognize in them a specifically romantic ring. The myth of the poet as a prophet had been revived and developed since the early days of romanticism, but to recall now some of the countless possible examples would take us too far from our subject. It will suffice to say that almost all the progressive-minded romantics upheld the belief in the avant-garde role of poetry, even if they did not use the term "avant-garde" and even if they did not embrace a didactic-utilitarian philosophy of art. The latter point is well illustrated by Shelley. A disciple of William Godwin—the author of the famous *Enquiry Concerning Political Justice* (1793)—Shelley was undoubtedly a liberal radical; but he thought, in his own words, that "a Poet . . . would do ill to embody his own conceptions of right or wrong, which are usually those of his time and place, in his poetical creations, which participate in neither."[14] If poetry, whose essence is imagination, is to have a moral effect, this can be brought about only by an enlargement of the imagination: "A man, to be greatly good, must imagine intensely and comprehensively. . . . Poetry enlarges the circumference of the imagination." In other words, poetry has to play a great social role not because it can "popularize" some idea or other, but simply because it stimulates the imagination.

These opinions were expressed in the posthumously published "Defence of Poetry," written in 1821. Shelley wanted to refute the thesis of T. L. Peacock, who contended, in his satiric essay on "The Four Ages of Poetry," that "a poet in our time is a semi-barbarian in a civilized community." For Shelley, the poet is not a relic of the past but a harbinger of the future. In the concluding part of "The Defence of Poetry," poets are specifically termed "heralds," and their minds are called "mirrors of futurity." "The Poet," Shelley writes, making a memorable statement, "is the unacknowledged legislator of the world."

We find in Shelley's essay—which might be considered the testimony of a great romantic poet in the debate we are focussing on—some of the ideas stressed in the writings of Saint-Simon and his disciples. First, the image of the poet (or the creative artist in general) as primarily a man of imagination. Then, the conception of the poet as a herald of the future. The unique social function of the artist is emphasized by both Saint-Simon and Shelley. But whereas Saint-Simon tends to favor a pedagogical and topical view of the artist's mission, Shelley seems to think that this same mission is carried out more naturally, and even unconsciously, through the display of the imaginative power, which is not governed by reason but by spontaneous inspiration. The essential contrast between Saint-Simon and Shelley would consist, then, in the former's prescribing a program for the imagination to fulfill (imagination having no real power without a "common impulsion" and a "general idea"), and the latter's placing an almost exclusive emphasis on imagination *per se,* regarded as the highest moral quality. Basically, the difference can be reduced to that between authoritarianism and libertarianism. This distinction is important for the understanding of the subsequent evolution of the idea of avant-garde both in the arts and in politics.

Saint-Simon's rival in political philosophy and social reformism, Charles Fourier, did not explicitly assign an avant-garde role to the artist, but implied the idea in more than one way in his doctrine. We should not, therefore, be surprised by the fact that one of his disciples, the obscure Gabriel Désiré Laverdant, conceived of the mission of the arts along much the same lines as those previously followed by Saint-Simon or Rodrigues. In his brief pamphlet entitled *De la mission de l'art et du rôle des artistes* (1845)—which, according to Renato Poggioli, can be taken as a perfect example of "the doctrine of art as an instrument for social action and reform, a means of revolutionary propaganda and agitation"[15]—Laverdant specifically writes, making significant use of the term avant-garde:

Art, the expression of Society, communicates, in its highest soaring, the most advanced social tendencies; it is the precursor and the revealer. So that in order to know whether art fulfills with dignity its role as initiator, whether the artist is actually of the avant-garde, one must know where Humanity is going, and what the destiny of our species is.[16]

Clearly, the wide appeal of Fourierism to a great assortment of artists did not lie in ideas like those expressed by Laverdant. What artists found attractive in Fourierism was the fact that—as Donald Egbert points out—Fourier's politics "verged on anarchism. . . . This strong element of individualism made Fourierism and anarchism alike appeal to some of those romantic individualists of the artistic avant-garde who subscribed to the doctrines of 'art for art's sake' and then to symbolism."[17] There were also some other elements in Fourier's philosophy that made it more attractive to artists than most of the other varieties of socialism that developed throughout the nineteenth century. "Fourier's conception of universal harmony," Donald Egbert writes, "was related to his ultimately Neo-Platonic belief in universal unity, which in turn led to his essentially romantic belief in what he regarded as 'universal analogies' (what Baudelaire was later to call 'correspondences'). Fourier drew analogies between colors, sounds, curves, passions, and rights. He thereby extended the analogy between colors and sounds which played so important a part in the art theory of romantics and later symbolists."[18]

The subsequent cultural use of the avant-garde metaphor should be seen as one of the signs of a larger modern tendency toward radicalism in both political thinking and aesthetics. Quite naturally, the nineteenth-century utopian reformers, socialists, and anarchists called for a committed, militant, politically responsible art. Interestingly, however, politically independent artists, and even some of the staunchest defenders of purist doctrines, were often tempted to borrow terms from the language of radicalism and use them in condemning the "official" culture of their time, with all its aesthetic and other taboos. Thus, toward the end of the nineteenth century, some of the most significant artistic statements contain notions directly derived from the vocabulary of politics. The most convincing example is perhaps Mallarmé's view, expressed in an important interview with Jules Huret (1891), that the modern poet is, simply and emphatically, "on strike against society" ("*en grève devant la société*").[19]

SOME MID-NINETEENTH-CENTURY WRITERS

AND THE AVANT-GARDE

By the mid-nineteenth century, the metaphor of the avant-garde—in both its primary political and its secondary cultural acceptation—had been used by social utopists, reformers of various sorts, and radical journalists, but, to my knowledge, had scarcely been used by literary or artistic figures. As has been pointed out, the idea that poets are endowed with visionary powers, that they are indeed "mirrors of futurity," and as such in advance of their time, was shared by many progressive-minded romantics. Victor Hugo was one of them, but he does not seem to have used the avant-garde simile before *Les Misérables* (1862), when he includes it in a passage that shows his enthusiastic approval of a broadly defined intellectual avant-garde:

> The encyclopedists, led by Diderot, the physiocrats, led by Turgot, the philosophers, led by Voltaire, and the utopists, led by Rousseau—these are the four sacred legions. They are the four *avant-gardes* [italics mine] of mankind as it marches toward the four cardinal points of progress—Diderot toward the beautiful, Turgot toward the useful, Voltaire toward truth, Rousseau toward justice.[20]

To get a better understanding of what avant-garde had come to mean toward the middle of the nineteenth century, we should also consider Balzac. In his grandiose and minute chronicle of his age, Balzac did not fail to notice that "avant-garde" had become a commonplace of revolutionary rhetoric. Significantly he does not use the word when writing as narrator, but only when reporting the speech of a particular character. This character, described as a "republican radical" (his prophetic revolutionism being in funny contrast to his very prosaic profession as a chiropodist), bears the ironical name Publicola Masson and makes a brief but memorable appearance in *Les Comédiens sans le savoir* (1846), a short novel that belongs, in the vast cycle of *La Comédie humaine*, to the section *Scènes de la vie parisienne*. Publicola Masson, while performing his not too pleasant job in the house of a famous painter, announces an imminent social overthrow, by comparison to which the Terror of the French Revolution would appear as benign—"We come after Robespierre and Saint-Just to improve on them," he proclaims.[21] The image he draws of the ideological avant-garde is, interestingly, that of a *subversive* force preparing the huge explosion that would blow up all the existing social structures and make a new and better world possible:

"Everything is conspiring to help us. Thus, all those who pity the people, and brawl over the question of the proletariat and salaries, or write against the Jesuits, or interest themselves in the amelioration of anything whatsoever—Communists, Humanitarianists, philanthropists . . . you understand—all these men are our *avant-garde* [italics mine]. While we lay in the powder, they are braiding the fuse, and the spark of circumstance will set fire to it."[22]

The first important modern literary critic to make use of the term avant-garde in a figurative sense seems to have been Sainte-Beuve, in his *Causeries du Lundi*. In his second review-article (dated 22 December 1856) on Hippolyte Rigault's *Histoire de la querelle des anciens et des modernes*, Sainte-Beuve spoke of the "avant-garde zeal" of the eighteenth-century *abbé* de Pons. In the famous *Querelle* de Pons was, evidently, in favor of the "moderns" and opposed—in a passage quoted by Sainte-Beuve—to the "stupid erudite scholars," and in fact the idea of authority (". . . dare think by yourselves and do not take orders from those stupid erudites who have sworn to be faithful to Homer no matter what. . ."). Sainte-Beuve comments as follows: "We can easily see that the *avant-garde zeal* [italics mine], the heat of the skirmish have made the *abbé* de Pons fly into a passion and he, ordinarily so polite, comes to use really coarse words."[23] It is interesting to note that, as Sainte-Beuve put it, de Pons "claimed that in matters of poetry and belles-lettres one should be exactly as free from judgments of authority *and even tradition* [italics mine] as one had been in matters of philosophy since Descartes."[24] As for the use of the term avant-garde, it is clear that Sainte-Beuve had in mind its military and *polemic* connotations; it is also clear that he did not approve of the exaggerations implied by the *"zèle d'avant-garde."*

Frequently used in the political language of radicalism, the term avant-garde, when applied to literature or the arts, tended to point toward that type of commitment one would have expected from an artist who conceived of his role as consisting mainly in party propaganda. That was perhaps one of the reasons why Baudelaire, in the early 1860s, disliked and disapproved of both the term and the concept. He voiced quite unambiguously his bitter disdain of the *"littérateurs d'avant-garde"* in some very characteristic entries in his personal notebook, published posthumously under the title *Mon Coeur mis à nu.* Baudelaire's profound intelligence was struck by the paradox of the avant-garde (as understood at the time): nonconformism reduced to a kind of *military* discipline or, worse, to herdlike conformity. His own individualism was repulsed by what he called the "predilection of the French for military metaphors." There is an intensely sardonic quality to Baudelaire's remarks on the avant-garde:

> On the Frenchman's passionate predilection for military metaphors. In this country every metaphor wears a moustache. The militant school of literature. Holding the fort. Carrying the flag high. . . . More military metaphors: the poets of combat. The littérateurs of the

avant-garde. This weakness for military metaphors is a sign of natures that are not themselves militarist, but are made for discipline—that is to say, for conformity—natures congenitally domestic, Belgian natures that can think only in unison.[25]

It is true that when Baudelaire so drastically rejected it, the term avant-garde had not yet come to be associated with that kind of artistic extremism and "experimental" spirit that were later to become essential elements in the aesthetics of the avant-garde. Baudelaire's point, however, was not merely topical, and we can say that his dismissal of the avant-garde had a certain prophetic quality that makes it relevant to the problem of the avant-garde in general. For is it not the case that the systematic nonconformism of the avant-garde generates a new type of conformity (however iconoclastic)? It would not be wrong, then, to say that Baudelaire was, in a way, the first writer to point out some of the basic aporias that result from the cultural use of the concept of the avant-garde. This specific problem has confronted the most perceptive students of the avant-garde and has been dealt with at length in an excellent essay by the German poet Hans Magnus Enzensberger, "The Aporias of the Avant-Garde" (1962). Enzensberger writes, commenting on the opening statement of Breton's *First Surrealist Manifesto*:

> "Only the word freedom can still fill me with enthusiasm. I consider it suited to keep the old human fanaticism upright for an indefinite time yet to come." With these words, André Breton, in the year 1924, opens the first *Surrealist Manifesto*. The new doctrine crystallizes, as always, around its yearning for absolute freedom. The word *fanaticism* is already an indication that this freedom can be acquired only at the price of absolute discipline: within a few years, the surrealist guard spins itself into a cocoon of regulations.[26]

This argument clearly reminds us of Baudelaire's emphasis on the insoluble contradiction between the supposedly courageous nonconformism of the avant-garde and its final submissiveness to blind, intolerant discipline.

TWO AVANT-GARDES:

ATTRACTIONS AND REPULSIONS

In the 1870s in France, the term avant-garde, while still preserving its broad political meaning, came to designate the small group of advanced writers and artists who transferred the spirit of radical critique of social forms to the domain of *artistic forms*. This transference did not involve the artists' submission to a narrow political philosophy or their turning into mere propagandists. Propaganda, to be efficient, has to resort to the most traditional, schematic, and even simplistic forms of discourse. But what the artists of the new avant-garde were interested in doing—no matter how sympathetic toward radical politics they were—was to overthrow all the binding formal traditions of art and to enjoy the exhilarating freedom of exploring completely new, previously forbidden, horizons of creativity. For they believed that to revolutionize art was the same as to revolutionize life. Thus, the representatives of the artistic avant-garde consciously turned against the stylistic expectations of the general public, whom the political revolutionists were trying to win over through the use of the most platitudinous revolutionary propaganda. The seeds of a conflict between the two avant-gardes were there.

The new, aesthetically revolutionary state of mind of the advanced artists of the 1870s is well illustrated, to choose but one example, in some of the writings and letters of Arthur Rimbaud—for instance, in his famous "Lettre du voyant," addressed to Paul Demeny on May 15, 1871. Although the poet did not use the term avant-garde, the concept was unmistakably there, and with all its important notes. The "newcomers," Rimbaud wrote to Demeny, "are free to condemn the ancestors." The poet should strive to become a *seer*, to reach the *unknown*, to invent an absolutely *new* language. Thus poetry *will be in advance* (in Rimbaud's own words: "*La Poésie ne rhythmera plus l'action; elle sera en avant.... En*

attendant, demandons au poète du nouveau,—idées et formes"[27]).
The socialist-anarchist beliefs of the young Rimbaud are well known;
so are his outspoken sympathies for the Paris Commune of 1871. In
Rimbaud—but his case was not unique—the two avant-gardes, the
artistic and the political, tended to merge. Poggioli did not fail to
notice this interesting phenomenon. He saw the two as almost perfectly united for approximately one decade:

> For an instant the two avant-gardes appeared to march allied or
> united, thus renewing the romantic precedent or tradition estab-
> lished in the course of the generations enclosed by the revolutions of
> 1830 and 1848. . . . This alliance . . . survived in France down to the
> first of the modern literary magazines, significantly entitled *La Revue
> indépendante*. This magazine, founded about 1880, was perhaps the
> last organ to gather fraternally, under the same banner, the rebels of
> politics and the rebels of art, the representatives of advanced opinion
> in the two spheres of social and artistic thought. Abruptly afterward,
> what might be called the divorce of the two avant-gardes took place.[28]

At this point, I should make it clear that I find Poggioli's idea of
an abrupt and *complete* divorce of the two avant-gardes unacceptable. The pattern of the relationships between the two avant-gardes
is actually more complicated. It is true that what is currently called
in Europe the "new avant-garde" (which has developed mostly since
the 1950s) requires us to look at the whole problem of the avant-
garde from a point of view that Poggioli could not have possibly
adopted, his book having been conceived mainly between 1946 and
1950.[29] But even what is today called the "old" or "historical avant-
garde" was more than once politically inspired, and if the
movements that represented it never entirely succeeded in joining
up with the more or less parallel radical movements in politics, it
would be inaccurate to say that the two avant-gardes were separated
by an unbridgeable gap.

The whole avant-garde issue is rendered somewhat confusing,
however, by what we may call a quarrel of words. This was due
mainly to the positive connotations of the term avant-garde itself.[30]
Such connotations, which ended by overriding the pejorative ones

in the case of avant-garde as a literary term, were even more power-ful in the language of politics. All the future-oriented sociopolitical doctrines thought of themselves as being in the avant-garde: Saint-Simonians, Fourierists, anarchists (Kropotkin had published a magazine called *L'Avant-garde* in Switzerland in 1878), Marxists, et al. disputed the term and accommodated it to their own kind of rhetoric.

The use of avant-garde in Marxism offers a significant example. Although the term itself was not employed in Marx and Engels' *Communist Manifesto* (1848), the concept was clearly implied. That is why, as Donald Egbert points out in *Social Radicalism and the Arts,*

> by the 1880's, at least, Marxists were becoming accustomed to using avant-garde as a political term, one result being that during the 1890's numerous provincial French newspapers connected with the Marx-ists of the Parti ouvrier were named *L'avant-garde* or bore titles beginning with that word. But it was Lenin who developed the statement in the *Communist Manifesto* into the doctrine that the party constitutes the political "avant-garde" (his own term).[31]

Lenin first defined the party as the avant-garde of the working class in *What is to Be Done* (1902). Quite interestingly, in his article "Party Organization and Party Literature," written in 1905, Lenin uses the argument of the revolutionary avant-garde to condemn drastically any kind of literary activity that does not function like a little "cog" in the "great... mechanism" of social democracy, a mechanism that was to be set in motion exclusively by the party:

> Down with non-partisan literature. Down with literary supermen. Literature must become *part* of the common cause of the proletariat, "a cog and a screw" of one single great Social-Democratic mechanism set in motion by the entire politically-conscious avant-garde of the entire working class. Literature must become a component of or-ganized, planned and integrated Social-Democratic Party work.[32]

Reduced to the status of a little "cog," it is not difficult to under-stand that literature can have no independent claim at performing any sort of avant-garde role. Thus, since the early 1900s, but especially after the 1917 October Revolution in Russia, and with increasing emphasis during the whole Stalin era, the term avant-garde came to be almost automatically associated with the idea of the monolithic Communist party. That was true not only for the Soviet Union but for Marxist-Leninist orthodoxy all over the world. Because of the role it played in the Marxist-Leninist-Stalinist political idiom, the term developed, for the adherents of that doctrine, such highly reverent connotations that its use in other contexts would almost have been regarded as blasphemy. This might be one of the reasons why many Marxist critics (even in the West) dealing with avant-garde literature or art preferred to characterize it as "modernist" (a word that they used to oppose to "realist" or "socialist realist," and that had acquired for them definitely negative connotations) or "decadent," which had the advantage of leaving even less room for ambiguity. Georg Lukács, for example, while aesthetically condemning "modernism" as an expression of the historical predicament of the bourgeoisie, thought that truly avant-garde trends should be looked for in the works of the major contemporary realists.[33] Soviet criticism did not go that far; "socialist realist" literature and art—although extremely pedagogical—were never discussed in terms of the avant-garde because this would have led to the possibility of a twofold confusion: first, the confusion between the function of art and the actual "avant-garde" role of the party (which exerted its unquestionable leadership in all fields of social and intellectual life); and second, the confusion between "socialist realism" and bourgeois "decadent" art, which, abusively and misleadingly, called itself, or was called, "avant-garde" (employed in such a context, "avant-garde" was obviously the sign of an odious terminological usurpation). Here we have a clear example of a dogmatically prescriptive use of the term avant-garde for exclusively political purposes.

Meanwhile, the literary-artistic meaning of avant-garde—already distinct since the 1870s—continued to develop steadily in France and soon in other Neo-Latin countries. This semantic process would not have reached a stage of "crystallization" without the formation in these cultures, both in literature and the arts, of a *new style* with precise and prominent characteristics. In order to understand better what avant-garde had come to mean in the years previous to the First World War, it is useful to consider how it was used by Guillaume Apollinaire, one of the most outspoken representatives of the search for new forms in poetry and the arts. In an article about the first Italian Futurist exhibition in Paris, which opened on February 5, 1912, Apollinaire wrote, showing little sympathy for the experiments of the Italian artists: "The young Futurist painters can compete with some of our avant-garde artists, but they are still weak pupils of a Picasso or of a Derain."[34] In an earlier passage of the article, Apollinaire had stated that the Futurists "declare themselves to be opposed to the art of the more extreme French schools, and yet they are nothing other than their imitators." From this we can infer that for Apollinaire the avant-garde was constituted by these same "extreme schools."

AVANT-GARDE AND AESTHETIC EXTREMISM

Although credited with being one of the principal theorists of cubism, Apollinaire had very seldom employed the term "cubism" before the spring of 1913, when his book, *Les Peintres cubistes*, was published. Now it is known that the author of *Alcools* had not originally intended to publish a book on cubism; what he had in mind was simply a collection of his articles about "new painting," under the unpretentious title *Méditations esthétiques*. The first page proofs (which he received probably in September 1912) show that the term "cubism" had been used only four times throughout the whole book. It was only after that date that Apollinaire wrote a few short historical and theoretical sections specifically devoted to cubism, which he inserted in the book, changing its title at the same time. These details prove only that the poet paid little heed to schools and doctrines as such, being open-mindedly in favor of the new experimental and artistically revolutionary tendencies, wherever they might have appeared. Thus, in June 1913, forgetting not only his more or less bitter attack against the Futurist painters, but also the sharp accusations brought against him by one of the leading Futurists, Umberto Boccioni, he wrote his well-known *Manifeste synthèse. L'Anti-tradition futuriste* (1913). For Apollinaire, we may conclude, avant-garde was a synonym for what he was later to call the *"esprit nouveau"* (I am referring to his important lecture "L'esprit nouveau et les poètes," given in 1917 and published posthumously in *Le Mercure de France* of December 1918).

By the second decade of our century, avant-garde, as an artistic concept, had become comprehensive enough to designate not one or the other, but *all the new schools* whose aesthetic programs were defined, by and large, by their rejection of the past and by the cult of the new. But we should not disregard the fact that novelty was attained, more often than not, in the sheer process of the destruction of tradition; Bakunin's anarchist maxim, "To destroy is to create," is actually applicable to most of the activities of the twentieth-century avant-garde.

The possibility of grouping *all* the antitraditional extreme movements in a broader category succeeded in making avant-garde an important terminological instrument of twentieth-century literary criticism. The term subsequently underwent a natural process of "historicization," but at the same time, with increased circulation, its meaning took on an almost uncontrollable diversity, a diversity that can only be suggested here.

In his already mentioned book, Poggioli remarked that

> the term "avant-garde art" (perhaps the critical concept as well) belongs almost exclusively to the Neo-Latin languages and cultures. . . .
> That the term struck deeper roots and better acclimatized itself in France and Italy than elsewhere may demonstrate that a sensitivity to what the term implies is more alive in cultural traditions which, like

the Italian, are alert to the theoretical problems in aesthetics or which, like the French, are particularly inclined to view art and culture from the viewpoint of its social disposition or its sociability (or "antisociability").[35]

The situation has dramatically changed since the author of the *Theory of the Avant-Garde* wrote these lines. On the one hand, the term and the concept of avant-garde have taken hold both in English-speaking countries and in Germany, which had resisted them for some time; on the other hand, although preserving in some contexts its generic meaning, avant-garde tends to become a predominantly historical category, grouping the most extreme movements that emerged especially during the first half of our century. Even as an historical notion, avant-garde is employed in a bewildering variety of terminological oppositions. In American criticism, for instance, avant-garde is generally a synonym for *modernism* and is opposed to the previous movements of *romanticism* (especially its belated forms) and *naturalism*, as well as the more recent and apocalyptic *postmodernism*. In contemporary Italy, the "historicization" of the concept of avant-garde is evident in the distinction that is usually made between the old *"avanguardia"* (frequently designated as *"avanguardia storica"*) and *"neo-avanguardia"* or, sometimes, *"sperimentalismo."* A similar process took place in Spain, but there the notion of *"vanguardia"* was, from the very beginning, opposed to that of *"modernismo."* As far back as 1925, Guillermo de Torre affirmed the international character of avant-gardism and studied it in his book *Literaturas europeas de vanguardia.* It is interesting to note that its recent enlarged edition, brought up to date, specifies in its title the *historical* intent of the author: *Historia de las literaturas europeas de vanguardia* (Madrid: Ediciones Guadarrama, 1965, 1971). The term *"vanguardismo"* is widely used by contemporary historians of Spanish literature: the fourth volume of the almost standard *Historia de la literatura española*, by Angel Valbuena Prat, significantly bears the title: *Época contemporánea, o del Vanguardismo al Existencialismo.* In this case *avant-gardism* is distinguished from *existentialism*, whereas, in his already mentioned book, Guillermo de Torre considers existentialism as one of the post-World War II forms of avant-gardism.

Logically speaking, every literary or artistic style should have its avant-garde, for there is nothing more natural than to think of the avant-garde artists as being in advance of their own time and preparing the conquest of new forms of expression for the use of the majority of other artists. But the history of the term in its cultural sense—which I have only briefly sketched—points to the contrary. The avant-garde does not announce one style or another; it is in itself a style, or better, an antistyle. That is why, for instance, Eugène Ionesco, although starting his discussion of the avant-garde by stressing the military analogy suggested by the word itself (and by the *Petit Larousse*), is finally obliged to abandon the apparently normal line of thinking:

> I prefer to define the avant-garde in terms of opposition and rupture. While most writers, artists, and thinkers believe they belong to their time, the revolutionary playwright feels he is running counter to his time. . . . An avant-garde man is like an enemy inside a city he is bent on destroying, against which he rebels; for like any system of government, an established form of expression is also a form of oppression. The avant-garde man is the opponent of an existing system.[36]

Here again we should make it clear that the avant-garde proper did not exist before the last quarter of the nineteenth century, although every epoch has its rebels and negators. The most prominent students of the avant-garde tend to agree that its appearance is historically connected with the moment when some socially "alienated" artists felt the need to disrupt and completely overthrow the whole bourgeois system of values, with all its philistine pretensions to universality. So the avant-garde, seen as a spearhead of aesthetic modernity at large, is a recent reality, like the word that, in its cultural meaning, is supposed to designate it. In this case, the history of the word can be said to coincide roughly with the history of the phenomenon it designates. This particular situation has been noted by, among others, Roland Barthes, who wrote in an article published in 1956 (and later collected in his *Essais critiques*):

Our dictionaries do not tell us precisely when the term *avant-garde* was first used in a cultural sense. Apparently the notion is quite recent, a product of that moment in history when to certain of its writers the bourgeoisie appeared as an esthetically retrograde force, one to be contested. For the artist, most likely, the avant-garde has always been a means of resolving a specific historical contradiction: that of an unmasked bourgeoisie which could no longer proclaim its original universalism except in the form of a violent protest turned against itself; initially by an esthetic violence directed against the philistines, then, with the increasing commitment, by an ethical violence, when it became the duty of a *life style* to contest the bourgeois order (among the surrealists, for example); but never by a political violence.[37]

In the same article, Barthes is one of the first to speak of the death of the avant-garde: it was dying because it was recognized as artistically significant by the same class whose values it so drastically rejected. The death of the avant-garde, in fact, was to become one of the recurrent themes of the 1960s.

THE CRISIS OF AVANT-GARDE'S CONCEPT

IN THE 1960s

The inner contradictions of the avant-garde as a cultural concept, of which Baudelaire was prophetically conscious in the 1860s, had to wait a whole century to become the focal point of a broader intellectual debate. This occurrence coincided, in the post-World War II period, with the unexpectedly large public success of avant-garde art, and with the parallel transformation of the term itself into a widely used (and misused) advertising catchword. The avant-garde, whose limited popularity had long rested exclusively on scandal, all of a sudden became one of the major cultural myths of the 1950s and the 1960s. Its offensive, insulting rhetoric came to be regarded as merely amusing, and its apocalyptic outcries were changed into comfortable and innocuous clichés. Ironically, the avant-garde found itself failing through a stupendous, involuntary success. This situation prompted some artists and critics to question not only the historical role of the avant-garde but the adequacy of the concept itself.

The German poet Hans Magnus Enzensberger, in his previously cited "Aporias of the Avant-garde," pointed out that nothing genuinely new could come out of the movement's self-contradictory premises and attitudes.[38] The avant-garde was dead, as Leslie Fiedler argued in his essay on the "Death of Avant-Garde Literature" (1964), because from a shocking antifashion it had gone on to become—with the help of the mass media—a widespread fashion.[39] Irving Howe also came to postulate the "break-up of the avant-garde." In the 1960s the avant-garde was being absorbed into the surrounding culture. "In the war between modernist culture and bourgeois society," Howe wrote, "something has happened recently that no spokesman for the *avant-garde* quite anticipated. Bracing enmity has given way to wet embraces, the middle class has discovered that the fiercest attacks upon its values can be transported into pleasing entertainments, and the avant-garde writer or artist must confront the one challenge for which he has not been prepared: the challenge of success."[40]

For many writers the idea of an avant-garde in a culturally pluralistic age like ours was reducible to the type of gross error that springs from a *contradictio in terminis*. To prove that the concept was simply irrelevant in the new historical context, the etymology of the term was brought into focus. Etymologically, two conditions are basic to the existence and meaningful activity of any properly named avant-garde (social, political, or cultural): (1) the possibility that its representatives be conceived of, or conceive of themselves, as being in advance of their time (obviously this does not go without a progressive or at least goal-oriented philosophy of history); and (2) the idea that there is a bitter struggle to be fought against an enemy symbolizing the forces of stagnation, the tyranny of the past, the old forms and ways of thinking, which tradition imposes on us like fetters to keep us from moving forward.

But what if there are no valid or convincing criteria to establish that a certain trend is in advance of any other? This point of view is posed by, among others, Leonard B. Meyer, in his book *Music, the Arts, and Ideas* (1967). And if he is right in speaking of contemporary art as fundamentally "anti-teleological" and in characterizing it in terms of stasis (illustrated by the notion of a "fluctuating steady-state"), then he is also right in dismissing the idea of an avant-garde: "The concept of an avant-garde implies goal-directed motion. . . . If the Renaissance is over, the avant-garde is ended."[41] Such clear-cut statements, however, do not prevent the author from using the term avant-garde throughout his book to distinguish between extreme antitraditional contemporary manifestations and more traditional ones. Is this an inconsistency or simply a proof that, irrespective of its etymology and theoretical implications, avant-garde may still be a useful term?

The existence of a contemporary cultural enemy—the second indispensable condition for an etymologically defined avant-garde—has also been questioned. Angelo Guglielmi, one of the critics associated with the Italian *Gruppo 63*, maintains that the adversary against whom the avant-garde should fight—namely, official culture—has simply vanished, being replaced by the intellectual relativism of modernity. Furthermore, inasmuch as the military associations contained in the notion of a cultural avant-garde have always been potentially distasteful, it becomes devastating in a time of almost boundless permissiveness like ours to stress the martial nature of the avant-garde (with all its connotations of iron discipline, blind obedience, strict organizational hierarchy, etc.). To expand the original military metaphor and, moreover, to point out that today's avant-garde has actually no enemy to fight is not only to deny its validity but also to make fun of it. For such a treatment of the avant-garde—which is basically a *reductio ad absurdum*—it is

enlightening to consider Guglielmi's comparison between the "old"
or "historical" avant-garde and what he calls "experimentalism":

> The situation of contemporary culture is similar to that of a city from
> which the enemy, after laying mines, has fled. What will the victor,
> who is at the gates of the city, do? Will he send assault troops to
> conquer a city that is already conquered? If he did so, this would
> create chaos and provoke new, useless destruction and death. Instead
> he will have specialized sections of the rearguard sent in which will
> advance into the abandoned city not with machine guns but Geiger
> counters.[42]

In this comparison (Guglielmi obviously has Marinetti's warlike
futurism in mind) the old avant-garde would be represented, in
today's cultural atmosphere, by the grossly inadequate assault
troops. By contrast, experimentalism appears as a highly specialized
rearguard that would use, instead of the noisy, brutal, and utterly
needless machine guns, the more peaceful and sophisticated prob-
ing devices characteristic of our electronic age. The soldier, with his
heroic boastfulness, is replaced by the specialist, and the whole
strategy of the old avant-garde has become, in face of the changed
situation, preposterously obsolete.

In the midst of today's general tolerance (which is nothing but a
disguise of an objective lack of criteria for choosing among a variety
of conflicting potentialities), Guglielmi's own *intolerance* toward the
avant-garde may appear as a curious relic of the past. Even the term
is irritating to him. Hence, his trenchant rejection of the label
"neo-avanguardia" and its replacement by the ideologically neutral
"sperimentalismo." Guglielmi's option, however, was not followed
by other members of the *Gruppo 63*, who continued to see themselves as representatives of a new avant-garde.

This last example may suggest that, despite the crisis it had to
face in the 1960s, the concept of the avant-garde did not collapse. It
was secretly protected by its inner contradictions, indeed by its
innumerable aporias (extreme forms of modernity's insoluble an-
tinomies), and, paradoxically, by its long and almost incestuous as-

sociation with both the idea and the praxis of cultural crisis. The fact is that from its very outset the artistic avant-garde developed as a culture of crisis.

Broadly conceived, modernity itself can be seen as a "culture of crisis," as has been argued in the first part of the book. But it should not be surprising when, within the large context of modernity, the label "culture of crisis" is applied specifically to the avant-garde. The avant-gardist, far from being interested in novelty as such, or in novelty in general, actually tries to discover or invent new forms, aspects, or possibilities of *crisis*. Aesthetically, the avant-garde attitude implies the bluntest rejection of such traditional ideas as those of order, intelligibility, and even success (Artaud's "No more masterpieces!" could be generalized): art is supposed to become an experience—deliberately conducted—of failure and crisis. If crisis is not there, it must be created. In this respect, certain parallelisms between the apparently contradictory notions of avant-garde and "decadentism" are inescapable. As a culture of crisis, the avant-garde is consciously involved in furthering the "natural" decay of traditional forms in our world of change, and does its best to intensify and dramatize all existing symptoms of decadence and exhaustion. This aspect will be discussed in more detail in the chapter devoted to the idea of decadence. For now, it will suffice to stress that the "decadentism" of the avant-garde is not only self-conscious but also openly ironical and self-ironical—and joyfully self-destructive.

From this point of view, the "death of the avant-garde" (an extremely apt expression) cannot be confined to any one moment in this century—such as before or after the last World War—simply because the avant-garde has been dying all along, consciously and voluntarily. If we admit that Dada's nihilism expresses an "archetypal" trait of the avant-garde, we can say that any true avant-garde movement (older or newer) has a profound built-in tendency ultimately to negate itself. When, symbolically, there is nothing left to destroy, the avant-garde is compelled by its own sense of consistency to commit suicide. This aesthetic thanatophilia does not contradict other features usually associated with the spirit of the avant-garde: intellectual playfulness, iconoclasm, a cult of unseriousness, mystification, disgraceful practical jokes, deliberately stupid humor. After all, these and other similar features are perfectly in keeping with the death-of-art aesthetics it has been practicing all along.

AVANT-GARDE, DEHUMANIZATION,
AND THE END OF IDEOLOGY

Historically, the emergence and the development of the avant-garde seem to be closely linked to the crisis of Man in the modern desacralized world. As early as 1925, Ortega y Gasset defined one of the striking characteristics of "new" or "modern" art (he did not use the term avant-garde): Dehumanization. According to him, this brought an end to the nineteenth-century "realism," which was in fact a "humanism." Ortega writes:

> During the nineteenth century, artists proceeded in all too impure a fashion. They... let their work consist entirely in a fiction of human realities. In this sense all normal art of the last century must be called realistic. Beethoven and Wagner were realistic, and so was Chateaubriand as well as Zola. Seen from the vantage point of our day Romanticism and Naturalism draw together and reveal their common realistic root. [43]

Today we can say that the antihumanistic urge of writers and artists during the first decades of the twentieth century was not only a "reaction" (against romanticism or naturalism) but a strangely accurate prophecy. Distorting and often eliminating man's image from their work, disrupting his normal vision, dislocating his syntax, the cubists and the futurists were certainly among the first artists to have the consciousness that Man had become an obsolete concept, and that the rhetoric of humanism had to be discarded. However, the demythologization of Man and the radical critique of humanism had been initiated earlier.

Nietzsche, one of the main sources of Ortega's philosophy, announced the final demise of Man and the advent of the Superman in the 1880s. Nietzsche's identification of modernity and decadence, and its main implications, will be discussed in the chapter on decadence. It will suffice here to point out that within the framework of his thought, the death of God and the death of Man (both metaphors signifying the final collapse of humanism under the corrosive influence of modernity's *nihilism*) were linked to one another. Like God, Man had been throughout the moral history of mankind an embodiment of *ressentiment* (see n. 58, p. 298), a deception successfully worked out by the "slaves" in order to subvert the values of life, that is, the values of the "masters." For Nietzsche, modernity, while being an exacerbated manifestation of the same age-old "will to death," had at least one clear-cut advantage over traditional humanism: it recognized that humanism was no longer viable as a doctrine, and that once God was dead, Man too had to clear the stage of history.

More relevant to the student of the avant-garde is the leftist critique not only of religion and religious humanism but also of humanism in general, seen as an *ideological* manifestation. The first symptoms of the crisis of Man's concept in the thought of the social and political avant-garde are clearly present in Marx, and there is little doubt, on a more general plane, that the de-individualization (if not the downright dehumanization) of history was to a large extent a contribution of nineteenth-century revolutionary radicalism. In Marxism, for instance, Man has often been described as an essentially bourgeois concept, the ideological heritage of the revolutionary struggles of the bourgeoisie against feudalism. In those struggles the concept of Man was used as a weapon against the concept of God, on which the whole feudal system of values had been based. But Man—even the most orthodox Marxist would admit—is only an abstraction. History could not possibly be made by Man: it is a product of class struggle (which is, according to Engels' well-known technological metaphor, the "engine" setting the historical process in motion). Marxism drastically questions, therefore, Man's Promethean capability of both making and transcending history (an intellectual myth resulting from the Enlightenment and reaching its climax in the "hero worship" of romanticism). Humanism is only an "ideology," and insofar as Marxism proclaims itself a "science," it is logically supposed to take an anti-ideologic and, implicitly, antihumanistic stand. This view is defended by one of the most influential (and fashionable) Marxist-Structuralist thinkers in Western Europe, Louis Althusser, and the fact that he is highly respected in the circles of the intellectual Parisian avant-garde is not a mere coincidence.

Whether Marx was a "humanist" (as the so-called humanist Marxists argue on the basis of Marx's early writings and especially of his concept of "alienation" as defined in the *Economic and Philosophical Manuscripts of 1844*) or a theoretical antihumanist (as Althusser maintains) is of little importance here. Personally, I think that both approaches have some justification; what is really interesting is that the antihumanistic interpretation of Marx had to wait until the 1960s to be undertaken more systematically. In fact, it was not before the general crisis of humanism had reached a certain depth that Marx was proclaimed an antihumanist. Rejecting the "humanist" interpretation of Marx (with all its sinister "petty bourgeois" implications), Althusser writes in his essay entitled "Marxism and Humanism" (1963):

> So, to understand what was radically new in Marx's contribution, we must become aware not only of the novelty of the concepts of historical materialism, but also of the depth of the theoretical revolution they imply and inaugurate. On this condition it is possible to define humanism's status, and reject its *theoretical* pretensions while recognizing its practical function as an ideology. Strictly in respect to theory, therefore, one can and must speak of *Marx's theoretical antihumanism*, and see in this *theoretical antihumanism* the absolute (negative) precondition of the (positive) knowledge of the human

world itself, and of its practical transformation. It is impossible to *know* anything about man except on the absolute precondition that the philosophical (theoretical) myth of man is reduced to ashes.[44]

For a correct understanding of these statements we should make it clear that Marxism is in Althusser's view only theoretically (philosophically) antihumanistic (and anti-ideologic).[45] Practically, as a revolutionary political doctrine, it can and does promote its own ideology, and consciously so. This ideology is supposed to oppose bourgeois ideology, and for tactical purposes it can use whatever weapons it may consider fit (including humanism, but certainly a "new" kind of humanism, purified of all its bourgeois and petit bourgeois elements).

Going beyond Althusser's subtle, trendy, but ultimately dogmatic approach, we observe that it is the basic ambiguity between science and ideology that makes Marxism such a stupendously elastic doctrine (and by way of reaction against this elasticity, a doctrine so easily hardened in the most arbitrary orthodoxies). This ambiguity can explain, among other things, the appeal of Marxism to the aesthetically rebellious avant-garde from Dada and surrealism to the diverse neo-avant-garde movements of our day. It can also account for the particular position occupied by Marxism in the framework of the contemporary crisis of ideology. Evidently, the following remarks are restricted to the attitude toward Marxism of the representatives of the literary and artistic new avant-garde. In this respect Guglielmi's example is again symptomatic.

No ideology—Guglielmi argues in *Avanguardia e sperimentalismo*—can any longer give us a convincing rationale of the whole reality; no ideology is capable nowadays either of explaining the *whole* world coherently or of persuading us that it could do so.[46] What existing ideologies can still do is only to instruct us how to behave as men "with civil and social responsibilities."[47] In the West, Guglielmi goes on to point out, even the deep influence of Marxism does not go beyond the limits of social life and action, its recommendations being utterly irrelevant to the philosophical and aesthetic problems that artists face. Thus, he writes, "we give our votes to the leftist parties and we reject not only socialist realism, but any kind of literature whose character is determined by content in the traditional sense, that is, any kind of literature which presupposes the existence of objective contents and, therefore, a complex of prearranged and unchanging values."[48] With such limitations, the appeal of Marxism remains great; this is due mainly to the fact that it is, Guglielmi believes, the only system of thought "in which incoherence appears as a virtue."[49] Such a view of Marxism's incoherence (which can easily be reduced to the "dialectic" ambiguity between ideology and anti-ideology) may give us a hint as to why so many neo-avant-garde writers and artists are directly or indirectly connected with the activities of various New Left groups that claim to derive from Marx (as seen by one or another of his interpreters, Lenin, Trotsky, Mao, Che Guevara, etc.). This may also explain why in most works of the neo-avant-garde (whatever the declarations of their authors) there is hardly any trace of political allegiance.

It would be wrong, however, to consider that only Marxism is relevant to a discussion of today's cultural avant-garde. The interesting fact is that even artists who seem politically committed to Marxism in one or another of its variants often practice, consciously or unconsciously, an anarchist type of aesthetics. The "Anarchist Renaissance" in the arts, of which André Reszler speaks in a recent article about "Bakunin, Marx and the Aesthetic Heritage of Socialism,"[50] not only applies to those who express a specifically anarchist creed but also embraces a great many of those who believe themselves Marxists. Insofar as anarchism as an attitude implies a veritable mystique of crisis (the deeper the crisis the closer the Revolution), I think that this trend confirms the validity of the more general equation between the cultural avant-garde and the culture of crisis.

Returning to the crisis of Man, it has lately reached the stage where the apocalyptic notion of the Death of Man has become a widely used philosophical cliché. In this respect, the perfect example is Michel Foucault, who has rightly been labeled "the philosopher of the death of Man." It is noteworthy that Foucault is close to, if not directly involved in, the activities of the French new avant-garde, with which he shares at least his strong interest in the theory of language and, more generally, in semiotics. In his main work, *Les Mots et les choses* (1967), in which he uses his antihistorical and antipositivist method called *"l'archéologie du savoir,"* he tries to establish the exact date when Man appeared "as epistemological consciousness of himself" and, similarly, the date of Man's demise. Man's actual history has been very short, Foucault believes. One of the most publicized conclusions he reaches is that for the Western world "man is a recent invention" (dating back to the end of the eighteenth century); and this invention seems already to have become obsolete.[51]

For another French philosopher, who also belongs to the fashionable intellectual avant-garde, man is simply "une machine désirante." I refer to Gilles Deleuze, and specifically to his recent book (written in collaboration with Félix Guattari): *L'Anti-Oedipe.*[52] The mechanical association quoted above (man is a machine) is not at all fortuitous. The book is meant as a radical critique of the orthodox psychoanalytical view of the unconscious, a view subordinated by Freud to his "expressive conception" of the human psyche. But the unconscious is not—the authors of *L'Anti-Oedipe* maintain—a restaging of a Greek tragedy in which human-mythical characters confront each other. Freud's "expressive" approach, with all its theatrical associations, should be dismissed and replaced by a nonanthropomorphic "productive theory": the unconscious works like an industrial unit, it is a factory of desire. Freud is drastically revised through Marx, whose theory of production supposedly contains all the key concepts needed for a functional description of the unconscious. The authors' position, however, is not so much Marxist as anarchist. Interestingly, their wide use of technological imagery and notions—quite in keeping with the mystique of technology promoted by certain branches of modern anarchism—tends to confirm Renato Poggioli's general observation concerning the relationships between avant-garde and "technologism": "The avant-garde thinker or artist," Poggioli writes in his *The Theory of the Avant-Garde*, "is . . . particularly susceptible to the scientific myth."[53] It needs to be emphasized, however, that what is important for the avant-garde is not science as such, but only its myth. The scientifism cultivated by the avant-garde for the sake of its antiartistic and antihumanistic metaphoric potential is both philosophically and aesthetically adapted to the strategy of dehumanization; more than that, it clearly rejects any one of the organic or biological assumptions that constitute the heritage of romantic philosophy and literary theory (the world viewed as a living creature, genius paralleled to a natural vital force, creation seen as a process of organic growth, etc.).

One of the consequences of the crisis of ideology in general, and of the crisis of humanism in particular, is a rather generalized axiological relativism. Even in literary criticism value judgments are considered increasingly irrelevant. The structuralist method is overtly against any kind of preoccupation with value. But the structuralists are not alone in this respect. Some left-oriented critics (prompted by a kind of anarchist instinct) find moral reasons for rejecting what seems to them the elitist interest in maintaining a hierarchic conception of literature and aesthetic value. This egalitarian antihierarchic drive is perhaps best illustrated in the recent criticism of Leslie Fiedler, one of the prophets of postmodernism, who advocates the rather funny idea that criticism ought to go Pop. While his zeal is perhaps that of a new convert, his approach is highly symptomatic, especially when he writes that he has become increasingly interested in the "kind of books no one has ever congratulated himself on being able to read" (i.e., Westerns, cheap best sellers, pornographic novels, and other sorts of books representative of contemporary popular literature). At one point, Fiedler draws a clear-cut distinction between "the elitist exile" of the author with a small audience and "best-sellerdom" as a form of communicating with a larger public via Pop (little thought seems to be given to the fact that best sellers are not so much selected by the public as *imposed* upon it through the commercial manipulation of taste by the publishing business). It is curious to observe that, in his new passion for Pop (often impossible to distinguish from sheer commercial kitsch), Fiedler believes himself a radical, even an anarchist: "I am quite aware," his recent profession of faith reads, "that there is a kind of politics implicit in the critical position I take in these essays, a populist, even anarchist stance based on an impatience with all distinctions of kind created on the analogy of class-structured society."[54]

The crisis of ideology is reflected in another highly significant phenomenon that is characteristic of a great deal of avant-garde art, both older and newer: its "anti-teleological" drive, to use L. B. Meyer's label. "The music of the avant-garde," Meyer writes in *Music, the Arts, and Ideas*, "directs us toward no point of culmination—establishes no goals toward which we move. It arouses no expectations, except presumably that it will stop. . . . Such directionless, unkinetic art, whether carefully contrived or created by chance, I shall call anti-teleological art."[55] This question will later be dealt with at more length.

AVANT-GARDE AND POSTMODERNISM

A sense of dramatic rupture in the modern tradition accounts for the use in recent American criticism of a terminological distinction that recalls the Continental distinction between avant-garde and neo-avant-garde, but whose implications and consequences are both farther reaching and more confusing. I refer to the distinction between *modernism* and *postmodernism*. The whole matter becomes particularly odd when we realize that insofar as literary criticism is concerned, "postmodernism" is not just a classifying label with slightly derogatory connotations (as it was in the 1930s when Federico de Onís spoke, in the Hispanic context, of *postmodernismo* as a kind of exhausted and mildly conservative *modernismo*),[56] but a highly controversial concept with enemies and adherents, which apparently involves a whole distinctive philosophical, political, and aesthetic program on the part of its partisans. Other terms have been proposed for what is currently called postmodernism—we may recall Frank Kermode's not too felicitous distinction between "paleomodernism" and "neomodernism"[57]—but postmodernism, associated with the broader notion of a "post-Modern" age, seems to have easily won out.

The prefix *post* is a common terminological instrument in the language of history, and it is quite often a neutral and convenient means of indicating the position in time of certain events by referring them to an outstanding previous moment. The fact that a specific phenomenon is characterized in terms of its posteriority to another phenomenon is by no means suggestive of inferiority. What the prefix *post* implies, however, is an absence of *positive* periodizing criteria, an absence which in general is characteristic of transitional periods. Moreover, insofar as historical periods are hierarchic constructs, they cannot be totally free from evaluative biases, and this is even more true of cultural history. Thus, from the point of view of literary modernity, we may sometimes feel justified to value precursory trends and, by contrast, look down upon intervals that can merely be described as coming in the aftermath of certain crucial cultural changes. The epithet "preromantic," for instance, not only singles out some late eighteenth-century poets but, by making them into forerunners of the great romantic revolution, sets their efforts in a favorable historical perspective; conversely, the epithet "postromantic" may be used to designate the epigoni of romanticism or, less scornfully, those writers who tried to break away from the romantic influence but without being able to shake it off completely and acquire an actually new literary identity.

The epithet "post-Modern" was apparently coined by the historian-prophet, Arnold J. Toynbee, in the early 1950s. Toynbee thought that Western civilization had entered a transitional phase during the last quarter of the nineteenth century. This transition—

toward what, he could not tell—appeared to him rather as a "mutation" and a dramatic departure from the traditions of the Modern
Age of Western history. In the later volumes of his *Study of History*
(VIII-XIII, published since 1954) he chose to call this time of social
unrest, world wars, and revolutions, the "post-Modern Age." Toynbee's periodization of Modern Western civilization distinguishes between Early Modern (the early Renaissance), Modern (the Renaissance proper and its aftermath), Late Modern (a period starting at
the turn of the seventeenth and eighteenth centuries, with what
Paul Hazard called *La Crise de la conscience européenne*,[58] and extending through the Enlightenment well into the nineteenth century), and, finally, post-Modern (an age which "has opened in the
seventh and eighth decades of the nineteenth century").[59]

By and large, the post-Modern Phase of Western civilization—
which as we see is already a century old—might be characterized as
an age of *anarchy*. The author of *A Study of History* makes use of
this very term when he speaks of the collapse of the rationalist world
view bequeathed to the West by Hellenic philosophers. The belief
in the conscious mind, reinforced throughout the Modern Age of
Western civilization as a consequence of the Renaissance rediscovery of antiquity, was drastically challenged during the Late Modern
period, and with increased intensity after the 1850s. Within the
broad framework of intellectual history, for instance, this challenge
is seen, among other things, in the rapid development of a series of
new sciences—psychology, anthropology, political economy,
sociology—which Toynbee considers characteristically "post-
Modern." "In the field of Psychology," he writes, "the post-Modern
Western scientific mind was verifying by observation Pascal's intuition that 'the Heart has its reasons, of which the Reason has no
knowledge.' In the twentieth century of the Christian Era a post-
Christian Western science of Psychology was beginning to explore
the subconscious abyss of the Human Psyche and to discover 'laws of
Nature,' reigning there, which were not the laws of Logic but were
laws of Poetry and Mythology."[60] Such discoveries, according to

Toynbee, account for the total relativism of the *"intellectually anarchic* [italics mine] Late Modern and post-Modern Age."[61]

In social terms, Modern Western civilization appears to Toynbee as *the* middle-class or bourgeois era: ". . . The word 'modern' in the term 'Modern Western Civilization' can, without inaccuracy, be given a more precise and concrete connotation by being translated 'middle-class.' Western communities became 'modern,' in the accepted Modern Western meaning of the word, just as soon as they had succeeded in producing a bourgeoisie that was both numerous enough and competent enough to become the predominant element in society. We think of the new chapter of Western history that opened at the turn of the fifteenth and sixteenth centuries as being modern' *par excellence* because, for the next four centuries and more, until the opening of a 'post-Modern Age' at the turn of the nineteenth and twentieth centuries, the middle class was in the saddle in the larger and more prominent part of the Western World as a whole."[62] The post-Modern Age is "marked by the rise of an industrial urban working class,"[63] and, more generally, by the advent of a "mass society" with a corresponding system of "mass education" and "mass culture." The latter-day chapter of Western history is clearly a "Time of Troubles," in which all the symptoms of disintegration and breakdown are present, although there are still hopes that the final collapse of Western civilization might be avoided.

Toynbee has been characterized as a prophet rather than an historian, and this characterization applies perfectly to his conception of the "post-Modern Age." Although this rather striking term occurs frequently in the last volumes of *A Study of History*, it never forms the object of systematic definition or analysis. As it stands, "post-Modern" is a hazy, quasi-apocalyptic notion referring to obscure demonic forces, which, if completely unleashed, could overthrow the very structures of Modern Western civilization. "Post-Modern" in Toynbee's prophetic language suggests irrationality, anarchy, and threatening indeterminacy, and from the various contexts in which the term is used, one thing becomes clear beyond doubt, namely, that "post-Modern" has overwhelmingly negative—although not necessarily derogatory—connotations. In spite of his criticisms of Spengler, Toynbee has often been compared to the German philosopher of *The Decline of the West*, and such a comparison seems justified by, among other things, some obvious parallelisms between the former's concept of the "post-Modern Age" and the latter's *Untergang* (decline) as applied to contemporary Western culture. This does not mean, however, that "post-Modern," even in Toynbee, should be taken as just another word for "decadence."

Toynbee's pessimistic label was successful not so much with historians as with literary critics. By the 1950s, both "modern" and "modernism" had acquired a distinct historical-typological meaning in the language of criticism to the extent, as we have seen earlier, that it was possible to oppose "modern" and "contemporary." The epithet "postmodern" and then the noun "postmodernism" seemed to convey, with appropriate vagueness, the new sense of crisis that was experienced after World War II. The feeling that modernist literature (Eliot, Pound, Yeats, Kafka, Mann, etc.) was no longer relevant to a dramatically changed social and intellectual situation was growing steadily among the younger generations. Used at first rather tentatively, and not without a touch of pessimism with regard to the fate of culture in a consumer society in which older intellectual standards appeared threatened, "postmodernism" was soon to become an almost honorific word. Interestingly, "postmodernism" was adopted as the battlecry of a new optimism, populist and apocalyptic, sentimental and irresponsible, which is perhaps best synthesized in the notion of a "counterculture." The apparently innocuous prefix "post" was itself semantically deneutralized and used rhetorically to convey a secret sense of exhilaration. Magically, the prefix seemed to do away with old restrictions and prejudices and to free the imagination for new, undefined, but extremely exciting experiences. Rereading recently Leslie Fiedler's essay "The New Mutants" (1965), I decided to underline all the words starting with this prefix. The result may give a close idea not only of the "mythological minority" that represented the young generation ten years ago, but also of the quasi-magical use of "post." The world of the "new mutants" is characterized as "post-Modernist," "post-Freudian," "post-Humanist," "post-Protestant," "post-male," "post-white," "post-heroic," "post-Jewish," "post-sexual," "post-Puritan."[64] Read in their contexts, all these words have intensely approbative connotations.

Among the first critics to make use of the epithet "postmodern" was Irving Howe, in his "Mass Society and Postmodern Fiction," published in *Partisan Review*.[65] In Howe's view, the passage from modernism to postmodernism is accounted for by the emergence of a "mass society," in which class distinctions become more blurred than ever in the past; in which "traditional centers of authority, like the family, tend to lose some of their binding power upon human beings; in which passivity becomes the general social attitude and man is transformed into a consumer, himself mass-produced like the products, diversions, and values that he absorbs."[66] Postmodern novelists were confronted with the historically new difficulty of giving "shape to a world increasingly shapeless and an experience increasingly fluid."[67] I would say that in this essay Howe's attitude toward postmodernism was not unsympathetic. More recently, in such an essay as "The New York Intellectuals," his approach has changed dramatically:

> We are confronting, then, a new phase in our culture, which in motive and spring represents a wish to shake off the bleeding heritage of modernism. . . . The new sensibility is impatient with ideas. It is impatient with literary structures of complexity and coherence, only yesterday the catchwords of our criticism. It wants instead works of literature—though literature may be the wrong word—that will be as absolute as the sun, as unarguable as orgasm, and as delicious as a lollipop. . . . It has no taste for the ethical nail-biting of those writers of the left who suffered defeat and could never again accept the narcotic of certainty. It is sick of those magnifications of irony that Mann gave us, sick of those visions of entrapment to which Kafka led us, sick of those shufflings of daily horror and grace that Joyce left us.

It breathes contempt for rationality, impatience with mind. . . . It is bored with the past: for the past is a fink.[68]

What Irving Howe seems to resent most is postmodernism's taste for public acclaim. Modernism was a "minority culture" that defined itself through opposition to a "dominant culture." But "the new sensibility is a success from the very start. The middle-class public, eager for thrills and humiliations, welcomes it: so do the mass-media . . . ; and naturally there appear intellectuals with handy theories."[69]

Borrowing the epithet "postmodern" from Arnold Toynbee, Harry Levin also makes the distinction between modern and post-modern. Thus, in a note introducing his essay "What Was Modernism?" (1960), he writes:

> Insofar as we are still moderns, I would argue, we are the Children of Humanism and the Enlightenment. To identify and isolate the forces of unreason, in a certain sense, has been the triumph of the intellect. In another sense it has reinforced that anti-intellectual undercurrent which, as it comes to surface, I would prefer to call post-modern.[70]

We note that for Harry Levin—as well as for Irving Howe—"modern" and "postmodern" are far from being merely neutral historical or cultural labels, employed for classifying purposes; they imply value judgments (and prejudgments as well). Thus, in the context in which Levin makes use of it, "postmodern" conveys a clear and strong sense of disapproval; this sense would come out even more strongly and clearly when examined against the background of Levin's critical conception as a whole. In a recent "Personal Retrospect," meant as an introduction to his volume *Grounds for Comparison* (1972), Levin ranges himself (not without a subtle trace of self-irony) among the "stodgy old humanistic liberals" whose positions are threatened by the contemporary wave of anti-intellectual apocalypticism. "If we now are facing an apocalypse," Levin writes, "then perhaps we may need critics with apocalyptic sensibilities, like George Steiner, rather than stodgy old humanistic liberals like Professor Trilling and myself."[71]

The death of modernism was joyous news for other critics who employ "postmodern" and "postmodernist" in an emphatically positive sense. Modernism had been highbrow, arrogant, and esoteric, and there was no need to mourn its death. The only trouble was that modernism had passed away in a discreet aristocratic fashion, and not everybody was aware that it was actually dead. Hence the need to proclaim its demise. Fiedler wrote in 1970:

> We are living, have been living for two decades—and have become actually conscious of the fact since 1955—through the death throes of Modernism and the birth pangs of Post-Modernism. The kind of literature which had arrogated to itself the name Modern (with the presumption that it represented the ultimate advance in sensibility and form, that beyond it newness was not possible), and whose moment of triumph lasted from a point just before World War I until one just after World War II, is *dead*, i.e., belongs to history not actuality.[72]

The new age is, in perfect contrast to the self-aware spirit of "analysis, rationality, anti-Romantic dialectic" embodied in modernist literature, "apocalyptic, antirational, blatantly romantic and sentimental; an age dedicated to joyous misology and prophetic irresponsibility; one, at any rate, distrustful of protective irony and too great self-awareness."[73]

Comparing the postmoderns to the moderns has become the latest form taken by the century-old Quarrel between the Ancients and the Moderns. An interesting example is provided us by Ihab Hassan, who treats this theme in "POSTmodernISM: A Paracritical Bibliography," which first appeared in 1971 in *NLH*[74] and was later collected in *Paracriticisms* (1975). In this article Hassan makes a full-scale comparison between modernism and postmodernism, a comparison that—though it does not specifically touch upon the question of value—tends to demonstrate that postmodernism, being in all respects different from modernism, is in no way less significant a cultural phenomenon. This comparison deserves to be discussed at some length.

Hassan's notion of modernism—which does not differ much from that of a wide range of contemporary English and American critics—includes the "historical" avant-garde in the Continental sense (namely, futurism, dadaism, constructivism, surrealism, etc.) but is far more comprehensive than that, including virtually every movement and almost every personality of any importance in the Western culture of the first half of our century. This extremely broad approach underlines the fact that practically no distinction is made by most American critics of twentieth-century literature between modernism and avant-garde. Implicitly, and sometimes explicitly, the two terms are taken as synonymous. Here is one of a host of possible recent examples, excerpted from a review of Poggioli's *Theory of the Avant-Garde*, published in *Boundary 2*. The author, Robert Langbaum writes: "For *avant-garde* in the title read *modernism*. The late Professor Poggioli of Harvard means by avant-garde what most of us mean by *modernism*, and has in fact written what is probably the best book on modernism."[75] This equivalence is surprising and even baffling for a critic familiar with the Continental usage of the term avant-garde. In France, Italy, Spain, and other European countries the avant-garde, despite its various and often contradictory claims, tends to be regarded as the most extreme form of artistic negativism—art itself being the first victim. As for modernism, whatever its specific meaning in different languages and for different authors, it never conveys that sense of universal and hysterical negation so characteristic of the avant-garde. The antitraditionalism of modernism is often subtly traditional. That is why it is so difficult, from a European point of view, to conceive of authors like Proust, Joyce, Kafka, Thomas Mann, T. S. Eliot, or Ezra Pound as representatives of the avant-garde. These writers have indeed very little, if anything, in common with such typically avant-garde movements as futurism, dadaism, or surrealism. So, if we want to operate consistently with the concept of modernism (and apply it to such writers as those mentioned above), it is necessary to distinguish between modernism and the avant-garde (old and new). It is true that modernity defined as a "tradition against itself" rendered possible the avant-garde, but it is equally true that the latter's negative radicalism and systematic antiaestheticism leave no room for the artistic reconstruction of the world attempted by the great modernists.

To better understand the strange relationship between modernism and the avant-garde (a relationship both of dependence and of exclusion), we may think of the avant-garde as, among other things, a deliberate and self-conscious *parody of modernity* itself. The status of parody is much more ambiguous than one might suspect. On the surface, a parody is meant to castigate, usually by exaggeration, certain hidden defects or incompatibilities in the original by which it is inspired. On a more profound level, however, the parodist can secretly admire the work he sets out to ridicule. A certain amount of praise for an author is even required on the part of his would-be parodist. Who tries to parody something that one believes completely insignificant or worthless? Moreover, a successful parody should convey, together with its criticism of the original, a degree of resemblance, a degree of faithfulness to both the letter and the spirit of the original. Ideally, a parody should at the same time appear to be a parody and offer the possibility of being nearly mistaken for the original itself. Seen as a parody of modernity, the avant-garde illustrates all these ambiguities, and while it is often gross and crude (as most actual parodies are), it can sometimes come so close to its model as to be confused with it.

Returning to Hassan's position, its interest lies in the fact that it synthesizes an approach characteristic of a recent line of development in Anglo-American criticism (a line that illustrates the reaction against the New Criticism, and more generally, against formalism). In his case, postmodernism is much more than a new critical label: it communicates a sense of commitment, as opposed to the requirement of detachment and objectivity of the formalists, and a sense of freedom from tradition (including the modernist self-critical tradition); hence the discovery of "paracriticism," and a certain playful quality perceivable throughout the essay. Hassan's comparison between modernism and postmodernism, although not a systematic one, proceeds by dividing the two cultural periods into a series of rubrics that are agreed upon by the most prominent students of modernity in literature and the arts, from Ortega to Poggioli: Urbanism, Technologism, "Dehumanization," Primitivism, Antinomianism, and Experimentalism. Hassan indicates both the modernist and postmodernist flavoring of each term.

Urbanism, for instance, is characterized in postmodernism by the following traits, enumerated in a deliberately telegraphic style:

> The city and the Global Village (McLuhan) and Spaceship Earth (Fuller). The city as cosmos.—Meanwhile, the world breaks into untold blocs, nations, tribes, clans, parties, languages, sects. Anarchy and fragmentation everywhere. . . .—Nature recovered partly in ecological activism, the green revolution, urban renewal, etc.— Meanwhile, Dionysus has entered the city: prision riots, urban crime, pornography, etc.

Concerning *technologism,* the author emphasizes the "runaway technology, from genetic engineering and thought control to the conquest of space," remarking subsequently that art is "following the trend of ephemeralization" and confronting the reader with the dilemma: "The computer as substitute consciousness or as extinction of consciousness?"

As regards *dehumanization,* to give a last example of the way Hassan works out his comparison, Ortega's powerful idea is developed in a new historical context: while the old dehumanization was carried out mostly along elitist lines, postmodernism is characterized by a profound "anti-elitism, anti-authoritarianism. Diffusion of the ego. Participation. Art becomes communal, optional, gratuitous, or anarchic.—Irony becomes radical, self-consuming play. Black canvas or black page. Silence. Also comedy of the absurd, black humor, insane parody."

Hassan's conclusion is that modernism "created its own forms of Authority," whereas postmodernism "has tended toward Anarchy, in deeper complicity with things falling apart."

I have quoted extensively from this article not only to point out some interesting ideas or suggestions but also to show the danger implied in the use of excessively broad concepts. Taking the term avant-garde in its Continental acceptation we can argue that what Hassan calls postmodernism is mostly an extension and diversification of the pre-World War II avant-garde. Historically speaking, many of the postmodernist notes defined by Hassan can easily be traced back to Dada and, not infrequently, to surrealism. Thus, antielitism, antiauthoritarianism, gratuitousness, anarchy, and, finally, nihilism are clearly implied in the dadaist doctrine of "antiart for antiart's sake" (the formula of Tristan Tzara). As for the found object and the signed soup can, they are obviously a continuation—somewhat epigonous, and, I would suppose, deliberately so—of Marcel Duchamp's and Man Ray's famous "ready-mades." The idea of chance is also a discovery of Dada, and it was theorized and applied not only by the dadaists but also by the surrealists in their doctrines of "automatic writing" and the "surrealist object."

Hassan's specious parallel is carried out more than once by contrasting neo-dadaist or neo-surrealist trends in recent culture with explicitly elitist or purist recommendations of some outstanding modernists (T. S. Eliot, for instance); or by contrasting the leftist radicalism so widespread in postmodernism with the "crypto-fascist" attitudes of Yeats, Lawrence, Pound, or Eliot (considered, all of them, as illustrative of that aspect of modernism). But what about other writers whose names are as often cited as examples of modernism? What about Kafka, Proust, Gide, Thomas Mann, Hermann Broch, Malraux, and so many others? Hassan's is a hasty generalization. Also, he seems to forget that his concept of modernism includes the Continental avant-garde and that the avant-garde was on the whole antielitist and—with some notable exceptions among the Italian futurists—strongly attracted to various forms of leftism (Communism, Trotskyism, Anarchism, etc.).

Certainly, the notion of an elite was implied in the concept of the avant-garde, but this elite, as we have seen earlier, was committed to the destruction of all elites, including itself. The idea was taken quite seriously by all the genuine representatives of the avant-garde. This involved, among other things, the blunt rejection of the principle of hierarchy in all walks of life and primarily, obviously, in art itself. In this respect, the claim of the surrealists that they had no talent—and their view that talent was indeed the worst insult that could be hurled in their face by opponents or even well-intended but naïve supporters—is consistent with the spirit of the whole avant-garde. The argument that postmodern culture is antielitist *because* it is popular—in the specific case of writers, because they are no longer ashamed of "best sellerdom"—seems utterly sophistic. To be popular in our age is to create for the market, to respond to its demands—including the eager and quite recognizable demand for "subversion." Popularity is equivalent to accepting if not the "System," then its most direct manifestation, the Market. The result of submission to the forces of the Market is neither elitist nor antielitist (both notions have been overworked to the point of being emptied of content). As for the truly great artists that represent the spirit of postmodernism—for instance, Beckett or even Pynchon—they are by no means more "popular" and accessible to the public at large than were the most sophisticated among the modernists or the avant-gardists.

INTELLECTUALISM, ANARCHISM, AND STASIS

Compared to the old avant-garde, the new, postmodernist avant-garde seems, in one of its main directions, more systematically involved in theoretical thinking. This highly intellectualized type of neo-avant-garde is most active in continental Europe. The former members of the *Gruppo 63* (Edoardo Sanguineti, Umberto Eco, Nani Balestrini, etc.), the French novelists comprised under the label of the "nouveau roman" (Robbe-Grillet, Claude Simon, Robert Pinget, etc.), the Parisian group *Tel Quel*, whose members, monomaniacs of the idea of Revolution, combine with impunity the Marquis de Sade and Marx, Mallarmé and Lenin, Lautréamont and Mao (Phillipe Sollers, Julia Kristeva, Marcelin Pleynet, etc.), the Stuttgart group of concrete poets led by the scientist Max Bense— are among the best known and most influential representatives of this new avant-garde.

In England and the United States a more spontaneous and, as it were, anarchistic trend began to assert itself with the Beat movement of the 1950s (Jack Kerouac, Allen Ginsberg, etc.), with the Liverpool group of Pop poetry (Adrian Henry, Roger McGough, Brian Patten), with the now dead Living Theatre (Julian Beck, Judith Malina), and, in music, with John Cage. But, as the case of John Cage clearly shows, the disruptive techniques—aleatory or otherwise—characteristic of aesthetic anarchism do not go without a high degree of sophistication and awareness of theoretical issues. The attempt at "discovering means to let sounds be themselves rather than vehicles for man-made theories or expressions of human sentiments"—as Cage puts it in his book *Silence*[76]—may be meaningful only to the connoisseur or to the snob, not to the man in the street who is likely to be a sincere consumer of kitsch and not care about pure sounds, stripped of their human significance. The same applies to the speculations about the "sensuous immediacy" of the image promoted to the rank of aesthetic norm in Susan Sontag's *Against Interpretation*.[77] It is not fortuitous that such theories turn out to be perfectly parallel to those about literalness (*littéralité*) upheld in France by representatives of the "nouvelle critique" (some of them associated with *Tel Quel*). Thus, modern poetry— according to Gérard Genette—tends to suppress any distance between letter and meaning, and to abolish the old transcendence of meaning in relation to the text. Today, "the literalness of language," Genette writes, "appears as the being itself of poetry and nothing would be more disturbing for one who adheres to such a view than the idea of a possible translation, of a certain space separating the letter from the meaning."[78]

In the long run, despite the apparent gap, there is an essential similarity between what we have called the intellectualist neo-avant-garde and the anarchistic trend. The unifying principle of the two main aspects of neo-avant-garde art is their common *antiteleological* drive. As Leonard Meyer rightly points out, what is involved in contemporary art is "a radically different set of ends, whether these ends be achieved by careful calculation as in the music of Stockhausen, the paintings of Tobey or Rothko, and the writings of Beckett and Alain Robbe-Grillet, or by random operations as in the music of Cage, the paintings of Mathieu, or the chance theater of MacLow's *The Marrying Maiden*. And underlying this new aesthetic is a conception of man and universe, which is almost the opposite of the view that has dominated Western thought since its beginnings."[79]

One of the characteristics of our time, as revealed in the public situation of the new avant-garde, is that we have begun to get accustomed to change. Even the most extreme artistic experiments seem to arouse little interest or excitement. The unpredictable has become predictable. Generally, the increasing pace of change tends to diminish the relevance of any particular change. The new is no longer new. If modernity has presided over the formation of an "aesthetic of surprise," this seems to be the moment of its total failure. Today the most diverse artistic products (covering the whole range from the esoterically sophisticated to sheer kitsch), wait side by side in the "cultural supermarket" (a notion ironically homologous to that of Malraux's "imaginary museum") for their respective consumers. Mutually exclusive aesthetics coexist in a sort of stalemate, no one being able to perform an actually leading role. Most of the analysts of contemporary art agree that ours is a pluralistic world in which everything is permitted on principle. The old avant-garde, destructive as it was, sometimes deluded itself into believing that there were actually new paths to break open, new realities to discover, new prospects to explore. But today, when the "historical avant-garde" has been so successful as to become the "chronic condition" of art, both the rhetoric of destruction and that of novelty have lost any trace of heroic appeal. We could say that the new, postmodernist avant-garde reflects at its own level the increasingly "modular" structure of our mental world, in which the crisis of ideologies (manifesting itself by a strange, cancerous proliferation of micro-ideologies, while the great ideologies of modernity are losing their coherence) makes it more and more difficult to establish convincing hierarchies of values.

This situation in regard to the arts has been perceptively described in Leonard Meyer's *Music, the Arts, and Ideas* (the chapter entitled "History, Stasis, and Change"). History, the author argues, is a "hierarchic construct," and periodization—"more than a convenient way of dividing up the past"—is a necessary consequence of the graded character of history, which would become incomprehensible "were it not hierarchically articulated into reigns, epochs, style periods, movements and the like. . . ."

But such an approach would be inappropriate insofar as our time is concerned. The arts today are characterized, Meyer believes, by a "fluctuating steady-state." Change is everywhere but we live, culturally, in a perfectly static world. The contradiction is only apparent, for stasis "is not the absence of novelty and change—a total quiescence—but rather the absence of ordered sequential change. Like molecules rushing about haphazardly in a Brownian movement, a culture bustling with activity and change may nevertheless be static."[80]

This stasis appears to me as one consequence of the irreducible contradictions involved in modernity's concept of time. Such contradictions have been self-consciously exaggerated by the avant-garde, which has endeavored to bring every single art form to the point of deepest crisis. In this process, both modernity and the avant-garde have displayed an extraordinary imagination of crisis; and they have jointly succeeded in creating a complex, often ironic and self-ironic sensitivity for crisis, which seems to be both their ultimate achievement and their nemesis.

As a result, old and new, construction and destruction, beauty and ugliness have become through relativization almost meaningless categories. Art and antiart (the latter notion taken not only in the dadaist polemical sense but referring also to the immense variety of products of kitsch) have merged. And stasis is just the most observable aspect of a crisis that seems to have become the major criterion of any significant artistic activity.

THE IDEA OF DECADENCE

All things considered, the century of the end will not be the most refined or even the most complicated, but the most hurried, the century in which, its Being dissolved in movement, civilization, in a supreme impulse toward the worst, will fall to pieces in the whirlwind it has raised. Now that nothing can keep it from being engulfed, let us give up practicing our virtues upon it, let us even manage to discern, in the excesses it delights in, something exalting, something which invites us to moderate our outrage and reconsider our scorn. In this fashion, these specters, these automata, these zombies are less detestable if we reflect upon the unconscious motives, the deeper reasons for their frenzy: do they not feel that the interval granted them is shrinking day by day and that the dénouement is taking form? And is it not to ward off this notion that they immerse themselves in speed? . . . Of so much haste, of so much impatience, our machines are the consequence and not the cause. It is not they that are driving civilized man to his doom; rather he has invented them because he was already on his way there; he sought means, auxiliaries to attain it faster and more effectively. Not content to run, he preferred to *ride* to perdition. In this sense, and in this sense alone, we may say that his machines allow him to "save time."

E. M. Cioran, *The Fall into Time* (1964),
trans. from the French by Richard Howard

VERSIONS OF DECADENCE

If the Latin noun *decadentia*, from which related words in modern European languages derive ("decadence" in English, *décadence* in French, *decadenzia* in Italian, *Dekadenz* in German, etc.), was not used before the Middle Ages, the idea of decadence itself is certainly much older, and probably as old as man himself. The myth of decadence was known, in one form or another, to nearly all ancient peoples. The destructiveness of time and the fatality of decline are among the outstanding motifs of all great mythical-religious traditions, from the Indian notion of the Age of Kali to the terrifying visions of corruption and sinfulness conveyed by the Jewish prophets; and from the Greeks' and Romans' disillusioned belief in the Iron Age to the Christians' sense of living in a malignant world that was approaching the dominion of absolute evil (the reign of Antichrist), as announced in the *Apocalypse*.

"The men of early times," thought Plato, "were better than we and nearer to the Gods" (*Philebus*, 16c).[1] This is just one example of how the present—even in an age that was subsequently regarded as glorious and exemplary—deemed itself inferior to earlier and more blissful times. Ancient Greece was very much in "the grip of the past,"[2] and in this respect it was not significantly different from any of the civilizations that flourished before the combined ideas of modernity and progress took hold of the Western mind. We all know how pervasive the myth of the Golden Age (as opposed to the Iron Age) was in Greece, then in Rome, but we are barely aware of the manifestations of the idea of decadence in classical metaphysics, outside of the obvious domain of poetico-historical speculation. In this context, it would be tempting to consider Plato himself as perhaps the first great Western philosopher to build up a whole complex ontology on the idea of decadence. For the Platonic theory of Ideas cleary implies a metaphysical concept of decadence (or degeneration) when it describes the relationship between those archetypal, perfect, unchanging, real models of all things and their mere "shadows" in the sensible world of perceived objects, where everything is subject to the corrupting influence of time and change. Closer to our concern with historical decadence, Plato's view of history and society summarizes the widespread Greek belief that time was nothing but a continuous decline. "With Plato," writes the French religious historian Henri-Charles Puech,

> the Greeks speculated on the models or ideal schemata of states or social forms, from which they derived a necessary, a temporal succession applicable to any event whatever. The resultant laws were "laws of decadence rather than of development" [Émile Bréhier]: they represent change as a fall from an ideal primitive state conceived in terms of myth; political states do not improve, they become corrupted; and the history of governments is a history of decadence. Here we perceive the core of the Greeks' feelings about time: it was experienced as a "degenerescence"—the notion of a continuous progress was unheard of.[3]

But to understand the formation of the *modern* idea of decadence and its applications to certain outstanding aspects of cultural modernity (illustrated terminologically by the appearance, toward the mid-nineteenth century, of the adjective and the noun "decadent," and, a few decades later, of the notion of "decadentism"), we have to consider in the first place, as we did in our account of the development of modernity's concept, the view of time and history brought about by the Judeo-Christian tradition. The originality of the Jewish and then Christian philosophy of history comes from its *eschatological* character, from its belief—which makes the progression of time linear and irreversible—in an end to history, in a *last* day (*eschatos* in Greek means "last"), after which (in the Christian view) the elect will enjoy the eternal felicity for which Man was created, while the sinful will forever suffer the tortures of hell. The approach of the Day of Doom is announced by the unmistakable sign of profound decay—untold corruption—and, according to apocalyptic prophecy, by the satanic power of Antichrist.

Decadence thus becomes the anguishing prelude to the end of the world. The deeper the decadence, the closer the Last Judgment. From the early Middle Ages on, countless sects and movements within Christianity upheld the belief in the millennium, indulging in the most somber expectations of imminent cosmic collapse and doom, which were to precede the end of time. Chilianism, rejected as early as St. Augustine and subsequently condemned by a series of Councils, managed to survive and reemerge with renewed powers during the troubled period of the Reformation. The vitality of a modern, secularized millennialism is apparent in diverse revolutionary and utopian doctrines, among them Marxism, with its eschatological vision of communism as the end of human alienation (it is not fortuitous that the idea of decadence—of the advanced *putrefaction* of modern-day capitalism, and of its dying culture—is so important in Marxism).

Christian time, it has been said, organizes itself *horizontally*, while Greek time might be characterized as essentially *vertical*. This analogy, even though it should not be taken too literally, is actually very suggestive. The opposition between Greek and Christian time has been elaborated upon by, among others, Henri-Charles Puech, who has pointed out some of the implications of the horizontal/vertical metaphor as applied to the contrasting views of time and change:

> The vertical interpretation of the world's changing appearances through the fixed and atemporal, archetypal realities of the upper, intelligible world, gives way—in ancient Christianity—to a horizontal interpretation of the segments of time through one another: the past announces and prepares the future; or... the earlier events are the 'types' or 'prefigurations' of the subsequent events, and these in turn are the realization of the events which precede them and which are related to them as the shadow is related to full, authentic reality. Thus we might say that here the image anticipates the model, while in Greek thought the transcendent model is for all eternity

prior to the image. Greek exemplarianism is diametrically reversed.[4]

If the horizontal-temporal relationship between "prefiguration" or "shadow" and "full reality" applies exclusively to ancient Christianity, the broad horizontal view of time and the ensuing stress on *historicity* (that is, on an irreversible succession of unique events, even if these can be seen as a fulfillment of prophecy) constitute a characteristic of Christianity as a whole.

What is new in the Christian view of decadence (by contrast with the more passive attitude of the ancients, whether they favored stoical resignation and indifference, or cultivated the hedonistic philosophy of *"Carpe diem"*) is an acute and feverish sense of urgency. Decadence is felt, with an intensity unknown before, as a unique crisis; and, as time is running short, it becomes of ultimate importance to do, without waiting any longer, what one has to do for one's own and one's fellow man's Salvation. In the perspective of the rapidly approaching end of the world every single instant can be decisive. The consciousness of decadence brings about restlessness and a need for self-examination, for agonizing commitments and momentous renunciations. Christian apocalypticism, even when it does not manifest itself overtly, results in a dramatically increased time awareness. This may have been a significant psychological factor in the preparation of the Renaissance discovery of secular time and the high valuation of temporality.

At this point it may be worth observing that the Renaissance did not assert the value of time in anything like a serenely optimistic perspective of open-ended historical development. Many of the most outstanding representatives of the Renaissance were pessimists, and the consciousness of crisis was widespread. Summing up a whole line of research, an intellectual historian of the modern sense of decadence can write about the "myth" of Renaissance optimism:

> But the gradual replacement of Christian supernaturalism by a naturalist and secular outlook did not necessarily lead to a more cheerful view of history. . . . Thus one of the most naturalist minds of

the Renaissance, Leonardo da Vinci, was obsessed with visions of a catastrophic end of the world, an event that he no longer envisaged as a divine judgment, but as a disaster in which all men, regardless of their merits, would suffer the same torments. . . . The wide response to Savonarola's virulent denunciations of Renaissance society also indicates that many Italians of the end of the fifteenth century looked upon their age as a period of crisis and corruption. In other words, the exuberant optimism of the Renaissance is little more than a myth.[5]

Leonardo's case is indeed revealing, and it is highly significant that his visions were centered around the characteristically Christian idea of an apocalyptic disaster, which, for being emptied of its religious significance, became only more ominously oppressive and anguishing.

The ideas of modernity and progress on the one hand, and the idea of decadence on the other, are mutually exclusive only at the crudest level of understanding. As soon as we take into consideration the way they were actually used in various phases of their history we become aware of the dialectical complexity of their relationships. Bernard de Chartres's famous simile is a good example. In the analogy of the dwarfs who stand on the shoulders of giants and are thus able to see farther, progress and decadence imply each other so intimately that, if we were to generalize, we would reach the paradoxical conclusion that progress *is* decadence and, conversely, decadence *is* progress. Bernard's metaphor has the merit of showing convincingly how such a blatant and logically unacceptable paradox can, as an image (or a projection of imagination), be received as a perfectly sound insight.

Like progress, decadence is a relative concept, and this relativity is rendered only more elusive by the fact that, as V. Jankélévitch points out in a remarkable philosophical essay on decadence, "there are no historical contents that can be characterized as decadent 'in themselves.' Decadence is not *in statu* but *in motu*."[6] Decadence is therefore not a structure but a direction or tendency.

We also note that the usual associations of decadence with such notions as decline, twilight, autumn, senescence, and exhaustion, and, in its more advanced stages, organic decay and putrescence—along with their automatic antonyms: rise, dawn, spring, youth, germination, etc.—make it inevitable to think of it in terms of natural cycles and biological metaphors. These organic affinities of the idea of decadence explain why progress is not its unqualified opposite. It is true that in earlier periods progress was conceived by analogy with growth and particularly with the intellectual development of the human individual (we recall Saint Augustine's comparison between the gradual development of mankind and that of a single man). But after centuries of close association with scientific research and technological advance, the concept of progress reached a level of abstraction at which older organic and specifically anthropomorphic connotations could no longer be retained. Progress came to be regarded as a concept having more to do with mechanics than with biology.

There is only a short distance from here to the view, not infrequent in our century, that progress is an enemy of life. The critique of the myth of progress was started within the romantic movement, but it gained momentum in the antiscientific and antirationalist reaction that marks the late nineteenth century and prolongs itself well into the twentieth. As a consequence—and by now this has become almost a truism—a high degree of technological development appears perfectly compatible with an acute sense of decadence. The fact of progress is not denied, but increasingly large numbers of people experience the *results* of progress with an anguished sense of loss and alienation. Once again, progress *is* decadence and decadence *is* progress. The true opposite of decadence—as far as the biological connotations of the word are concerned—is perhaps regeneration. But where are the barbarians who will regenerate our exhausted world?

Without entirely subsiding, the exhilarating belief in progress has been replaced during the last one hundred years or so by the infinitely more ambiguous (more ambiguous because more self-critical) myths of modernity, the avant-garde, and decadence. I am, of course, limiting my remarks to the way these myths function within the scope of the literary and artistic imagination of our age. So, I am particularly interested here in the passage from the old and general sense of decadence to the new and more specific notion of *cultural decadence* as it evolved in the nineteenth century, culminating with the appearance of the aesthetic-historical category of "decadentism." In other words, I am concerned with the process through which decadence becomes self-consciously modern. In this process, as we shall see, a complete reinterpretation and reevaluation of the concept of decadence is achieved.

FROM "DECADENCE" TO
"STYLE OF DECADENCE"

Although most literary historians agree that the modern aesthetic idea of decadence originates from romanticism—an assertion that is basically correct—the romantics themselves did not consciously identify with anything like a well-articulated or even a vague program of decadence. Their occasional pronouncements on whatever aspects of decadence they might have observed in the life of contemporary society are largely irrelevant to our subject because the use of the concept in such instances had neither originality nor anticipatory value. Ironically, decadence was employed in a *cultural* and specifically *aesthetic* sense—even though it preserved its traditional derogatory connotations—by adversaries of romanticism. This happened in France, where neoclassicism was, at the beginning of the nineteenth century, stronger than anywhere else in Western Europe.

The first to introduce the theoretical notion of a "style of decadence," defined by a number of recognizable and recurrent characteristics, was the antiromantic and conservative French critic Désiré

Nisard. Without referring directly to the romantics, who were rebelling against the strict rules of neoclassical poetics, Nisard wrote his *Etudes de moeurs et de critique sur les poètes latins de la décadence* (published in Brussels in 1834) with what he considered the romantic excesses and abuses in mind. Although his book is ostensibly devoted to the poetry of the late Roman Empire, the actual target of his strictures is undoubtedly romanticism. Interestingly, Nisard's arguments—and especially his view that a "decadent style" of art places such emphasis on detail that the normal relationship of a work's parts to its whole is destroyed, the work disintegrating into a multitude of overwrought fragments—have been quite influential, even though the name of their originator has sunk into oblivion. It is indeed fascinating (for those who are interested in the strange life of ideas) to discover to what an extent Paul Bourget's famous description of *"style de décadence"* (which, as is known, was readily borrowed by Nietzsche) is indebted to Nisard's approach half a century earlier. [7]

The decadence and final collapse of the Roman Empire had long been a subject of meditation for historians, but it was not until the eighteenth century that it received a consistently modern (i.e., non-theological) treatment. The best example of this new, immanent approach (in the sense that it discounts the intervention in history of any transcendental factor) is Montesquieu's *Considérations sur les causes de la grandeur des romains et de leur décadence* (1734). But in this essay, which lays the foundation for and in certain respects anticipates the vast synthesis of *L'Esprit des lois* (1748), Montesquieu does not consider the literature of decadent Rome, but limits his analysis to the sociopolitical, moral, and military causes that led to the downfall of antiquity's most powerful empire.

In his *Cahiers*, however, when meditating on the issues of the *Querelle des Anciens et des Modernes*, Montesquieu came close to formulating a general law of decadence, seen in its paradoxical interrelationship with prosperity. This law would also apply to cultural decadence, and Montesquieu suggests that the very richness and diversity of the moderns' literary achievement might have been taken as a sign that decadence was in the offing: "In the history of empires, nothing is closer to decadence than great prosperity; likewise, in our literary republic, one worries lest prosperity lead to decadence."[8]

In his *Essai sur les moeurs et l'esprit des nations* (1756), Voltaire also employs the term "decadence" in connection with the decline of the Roman Empire, elaborating on its causes (the advent of Christianity and the subsequent social turmoils that weakened the Empire in the face of growing barbarian threat), but, like his predecessor, he gives no attention to the specifically literary forms of Roman decadence. Voltaire speaks of decadence in a literary sense only when he complains of the corruptions of taste in his own time as compared to the glorious achievements of the *Siècle de Louis XIV* (1739–68).

During the eighteenth century, however, the idea emerged that an historical period (be it one of growth and progress or one of decadence) should be perceived as a "totality," and that sociopolitical phenomena and artistic manifestations are *organically* interrelated. This broader concept of history is central to Madame de Staël's approach in *De la littérature considerée dans ses rapports avec les institutions sociales* (1800). This work, which has sometimes been considered a document of early romanticism, is in fact little more than a synthesis of Enlightenment aesthetic ideology. In a most optimistic eighteenth-century fashion, Madame de Staël shares the belief in indefinite progress and is deeply convinced of the overall superiority of the moderns over the ancients. Set in such a perspective, the decadence observed in certain past periods appears as an accidental phenomenon, to be explained by isolated deviations from the ideal and practice of freedom. Madame de Staël writes:

> It has been maintained that the decadence of arts, letters and empires comes necessarily after a certain period of splendor. This idea is wrong. The arts have a borderline beyond which, I believe, they

cannot advance; but they can keep up the level they have reached; and in all knowledge which lends itself to development, the moral nature tends to improve.[9]

Madame de Staël naturally mentions Roman decadence—whose main cause she assigns to tyranny—and admits that it resulted in the corruption of previous standards of taste. But even in such a period of decadence, she maintains, the principle of progress was subtly at work, and the Roman writers of the imperial period, being artistically inferior, "were, as thinkers, superior to those of the Augustan era."[10] As for her own time, Madame de Staël felt assured that, with the beneficial and irreversible influence of "les lumières," there was no longer any threat of decadence. For her, decadence was exclusively a matter of the past:

> The decadence of empires is not more in the natural order than is that of letters and of enlightenment [lumières]. ... European civilization, the establishment of Christianity, scientific discoveries... have... destroyed the ancient causes for barbarism. So the decadence of nations, and consequently of letters, is less to be feared nowadays.[11]

Like many of her eighteenth-century predecessors, Madame de Staël did not dwell on the question at more length because she simply ruled out the possibility of any future decadence.

Nisard, the first critic to devote more sustained attention to literary decadence as a "style," was infinitely less optimistic than Madame de Staël. We have already noted that his preoccupation with the decadence of Latin literature had been prompted by contemporary issues, as perceived from the standpoint of an embattled defender of neoclassical values in a time favorable to romanticism. As he pointed out in the preface to the first edition of his *Etudes*, Nisard was interested in the *recurring traits* of literary decadencies:

> I offer a developed theory on the common characteristics of decadent poetries. ... I try to explain what imperceptible, successive needs have led the human spirit to this unusual state of exhaustion in which the richest imaginations can do nothing for true poetry, and are left with only the power to destroy languages scandalously.[12]

So we are not surprised to find Nisard applying his theory of decadence (only two years after the publication of his book on the Silver Age of Latin poetry) to the foremost French romantic poet, Victor Hugo. Earlier, in 1829, Nisard had been a champion of Hugo, but during the following years he underwent such a complete change of heart that in 1836 he became probably the most articulate, if not the most outspoken critic of the great poet. In his article "M. Victor Hugo in 1836," the author of *Etudes* discovers in Hugo's *Chants du crépuscule* all the main signs of decadence—the profuse use of description, the prominence of detail and, on a general plane, the elevation of the imaginative power, to the detriment of reason. Nisard's strictures against Hugo amount, theoretically, to an attack against imagination and novelty (the profound *antimodern* character of this attack can be better grasped if we compare it to Baudelaire's passionate praise of imagination, "the queen of faculties"). Nisard writes:

> When we say that [Victor Hugo] has been an innovator, we are not praising him. In France, a country of practical and reasonable litera-ture, a writer who has only imagination, though it be of the rarest sort, cannot be a great writer. . . . In him the imagination takes the place of everything; imagination alone conceives and performs: it is a queen who governs unchecked. Reason finds no place in his works. No practical or applicable ideas, nothing or next to nothing of real life; no philosophy, no morals.[13]

Imagination, Nisard thinks, when it is no longer under the control of reason, loses sight of the whole of reality and of the actual hierarchy of things, focussing on details (in which, he is quite willing to con-cede, Hugo excels).[14] Another noteworthy feature of Nisard's theory is that it stresses the *dangerously deceptive* character of decadent art, its power to seduce. The harmfulness of decadence is in direct proportion to its capacity for deception. Anticipating once again Nietzsche's view of decadence, as expressed in the latter's famous critique of Wagner, Nisard calls Victor Hugo a "seducer."[15]

The sense of decadence in the nineteenth century was certainly not restricted to France, but it was in that country, perhaps because of "the feeling that the nation's power and prestige in the world were declining,"[16] that the theme of decadence not only became more compelling and obsessive but also was charged with the intensely contradictory meanings that define, culturally, a typical love-hate relationship. In other words, in France, to a larger extent than elsewhere, the idea of decadence, with all its old and new ambiguities, provided an occasion for cultural self-identification. The opening line of Verlaine's famous sonnet "Langueur" (1884)— *"Je suis l'empire à la fin de la décadence"*—sums up poetically the feelings of a significant section of the French intelligentsia, especially after the failure of the 1848 Revolution and, with increased dramatism, after France's collapse in the 1870 Prussian War and the subsequent uprising that led to the ephemeral Paris Commune of 1871.

Obviously, a wide variety of attitudes and standards flourished among the numerous French intellectuals who shared an awareness of decadence. Some cultivated a "regenerationalist" concept of decadence, decrying the effects of decline and believing in the possibility of a future "renascence," to which they were deeply committed. Others—and they are of primary interest to us—relished the feeling that the modern world was headed toward catastrophe. Most of the latter group were artists, conscious promoters of an aesthetic modernity that was, in spite of all its ambiguities, radically opposed to the other, essentially bourgeois, modernity, with its promises of indefinite progress, democracy, generalized sharing of the "comforts of civilization," etc. Such promises appeared to these "decadent" artists as so many demagogical diversions from the terrible reality of increasing spiritual alienation and dehumanization. To protest precisely such tactics, the "decadents" cultivated the consciousness of their *own* alienation, both aesthetic and moral, and, in the face of the false and complacent humanism of the day's demagogues, resorted to something approaching the aggressive strategies of antihumanism and of what, as we have seen, Ortega y Gasset was to call a few decades later the "dehumanization of art." Furthermore, the "decadents" often upheld revolutionary beliefs (anarchism was particularly attractive to them) and so they were not unjustly perceived as representatives of the avant-garde. In the 1880s, literary decadentism and literary avant-gardism had come to be, if not completely synonymous, very closely related notions. We shall deal with this relationship later.

Resuming our historical account, we note that toward the middle of the nineteenth century an increasing number of French intellectuals, both within the Art for Art's Sake movement and outside it, speculate on literary decadence and, unlike the ultraconservative Nisard, feel inclined to reevaluate it, at least partially. Here the testimony of the young Ernest Renan is significant. Before becoming the passionate advocate of the idea of progress in his still youthful *Avenir de la science* (written in the late 1840s but not published until 1890), Renan had been preoccupied with the question of decadence in the philosophical diary of his formative years, which is known under the title *Cahiers de jeunesse* (1846–47). Periods of decadence, Renan argued, are inferior to classical periods only insofar as the sheer power of imaginative creation is concerned, but they are clearly superior in *critical* ability: "These periods of decadence are strong in criticism, often stronger than periods of greatness,"[17] Renan wrote, and defending the value of criticism, he declared:

> In a sense, criticism is superior to composition. Till now criticism has adopted a humble role as a servant *et pedis sequa*; perhaps the time has come for criticism to take stock of itself and to raise itself above those whom it judges. Thus this century is thin in producing fiction of the original classical type. Does this mean that the century is inferior? No, because it is more philosophical.[18]

Renan also noted his time's special interest not only in past periods of decadence but also in periods of primitivism. The taste for both decadence and primitivism, Renan rightly observed, derived from a certain impatience with classicism as such:

> What a curious fact of literary history is the craze of our time for non-classical literatures. It is not that there is no interest in Greek,

Latin, and French literatures but it is mostly their pre-classical and post-classical periods that are studied. All interest lies in what is called the origins and the decadent eras.[19]

Renan is probably the first to have been aware of the remarkable fact that the fascination with decadence and the apparently contradictory fascination with origins and primitivism are actually two sides of one and the same phenomenon. The intimate relationship between the craze for the oversophisticated, excessively refined products of decadence, and the craze for the naïve, awkward, immature manifestations of "primitive" creativeness has been demonstrated over and over again by the development of modern literature and art since the late nineteenth century.

The first entirely approbative and widely influential view of decadence as a *style* occurs in the preface that Théophile Gautier wrote in 1868 for Baudelaire's *Fleurs du Mal*. A champion of Art for Art's Sake, Gautier had expressed his admiration for certain literary themes usually associated with decadence as early as 1836, when *Mlle de Maupin*, with its famous preface, had been published. His application of the concept to Baudelaire's poetry remains, however, Gautier's crucial statement, although we note that he was not too happy with the term "decadence" itself (an important nuance that is all too often skipped over by students of decadence):

> The style inadequately called of decadence is nothing but art arrived at the point of extreme maturity yielded by the slanting suns of aged civilizations: an ingenious, complicated style, full of shades and of research, constantly pushing back the boundaries of speech, borrowing from all technical vocabularies, taking color from all palettes and notes from all keyboards, struggling to render what is most inexpressible in thought, what is vague and most elusive in the outlines of form, listening to translate the subtle confidences of neurosis, the dying confessions of passion grown depraved, and the strange hallucinations of the obsession which is turning to madness.[20]

The object of Gautier's article, Baudelaire himself, was not unacquainted with the new approach to the problem of decadence. It is true that Baudelaire sometimes openly rejects both the term and the concept, but at least as frequently he has something favorable to say about decadence. Let us consider, for instance, the curious note that, in the first edition of *Les Fleurs du Mal* (1857), accompanied the poem in medieval Latin, "Franciscae meae laudes." More than an explication, the note was meant to express Baudelaire's adherence to a certain style, which he defined as at once *decadent, spiritual,* and *modern.* The relationship established in the text among these three key notions is typical of Baudelaire's way of thinking:

> Does not the reader think, as I do, that the late Latin decadence—a supreme sigh of a robust person already transformed and prepared for spiritual life—is uniquely appropriate for expressing passion such as the modern poetic world has understood and felt it?[21]

Baudelaire, whose work was to serve as an example for various definitions of decadence from Gautier to Bourget and later, never addressed himself to the problem of developing a unified theory on the subject. His criticism, however, contains a number of insights that demonstrate their author's central role in the further promotion of the modern concept of artistic decadence. The young Baudelaire of the "Salon of 1846" makes use of the term "decadence" to characterize Victor Hugo. This clearly reminds us of Nisard's earlier (1836) critique of Hugo. But Baudelaire, even though he retains some elements of Nisard's definition (for instance, the idea that a poet of decadence will try to obtain by means of words effects characteristic of other artistic media, such as painting or music), is totally opposed to the main thrust of Nisard's antiromantic and anti-imaginative approach. When he compares Delacroix to Hugo, Baudelaire exalts the former as a *true* romantic (a creator endowed with *"l'imagination la plus voyageuse"*), while rejecting the usual characterization of Hugo in terms of romanticism. According to the author of the "Salon of 1846" Victor Hugo was "a workman more ingenious than inventive, a craftsman more industrious and correct than creative. . . . He is a composer of decadence. . . . Mr. Hugo had been a natural member of the Academy even before being born."[22] Here, decadence is equated with the sterility of academicism.

More than a decade later, in the article entitled "L'Art philosophique" (written probably in 1859 but published posthumously), Baudelaire speculates on decadence in more general terms and develops his earlier idea that the main characteristic of decadence is its systematic attempt to break down the conventional boundaries between diverse arts. As in the 1857 note on "Franciscae meae laudes," Baudelaire establishes a direct connection between *decadence* and *modernity*. After centuries during which the history of art had tended toward an increasingly marked "separation of powers" and specialization (with the result that "there are subjects which belong to painting, others to music, others to literature"), Baudelaire observed the dominance in contemporary art of a directly opposite principle:

> Is it an inevitable result of decadence that every art today reveals a desire to encroach upon neighboring arts, and the painters introduce musical scales, sculptors use color, writers use the plastic means, and other artists, those who concern us today, display a kind of encyclopedic philosophy in the plastic arts themselves?[23]

Considering Baudelaire's commitment to modernity, and specifically his deep conviction regarding the essential unity of the arts, this view of decadence can hardly be regarded as a negative one. And the poet's acceptance of decadence—understood as a free interchange of means and procedures among the arts—becomes even clearer when we think of his open advocacy of "total" or "synthetic" art, and of the way he applied the two kindred principles of universal analogy and synaesthesia to his discussion of Richard Wagner. Speaking of Wagner in 1861, Baudelaire specifically praised the German composer for his conception of "dramatic art" as the "reunion, the *coincidence* of several arts," that is, "*l'art par excellence, le plus synthétique et le plus parfait.*"[24] To exemplify Wagner's drive toward a synthesis of the arts, Baudelaire lays special emphasis on the *visual* quality of Wagnerian music:

> No musician excels in painting space and background like Wagner. . . . It seems at times, listening to that ardent and despotic

music, that one discovers dizzy conceptions of opium painted on a background of half-lights, torn by revery.[25]

It may be interesting to point out here that Baudelaire's acknowledged master, Eugène Delacroix, was also sensitive to the phenomenon of decadence, as his *Diary* amply proves. Periods of decadence, Delacroix thought, are always more complex, more refined, and more analytical than those that precede them. There seems to be an inevitable progression in man's consciousness of his own sentiments. For an artist, to go against the grain and cultivate some kind of archaicism would be simply ridiculous:

> The essence of my idea was the need to belong to one's time. Therefore, the foolishness of going against the tide and being old fashioned. Racine seems already refined in comparison to Corneille; and how much more refined have we become since Racine. . . . Our modern artists do not depict only feelings; they describe the external world and analyze everything.[26]

And in another entry made a few days later, on April 16, 1856, Delacroix goes on to establish a clear connection between decadence and the need for refinement:

> On the need for refinement in times of decadence. The greatest spirits cannot avoid it. . . . The English, the Germanics have always pushed us in that direction. Shakespeare is very refined. Painting with a great depth feelings which ancient artists neglected or did not know, he discovered a small world of emotions which all men in all times have experienced in a state of confusion. . . .[27]

For the French writers and artists of the 1850s and 1860s, the idea of decadence is quite often related either directly to the notion of progress or indirectly to the effects of the "hysteria" of modern development on human consciousness. The Goncourt brothers speak, in 1864, of a "modern melancholy," which they see as a result of the unbearable strain put on the mind by the demands of a society in a rage for "production" in all senses. It would be hard to find a view in sharper contrast to the optimistic Enlightenment concept of progress than the following passage from the *Diary* of the Goncourt brothers, where progress and neurosis are one and the same thing:

> Since the time mankind exists, its progress, its acquisitions have all been of the order of sensibility. Each day, it becomes nervous, hysterical. And in regard to this activity... are you certain that modern melancholy does not result from it? Do you know if the sadness of the century does not come from overwork, movement, tremendous effort, furious labor, from its cerebral forces strained to the breaking point, from overproduction in every domain?[28]

Contemporaneously with the Goncourt brothers, Émile Zola spoke of a "sickness of progress," whose symptoms he discovered in all the manifestations of his time, literature included: "We are sick, that's certain, sick with progress.... This triumph of nerves over blood has determined our ways, our literature, our entire epoch."[29]

Terminologically, this increased consciousness of decadence explains the revival of the epithet *"décadent,"* which had circulated in the French of the sixteenth century (Brantôme) but had since been abandoned, probably because of its neologistic ring, which did not fit the purist demands of seventeenth-century neoclassicism. In England, the OED tells us, "decadent" was used as early as 1837 (in his famous *History of the French Revolution*, Carlyle spoke of "those *decadent* ages in which no Ideal either grows or blossoms"). It may be that Carlyle had come across this word during his research on the French Revolution; the fact is, however, that the major dictionaries of the French language (Littré, Hatzfeld, Robert) do not give any examples concerning the usage of the epithet during the first half of the nineteenth century. Even if it enjoyed some kind of sporadic circulation before the 1850s, it was, significantly, after that date that *"décadent"* underwent a process of semantic enrichment, which, during the 1880s, resulted in a series of new and sometimes ironical-fanciful coinages, such as the verb *"décader,"* or the labels *"décadisme"* or *"décadentisme."* As we shall see later, only the latter term managed to survive and to become—not in its country of origin but in Italy—a major critical category (*"decadentismo"*).

The obsession with decadence and the growing circulation of words related to that notion account for a semantic occurrence unparalleled in the first half of the nineteenth century, namely, the formation, from the adjective, of the corresponding homonymous noun: *"décadent"* (one that is a decadent). This noun is used during the 1860s by the Goncourt brothers in their *Journal*—for instance, in the entry where Théophile Gautier is quoted as saying to the authors: "We three and two or three others, we are sick. We are not *decadents* [my italics], but rather primitives. No, still no, but strange, undefined, exalted individuals."[30] During the early 1880s the Goncourt brothers themselves came to be regarded— and this was *before* the specifically "decadentist" movement started in 1886—as *decadents,* and even more than that, as the foremost representatives of contemporary decadent style, as *"des décadents de parti pris"*—decadents by their own choice.[31]

Paul Bourget, who was responsible for this characterization of the Goncourt brothers, was the first French writer to accept unwaveringly (unlike Baudelaire or even Gautier) both the term and the fact of decadence, and to articulate this acceptance in a full-blown, philosophic and aesthetic theory of decadence as a style. Even though Bourget had almost certainly read Nisard,[32] his view of decadence was not only free from Nisard's too obviously conservative polemicism but was qualitatively different—by far more complex and profound, as a consequence, among other things, of his *personal* identification with the "terrible" reality of decadence. Bourget spoke of decadence from within, with unmistakably dramatic accents, in a manner that prefigured Nietzsche's treatment of decadence a few years later. Even Bourget's earliest pronouncement on decadence (in 1876) conveys that sense of personal involvement:

> We accept . . . this terrible word *decadence.* . . . It is decadence, but vigorous; with less accomplishment in its works, decadence is superior to organic periods because of the intensity of its geniuses. Its uneven, violent creations reveal more daring artists, and audacity is a virtue which despite ourselves elicits our sympathy.[33]

Bourget formulates a *"Théorie de la décadence"* (his own phrase) in his article on Baudelaire, published in the *Nouvelle revue* (15 November 1881) and reprinted in *Essais de psychologie contemporaine* (1883). His approach to decadence, before becoming specifically stylistic, is broadly sociological and obviously influenced by the prevailing scientific fashions of the time (the biological interpretation of social phenomena, evolutionism, the theory of heredity, etc.). There are, Bourget argues, "organic societies" (in which the energies of the components are *subordinated* to the goals and demands of the "total organism") and societies in decadence, which are characterized by a growing degree of "anarchy," by a gradual loosening of the hierarchical relationships among the various elements of the social structure. Decadent societies are highly *individualistic*: "The social organism becomes decadent as soon as individual life becomes exaggeratedly important under the influence of acquired well-being and heredity."[34] So far nothing too original. Bourget's theory becomes truly interesting and fruitful only when he establishes an analogy between the social evolution toward individualism and the "individualistic" manifestations of artistic language, which are typical of *"le style de décadence"*:

> One law governs both the development and the decadence of that other organism which is language. A style of decadence is one in which the unity of the book breaks down to make place for the independence of the page, in which the page breaks down to make place for the independence of the sentence and in which the sentence breaks down to make place for the independence of the word.[35]

If we admit that the concept of individualism is central to any definition of decadence it is clear that, besides having their disadvantages from the point of view of nationalism and sheer military might, decadent periods should be favorable to the development of the arts and, more generally, should eventually bring about an aesthetic understanding of life itself. To prefer decadence to its radical opposite (that is, barbarism) appears, at least culturally, to be a legitimate choice. Thus, we are entitled, Bourget goes on to say, "to prefer the defeat of decadent Athens to the triumph of the violent Macedonian."[36] The same applies to literary decadence. Here the author takes on an almost evangelistic tone: "Let us then indulge in the unusualness of our ideal and form, even though we imprison ourselves in an unvisited solitude. Those who come to us will be truly our brothers, and why sacrifice what is most intimate, special and personal to others?"[37] In Bourget, the borderline between intellectual recognition of the fact of decadence and aesthetic commitment to decadence as a cultural style becomes almost completely blurred. With him, we may say, the relativism of modernity has resulted in the theoretically unbounded, anarchic individualism of decadence, which, for all its socially paralyzing effects, is artistically beneficial. A style of decadence is simply a style favorable to the unrestricted manifestation of aesthetic individualism, a style that has done away with traditional authoritarian requirements such as unity, hierarchy, objectivity, etc. Decadence thus understood and modernity coincide in their rejection of the tyranny of tradition.

THE DECADENT EUPHORIA

In 1883, the year Bourget's article on Baudelaire was reprinted in *Essais de psychologie contemporaine,* Verlaine published in the magazine *Le chat noir* his famous sonnet "Langueur" (included in 1885 in his volume *Jadis et naguère*). This poem was to be adopted as a sort of manifesto by the group that, with the appearance of the magazine *Le Décadent* (1886), launched the short-lived movement known as *Décadisme:*

> Je suis l'Empire à la fin de la décadence
> Qui regarde passer les grands Barbares blancs
> En composant des acrostiches indolents
> D'un style d'or où la langueur du soleil danse. . . .

An event far more important for the history of the idea of modern decadence is the publication of Huysmans's novel *À Rebours* in 1884. For the readers of the approaching *fin de siècle*, *À Rebours* was more than just another book treating the theme of decadence: it was actually the *summa* of decadence, an encyclopedia of decadent tastes and idiosyncrasies in matters covering the whole range from cuisine to literature. Huysmans's novel appears as both a psychology—or better psychopathology—and an aesthetics of decadence, the two areas being virtually indistinguishable in this case.

To understand this book and its hero, Jean Floressas des Esseintes, it is important to keep in mind that the author totally equates modernity-artificiality-decadence. In the portrayal of des Esseintes, Baudelaire's already-mentioned aversion for nature (leading to the praise of modernity as artificiality) is pushed to its most extreme consequences. The cult of artificiality, as expounded in *À Rebours*, is based on an exclusively negative-destructive imagination. Des Esseintes is not really trying to isolate himself from nature; it would be more correct to say that his attitudes are dictated by his consuming desire to thwart, chastise, and finally *humiliate* nature. His aestheticism is not an escape but a perpetual violation of nature. His cult of artificiality is a cult of the perverse. The total aesthete will therefore congratulate himself whenever he is able to make outside or inner nature deviate from its norms and laws. Attracted by all that is aberrant, his imagination will voluptuously explore the realm of the abnormal in search of a beauty that is supposed to be both antinatural and absolutely new. The appeal of decadence comes as no surprise in such a context.

Des Esseintes's most refined pleasure is perhaps to find out that nature can sometimes obey the arbitrary orders of human fantasy. We recall how happy he is when, after having decided that "he wished real flowers would imitate artificial ones,"[38] he is presented with a collection of monstrous caladiums and other strange flowers grown by cranky horticulturists. His reflection is typical: "Most of the time nature by itself is incapable of begetting such sickly, perverse species. . . ."[39] Commenting on this passage in his perceptive study *The Idea of Decadence in French Literature (1830–1900)*, A. E. Carter points out the basically anti-Rousseauistic (that is anti-romantic) concept involved in Huysmans's view of the relationship man/nature: "Man's intervention, as always, produces something which is of necessity perverse and corrupt. Like all the rest of the cult of artificiality, this is orthodox Rousseauism turned inside out. . . . The Marquis de Sade's characters outraged nature by crime, Des Esseintes does it by artificiality."[40]

More directly linked to our concern with the *concept* of decadence, *À Rebours* contains, especially in chapters three (a description of Des Esseintes's Latin library) and fourteen (where the character's favorites among nineteenth-century writers are discussed), the main elements of a theory of literary decadence. It is intriguing to discover that most of the choices made in 1884 by Des Esseintes, and particularly those regarding the literature of the nineteenth century, have been validated by what we call the modern tradition. Huysmans's rejection of romanticism and romantic rhetoric, his displeasure with the kind of antiromanticism practiced by the Parnassians (the poetry of Gautier and Leconte de Lisle is finally dismissed as being too perfect and not *"ductile au rêve"*[41]), and his positive identification of what we might label "a poetics of crisis" (as reflected in Baudelaire and even more clearly in Mallarmé), indicate some of the most characteristic lines along which modern literary consciousness has subsequently developed. We should, however, note that if these and other aesthetic ideas of Huysmans have been retained, his own *rhetoric of decadence* has largely been abandoned. This rhetoric is all too obvious in the following praise of Mallarmé as the last of the poets (although the idea itself may strike us as not altogether indefensible, especially if we consider Mallarmé's own utopia of *the* Book, the ultimate and absolute text, which, once written, leaves the universe without any *raison d'être*):

> The decadence of a literature, irreparably damaged in its organism, weakened by the age of ideas, exhausted by the excesses of syntax, sensitive only to those curiosities that render the sick feverish, and

which, despite all this, hastens to express everything during its decline, is determined to make up for all omissions of pleasure, and bequeaths the most subtle memories of pain—this literature, on its death bed, found embodiment in Mallarmé, in the most consummate and exquisite fashion.[42]

À Rebours probably represents an absolute as far as the *aestheticization* of decadence is concerned. From this point of view, the period following the publication of Huysmans's novel, and during which the euphoria of decadence reached its climax, could not have been expected to produce anything new. The fact is, however, that the total aestheticism involved in the pure concept of decadence, as worked out by Des Esseintes, was actually an untenable position. In the novel, threatened by madness, Des Esseintes had to give up his cult of artificiality and experience the bitter sense of absolute failure, although the ending leaves open the prospect of his possible conversion to Christianity. Huysmans himself confessed, in his preface written twenty years after the novel, that composing À Rebours had been for him a sort of catharsis, and that in spite of the book's wilfully pessimistic outlook, the germs of hope were hidden in it, so much so that "this book has been a beginning of my Catholic work, which is entirely there, in embryo."[43]

After À Rebours, decadent aestheticism becomes more conscious of its critical-polemical functions and is less prone to take itself as *the* solution to the painful uncertainties and contradictions of modern life. Aestheticism, even in its most offensive forms, is no longer cut off from the various concerns of practical life and, more than that, can no longer be regarded as incompatible with the possibility of moral, religious, or political commitments by its adherents. This deserves to be stressed, because the preconception that aestheticism automatically means total disinterest in nonaesthetic matters is still widespread. The evolution of *Décadisme* toward open advocacy of revolutionary ideas is a good example that aestheticism and the cult of social involvement and even violence can go hand in hand. Before elaborating, let me note parenthetically that even a poet like Mallarmé (whose aesthetic aloofness is unmistakable, whether we consider it "decadent" or not), made no secret about his belief that it was the duty of the modern poet to be *"en grève devant la société,"* and was himself an overt sympathizer of anarchism. In England at the turn of the century, the most conspicuous representative of decadent aestheticism, Oscar Wilde, illustrates the same trend when he speaks in defense of utopia and indulges in futuristic considerations about the triumph of socialism (a socialism strongly tinged with anarchism).[44]

A year after the publication of *A Rebours,* decadence had become such a fashionable topic in Paris that it could be parodied and, moreover, such parodistic forgeries as *Les Déliquescences, poèmes décadents d'Adoré Floupette*[45] could be taken seriously. It is not certain whether Anatole Baju, the founder of *Le Décadent* (1886) and the proponent of *Décadisme,* intended the title of his magazine as an allusion to Verlaine's sonnet "Langueur" or whether he was inspired by the success of *Les Déliquescences.* What is beyond question is that Baju and his friends were attracted by the notion of decadence not only as a complete antithesis of bourgeois banality but also as a new means of shocking the middle class (*épater le bourgeois*). The primary purpose of the *Décadent* was clearly to scandalize. The aggressive tone of the various manifestoes (by Baju) printed in the magazine leaves little doubt as to that. Formally, these manifestoes may be classified among the early avant-garde exercises in the rhetoric of provocation (the use of the epithet avant-garde is doubly justified here: first, because the manifestoes clearly announce the sweeping style of the later declarations of the avant-garde; second, because they offer a good example of how the hyperbolic language of *political radicalism* came to be used for purposes of literary polemics). Not surprisingly, Baju's manifestoes are for the most part variations on the subject of decadence:

Not to recognize the state of decadence which we are in would be the height of insensibility.... religion, customs, justice, everything decays [*tout décade*].... Society comes apart under the corrosive action of a deliquescent civilization.... We commit this leaf to murdersome innovations, to stupefying audacities, to incoherences of thirty-six atmospheres at the furthest limit of their compatibility with those archaic conventions labeled by the term public morality. We will be the stars of an ideal literature.... In a word, we will be the Mahdis screaming and preaching eternally the dogma of elixir, the quintessential word of triumphant *décadisme*. [46]

But decadence, the readers of the second issue of *Le Décadent* learn, is simply awareness and acceptance of modernity. And even more, the true decadent will not only try to harmonize his work with the most outstanding features of modern civilization but will also resolutely and courageously express a progressive creed, a firm belief in what Baju calls *"la marche ascensionelle de l'humanité."* In other words, the decadent is in the avant-garde (although the term is not used):

The ancients belonged to their time. We want to belong to ours. Steam and electricity are the two indispensable agents of modern life. We ought to have a language and a literature in harmony with the progress of science. Is this not our right? And is this what is called decadence? Let it be decadence. We accept the word. We are decadent, since this decadence is nothing but the ascending march of humanity toward ideals which are reputed to be inaccessible. [47]

At the height of the decadent euphoria, Verlaine—the best-known contributor to *Le Décadent*—thought that Baju's coining of the label *Décadisme* was nothing less than a stroke of genius. In a letter addressed to *Le Décadent* (published in the issue of January 1, 1888), Verlaine wrote: *"Décadisme* is a word of genius, an amusing find which will last in the literary history; this barbarism is a miraculous sign. It is short, convenient, *handy,* and precisely removes the degrading notion of decadence; it sounds literary without being pedantic, it is flexible and breaks through." [48]

But Verlaine, whose enthusiastic remarks were used by *Le Décadent* solely for purposes of publicity and without any discretion or restraint, was soon to cool in his support of the decadent cause. We recall that after 1886, when Jean Moréas had published his manifesto *Symbolisme* in *Le Figaro,* a growing number of the antitraditional Parisian writers found the new label convenient. By 1888, those who declared themselves decadents tended to be identified simply as followers of Anatole Baju, whose own literary reputation was in no way capable of giving credibility to a true literary movement. Baju had probably been conscious of that when he tried to use Verlaine's name to boost his magazine and the tendencies it represented. But, understandably, Verlaine was quite reluctant to play a role that he was being forced into for reasons of literary tactics. Baju himself became increasingly politicized and in 1889 stopped publishing *Le Décadent* to devote all his efforts to the legislative elections of September 1889 and to his disastrous campaign as a socialist candidate for the National Assembly. At any rate, when it folded, *Le Décadent* was in the process of losing its best contributors. In 1891, Baju reminisced bitterly about his failure to overcome the "reactionary" prejudices of his former literary friends whom, for a moment, he had thought capable of participating in his vast and ambitious plan of undermining the bases of the bourgeois social edifice. Here Baju spoke as an anarchist committed to the ideal of total revolution:

> The number of my contributors, the variety of their learning, their talent were a force which, used for purposes of destruction, would have mined the base of the social structure. Some would have attacked ownership, religion, the family, others would have ridiculed marriage, and advocated free love. Others yet would have praised the benefits of cosmopolitanism and of universal association. Each one, according to his temperament, by means of books, the stage or newspapers, would have contributed to the formation in education of that synthesis of revolutionary action without which only partial and scanty progress can be made. I was taken in simply as a result of my imagination. Most of my contributors, proven reactionaries, were willing to mishandle some bourgeois prejudices, but they would not destroy these prejudices for anything in the world. Science was for them, naïvely, anathema and they thought art was incompatible with socialism. They were impervious to all of this.[49]

After 1889 all the signs were there that the euphoria was rapidly subsiding and that *Décadisme* had been just one among a large number of quickly passing fads in the restless intellectual atmosphere of *fin-de-siècle* Paris.[50] During the 1890s, however, the term *"décadent"* retained the positive artistic connotations it had acquired in the two previous decades, and Valéry could use it with the meaning of *"ultraraffiné."* But in this sense the word had become too vague to be really useful as a critical tool. The newly coined *"décadisme"* was challenged, and finally replaced, by the apparently more appealing *"symbolisme."* This may explain why today French critics use the label "decadentism" in only a very narrow historical sense, to designate the poets who, in the late 1880s, made the specific claim of being decadent and grouped themselves around such unequivocally entitled periodicals as *La Décadence* or *Le Décadent.* *"Symbolisme"* eventually had the same fate, and also came to mean one among a multiplicity of parallel or successive modern literary movements. (Curiously, as was noted in our discussion of modernism, French criticism does not have a unified and comprehensive concept—comparable in scope to romanticism—by means of which to designate the postromantic or "modern" age of literature, what Anglo-American criticism calls modernism, or what Italian criticism has agreed to name *"decadentismo."*)

In France, we may conclude, notions like *décadent, décadisme,* or *décadentisme* have been unable to shake off the memory of their short period of tremendous popularity. That is why, although it was in France that the gap separating the general view of decadence from the modern aesthetic *ideal* of decadence (as a form of radical antitraditionalism) was first bridged, we have to move outside France to follow the further development of the concept of cultural decadence as related to the idea of modernity.

NIETZSCHE ON "DECADENCE" AND "MODERNITY"

In one of his last works, *The Case of Wagner* (1888), Nietzsche points out that "decadence" has been the central theme of his philosophical career:

Nothing has preoccupied me more profoundly than the problem of decadence—I had reasons. "Good and evil" is merely a variation of that problem. Once one has developed a keen eye for the symptoms of decline, one understands morality, too—one understands what is hiding under its most sacred names and value formulas: impoverished life, the will to the end, the great weariness. Morality negates life.[51]

This short passage actually sums up the essential directions and insights of Nietzsche's thought, and it is hard to imagine a better way of characterizing his contribution in equally condensed and lapidary phrasing.

To understand adequately Nietzsche's passionate critique of decadence—and, indeed, the profound dialectical quality of his philosophy as a whole—we have to keep in mind all the time that he speaks of decadence from *personal experience,* as a man who knows the value of health for having been sick and who, therefore, cannot fail to recognize the philosophical value of sickness itself, without which health would be unable to achieve self-consciousness. In this sense, as he himself suggests quite unequivocally, his attack against the preeminent decadent, Richard Wagner, contains throughout, even in its moments of greatest bitterness, its own dialectical opposite, namely, gratefulness.

... Wagner is merely one of my sicknesses. Not that I wish to be ungrateful to this sickness. When in this essay I assert the proposition that Wagner is harmful, I wish no less to assert for whom he is nevertheless indispensable—for the philosopher. Others may be able to get along without Wagner; but the philosopher is not free to do without Wagner. He has to be the bad conscience of his time: for that he needs to understand it best.... I understand perfectly when a musician says today: "I hate Wagner, but I can no longer endure any other music." But I'd also understand a philosopher who would declare: "Wagner sums up modernity. There is no way out, one must first become a Wagnerian."[52]

In a famous passage in *Ecce Homo* (also written in 1888), Nietzsche speaks in a more general sense of his own dual nature. He characterizes himself ("already dead as my father, while as my mother I am still living and becoming old") as "at the same time a *decadent* and a *beginning*," and goes on to say quite emphatically: "I have a subtler sense of smell for the signs of ascent and decline than any other human being before me; I am the teacher *par excellence* for this—I know both, I am both."[53] In the same chapter ("Why I Am So Wise"), Nietzsche relates his experience of disease, to which he feels indebted for his "dialectician's clarity," dialectic itself being, as he does not fail to stress, "a symptom of decadence."[54] And the section I am quoting from ends with the following tribute to decadence, where pathos and irony fuse:

> A long, all too long, series of years signifies recovery for me; unfortunately it also signifies relapse, decay, the periodicity of a kind of decadence. Need I say after all this that in questions of decadence I am *experienced*? I have spelled them forward and backward. . . . Looking from the perspective of the sick toward *healthier* concepts and values and, conversely, looking again from the fullness and self-assurance of a *rich* life down into the secret work of the instinct of decadence—in this I have the longest training, my truest experience. . . . Now I know how, have the know-how, to *reverse perspectives*: the first reason why a "revaluation of values" is perhaps possible for me alone.[55]

Such assertions, useful as they may be in guarding against the all too often simplified accounts of Nietzsche's thinking (which tend to reduce its richness to vulgar black-and-white types of contrasts or, conversely, to a fundamental and insoluble "ambiguity"), suggest only partially the actual complexity of Nietzsche's idea of decadence. To be fully aware of this complexity, one has to realize first to what an extent the spirit of decadence is *deceptive*, that is, tries to pursue its destructive work under the most reassuring and healthy appearances. For Nietzsche, the strategy of decadence is typically that of the liar who deceives by *imitating* truth and by making his lies even more credible than truth itself. Thus, in its hatred of life, decadence masquerades as admiration of a higher life, and, because of its mastery in the art of seduction, it is able to make weakness look like force, exhaustion like fulfillment, cowardice like courage. Decadence is dangerous because it always disguises itself as its opposite.

Wagner, "the Cagliostro of modernity," is a "typical decadent who has a sense of necessity in his corrupted taste, who claims it is a higher taste, who knows how to get his corruption accepted as law, as progress, as fulfillment."[56] According to this logic, something that seems decadent, something that presents the unmistakable "signs of decay" may have little or nothing to do with decadence proper. For example, let us consider two aphorisms from *The Gay Science* (I, 23, 24). The first one, entitled "The Signs of Corruption," is clearly written with the period of Roman decadence in mind, and it turns out to be an attempt to rehabilitate and revaluate this period, to pierce beyond the clichés (corruption, superstition, exhaustion, moral decay, etc.) by which it is usually described. All these negative features reveal, to the penetrating eye of the philosopher, a latent positive content. Superstition, Nietzsche contends, "is actually a symptom of *enlightenment*," because "whoever is superstitious is always, compared with the religious human being, much more of a person; and a superstitious society is one in which there are many individuals and must delight in individuality."[57] And he goes on to show that the automatic association of corruption with exhaustion is also incorrect:

> What is generally overlooked is that the ancient national energy and national passion that became gloriously visible in war and warlike games have now been transmuted into countless private passions. . . . Thus it is precisely in times of "exhaustion" that tragedy runs through houses and streets, that great love and great hatred are born, and that the flame of knowledge flares up into the sky.

Such times of "corruption," we are told in the conclusion of the argument, "are those when the apples fall from the tree; I mean the individuals, for they carry the seeds of the future. . . . Corruption is merely a nasty word for the autumn of a people." As we shall see, for Nietzsche such a *natural* process is not necessarily linked to decadence, which is a phenomenon of the order of the *will*—decadence is a loss of the will to live, which prompts an attitude of revengefulness against life and which manifests itself through *ressentiment*.[58]

Thus understood, decadence—which always involves self-deception—is a permanent danger and belongs to every age, not only to those traditionally called decadent. The aphorism entitled "Diverse Dissatisfaction" comes much closer to the problem of actual decadence than the one just cited. But here again Nietzsche, in the demystifying mood that pervades the whole of the *Gay Science*, chooses to point out some of the advantageous consequences of real decadence (as opposed to the frightening alternative of what he calls "Chinese 'happiness'"). The aphorism opens with a typical Nietzschean distinction between the weak and quasi-feminine type on the one hand and the strong or masculine type on the other, but this distinction is developed in an unexpected fashion, at least for the reader who is influenced by popular clichés about Nietzsche. The feminine type, endowed with a "sensitivity for making life more beautiful and profound," has been prevailing in Europe since the Middle Ages. It has been deceived occasionally and has settled "for a little intoxication and effusive enthusiasm, although it can never be satisfied altogether and suffers from the incurability of its dissatisfaction." This type is responsible, Nietzsche stresses, for the "*continuation* of the real misery," but, at the same time, without it "the celebrated European capacity for constant *change* might never have come into existence, for the requirements of the strong among the dissatisfied are too crude."

The opposite has happened in China, where "large scale dissatisfaction and the capacity for *change* have become extinct centuries ago." Confronted with the Chinese alternative, European "feminine dissatisfaction" turns out to be a real blessing:

> Socialists and state idolaters of Europe with their measures for making life better and safer might easily establish in Europe, too, Chinese conditions and a Chinese "happiness," if only they could first extirpate the sicklier, tenderer, more feminine dissatisfaction and romanticism that at present are still superabundant here. Europe is sick but owes the utmost gratitude to her incurability and to the eternal changes in her affliction: these constantly new conditions... have finally generated an intellectual irritability that amounts to genius and is in any case the mother of genius.[59]

Nietzsche's fondness for the European spirit (which he opposed to the suffocating narrowness of German nationalism) and his famous maxim about living dangerously should be understood in light of ideas such as those just cited. As for decadence, the most important thing is to recognize it, to become conscious of it, and to resist being misled by its various tricks and disguises. This point is made in a series of notes included by the editors of Nietzsche's late *Nachlass* in *The Will to Power.* Insofar as it is an unavoidable aspect of life, decadence is nothing *to be fought;* it is a necessary phenomenon and belongs to every age and every people. What should be fought, however, is the contagion of the healthy parts of the organism.[60] One should always keep in mind that for Nietzsche this *contagion* is not a matter of physiology (where decay is as natural as growth) but exclusively a matter of psychology.

Thus, one can be sick or weak without being a decadent: one becomes a decadent only when one *wants* weakness. The distinction is that between actual sickness and *sickliness* (the latter's moral corollary being "resignation and meekness in face of the enemy"). Nietzsche stresses: "Health and sickness are not essentially different. . . . One must not make of them distinct principles or entities that fight over the living organism and turn it into their arena. That is silly nonsense. . . ."[61] Decadence, then, appears as a form of psychological, moral, or aesthetic self-deception, as a result of which weakness becomes a *task,* as Nietzsche puts it.

The first and most harmful mystification of decadence leads to a confusion between cause and effect. The spirit of decadence falsifies the normal perspective and makes its own consequences appear as its causes. If this misconception is not dispelled, fighting against decadence (against its supposed causes, which are in fact only its effects) is an entirely quixotic enterprise that achieves nothing but the opposite of its goal, namely, a promotion of decadence. Nietzsche has emphasized this crucial point several times:

> One confuses cause and effect: one fails to understand decadence as a physiological condition and mistakes its consequences for the real cause of the indisposition; example: all of religious morality.[62]

If we take Jaspers's well-known methodological advice and look in Nietzsche for passages contradicting those quoted above, we soon realize that they are not at all difficult to find and that in fact the philosopher is, in a large sector of his work, a straightforward defender of the conception of man as a "fantastic animal" whose greatness is measured by his *will to illusion* and by his ability to work out a whole web of delusional concepts and deceptive mechanisms that falsify reality. There are indeed numerous aphorisms in which mathematical and logical concepts, laws of science and such fundamental philosophical notions as reason, truth, cause, effect, subject, and object are seen merely as fictions, and in which human knowledge is viewed as an entirely metaphorical activity. In his *Philosophy of 'As If,'* Hans Vaihinger devotes an important chapter to Nietzsche and offers a rich—if somewhat biased—collection of quotations that support his contention that the author of Zarathustra is a philosopher of the *will to illusion* and a forerunner of the "Metaphysic of As-if."[63] Vaihinger is obviously aware of the relevance of such ideas to both aesthetics (whence they are derived) and ethics, but his discussion is confined to matters of epistemology alone. As a consequence, we may reproach him with having avoided a series of questions that, no matter how difficult, should be asked and answered by a student of Nietzsche's *work as a whole.* For instance, if it is the nature of art to be aesthetic play and longing for illusion, why is Wagner accused as an illusionist and a liar? What is so wrong with Wagner's lying, especially for someone who can write (the quotation figures in Vaihinger): "Ah, now we must embrace untruth, now at last error becomes a lie. . ."?[64]

As a rule, Vaihinger selects only the passages in which Nietzsche speaks positively of lying, mythologizing, and fiction, and leaves out all those in which the apparently opposite ideas are expressed. The fact that Nietzsche could sometimes take fictions *in malo sensu* is mentioned only briefly and inconsequentially, although the relationship between "bad fictions" and "the concepts on which morality is based" is pointed out.[65] But Vaihinger clearly does not share Nietzsche's antireligious feelings. This makes him speculate, in the conclusion of the chapter on Nietzsche, about what directions the philosophy of the latter would have taken if his career had not been cut short by illness. "He would not have revoked his *Antichrist*... , but he would have presented the 'obverse of evil things' with the same relentless frankness: he would have 'justified' the utility and necessity of religious fictions."[66] Who knows?

At any rate, to understand Nietzsche's approach to decadence, it is important to realize that for him neither truth nor error, fiction, or lie has any value whatsoever in and by itself. They can have positive or negative value only in relation to life and to whether they promote or hinder life. Nietzsche, as Georg Simmel has pointed out in his essay on "The Conflict in Modern Culture" (1914, pub. 1918),

> finds in life itself the purpose of life which it is denied from the outside. This life by its nature is increment, enrichment, development towards fulfillment and power, towards a force and beauty flowing from itself. . . . It is only the original fact of life which provides meaning and measure, positive or negative value.[67]

It is this supreme valuation of life which justifies Nietzsche's grandiose project of a transvaluation of all values and which accounts for the feverishly dialectical quality of his thought.

Thus, Nietzsche can argue in favor of lying in an extramoral sense (as in the 1873 fragment *Ueber Warheit und Lüge im aussermoralischen Sinne*, whose importance Vaihinger stresses) and, without actually contradicting himself, reject Wagner's music as an example of decadent (moral) lying. The whole question is one of perspective, and it may be useful here to recall that Nietzsche has characterized his own philosophy as "perspectivism." There is a great difference between the perspective from which one can realize that truth is a *fiction* (a creation of life meant to help life achieve its purposes) and the perspective from which the decadent ascribes *a character of truth* to a fiction which as fiction, and under particular circumstances, might even have been justified in the name of life. If we place ourselves in the first perspective, we engage our mind in a fruitful direction in which illusion becomes self-conscious—and self-consciousness is usually a liberating and life-enhancing force. On the contrary, when we treat illusion as a reality, when we endow it with the "moral" prestige of truth, we blind ourselves to its nature and become the slaves of a lifeless dogma. Morality, Nietzsche seems to suggest, kills the vital aspects of illusion (those same that consciousness could render more intense) and opens the door to bad faith and self-deception. There is actually no inconsistency in Nietzsche's view that the complex relationships between truth and falsehood, reality and fantasy, or knowledge and invention, can be exploited with equal effectiveness for the purposes of life and, conversely, for those of *ressentiment* and the revenge against life.

From a terminological point of view, it is interesting to note that Nietzsche started using the term *"décadence"* (with the French spelling) at a relatively late stage. It was argued that the reading of Paul Bourget's *Essais de psychologie contemporaine* (1883) was decisive in Nietzsche's adoption of the term, but Walter Kaufmann dispelled this error by pointing out that the word first occurred in a text written around 1878, that is, five years before the publication of Bourget's *Essais.* In that text, Nietzsche said that Cervantes's *Don Quixote* "belongs to the decadence of Spanish culture."[68] There should be little doubt, however, that Nietzsche picked up the noun *décadent* from Bourget, who was the first prominent French writer to use it (as we have seen, it occurs in earlier dated entries of the *Diary* of the *frères* Goncourt, but the *Diary* only began to be published in 1887). It is also clear that it was after having read Bourget that Nietzsche employed the specific phrase "style of decadence." More than that, Nietzsche clearly paraphrased Bourget in *The Case of Wagner,* in his famous definition of the "style of decadence":

> What is the sign of every *literary decadence*? That life no longer dwells in the whole. The word becomes sovereign and leaps out of the sentence, the sentence reaches out and obscures the meaning of the page, the page gains life at the expense of the whole—the whole

is no longer a whole. But this is the simile of every style of decadence: every time, the anarchy of atoms, disaggregation of the will. . . .[69]

The striking fact about this borrowed passage is that, read in the context of *Der Fall Wagner* and the other works of Nietzsche's last period, it both sounds and *is* original; and this is so because it is enriched by the complex and dialectically ambivalent significances that Nietzsche attaches to the idea of decadence—enriched to the point that one can see it, as Walter Kaufmann does, as a description of Nietzsche's own "monadologic" style.[70] In this light the philosopher's claim to have been a *decadent*—a "self-overcoming" *decadent*—should be taken in all seriousness. Also, the fact that such an obvious paraphrase can acquire meanings and qualities that are missing in the original (paradoxically, Bourget seems to be remembered today largely because Nietzsche praised him) should speak against exaggerating the "influence" of this particular French writer over the German thinker. It would be more correct to say that Nietzsche's adoption of the French words *décadence* and *décadent* (the latter almost certainly taken from Bourget), as well as certain aspects of his theory of cultural decadence, were results of his long and close familiarity with French literature and philosophy, and of his meditations on the broader theme of French decadence since the seventeenth century. As we have seen earlier, the sense of decadence was widespread in France after 1848 and, with dramatically increased acuteness, after 1870. Nietzsche's indebtedness to Bourget should be seen against the larger background of Nietzsche's well-known affinity for French culture, a subject that has been satisfactorily studied by, among others, W. D. Williams in his book *Nietzsche and the French*.[71]

The terms *décadence* and *décadent* offered Nietzsche the opportunity to synthesize and unify a great many related ideas (decline, degeneration, sickness, etc.) that had become constitutive elements of his dialectic of life against death. His concept of decadence actually originated, more than in his attitude toward French culture, in his reaction to German cultural modernity (evident as early as 1873–74 in his powerful idea of "untimeliness") and in his critique of romanticism, whose relevance to modernity he was one of the first to stress. Nietzsche's rejection of romanticism as a manifestation of decadence reminds us of Goethe's famous dictum, "*Classisch ist das Gesunde, Romantisch ist das Kranke*" (Classic is the healthy, romantic is the sick). Another central idea of Nietzsche's vitalistic philosophy may be associated with Goethe's no less famous thought that "the purpose of life is life itself." We may say that Goethe had an infinitely deeper impact on Nietzsche as a critic of romanticism than did French conservative criticism since Nisard, with its explicit pairing of romanticism and decadence. To a large extent it was what he most admired in Goethe that enabled Nietzsche to diagnose the "romantic sickness" from which the two great models of his youth, Schopenhauer and Wagner, had suffered. Nietzsche probably owed to Goethe even his early distinction between the Dionysian and the Apollonian, but he certainly was indebted to the author of "the best German book that there is" (*Conversations with Eckermann*) for the later revision of that distinction, in which the Dionysian, *including* the Apollonian, came to be opposed to *decadent romanticism*. Interestingly, it was the old Goethe who embodied the Dionysian spirit as Nietzsche conceived it toward the end of his career. Goethe, he wrote in *The Twilight of the Idols* (published in early 1889), is "not a German event, but a European one":

> ... a magnificent attempt to overcome the eighteenth century by a return to nature, by an *ascent* to the naturalness of the Renaissance—a kind of self-overcoming on the part of the century.... He surrounded himself with limited horizons; he did not retire from life but put himself in the midst of it; he was not faint-hearted but took as much as possible upon himself, over himself, into himself. What he wanted was totality.... In the midst of an age with an unreal outlook, Goethe was a convinced realist: he said Yes to everything that was related in this respect—and he had no greater experience than that *ens realissimum* called Napoleon.... Such a spirit who has *become free* stands amid the cosmos with a joyous and trusting fatalism, in the *faith* that only the particular is loathsome,

and that all is redeemed and affirmed in the whole—*he does not negate any more*. Such a faith, however, is the highest of all possible faiths: I have baptized it with the name of *Dionysus*.[72]

Goethe as an historical personality is perhaps the closest approximation that Nietzsche cared to give, in more concrete terms, of what he understood by "overman." But Goethe had been a "mere interlude" in a period of decadence, "chaos," and "utter bewilderment," dominated by an "instinct of weariness" and "romanticism of feeling": "Is not the nineteenth century... merely an intensified, *brutalized* eighteenth century, that is, a century of *decadence?*"[73]

Nietzsche's theory of decadence reveals its entire philosophic and aesthetic significance only when, together with his admiration for what Goethe symbolized, the details of his critique of Schopenhauer and Wagner are considered. Nietzsche's polemic against both, full of the most intense and genuine intellectual pathos, is more illuminating in regard to his concept of decadence than anything he has to say about the French decadents from Rousseau (by far the most ferociously attacked of all the French thinkers) to Baudelaire. An examination of the relation of Nietzsche's philosophy to Schopenhauer would take us too far into matters with which we are not directly concerned here, so I shall limit myself to discussing the "case" of Wagner. This will offer an opportunity to place Nietzsche's view of decadence within the larger framework of his conception of art in general.

Like philosophy, art is designed to serve life, its specific task being that of organizing experience in an aesthetically meaningful way. The problem is: what kind of life is art promoting? Says Nietzsche,

Every art, every philosophy, may be considered a remedy and aid in the service of either growing or declining life: it always presupposes suffering and sufferers. But there are two kinds of sufferers: first, those who suffer from an *overfullness* of life and want a Dionysian art as well as a tragic insight and outlook on life—and then those who suffer from an *impoverishment* of life and demand of art and philosophy, calm, stillness, smooth seas, or, on the other hand, frenzy, convulsion, and anesthesia. Revenge against life itself—the most voluptuous kind of frenzy for those so impoverished![74]

In the genealogy of the arts, Nietzsche thought, music in general is a latecomer, it appears as a typically autumnal product in any particular culture:

> Music makes its appearance as the last plant among the arts, . . . it arrives last, in the fall, when the culture which belongs to it is fading. . . . Only Mozart transformed the age of Louis XIV and the art of Racine and Claude Lorrain into ringing gold; only in the music of Beethoven and Rossini did the eighteenth century sing itself out. . . . All true, all original music, is swan song.[75]

This does not mean, however, that all music is decadent. As pointed out earlier, for Nietzsche decadence is a question of "will" and an "ideal," not decline as such (a fact of life that would be cowardly to deny) but *acceptance and promotion* of decline. Even within the overwhelmingly decadent context of modernity, Nietzsche recognizes the possibility of a music "that would no longer be of romantic origin, like German music—but Dionysian."[76] The first section of *The Case of Wagner* offers an example: Bizet's *Carmen*, conceived as an absolute counterpart of Wagnerian decadence. If we reverse the terms of Nietzsche's characterization of Bizet, we obtain in a concentrated form his main arguments against Wagner.

> This music seems perfect to me. It approaches lightly, supplely, politely. It is pleasant, it does not *sweat*. . . . This music is evil, subtly fatalistic: at the same time it remains popular—its subtlety belongs to a race, not to an individual. It builds, it organizes, finishes: thus it constitutes the opposite of the polyp in music, the "infinite melody." Have more painful tragic accents been heard on the stage? Without grimaces. Without counterfeit. Without the *lie* of the great style.[77]

As for Wagner, who pushes the romantic spirit of decadence to the extreme—he is the great liar: his "music is never true. But it is *taken for true*. . . ."[78] "True" here is meant in the restricted sense of being "true" to the genius of music *qua* music, of music as an autonomous art, justified aesthetically by this very autonomy. Wagner's lying consists in his using music for essentially nonmusical purposes. Here Nietzsche employs a concept that had been common in the theory of decadence since Nisard, who, as we recall, accused Victor Hugo of painting with words, that is, of using words to obtain effects characteristic of an art other than poetry. But Nietzsche's insight is infinitely more profound than that of Nisard and other previous theorists of decadence. Wagner's perversion of music does not represent an accidental deviation from the specificity of an art—it is expressive of the whole crisis of modernity, which manifests itself by what Nietzsche calls quite suggestively, *theatrocracy*. Wagner is an "incomparable *histrio*," an *actor*. He is not a musician who errs, he is not a poet either, he is only an *actor* of genius—"he became a musician, he became a poet because the tyrant within him, his actor's genius, compelled him." So,

> Wagner was not a musician by instinct. He showed this by abandoning all lawfulness and, more precisely, all style in music in order to turn it into what he required, theatrical rhetoric, a means of expression, of underscoring gestures, of suggestion, of the psychologically picturesque. . . . He is the Victor Hugo of music as language. Always presupposing that one first allows that under certain circumstances music may not be music but language, instrument, *ancilla dramaturgica*. Wagner's music, if not shielded by theater taste, which is very tolerant taste, is simply bad music, perhaps the worst ever made.[79]

The comparison between Wagner and Victor Hugo is extremely interesting. Was Nietzsche aware, beyond Bourget, of Nisard, who had applied his theory of decadence specifically to Victor Hugo? In any case, Nietzsche—considering his philosophic and aesthetic beliefs—was naturally inclined to dislike Victor Hugo's personality as a whole, and particularly Hugo's *social* romanticism. And even if Nietzsche was familiar with Nisard's rejection of Hugo, by comparing the latter to Wagner he opens an entirely new perspective on the phenomenon of modern decadence. In contrast to the "elitist" view of decadence, Nietzsche is among the first to stress the crowd-pleasing quality of decadent art as illustrated in both Hugo and Wagner:

> Victor Hugo and Richard Wagner—they signify the same thing: in declining cultures, wherever the decision comes to rest with the masses, authenticity becomes superfluous, disadvantageous, a liability. Only the actor still arouses great enthusiasm.[80]

It is noteworthy that, while stressing the "popular" quality of Bizet's music, Nietzsche speaks of the *mass* appeal of such artists as Hugo and Wagner. Modernity leads to theatrocracy because "the theater is a form of demolatry [worship of the masses] in matters of taste: the theater is a revolt of the masses [*ein Massen-Aufstand*], a plebiscite against good taste.—*This is precisely what is proved by the case of Wagner*: he won the crowd, he corrupted taste, he spoiled even our taste for opera."[81] Here Nietzsche is very close to proposing a definition of what was going to be designated toward the middle of the twentieth century by the term *kitsch*—bad taste as an aesthetic category. Also, Nietzsche introduces here the larger theme of "the revolt of the masses"—a theme rendered notorious by the controversial book Ortega y Gasset devoted to it in 1930, *La rebelión de las masas.*

Nietzsche was certainly aware of the modern crisis of Christianity. The great religion of decadence had undergone a process of disintegration started, on a larger scale, during the eighteenth century, that same century in which the philosopher discovered the first unmistakable signs of modernity. But why, then, did he describe modernity as essentially decadent? The answer to this question measures the originality of Nietzsche's thought as compared to that of previous and contemporaneous philosophers of history: what modernity had inherited from Christianity was not a set of symbols (some of which attracted Nietzsche to the point of fascination) but the deep spirit of *ressentiment*, the hostility against life. And this hostility was perfectly able to do without the specific symbols and dogmas of Christianity, using for its purposes the whole range of "modern" secular intellectual myths. Nietzsche had the penetrating intuition that the time consciousness of modernity was not substantially different from the Judeo-Christian concept of time, and it was this intuition that led him to make the idea of "eternal recurrence" the core of his philosophy.

Nietzsche was one of the first Western thinkers to point out the secret indebtedness of apparently anti-Christian modernity to Christianity. The idea gained acceptance and, half a century later, Ortega y Gasset—perhaps the most brilliant follower of Nietzsche— could stress the impact of Christianity upon modernity almost as a matter of course. In the chapter "Valuations of Life" in *The Modern Theme,* Ortega writes:

> Modern times represent a crusade against Christianity.... By the middle of the eighteenth century the divine world to come had evaporated. This life was all that remained to man. ... The thought of the last centuries, though anti-Christian, is seen nevertheless to have adopted an attitude in regard to life which has a strong resemblance to that of Christianity.

And this is so because the modern "doctrine of culture" is nothing but "a Christianity without God." In the perspective of modern cultural "progressivism," Ortega emphasizes,

> The meaning and value of life, which is essentially present actuality, are forever awaking to a more enlightened dawn, and so it goes on. Real existence remains perpetually on the subordinate level of a mere transition toward an utopian future. The doctrines of culture, progress, futurism and utopianism are a single and unique ism.[82]

In the ancient world, Ortega concludes very much in Nietzsche's spirit, life had been less affected by "trans-vital values" than in both Christianity and modernity.

Trans-vital values, Nietzsche would argue, are basically antivital values, and as such are signs of decadence. Decadence turns against life whenever it ascribes to life meanings other than those of life itself, whenever it introduces the idea of a redeeming "beyond"—whether this "beyond" is conceived in terms of the Christian "afterlife" or in terms of the modern secular utopia. Aes-

thetically speaking, the modern decadent—personified by Wagner—can easily pass from revolutionism to nihilism to Christianity—
all these alternatives express the same basic need for redemption
and try to subvert the "Yes-saying" spirit of authentic life. But
how can life become self-conscious of its meaning in a world without
decadence? How can one practice the essential art of self-overcoming
if there is no decadence—no temptation? Nietzsche leaves such
questions unanswered. Without decadence—without a real danger—the notions of moral (or immoral) courage, drama, tragic consciousness, and many other central concepts of Nietzsche's philosophy—would simply become meaningless. After all, Nietzsche did
not only overcome himself as a decadent—ironically, he also composed the most complete *laus decadentiae.*

Nietzsche's theory of decadence is ultimately a theory and
critique of ideology. Although the current notion of ideology in the
sense of "false consciousness" comes from Marx, it should be observed that Nietzsche's analysis of decadence, and specifically of
modern decadence, constitutes the first attempt at a comprehensive
and radical critique of ideology in general, with a particular emphasis on modern bourgeois ideologies (political, social, cultural),
including the ideologies of modernity. If we exclude the fragmen-
tary views on the question of ideology advanced by Marx and Engels, there is nothing in the whole nineteenth century that begins to
approach the dialectic complexity and profundity of Nietzsche's philosophy of decadence. Karl Mannheim, the leading figure in the
twentieth-century sociology of knowledge, has recognized in Marx
and Nietzsche the two major precursors of the new critique of ideology. About Nietzsche, he writes:

> The other source of the modern theory of ideology and of the sociol-
> ogy of knowledge is to be found in the flashes of insight of Nietzsche
> who combined concrete observations in this field with a theory of
> drives and a theory of knowledge which remind one of prag-
> matism.... From Nietzsche the lines of development lead to the
> Freudian and Paretian theories of original impulses and to the

methods developed by them for viewing human thought as distortions and as products of instinctive mechanisms.[83]

THE CONCEPT OF DECADENCE IN

MARXIST CRITICISM

In 1963, speaking at a Conference of European Writers convened in Leningrad, Jean-Paul Sartre felt the need to dissent from the rigid views on the question of "decadentism" upheld by Soviet writers and critics. By that time Sartre had come to regard himself—and to be regarded—as a Marxist. He was by no means inimical to the Soviet experience as a whole, although he did not identify with some of the basic dogmas of official Soviet ideology. Moreover, he was strongly sympathetic to the process of de-Stalinization, which was then in full swing and seemed to justify a good deal more optimism than was actually warranted. So, he may have thought that the moment had come to reject the concept of "decadentism," in which he saw a survival of Zhdanovism, the specifically cultural form of all-pervading Stalinist terror. "Our friends" [the Soviet writers], Sartre argued very politely, are superficial when they deal with the problem of cultural decadence:

> When they speak of Proust, Joyce and Kafka as decadent authors, very often they have not read them. . . . However, this is not the problem. The real problem is an ideological one, and it must be stressed. Either we accept an utterly naïve and simple Marxism, and say: "such and such a society is decadent, therefore the writers who express it are decadent.". . . Or we say: "a decadent society poses new problems for a writer, tortures him in his own consciousness and in his creative activity." Otherwise, would there be any progressive people in a decadent society? Thus we must certainly consider that

this society, which contains and produces the artist, also conditions him; but we are not by any means compelled to think of this author strictly as a decadent. On the contrary, he can be recuperated by a new society; and there is no certainty that in his struggle against his own contradictions he may not have invented the forms of the ideas which will be used by the liberated society.[84]

To fight a "naïve" point of view can be dangerous intellectually; the polemicist himself can become unwittingly naïve and elementary. This is even more likely when the polemicist does not want to annoy those whose narrow-mindedness he is resisting. But, in spite of the simplistic character of his remarks, Sartre was making a valid point insofar as the Marxist concept of decadence was concerned, namely, that this concept could not and should not be indiscriminately applied to the matter of aesthetics. Marx himself had pointed out the transideological character of great art and insisted on the immanence of aesthetic development in a famous passage (in *Introduction* to *The Critique of Political Economy*, 1857), where he spoke of "the unequal relation between the development of material production and e.g., artistic production," and where, stressing the backwardness of the civilization of ancient Greece, he noted the permanence and even the absolute superiority of Greek standards of beauty: "The difficulty does not lie in understanding that the Greek art and epos are bound up with certain forms of social development. It rather lies in understanding why they still afford us aesthetic enjoyment and in certain respects prevail as the standard and model beyond attainment."[85] Nowhere in Marx or Engels is there any suggestion that would legitimize the view of a compelling parallelism between declining social forms and artistic decadence. On the contrary, as Marx put it, the decline of certain classes "such as the medieval knights, provided the raw material for magnificent and tragic works of art."[86]

In connection with the idea of artistic decadence in the context of Marxist thought, Sartre made a more complete and courageous statement a year after the Leningrad Conference, at a Symposium on the Question of Decadence held in Czechoslovakia (other partic-

ipants were Ernst Fischer, Edouard Goldstücker, and Milan Kundera). Sartre said on that occasion,

> I think that before anything else we must reject *a priori* the concept
> of decadence. It is evident that decadence has existed. . . . It is only
> on a strictly artistic basis that the concept of decadence can be de-
> fined and applied. To the question: Can art be decadent? I answer: It
> can be, but only if we judge it by its own artistic criteria. If we wanted
> to show that Joyce, Kafka or Picasso are decadent we would have to
> do this primarily on the basis of their own works.[87]

What Sartre's point of view amounts to is a clear-cut distinction
between artistic immanence and ideology. The latter can certainly
influence art in a variety of ways, but aesthetic value is never entirely determined by ideology; as a matter of fact, aesthetic value
deserves its name only insofar as it transcends ideology.

Significantly, neither Marx nor Engels addresses himself to the
question of *artistic* decadence. They do not even use the term. The
concept of decadence taken in a broad sense and applied socially,
however, is a constitutive element of their historical materialism.
This concept is conveyed by a large variety of terms suggesting the
decline, decay, and inevitable collapse of ruling classes when they
no longer play the progressive role that helped them rise to power.
A product of class struggle, history illustrates at every stage the
clash between the forces of the new and those of the old. The
conflict manifests itself first on the level of màterial production,
which is the determining factor in history: new and more effective
means of production appear, promoted by a rising class; the old
social forms (institutions, laws, etc.) supported by the ruling class
become increasingly incompatible with the further development of
the means of production, and when this incompatibility reaches the
point of crisis the whole society finds itself in the midst of revolutionary turmoil. As a result a new order is established. Basically,
structural change in history is explained within the framework of a
dialectic of content and form, implying the transformation of quantity (the means of production that develop slowly and steadily, illustrating the principle of gradual evolution) into quality (the new so-

cial structure that is brought about by revolution). *Evolution* leads to *revolution*, and a declining class opposes both, practically as well as ideologically.

But is the artistic culture of a period of crisis and decay (at least insofar as the ruling classes are concerned) a decadent one? Or, to be more specific, is an artist who chooses to defend an ideologically reactionary position a decadent? There is absolutely no suggestion in either Marx or Engels that such a relationship between ideological content and aesthetic achievement can be established. On the contrary, a great artist remains great even when his conscious options clearly go against the mainstream of history. Here the often quoted statement of Engels on Balzac is relevant:

> Well, Balzac was politically a legitimist; his great work is a constant elegy on the irreparable decay of good society; his sympathies are with the class that is doomed to extinction. But for all that, his satire is never keener, his irony never more bitter, than when he sets in motion the very men and women with whom he sympathizes most deeply—the nobles. And the only men of whom he speaks with undisguised admiration are his bitterest political antagonists, the republican heroes of the Cloître Saint Méry, the men who at that time (1830–36) were indeed representatives of the popular masses.
>
> That Balzac was thus compelled to go against his own class sympathies and political prejudices, that he *saw* the real men of the future where, for the time being, they alone were to be found—that I consider one of the greatest triumphs of realism, and one of the greatest features in Balzac.[88]

Neither the concept nor the term "decadence" played any significant role in the Marxist interpretation of art before the early twentieth century. If we dismiss certain purely accidental occurrences of the word in Marxist critical texts at the turn of the century (when the French epithet *décadent* had achieved something of an international popularity that went far beyond the literary squabbles of Parisian cultural life), the first Marxist to propose a fully articulated theory of artistic decadence was a Russian, the revolutionary philosopher and critic G. V. Plekhanov (1856–1918). Although Plekhanov's version of Marxism was different from Lenin's—a difference that was under-

scored by Plekhanov's joining with the Mensheviks and subsequently rejecting the Leninist view of the Russian socialist
revolution—his approach to aesthetics and his doctrine of "scientific
criticism" were readily accepted and later "canonized" by party
ideologists in the Soviet Union. Plekhanov's aesthetic writings have
been widely published and publicized, and some of his ideas—
especially his account of the decadence of Western bourgeois
culture—have become standard themes of Soviet criticism, reinforced in the period of Zhdanov's intellectual terror, and accepted as
a matter of course even after the collapse of Stalinism. Thus, it
should not seem surprising to discover that the article on "Decadence" in the 1970 edition of the *Great Soviet Encyclopedia* is
based entirely on the theoretical authority of Plekhanov (obviously,
Zhdanov and a host of other Stalinist experts on decadence had to be
dropped for cosmetic reasons).[89]

It is important to point out that, no matter how genuine a Marxist he was, Plekhanov's denunciation of decadence in modern literature was much closer to certain nineteenth-century Russian intellectual traditions (in particular the *ethical view* of art promoted by
such diverse authors as V. G. Belinsky, Chernyshevsky, or Tolstoy
in his religious-anarchist essay *What Is Art?*) than it was to the spirit
of Marxism. Plekhanov as a theorist of decadence unwittingly
brings into Marxist criticism the longtime Russian ambivalence toward Western modernity and its artistic expressions. It seems,
therefore, correct to say that the twentieth-century orthodox Marxist critique of decadence is largely if not exclusively a Russian
contribution.

Plekhanov's views on modern art and decadence are summed up
in his essay "Art and Social Life" (1912), where he establishes a
direct historical link between the romantic hostility to the bourgeois
mode of life and decadent (or neoromantic) negativism; both attitudes are not only sterile and self-defeating but—in spite of their
pretense not to be committed to any kind of utilitarian ideal—are
definitely conservative and even reactionary. Neither the romantics
nor the neoromantics actually fought the bourgeoisie: in fact, they

approved of bourgeois society, the former "instinctively," the latter "consciously." Decadence is therefore nothing but a case of duplicity. Plekhanov writes:

> The tendency towards art for art's sake arises and becomes established wherever insoluble disaccord is to be found between those engaged in art and the social environment in which they live. . . . Although in revolt against the vulgarities of the society they lived in, the Romantics, Parnassians and realists in no way rebelled against the social relations in which these vulgarities were rooted. On the contrary, whilst denouncing the "bourgeois," they approved of bourgeois society—at first instinctively, and later, quite consciously. And the more the emancipation struggle against the bourgeois social system developed, the more conscious became the attachments to this system of the French adherents of art for art's sake. And the more conscious the attachment became, the less were they able to remain indifferent to the ideological content of their own work. But their blindness towards the new trend, which was seeking to regenerate the whole of social life, made their ideas mistaken, narrow and bigoted. It depreciated the quality of the ideas expressed in their works. As the natural result of all this, French realism found itself at a dead-end, out of which were to develop . . . decadent and mystical tendencies.[90]

Plekhanov's approach to the question of decadence not only is rigid and crudely schematic but also involves blatantly contradictory assumptions without making even the slightest effort to reconcile them. The fundamental inconsistency of his theory comes from his treatment of decadence simultaneously as (1) a natural phenomenon, the inevitable form of a dying culture produced by a dying society (". . . an apple tree must produce apples and a pear tree pears"; likewise, art in the period of capitalism's demise must be decadent),[91] and (2) the result of a free and consciously reactionary choice by writers and artists. The decadents, we are told, "want a movement. But the movement they desire is a conservative movement, opposed to the emancipation movement of our time. . . . This is why even the best of them cannot produce the fine work of which they might have been capable had their social sympathies and way of thinking been different."[92] But such a flat statement amounts to saying that, after all, an apple tree might have produced pears if it had chosen to do so! The second point, however, is essential to Plekhanov's highly politicized view of decadence, and it entitles him to bring most serious moral charges against the decadents, a thing that would have been impossible if he had limited himself to the "natural" explanation.

A revolutionary Puritan, Plekhanov accuses the decadents of counterrevolutionary sloth: "What the present-day aesthetes need is a social order that will force the proletariat to work while they give themselves up to elevated pleasures . . . such as the drawing and coloring of cubes and other geometrical figures."[93] Cubism (which also comes under fierce attack elsewhere in the article), like other manifestations of the early artistic avant-garde, is the object of a blanket rejection, and this direction has been followed not only by the mainstream of official Soviet criticism but also by better informed and more sophisticated Marxist intellectuals such as Georg Lukács or Christopher Caudwell. In his blunt style, Plekhanov goes on to point out that, "Constitutionally incapable of serious work, they [i.e., the decadents] are filled with most sincere indignation at the thought of a social order in which there will be no idlers."[94] The slothful decadent is also greedy and in total collusion with the bourgeoisie, which he pretends to despise: "*Art for art's sake* . . . has become art for money's sake. . . . Is it in the least surprising that, in a generally mercenary age, art too has become mercenary?"[95]

In Plekhanov, the traditional Russian ethical censure of the aesthetic reaches the stage of unwitting self-parody, a parody that will be carried to incredible extremes during the days of Stalinism. Leaving aside the crude polemical clichés and the dreary quality of Plekhanov's style and thought, we may say that he is perhaps the first notorious representative of vulgarized Marxism in literary criticism. The broad and flexible economic reductionism of Marx becomes explicitly and almost exclusively political in Plekhanov, and clearly announces the total politicization of literary criteria, which will mark both the theory and the practice of socialist realism. Plekhanov's theory of decadence was probably the most important single prerequisite for the emergence, two decades later, of socialist realism. The link between the two is so strong that if we dismiss the idea of decadence (as Plekhanov and, then, the cultural Stalinists conceived of it), the label socialist realism becomes simply meaningless. This link (how dialectical) is emphasized in the article on "Decadence" in the latest edition of the *Great Soviet Encyclopedia*:

> Many motifs of the decadent frame of mind have become the property of various modernist artistic currents. Progressive realist art, and above all the art of socialist realism, develops in a constant struggle against them. In criticizing various manifestations in art and literature of the attitudes of decay and decline, Marxist-Leninist aesthetics proceeds from the principles of high ideological content, identification with the people, and party-mindedness in art.

In spite of its elementary and hopelessly mechanistic (reductionist) character, the Soviet theory of bourgeois cultural decadence, with its arbitrary identification of decadentism, modernism, and the avant-garde, went unchallenged between the 1930s and the 1960s not only in the Soviet Union but also in orthodox Marxist circles throughout the Western world. Even the best intellectually equipped Western communists accepted the banalities implied in the Stalinist view of bourgeois decadence as a matter of course, apparently unaware of its preposterous philosophical simple-mindedness and of the gross misconceptions (even from the Marxist standpoint) that its application was bound to bring about. Some of the writings of the English Marxist Christopher Caudwell offer a good example. Caudwell's concept of decadence (the decay of bourgeois civilization as embodied in the "dying culture" of Western modernity) is certainly not as crude as the one inherited by Soviet criticism from Plekhanov. The author of *Studies in a Dying Culture* (1938) and *Further Studies in a Dying Culture* (1949), both posthumous collections, is not willing to accept that Art for Art's Sake is just art for money's sake. He distinguishes between "commercialized art" and the "reaction against such an evident degradation of the artist's task," but, because both are products of the same bourgeois decay, he denies them aesthetic or any other kind of relevance. In his essay on "Beauty: A Study in Bourgeois Aesthetics," Caudwell writes:

> Because it is not realized that beauty is a social product, there is a degradation even of the "purest" forms of art products. We have commercialized art, which is simply affective massage. . . . Hence wish-fulfillment novels and films, hence jazz. The bourgeois floods the world with art products of a baseness hitherto unimaginable. Then, reacting against such an evident degradation of the artist's task, art withdraws from the market and becomes non-social, that is personal. It becomes "highbrow" art, culminating in personal fantasy. The art work ends as a fetish because it was a commodity. Both are equally signs of the decay of bourgeois civilization due to the contradictions in its foundation.[96]

Both the individualist avant-gardists (the dadaists and the surrealists are mentioned)[97] and the producers of bourgeois muck have as their objective the destruction of art, an unavoidable consequence of the moribund phase of capitalism. Caudwell's essential model is clearly Stalinist, which makes it all the more remarkable that some of the analyses in *Studies*, especially some of the aesthetic considerations in his major critical work, *Illusion and Reality* (1937), manage to escape the helpless obtuseness of the vulgarized Marxist approach promoted by the literary *apparatchiks* of the international communist movement.

The striking resemblances between the Soviet condemnation of decadence (in the name of socialist realism) and the Fascist rejection of the "sick art" of modernism (in the name of a healthy and beautiful art enjoyed by the people) went unnoticed by communist intellectuals. It was not until the mid-1960s that the crisis of conscience brought about by de-Stalinization prompted certain Western Marxists associated with the communist movement to reexamine the Soviet dogma of decadence and its implications. The case of the Austrian philosopher and critic, Ernst Fischer, formerly a Stalinist, is worth mentioning here. In his book *Kunst und Koexistenz* (1966), which was translated into English under the title *Art*

Against Ideology, Fischer felt the need to revise his earlier view of decadence as a matter of "formalism" versus content-oriented and realistic art, a view that was very much in line with the official Soviet concept of decadence. Fischer's book as a whole is a good illustration of the post-Stalin revival of humanist Marxism within the communist movement in Western Europe. This new spirit was never accepted by Moscow, and the brutal suppression in August 1968 of the Czechoslovak experiment in socialism "with a human face" showed quite clearly that the Kremlin ideologists were not prepared to tolerate anything like a real de-Stalinization. Not surprisingly, Fischer was expelled from the tiny pro-Muscovite Austrian Communist party as a result of his outspoken disagreement with the invasion of Czechoslovakia.

Returning now to the question of decadence, we might observe that Fischer's new treatment of it in the early and mid-1960s does not represent an abandonment of Marxism but rather a discovery of certain vital (if highly "unorthodox") aspects of Western Marxist thought. That is why Fischer's revised notion of decadence—with its new insistence on the "ideological" and "false" character of actually decadent art—comes very close to the preoccupation of the Frankfurt School with aesthetic "falsehood" and, more generally, with the various forms of "false consciousness" that characterize modernity. In other words, Fischer's "decadence" stands for much of what we would call "kitsch," and more precisely, as we shall see in the last chapter of this book, "political kitsch."

The diverse innovative movements that constitute the broad phenomenon of modernism are no longer considered decadent by Fischer. Significantly, he discovers now the positive justification of the devaluation of the subject in modern painting: "For a long time," he writes in "The Problem of Decadence,"

> I was inclined to see in this devaluation of the subject, in this eclipse of the "what" by the "how," a symptom of decadence, and I put forward this view in my book *The Necessity of Art.* Today I believe I was wrong... because in this devaluation of the subject we can rec-

ognize a certain rejection of "ideology" as false consciousness. . . . Are battles, coronations, historical events really so much more significant than the "little" subjects "seen under a light," the light discovered by impressionism?. . . Impressionism did not represent a decay but a fresh start toward new possibilities.[98]

And Fischer goes on to ask himself whether instead of considering decadent such artists as Kollwitz and Barlach, Klee and Kandinsky, Becker-Modersohn and Kokoschka (whose works were exhibited in the 1937 "Degenerate Art" show opened by Hitler himself), one should not rather characterize as "hopelessly decadent" the boastful emptiness and routine sublimity of Nazi art. And how about socialist realism, in whose perspective the above-mentioned artists were also typically degenerate examples of bourgeois decadence? There is little doubt for the perceptive reader of this essay that Fischer was perfectly conscious of the troublesome parallels between Fascist art and the Stalinist version of socialist realism, as well as of the analogies between the Nazi and Soviet treatments of the problem of decadence. In regard to the latter point, the only difference is that Hitler saw the decadents as representatives of "destructive Marxism" whereas the Marxists rejected the same as spokesmen of monopoly capitalism in its last stage of putrescence! Were it not for this difference, the following passage from one of Hitler's speeches (quoted by Fischer) could easily be mistaken for a corresponding denunciation of "bourgeois" decadence by any official Soviet ideologist from Zhdanov to Khruschev:

> Our healthy, unspoilt people will no longer tolerate an art which is remote from life and contrary to nature. . . . This degenerate art is destruction, stemming from destructive Marxism, that mortal enemy of everything that is natural and folklike. . . . We shall from now on wage a merciless mopping-up campaign against the last elements of disintegration in our culture![99]

The conclusion of Fischer's essay advances a viewpoint that is tantamount to an *a priori* dismissal of any *general* theory of cultural decadence within Marxist criticism:

> We must distinguish between the decline or rise of mankind as a
> whole, the decline and rise of classes, nations and social systems, and
> the decline or rise of the arts (or of a particular branch of the arts)
> within classes, nations and social systems. . . . All these things interact
> with one another, condition and interpenetrate one another in a mul-
> titude of ways, forming a continual reciprocal process, without ever
> becoming a rigid mechanism. This in itself provides many pos-
> sibilities of applying and misusing the concept of "decadence," and
> makes it necessary to concretize it in every particular case.[100]

Like Sartre at about the same time, Fischer cannot help concluding
that the concept of decadence should be used very cautiously and
only in very precisely defined and circumscribed cases, any
generalization being potentially misleading and harmful. Insofar as
art is not ideological (and all the more so when it is directly, deliberately anti-ideological), it cannot be qualified as decadent. Thus, only
ideological art can be decadent. But ideological art—a characteristic
of modernity insofar as modernity is an age of ideology—can be
better described in terms of kitsch. In spite of his excellent intentions, when he speaks of ideological art as decadent Fischer misuses
the term "decadence" once again, although the connections—often
of the order of contrast—between kitsch and decadence are numerous and significant, and the relationship between the problem of
decadence and the problem of ideology should by no means be
ignored.

As a matter of fact, it can be said that what makes the orthodox
(Soviet) Marxist theory and critique of decadence so unsatisfactory,
indeed so obviously crude and cliché-ridden, is the totally undialec-
tical use of the concept of ideology. The approach of Marx and
Engels to the question of ideology, although never developed into
anything close to a full-fledged theory, contained certain highly
original insights, which, for reasons that cannot be discussed here in
any detail, were simply abandoned by Lenin and then by the whole
Marxist-Leninist orthodoxy. Perhaps the main cause of this veritable
intellectual betrayal of original Marxism was, ironically, an ideological one, namely, the need of the totalitarian Soviet state for simple,
easily identifiable notions to be used as propaganda—against

"bourgeois ideology," in support of "revolutionary ideology," etc. The predictable result was that, enforced by the all-pervading censorship of Stalinist terror, this kind of extremely primitive propaganda ended up becoming the official ideological line of the party, and as such it had to be followed in the most literal sense by everybody. Any attempt at original thought, even within the dialectical tradition of Marxism, was brutally stifled. The "decadence" of bourgeois ideology and the triumphant assertion of the opposite, "scientific ideology" of Marxism-Leninism became articles of imposed faith.

The novelty of Marx's concept of ideology and its numerous possible applications to various areas of knowledge went unnoticed for a long period, but the ideas were finally discovered and utilized—not by the Marxist orthodoxy but by thinkers who read and interpreted Marx in an independent and often heterodox fashion, such as Karl Mannheim in his *Ideology and Utopia* (1929–31) or in his essays on the "sociology of knowledge." If the leftist critique of ideologies was slow to develop its original potentialities, on the right the enormous influence of Nietzsche at the turn of the century was responsible for a more profound and more genuinely dialectical attack against the main ideologies of the time (including socialism).* Without directly employing ideology as a nominal category, Nietzsche's theory of decadence as derived from his analysis of modernity clearly implied the notion of "false consciousness." We might also recall that Nietzsche as a dialectician had become aware of the ambiguity of truth itself—truth being sometimes a servant of decay and death, in which case "self-conscious illusion" was the vital alternative.

Ideological deception and self-deception as characteristics of modernity constitute the theme of perhaps the most important

---

*The distinction between "right" and "left" in questions of modern intellectual history as well as in many other respects is often not only arbitrary—like any convention—but dangerously misleading, and it can serve as a justification for the crudest type of political reductionism. It is used here only as a matter of practical convenience.

philosopher of culture influenced by Nietzsche, that is, Oswald Spengler. It is interesting here to point out that Spengler's *Untergang des Abentlandes* (published in 1918) and more generally the right-wing philosophical explanations of Western decline were somehow taken as a challenge by certain independent Marxist thinkers. This seems to be the case of at least some of the members of the Frankfurt School. In an article entitled "Spengler Today" (1941), T. W. Adorno, while being sharply critical of Spengler's "positivist" metaphysics of history, not only recognizes the force of his thought but also makes the following admission:

> Spengler stands, together with Klages, Moeller van den Bruck, and also Jünger and Steding, among those theoreticians of extreme reaction whose criticism of liberalism proved superior in many respects to that which came from the left wing. It would be worthwhile to study the causes of this superiority. It is probably due to a different attitude towards the complex of "ideology." The adherents of dialectical materialism viewed the liberal ideology which they criticized largely as a false premise. They did not challenge the ideas of humanity, liberty, justice as such, but merely denied the claim of our society to represent the realization of these ideas. Though they treated the ideologies as illusions, they still found them illusions of truth itself. . . . Above all the leftist critics failed to notice that the "ideas" themselves, in their abstract form, are not merely images of the truth that will later materialize, but that they are ailing themselves, afflicted with the same injustice under which they are conceived and bound up with the world against which they are set. On the right, one could the more easily see through the ideologies the more disinterested one was in the truth these ideologies contained, in however false a form. All the reactionary critics follow Nietzsche inasmuch as they regard liberty, humanity, and justice as nothing but a swindle devised by the weak as a protection against the strong.[101]

That, just a few lines later, Adorno could characterize this right-wing "critique of ideologies" as "comfortable" and even "cheap," while still considering it superior to what most of the leftist critics of ideology had to say, measures his contempt for the latter's philosophical crudeness. Not surprisingly, then, Adorno feels compelled to reject both the Nietzsche-Spengler and (implicitly) the prevailing leftist interpretation of decadence. Bringing in the major theme of his thought, namely, that of *negation* and *negativity*—a theme which was later to be developed into one of his major philosophical works, *Negative Dialectics* (1966)—he goes on to vindicate the much-abused—from the right as well as from the left—notion of decadence. It is precisely by its merciless negativity that decadence is the refuge of a "better potentiality" and that it is able to set free the hidden forces of Utopia. The article on Spengler ends with the following passage, which deserves to be quoted in full:

> Spengler has the prying glance of the hunter who strides mercilessly through the cities of mankind as if they were the wilderness they actually are. But one thing has escaped his glance: the forces set free by decay. "How does everything that is to be appear so ill" ("Wie scheint doch alles Werdende so krank")—this sentence of the poet Georg Trakl transcends Spengler's landscape. There is a passage in the first volume of the *Decline of the West* that has been omitted in the English translation. It refers to Nietzsche. "He used the word decadence. In this book, the term Decline of the West means the same thing, only more comprehensive, broadened from the case before us today into a general historical type of epoch, and looked at from the bird's-eye view of a philosophy of Becoming." In the world of violence and oppressive life, this decadence is the refuge of a better potentiality by virtue of the fact that it refuses obedience to this life, its culture, its rawness and sublimity. Those, according to Spengler, whom history is going to thrust aside and annihilate personify negatively within the negativity of this culture that which promises, however weak, to break the spell of culture and to make an end to the horror of pre-history. Their protest is our only hope that destiny and force shall not have the last word. That which stands against the decline of the West is not the surviving culture but the Utopia that is silently embodied in the image of decline.[102]

It is important to note here that not only Adorno but all those who were interested in aesthetics among the members of the Frankfurt School (moved after 1933 to France, and after the invasion of France during World War II to the United States) were aware of the fact that art (*true* art) and ideology are mutually exclusive concepts. But ideology can manifest itself, among other things, through art, *falsifying* it to serve the achievement of specifically ideological purposes. The question of *falsehood* in art and of the consequences of its growing importance in our time (through commercialization, ideological manipulation, etc.) is discussed in many essays by Adorno, beginning with his famous *Philosophy of Modern Music* (written in 1940–41, published in 1949). Because of this proliferation of falsehood and the ideologically successful (mis)use of practically all known art forms, the genuine modern artist is compelled to look for new means of expression, whose novelty, according to Adorno, is measured exclusively by their negativity, by the ever more complex rejections that their choice involves. This inflexibly negative asceticism is exemplified in the personality of Arnold Schönberg, to whom, in the *Philosophy of Modern Music*, Stravinsky is opposed as an example of aesthetic compromise. (Stravinsky's case is discussed in the introduction under the unequivocal heading of "False Musical Consciousness.")[103]

The dialectical analysis of "false consciousness" (in philosophy, aesthetics, and elsewhere) led Adorno to an increasingly uncompromising and austere pessimism—and this is especially true of his last years, when he felt compelled to admit: "Philosophy, which once seemed obsolete, lives on because the moment to realize it was missed. The summary judgment that it had merely interpreted the world, that resignation in the face of reality had crippled it in itself, becomes a defeatism of reason after the attempt to change the world miscarried."[104] The allusion to Marx's famous antiphilosophical thesis on Feuerbach—"So far philosophers have been content to interpret the world; what matters is to change it"—is quite transparent.

Understanding decadence as a culture of negation (which brings it very close to some definitions of modernism or the avant-garde), Adorno suggests the possibility of a revaluation of the concept of aesthetic decadence within the limits of a Marxist and dialectical theory of ideology. The expression of a precise historical moment, decadence no longer appears as a poisonous manifestation of "bourgeois ideology" but, on the contrary, as a reaction against it and, moreover, as a deep and authentic awareness of a crisis to which no easy (or even difficult) solutions can be prescribed.[105] However, neither Adorno nor any of the other members of the Frankfurt School undertook a more systematic or explicit analysis of the concept of decadence understood along such lines. They were, as cultural critics and sociologists of culture, more inclined to devote their attention to directly ideological phenomena, and in this respect their achievements are remarkable: they were among the first to propose a consistent theory of popular or mass culture (as related to mass society) and to elaborate on the various aspects and functions of the modern cultural market, mass cultural consumption, and what Adorno and Horkheimer called the "culture industry." (These contributions will be referred to more specifically in the final essay on kitsch.)

The fact that Adorno's more or less accidental insights into the question of artistic decadence were potentially fruitful has been demonstrated by the independent but in certain ways similar treatment given the concept of decadence in Italy. As a result, much of contemporary Italian criticism uses the term *"decadentismo"* as a major historical category, sometimes as broad and complex as the concept of modernity. The fact that some modern Italian critics are Marxist or at least influenced by Marxism (although not by the orthodox Leninist-Stalinist kind) is perhaps not unrelated to this specific terminological preference.

IL DECADENTISMO

While, for one reason or another, the literary labels of "decadence" or "decadentism" were either narrowed down to a strictly limited historical sense (the 1880s in France, the late Victorian period illustrated by writers like Pater, Oscar Wilde, Arthur Symons, etc., in England), or simply dropped by most West European schools of criticism, the Italians seem to have reached early in the century some kind of a consensus with regard to the application of the two related notions, and have since gone on utilizing them and speculating about them. Today *decadentismo* constitutes one of the major historical and aesthetic categories of Italian literary scholarship, comparable in complexity and scope with such concepts as romanticism, naturalism, or modernism. In the introduction to his anthology *Il decadentismo e la critica* (1963), Riccardo Scrivano proposes a periodization of the development of *decadentismo* in Italian criticism, one that is helpful for the broadly expository purposes of this essay.

There are, according to Scrivano, three main phases in the evolution of the concept: (1) The first period starts at the turn of the century, when the term *decadentismo* was used in connection with contemporary European and especially French literature (as in Vittorio Pica's *Letteratura d'eccezione*, published in 1898), and extends to the early 1920s. During this time span the most important critical pronouncements on *decadentismo* are those of Benedetto Croce, whose negative attitude toward the "voluptuous refinements" and "animal sensuousness" of the international decadent movement is expressed in various essays and articles collected in the six volumes of *La letteratura della nuova Italia*, in *Poesia e nonpoesia* (first published in 1923), *Poesia antica e moderna*, etc. (2) The beginning of the second phase is marked by Francesco Flora's treatment of decadence in his book *Dal romanticismo al futurismo* (1921). Although still a highly controversial concept, *decadentismo* tends to be regarded increasingly as a natural outgrowth of romanticism. Undergoing a broad process of historicization, the concept gradually loses its negative connotations. The second phase ends with the clear-cut rejection of the old moralistic condemnation of decadence as aesthetic pathology. The new attitude toward *decadentismo* is represented by Walter Binni's *Poetica del decadentismo* (1936). (3) The third and last phase, starting in the late 1930s and still continuing, is characterized, according to Scrivano, by diverse attempts to link the "cultural and literary experience of *decadentismo* to social and political phenomena."[106]

The notion of *decadentismo*, insofar as it is a distinctive category of Italian criticism, evolved largely as a reaction against Croce's insistent denunciation of modern decadence in literature and the arts. But Croce's approach to the question of decadence and decadentism, while almost totally negative, is often more complex and insightful than most of his philosophical adversaries would care to admit, and in some cases it clearly anticipates certain fruitful avenues of reflection. That is why it is probably safe to say that Croce is to a great extent responsible for the important role the concept of decadentism has played in twentieth-century Italian criticism and aesthetics. After all, this is not the first time in intellectual history that a powerful personality, by inspiring even an intensely negative reaction, has shaped a whole movement of ideas.

Croce's definition of *decadentismo* oscillates between a general aesthetic view of the matter of decadence (a view that equates decadence with Art for Art's Sake, formalism, or aestheticism[107]) and a more specific historical approach, which looks at the modern decadent movement as a direct product of romanticism.[108] Consistent with his cult for aesthetic fullness, Croce rejects not only decadentism but romanticism at large, the latter being held responsible for the deep crisis in art, which constitutes the outstanding characteristic of modernity. A comprehensive statement of Croce's recurrent and unyielding antiromanticism is found in his article on "Aesthetics" written for the 1929 edition of the *Encyclopaedia Britannica*:

> But the chief problem of our time, to be overcome by aesthetics, is connected with the crisis in art and in judgments upon art produced by the romantic period. . . . The crisis of the romantic period, together with sources and characteristics peculiar to itself, had a magnitude of its own. It asserted an antithesis between *naïve* and *sentimental* poetry, *classical* and *romantic* art, and thus denied the unity of art and asserted a duality of two fundamentally different arts, of

which it took the side of the second, as that appropriate to the modern age, by upholding the primary importance in art of feeling, passion and fancy. . . . Later, it was thought that the disease had run its course and that romanticism was a thing of the past; but though some of its contents and some of its forms were dead, its soul was not: its soul consisting in this tendency on the part of art toward an immediate expression of passions and impressions. Hence it changed its name but went on living and working. It called itself "realism," "verism," "symbolism," "artistic style," "impressionism," "sensualism," "imagism," "decadentism," and nowadays, in its extreme forms, "expressionism" and "futurism.". . . The tendency to destroy the idea of art is a characteristic of our age; and this tendency is based on the *proton pseudos* which confuses mental or aesthetic expression with natural or practical expression—the expression which passes confusedly from sensation to sensation and is a mere effect of sensation, with the expression which art elaborates, as it builds, draws, colours or models, and which is its beautiful creation. The problem for aesthetics to-day is the reassertion and defence of the classical against romanticism: the synthetic, formal theoretical element which is the *proprium* of art, as against the affective element which it is the business of art to resolve into itself, but which to-day has turned against it and threatens to displace it.

As we see, romanticism—by whatever name it calls itself—is *the* modern disease and the starting point of all decadence. Such a sweeping condemnation of romanticism reminds us, among others, of Nisard, and it turns out that Croce actually admired the author of *Etudes de moeurs et de critique sur les poètes latins de la décadence.* [109]

It should be noted that Croce distinguishes between *decadenza* (decadence proper) and *decadentismo*. *Decadenza* is a more general notion; it denotes decay in all walks of life—moral, political, religious, and artistic decadence are taken together as implying each other.[110] *Decadentismo* has a specialized aesthetic-historical meaning and it refers to various postromantic schools, movements, or "isms." In an essay dating from 1919 ("La storia delle arti figurative"), Croce speaks of a new direction that he characterizes as *decadentistica* and that he sees as subsuming such movements as "impressionism," "cubism," "futurism,"[111] that is, movements that considered themselves avant-garde.

Like the baroque, with which it has numerous points in common, decadentism is for Croce a concrete historical form of eternal aesthetic "sinfulness" or even, more generally, of human "sinfulness" (". . . *è un peccato estetico, ma anche un peccato umano, e universale e perpetuo, come tutti i peccati umani*").[112] However, while believing that true poetry is essentially unclassifiable and implicitly ahistorical or transhistorical, Croce tends to consider "artistic perversions" in rather precise historical terms, as if universal evil could manifest itself artistically only *in* and *through* history. Thus, for him, the baroque heresy dominates Europe from the end of the sixteenth century to the end of the seventeenth century;[113] as for decadentism, it is an outgrowth of late eighteenth-century and early nineteenth-century romanticism, and has exerted its increasingly obnoxious influence since the middle of the nineteenth century. That is why, referring to a poet like D'Annunzio—the unanimously recognized prototype of Italian *decadentismo*—one may be entitled to point out numerous traits of *barocchismo* in his works, but only when one has first realized that a D'Annunzio could have emerged only *after* romanticism and other related movements.[114] While historical labels can tell us nothing about the nature of great poetic works, they are justifiable and even necessary when we deal with aesthetic diseases or aberrations. Croce historicizes the concept of decadentism only to reject all that it stands for.

Although he frequently used the term and the critical concept of *decadentismo*, Croce never analyzed it (as he did the baroque) in a more systematic fashion. The first such analysis was attempted by Francesco Flora in 1921. In his book *Dal romanticismo al futurismo*, whose first chapter deals, significantly, with romantic decadence ("La decadenza romantica"), Flora discusses a variety of historical and stylistic aspects of what he calls the "age of decadentism" (aestheticism, sensuousness of the poetic word, fragmentarism in poetry, etc.). Other critics and literary historians of the 1920s feel attracted to the theme of literary decadence. Luigi Russo, for instance, in his 1922 book *Narratori*, examines the decadent prose of such writers as D'Annunzio, Fogazzaro, and Oriani, noting that while romanticism had been wholly nationalistic (Manzoni), decadentism manifested an opposite, "Europeanizing" tendency.[115]

The new concept of decadentism as a continuation of certain profound and aesthetically legitimate trends of romanticism is central to Mario Praz's important book *La carne, la morte e il diavolo nella letteratura romantica* (1930), translated into English under the title *The Romantic Agony* (1933). Praz's approach is directly and indirectly polemical with regard to Croce's conception of literature, which is based on a rigid metaphysical distinction between classicism and romanticism, a distinction that implies the severe condemnation (on ultimately moral grounds) of both romanticism and decadentism. Praz refuses to see decadentism as an exacerbation of the romantic sense of crisis; in his view, decadentism is wholly contained in romanticism and both are concrete historical forms of taste, which, as such, do not have to be justified by any transcendental or extrinsic criteria. That is, romanticism and decadentism—the latter being simply an *aspect* of the former—are aesthetically as legitimate as classicism or any other historical form of taste. But Praz goes much further: in "Byzantium," the last chapter of his book, he offers what I believe to be the most complete and sensitive description to that date of decadentism as an international phenomenon, observed in three major Western literatures, French, English, and Italian.

During the 1920s and 1930s, as a result of the insights of Flora, Russo, Praz, and others, the notion of *decadentismo* becomes a category of literary history and criticism purified of both pejorative and approbative connotations. The new status of the term is assessed by Walter Binni in the introduction to his *Poetica del decadentismo*. Decadentism, Binni points out, "should be seen as an historical phenomenon manifested concretely in single poetic individualities," as a "poetic climate" that does not imply any predetermined value approach. In other words, decadentism has produced, like other artistic movements, major *and* minor writers. "In brief," Binni concludes, "for us the label 'great decadent poet' does not sound more equivocal or absurd than the label 'great romantic poet.'"[116]

The concept that forms the basis of Binni's poetics of decadentism is significantly broader than the one that emerged from the late nineteenth-century French discussion of decadence. The central element in his *decadentismo* is the philosophic-aesthetic notion of decadence, which operates in Nietzsche's critique of Wagner and, more generally, in his analysis of West European modernity. For Binni, "the three legitimate fathers of decadentism are Schopenhauer, Nietzsche, and Wagner."[117] Seen in this light, the major developments in French poetry since Baudelaire appear as specifically decadent, and figures like Mallarmé, Rimbaud, Verlaine, the *symbolistes*, and Valéry become actual cornerstones in Binni's attempt to reconstruct the poetics of decadentism, that is, to discover the structural principles and aspects of decadentism's poetic self-consciousness. It may be worthwhile to recall here that by the 1930s French criticism had almost completely abandoned the notion of decadence and, as shown earlier, applied the epithet *décadent* only to a small group of minor writers of the 1880s. By the same time, critics in other Western countries had come to refer to what the Italians were calling *decadentismo* by a variety of other names—the enlarged version of *modernismo* in the Hispanic world (as used by Federico de Onís), "modernism" in the English-speaking world, etc.

The Italian preference for *decadentismo* and the subsequent enrichment of this concept can be explained, aside from the enormous influence of Croce and the complex reaction it provoked, by the historical coincidence between the Italians' discovery of the great innovative trends in post-Baudelairean French poetry and the strong impact of Nietzsche's philosophy, with its tragic dialectic and its identification of modernity and decadence. Through Nietzsche, the influence of Schopenhauer and Wagner at the turn of the century, as it exerted itself on, among others, D'Annunzio, also came to be seen as typically decadent. Nietzsche himself, perceived as a highly controversial thinker, became, more than a theorist, a representative of decadentism. If such an obstreperously avant-garde movement as futurism was declared *decadentistic* not only by adversaries like Croce but also by objective critics like Binni and many others, this was due in part to the adoption by the futurists of certain superficially understood Nietzschean ideas—*"vivere pericolosamente,"* the affirmation of life against history, the cult of violence and war, etc. I would venture to say that the terminological choice of *decadentismo* itself was determined primarily by the influence of Nietzsche, and only secondarily by that of Nietzsche's own French sources.

Binni's *Poetica del decadentismo,* although recognizing that there is a relationship between romanticism and decadentism, is, unlike Praz's *Romantic Agony,* interested in stressing the differences between the two rather than the similarities. The fundamental thesis of Binni is summarized in the observation that "between romanticism and decadentism there is the distance that separates the violent affirmation of the self from its more refined analysis."[118] As a culture of subjectivity, decadentism implies an expansion of the self beyond its traditionally established boundaries, and the "refined analysis" of which Binni speaks clearly entails the pursuit of the self in its venturesome discovery of the unconscious. In this sense, there is an intriguing parallelism between the development of literary decadentism and the appearance and evolution of modern psychoanalysis.[119] Such analogies, by which the aesthetic concept of decadentism is expanded to embrace and account for more general characteristics of intellectual modernity, point to the speculative inclination of twentieth-century Italian criticism as a whole, an inclination confirmed, among other things, by the fact that initially artistic notions such as *decadentismo* could be readily adopted and applied to nonartistic matters by cultural critics and even philosophers. The latter case is illustrated by Norberto Bobbio's book, *La filosofia del decadentismo* (1944), in which decadentism is identified with irrationalism in philosophy and specifically with existentialism.[120]

From the 1930s on, *decadentismo* has been a constant theme of discussion in Italian criticism. Luigi Russo and Francesco Flora[121] developed and refined their early insights into the question of decadentism, and a large number of other critics—among them Luciano Anceschi and A. Momigliano—contributed to the enrichment of the concept along aesthetic or cultural-historical lines. After World War II, two major factors have had a direct influence on the continuing debate around decadentism. First, the fall of Fascism and the ensuing sense of liberation stimulated a renewal of Italy's interest and participation in European cultural life, as a result of which, on a literary plane, the major representatives of Western modernism—Proust, Mann, Joyce, Kafka, etc.—enjoyed a wider diffusion and became starting points of new and fruitful critical explorations. Interestingly, these authors were usually studied within the framework of the concept of *decadentismo,* and as a natural consequence of such applications the concept itself had to undergo a subtle process of redefinition. For all practical purposes, today's *decadentismo* is a near-perfect synonym for our modernism, and a recent expository study such as Elio Gioanola's *Il decadentismo* (1972) might be taken by an English reader, if its would-be translator were to replace *decadentismo* by "modernism," as one more introduction to literary modernism.[122] The second postwar development with direct bearing on the question of *decadentismo* has been the emergence in Italy of a strong school of Marxist criticism.

Although occasionally the Italian Marxist interpretation of decadentism, especially during the 1950s, was unavoidably trapped in the simple-minded schematism of the Zhdanovist view of decadence, it was on the whole protected from the dangers of vulgar Marxism by the fact that the concept of *decadentismo* had already reached, as a result of the attack on Croce's aesthetic idealism, a degree of subtlety and complexity that no serious critic could possibly ignore. Also, the treatment of literary problems in Antonio

Gramsci's posthumous writings—the *Quaderni del carcere*—offered Italian Marxists an example of sociological and political analysis of literature that had little if anything to do with the strident slogans and clichés of the postwar official cultural line of Stalinism.[123] With regard to *decadentismo*, there are sometimes wide differences of opinion between individual Italian Marxists—and this is refreshing when we think of the painful uniformity of the Soviet ideological orthodoxy, which, as we have seen, has not revised its position vis-à-vis "bourgeois decadence" even after Stalin's death and the condemnation of the "personality cult."

Whether *decadentismo* appears as a broader or narrower historical period, whether it is seen as comprising the avant-gardes or as being distinct from them, whether it is identified with one or another particular aspect or phase of modernity, the Italian Marxist and, more generally, sociologically-oriented critics—I have in mind such critics as Giuseppe Petronio, Carlo Salinari, Leone de Castris—tend to agree on certain fundamental issues, and in the first place on the link between *decadentismo* and a *consciousness* of crisis. Even though its premises can be wrong, or false, or "mythical," decadentism is redeemed, and not only aesthetically, by the intense experience of the sense of crisis from which it originates. According to de Castris (*Decadentismo e realismo* [1959]), decadentism contains even the possibility of a new realism, a realism of inner life, of consciousness, interested primarily in the self that experiences the crisis and less in the naturalistic representation of the milieu.[124] Even a critic like Salinari, who is closer to Marxist "orthodoxy," and who defines decadentism as a "spiritualistic reaction within the context of the last progressive manifestation of nineteenth-century bourgeois thought, positivism," that is, as a negative phenomenon, recognizes that decadentism also has positive notes:

> Certainly, this reaction corresponded to an involutive process which affected the whole of European society and which brought about the drama of the First World War. But, on the other hand, this same reaction resulted in the separation from the ruling class of many

artists who openly adopted an attitude of opposition. The consciousness of crisis, the solitude of the artist severed from his natural historical *humus*, the despair of modern man are the great themes through which artists of various nations become aware of their alienation from contemporary society.[125]

Such a view is clearly a far cry from the official Soviet Marxist theory of decadentism as a *direct* and utterly obnoxious manifestation of bourgeois ideology. The actual nature of decadentism is infinitely more complex, contradictory, and intellectually challenging. The Italian Marxists were confronted with an aesthetically and historically sophisticated concept of *decadentismo* and, with few exceptions, they felt obliged to deal with it objectively and to pay attention to nuances and subtle, but essential, details.

KITSCH

Where there is an avant-garde, generally we also find a rear-guard. True enough—simultaneously with the entrance of the avant-garde, a second new cultural phenomenon appeared in the industrial West: the thing to which the Germans gave the wonderful name of *Kitsch*.... Kitsch is vicarious experience and faked sensations. Kitsch changes according to style, but remains always the same. Kitsch pretends to demand nothing of its customers except their money—not even their time.

Clement Greenberg,
"Avant-Garde and Kitsch" (1939)

KITSCH AND MODERNITY

In a note for his unfinished play *Kitsch*, written between February and May 1917 and published posthumously, the German dramatist and poet Frank Wedekind remarked that "Kitsch is the contemporary form of the Gothic, Rococo, Baroque."[1] This was perhaps the first time that the essence of modernity was specifically identified as kitsch, and that kitsch, for all its strong derogatory connotations, was seen as a broad historical style, as a distinctive embodiment of the modern *Zeitgeist*. Whether Wedekind meant his statement to be taken ironically or literally is a moot question. He may have wanted it to be taken ambiguously. The other notes and the actual scenes from *Kitsch* that he managed to write before his death in March 1918 support both the ironical and the literal interpretation. What remains indisputable, however, is that Wedekind establishes an intellectually disturbing equation between modernity and kitsch.

The spectacular growth and diversification of pseudoart in the period between the wars and after World War II has confirmed Wedekind's gloomy observation, and most contemporary critics would agree, however reluctantly, with Harold Rosenberg's assessment of popular culture (and kitsch criticism) in an article published in the late 1950s and collected in *The Tradition of the New*:

> Kitsch has captured all the arts.... When painter X or playwright Y begins to turn out X's and Y's for his readied audiences—kitsch. One of the best American poets has produced little else for years.... In each case no question of dishonesty, of "selling-out," but of muscular slackness associated with finding an audience responsive to certain norms.... In the present organization of society only kitsch can have a social reason for being.[2]

Modernity and kitsch—the notions might seem mutually exclusive, at least insofar as modernity implies antitraditional present-

ness, experiment, newness of Pound's "Make it new," commitment
to change, while kitsch—for all its diversity—suggests repetition,
banality, triteness. But in fact it is not difficult to realize that kitsch,
technologically as well as aesthetically, is one of the most typical
products of modernity. The link between kitsch (whose dependence
on fads and rapid obsolescence makes it the major form of expendable "art") and economic development is indeed so close that one
may take the presence of kitsch in countries of the "Second" or
"Third" world as an unmistakable sign of "modernization." Once
kitsch is technically possible and economically profitable, the proliferation of cheap or not-so-cheap imitations of everything—from
primitive or folk art to the latest avant-garde—is limited only by the
market. Value is measured directly by the demand for spurious
replicas or reproductions of objects whose original aesthetic meaning consisted, or should have consisted, in being unique and therefore inimitable. No one today is surprised that any masterpiece, say
Michelangelo's *Moses*, is available for "home use" in copies of different sizes and materials (from plaster, plastic, and china to real
marble). Now one can buy the masterpiece and, after placing it near
the fireplace, comfortably enjoy it every evening.

Alexis de Tocqueville in his famous book *Democracy in America*
was perhaps the first intellectual historian and sociologist to analyze
the effects of modern democracy on the arts and to explain why
democracy necessarily leads to a lowering of standards in both creation and consumption. In a modern democracy "the number of
consumers increases, but opulent and fastidious consumers become
more scarce." This general law explains why both the artisan and the
artist are "induced to produce with great rapidity a [large] quantity
of imperfect commodities" or art objects. Tocqueville described in
the 1830s one of the fundamental drives of modernity—"the hypocrisy of luxury":

> In the confusion of all ranks everyone hopes to appear what he is not,
> and makes great exertions to succeed in this object. . . . To mimick
> virtue is of every age; but the hypocrisy of luxury belongs more
> particularly to the ages of democracy. . . . The productions of artists

are more numerous, but the merit of each production is diminished. No longer able to soar to what is great, the artists cultivate what is pretty and elegant; and appearance is more attended than reality.[3]

The highly interesting passage that follows refers to an experience that today we would probably describe in terms of kitsch:

> When I arrived for the first time at New York, . . . I was surprised to perceive along the shore, at some distance from the city, a considerable number of little palaces of white marble, several of which were built after the models of ancient architecture. When I went the next day to inspect more closely the building which had particularly attracted my notice, I found that its walls were of whitewashed brick, and its columns of painted wood. All the edifices which I had admired the night before were of the same kind.[4]

From Tocqueville on, many social and cultural critics, conservatives and revolutionaries alike, agreed that artistic standards were rapidly deteriorating and attributed the main cause of the widespread corruption of taste to status-seeking and display. First the plutocrats and the *nouveaux riches*, then the petty bourgeois and certain segments of the populace were seen as trying to imitate the old aristocracy and its patterns of consumption, including the consumption of beauty. The art they liked, created and bought mainly as a sign of social status, no longer had to perform its difficult aesthetic function, and genuine artists were forced to turn their backs on an audience that applied exclusively pecuniary criteria in the matter of aesthetics.

Some radical social critics were led to generalize the situation of the mid- and late nineteenth century to encompass the whole of cultural history. Thus, for Thorstein Veblen, all culture was nothing but a consequence of aggressive showing-off as manifested in what he called in his *Theory of the Leisure Class* (1899) "conspicuous leisure" and "conspicuous consumption." Reacting against contemporary cultural hypocrisy, Veblen indulged in the somber illusion that all culture was reducible to the deceptive strategies of modern pseudoculture. Consumption for the sake of ostentation, he thought, had been the distinguishing feature of even the earliest cultures, promoted by warrior castes in barbarian societies in which all values (including those we call aesthetic) were simply symbols and means of economic differentiation. In spite of its more complex relationships, Veblen thought, modern society has preserved the basic characteristics of "predatory culture."

Surely art and even modern commercialized pseudoart cannot be explained merely by status seeking. Although true aesthetic experience may be rare to the point of being statistically irrelevant, and although it may be aided or impeded by various social factors, the need for art and the desire for prestige are different psychological entities. This distinction can be verified indirectly by the fact that even the consumption of pseudoart does not coincide with consumption for purposes of ostentation only. Lovers of kitsch may look for prestige—or the enjoyable illusion of prestige—but their pleasure does not stop there. What constitutes the essence of kitsch is probably its open-ended indeterminacy, its vague "hallucinatory" power, its spurious dreaminess, its promise of an easy "catharsis."* In numerous cases, like the true art that it counterfeits, kitsch has little if anything to do with Veblenian "conspicuous consumption." Stressing the basic modernity of kitsch, T. W. Adorno has rightfully observed:

> The historical necessity of such *kitsch* has been misjudged by Veblen. To him, the false castle is nothing but a reversion. He knows nothing of its intrinsic modernity and visualizes the illusionary images of uniqueness in the era of mass production as mere vestiges instead of "responses" to capitalistic mechanization which betray something of the latter's essence. The realm of objects which functions in Veblen's conspicuous consumption is actually a realm of artificial imagery. It is created by a desperate compulsion to escape from the abstract sameness of things by a kind of self-made and futile *promesse du bonheur.*[5]

Whether we accept the "status-seeking" theory or whether we prefer to see kitsch as a pleasurable escape from the drabness of

---

*Adorno's perceptive definition of kitsch as a "parody of catharsis" is discussed on page 241.

modern quotidian life, the whole concept of kitsch clearly centers around such questions as imitation, forgery, counterfeit, and what we may call the aesthetics of deception and self-deception.

Kitsch may be conveniently defined as a specifically aesthetic form of lying. As such, it obviously has a lot to do with the modern illusion that beauty may be bought and sold. Kitsch, then, is a recent phenomenon. It appears at the moment in history when beauty in its various forms is socially distributed like any other commodity subject to the essential market law of supply and demand. Once it has lost its elitist claim to uniqueness and once its diffusion is regulated by pecuniary standards (or by political standards in totalitarian countries), "beauty" turns out to be rather easy to fabricate. This fact may account for the ubiquity of spurious beauty in today's world, in which even nature (as exploited and commercialized by the tourist industry) has ended up resembling cheap art. Less than a century ago, nature used to imitate art, as Oscar Wilde put it in his famous "Decay of Lying." Certain sunsets, Wilde went on to say, had come to look like paintings by Corot. Nowadays, nature has little choice but to imitate mass-produced color reproductions, to be as beautiful as a picture postcard.

KITSCH, CAMP, AND HIGH ART

Earlier in the century, when modernism's victory over *pompier* academicism (one of the most gorgeous and self-righteous forms of kitsch) and other similar corruptions of taste seemed irreversible, the art world indulged in the optimistic illusion that the benevolent and sinister monster of kitsch would never again haunt its precincts. After a period of half triumph in the domain of "high art," kitsch was believed to be safely confined to the flea market or to the obscure—if thriving—industry of cheap imitations, humble religious art objects, vulgar souvenirs, and kinky antiques. But the polymorphous monster of pseudoart had a secret and deep-rooted power that few modernists were aware of—the power to please, to satisfy not only the easiest and most widespread popular aesthetic nostalgias but also the middle class's vague ideal of beauty, which still is, in spite of the angry reactions of various avant-gardes, the commanding factor in matters of aesthetic consumption and, therefore, production.

Other factors and influences have helped the recent reappearance of kitsch in the domain of high art. An extremely important "strategic" advantage has been the tendency of kitsch to lend itself to irony. From Rimbaud's praise of "poetic crap" and "stupid paintings"[6] through Dada and surrealism, the rebellious avant-garde has made use of a variety of techniques and elements directly borrowed from kitsch for their ironically disruptive purposes. Thus, when the avant-garde became fashionable, especially after World War II, kitsch came to enjoy a strange kind of negative prestige even in some of the most sophisticated intellectual circles. This seems to have been one of the main factors in the emergence of the curious camp sensibility, which, under the guise of ironic connoisseurship, can freely indulge in the pleasures offered by the most awful kitsch. Camp cultivates bad taste—usually the bad taste of yesterday—as a form of superior refinement. It is as if bad taste, consciously acknowledged and pursued, actually could outdo itself and become its own clear-cut opposite. This is at least what Susan Sontag suggests in her "ultimate" statement on camp, namely, "It is beautiful *because* it is awful."[7] Externally, however, camp is often hard, indeed impossible, to distinguish from kitsch.

The new camp fashion, born not long ago in intellectual (originally homosexual) circles in New York City, rapidly swept over the entire United States and has contributed substantially to the kitsch Renaissance in the world of high art. Still, one has reason to be surprised when one learns that a unanimously esteemed museum—with one of the best collections of modern art in the world—can house a show consisting mainly of magnificent kitsch, as redeemed by the sensibility of camp. In his *New York Times* review of the big exhibition of contemporary American art organized at the Art Institute of Chicago in the summer of 1974, Hilton Kramer suggestively groups the numerous painters representative of the camp spirit (the "grand master" being Andy Warhol) under the label of "The Flea Market School." He writes with acerbity ". . . I have passed many hours in real flea markets where the visual rewards were far greater."[8] Such examples of the proliferation and encroachment of kitsch in the domain of high art justify Kramer's rather melancholy reflection that "there are now no pockets of bad taste or vulgar display buried in the past that are not ready for exhumation."

If the avant-garde and camp fashions can resort to artistic forms and techniques clearly related to the most obvious varieties of kitsch, kitsch in its turn can mimic with profit the appearance of avant-gardism. This is another explanation of kitsch's constantly renewed power of survival within the domain of what is commonly regarded as high art. Certainly, the kitsch artist mimics the avant-garde only to the extent to which the latter's unconventionalities have proved successful and have been widely accepted or even turned into stereotypes. For kitsch, by its very nature, is incapable of taking the risk involved in any true avant-gardism.

Kitsch uses avant-garde procedures for purposes of what we may call "aesthetic advertising." A good literary example of this is the Soviet poet, Evgheni Yevtushenko, who a decade or so ago achieved the rapid celebrity of a rock star in both his native country and the West. An Italian essayist, Luigi Baldacci, has convincingly pointed out the kitsch quality of one of Yevtushenko's most characteristic poems, "The Hydroelectric Power Station of Bratsk."[9] Yevtushenko's "poetic kitsch" is defined by the poet's attempt to convey a plain and predictable political message by means of Mayakovsky's futuristic poetic language. The message by itself, even though extremely banal, cannot properly be called kitsch. The political content of the poem becomes kitsch, however, when it assumes a false identity and masquerades as poetry. The aesthetic falsification consists of the use of avant-garde expressive means that have nothing to do with the tenor of the poem and that have the unique function of sticking the label *"prodotto d'arte"* ("artistic product") on "a package which does not contain anything except a purely ideological message."[10] The difference between Mayakovsky and Yevtushenko is quite clear: the first was a genuine revolutionary, both poetically and politically (whether we like his politics or not), while the second is just a skillful propagandist trying to "sell" accepted ideological commonplaces as avant-garde poetry.

The possibility of the avant-garde's using kitsch elements and, conversely, of kitsch's making use of avant-garde devices is just an indication of how complex a concept kitsch is. We are dealing here indeed with one of the most bewildering and elusive categories of modern aesthetics. Like art itself, of which it is both an imitation and a negation, kitsch cannot be defined from a single vantage point. And again like art—or for that matter antiart—kitsch refuses to lend itself even to a negative definition, because it simply has no single compelling, distinct counterconcept.

ETYMOLOGY, CONTEXTS OF USAGE, AND

THE "LAW OF AESTHETIC INADEQUACY"

What, then, is kitsch? Can we be content with saying vaguely that it is bad art—artistic or literary rubbish, as its immediate etymology would suggest? Or should we favor the notion that kitsch is primarily false art and, therefore, to be judged in relation to such intriguing categories of falsehood as the counterfeit, forgery, or lie? And, if the relationship between kitsch and falsehood is admitted, how can this relationship account for the widespread view that kitsch is just a synonym for "bad taste"? And then what is bad taste? Is kitsch as bad taste to be discussed mostly in aesthetic terms or should it rather be conceived sociologically as a kind of ideological diversion? And, viewed as falsehood and diversion, does not kitsch also demand to be considered ethically? And, if the ethical approach is justified, can one not go further and conceive of kitsch theologically, as a manifestation of sin to be blamed, ultimately, on the influence of the devil? These and other similar questions have been raised in connection with kitsch, and the trouble is that, up to a certain point, they are all relevant.

Before trying to answer such questions, let us note that out of the numerous terms designating artistic bad taste in various modern languages, *kitsch* has been the only one to achieve a truly international status. In German, where it comes from, kitsch has a number of synonyms or near-synonyms, such as *schund* or *trivial*, and lexical compounds like *Schundliteratur* or *Trivialliteratur* are employed interchangeably to denote literary kitsch. In French, *camelote* suggests the cheapness and poor quality of many kitsch objects, but it cannot be used as an aesthetic concept. Also in French, the notion of *style pompier* refers to a pompous, academicizing variety of bad taste in painting, but it lacks both the semantic complexity and flexibility of kitsch. In Yiddish and then in American English words like *schlock* (stuff of low quality or value) or *schmaltz* (sentimental and exaggeratedly florid art) come close to certain shades of meaning implied by kitsch, but they are far from covering the whole area referred to by the latter concept. The Spanish *cursi*, as far as I know, is the only single word that suggests both the deceptive and the self-deceptive aspects of bad taste that are implied in kitsch. The aesthetic paradoxes involved in the notion of *cursi* are very similar to those of kitsch, as a reading of Ramón Gómez de la Serna's brilliant essay *Lo cursi* (1943) easily reveals.[11] The circulation of the term *cursi*, however, remains limited to the Hispanic world.

As close to kitsch as *cursi*, perhaps, is the Russian term *poshlust*, at least in its Nabokovian interpretation and transcription, in which "the first 'o' is as big as the plop of an elephant falling into a muddy pond and as round as the bosom of a bathing beauty in a German picture postcard" (*Nikolai Gogol* [Norfolk, Conn.: New Directions,

1944], p. 63). The ten pages or so in Nabokov's essay on Gogol in which *poshlust* is discussed are among the wittiest and most perceptive that have ever been written on the subject of kitsch and—although the German word is never mentioned—on the close affinities between what this notion signifies and certain outstanding traits of the German character. "Among the nations with which we came into contact," Nabokov writes, "Germany had always seemed to us a country where *poshlust,* instead of being mocked, was one of the essential parts of the national spirit, habits, and general atmosphere..." (p. 64). Indeed, this may be one of the reasons why kitsch, and not *poshlust,* has been adopted internationally: the Germans truly earned this courtesy of recognition. And, furthermore, kitsch is so easy to pronounce, as easy as "itch." And, if we were to follow for a moment Nabokov's paronomastic logic, don't we all have an itch for kitsch?

The term kitsch is, like the concept it designates, quite recent. It came into use in the 1860s and 1870s in the jargon of painters and art dealers in Munich, and was employed to designate cheap artistic stuff. It was not before the first decades of the twentieth century that kitsch became an international term. As frequently happens with such rather loose and widely circulating labels, its etymology is uncertain. Some authors believe that the German word derives from the English "sketch," mispronounced by artists in Munich and applied derogatorily to those cheap images bought as souvenirs by tourists, especially the Anglo-Americans (cf. Gero von Wilpert, *Sachwörterbuch der Literatur,* Stuttgart, 1969). According to others its possible origin should be looked for in the German verb *verkitschen,* meaning in the Mecklenburg dialect "to make cheap" (cf. *Trübners Deutsches Wörterbuch,* vol. 4, Berlin, 1943). Ludwig Giesz in his *Phänomenologie des Kitsches* also mentions the hypothesis that links kitsch to the German verb *kitschen,* in the sense of "collecting rubbish from the street" (*den Strassenschlamm zusammenscharren*); *kitschen* has indeed this specific meaning in the southwestern part of Germany; it can also mean "to make new furniture from old" (*neue Möbel auf alt zurichten*).[12]

These three main etymological hypotheses, even if erroneous, seem to me equally suggestive of certain basic characteristics of kitsch. First, there is often something sketchy about kitsch. Second, in order to be affordable, kitsch must be relatively cheap. Last, aesthetically speaking, kitsch may be considered rubbish or junk.

Let me add that, apart from those who derive kitsch either from the English (the "sketch theory") or from the German, there are writers who favor less plausible views. According to Gilbert Highet, kitsch comes from the Russian verb *keetcheetsya*, meaning "to be haughty and puffed up." Hence, his view that kitsch signifies "vulgar showoff" and "is applied to everything that took a lot of trouble to make and is quite hideous."[13] However improbable, such a derivation has the merit not only of stressing the basic uncertainties with regard to the word's origin, but also of suggesting the actual flexibility of its present-day meaning. Moreover, Highet is right to the extent that he points out that kitsch is not always easy to make, and that to produce bad art or poetry can sometimes require a great deal of effort.

Whatever its origin, kitsch was and still is a strongly derogatory word, and as such lends itself to the widest range of subjective uses. To call something kitsch is in most cases a way of rejecting it outright as distasteful, repugnant, or even disgusting. Kitsch cannot be applied, however, to objects or situations that are completely unrelated to the broad domain of aesthetic production or aesthetic reception. Generically, kitsch dismisses the claims or pretensions of quality of anything that tries to be "artistic" without genuinely being so. It may, then, apply derogatorily to architecture, landscaping, interior decoration and furnishing, painting and sculpture, music, cinema and TV programs, literature, and virtually anything subject to judgments of taste. If we think of kitsch in terms of aesthetic deception and self-deception, there are obviously as many types of kitsch as there are possibilities of misusing or counterfeiting the signs of art. Limiting ourselves, for the moment, to literature, we can distinguish two very comprehensive categories, each one comprising an indefinite number of species and subspecies: (1) Kitsch produced for *propaganda* (including political kitsch, religious kitsch, etc.) and (2) kitsch produced mainly for *entertainment* (love stories, Rod McKuen-type giftshop poetry, potboilers, slicks, etc.). We should recognize, however, that the division between the two categories can become extremely vague: propaganda can masquerade as "cultural" entertainment and, conversely, entertainment can be directed toward subtle manipulative goals. From the psychological point of view we can use the distinction proposed by Hans Egon Holthusen between "sweet kitsch"—the sentimental "saccharine type"—and the sour variety, with innumerable nuances in between.[14]

No matter how we classify its contexts of usage, kitsch always implies the notion of *aesthetic inadequacy*. Such inadequacy is often found in single objects whose formal qualities (material, shape, size, etc.) are inappropriate in relation to their cultural content or intention. A Greek statue reduced to the dimensions of a *bibelot* can serve as illustration. But the "law of aesthetic inadequacy" has a much wider scope, and we may well speak of kitsch effects in connection with combinations or arrangements of objects that, taken individually, have absolutely nothing kitschy about them. Thus, a real Rembrandt hung in a millionaire's home elevator would undoubtedly make for kitsch. Obviously, this is a hypothetical example and a caricature but it has the merit of suggesting the *use* of genuine great art as mere ostentatious decoration. An aesthetic object displayed as a symbol of affluence does not become kitsch itself, but the role it plays is typical of the world of kitsch. Certainly, the opposite happens more frequently, that is, a variety of easily affordable things, which have little if anything to do with art, may be given aesthetic significance and treated with the respect due to true art objects. We have only to think of the horrendous old "curiosities" that are on sale in the increasingly numerous nostalgia shops— rotten boots, broken cart wheels, porcelain night-pots, unwieldy rusty bathtubs of two or three generations ago, and innumerable other shabby and junky "antiques," which many people enjoy as poetic relics from the better world of our grandfathers. Between the two extremes of authentic art reduced to signifying mere wealth and patent nonart vested with aesthetic prestige, there are countless instances to which the concept of aesthetic inadequacy applies.

KITSCH AND ROMANTICISM

Although kitsch can occur in a great many different contexts, the concept almost completely lacks what I would call "historical depth," that is, it can hardly be used in connection with anything before the late eighteenth century or the early nineteenth century. This is another way of saying that kitsch—not only as a term but also as a concept—is essentially modern. Even if we can discover some formal relationship between kitsch and mannerist or baroque art, kitsch seems to be, historically, a result of romanticism. On the one hand, the romantic revolution—insofar as it was a consequence of the eighteenth-century Quarrel between the Ancients and the Moderns—brought about an almost complete relativization of the standards of taste; on the other hand, many romantics (some of them truly great poets or artists and obviously having nothing to do with kitsch) promoted a sentimentally oriented conception of art, which in turn opened the road to various kinds of aesthetic escapism. The point has been made before that the desire to escape from adverse or simply dull reality is perhaps the main reason for the wide appeal of kitsch.

More generally, romanticism is the first important *popular* literary and artistic movement, the main cultural product of the rise of modern democracy. A sociologist of institutions and intellectual life like Tocqueville could not fail to dwell upon the outstanding features by which literature in democratic ages (he did not use the

word "romanticism") is distinguished from the literature produced
in periods of aristocracy (he obviously had the great French poets of
the seventeenth century in mind). In democracies, men do not
think that the pleasures of mind "constitute the principal charm of
their lives; but they are considered as transient and necessary recre-
ations amidst the serious labours of life." And Tocqueville goes on to
describe in more detail the needs of average readers in a democratic
age:

> As the time they can devote to letters is very short, they seek to make
> the best use of the whole of it. They prefer books which may be easily
> procured, quickly read, and which require no learned researches to
> be understood. They ask for beauties, self-proffered, and easily en-
> joyed; above all, they must have what is unexpected and new. Accus-
> tomed to the struggle, the crosses, and the monotony of practical life,
> they require rapid emotions, startling passages.... Authors will aim
> at rapidity of execution, more than at perfection of detail. Small
> productions will be more common than bulky books.... The object of
> authors will be to astonish rather than please, and to stir the passions
> rather than charm the taste.[15]

Tocqueville is one of the first to remark that democracy encourages
commercialism in literature and the arts. Leaving aside a few great
authors, writers in a democracy work for the market:

> Democracy not only infuses a taste for letters among the trading
> classes, but introduces a trading spirit into literature.... Among aris-
> tocratic nations no one can hope to succeed without immense exer-
> tions, and... these exertions may bestow a great deal of fame, but
> can never earn much money; whilst among democratic nations, a
> writer may flatter himself that he will obtain at a cheap rate a meager
> reputation and a large fortune.[16]

What is remarkable about passages such as these is that many of the
points they make might well apply to kitsch: art as recreation and
entertainment, easiness of access, quick and predictable effects,
"trading spirit" on the part of writers (who are more interested in
immediate financial rewards than in achieving fame), the reading

public's psychological need for escape from the dullness of quotidian life—these are some of the recurring elements in most sociologically oriented definitions of kitsch.

The relationship between romanticism and kitsch can also be discussed from an aesthetic vantage point. Hermann Broch, for instance, links the modern rise of kitsch to the change brought about by romanticism in the conception of the aesthetic ideal. Before romanticism the aesthetic ideal had been considered as *transcendent* in regard to any possible work of art: Beauty appeared as an absolute, practically never attainable, model and criterion of value. But during the romantic era the aesthetic ideal lost all trace of its former transcendence and came to be perceived exclusively in terms of its immanence in particular, finite works of art. Value systems before romanticism were, according to Broch, *open* (in the sense that the goal to be attained remained outside the system). In an essay written in 1950 he observed,

> Romanticism is inclined in exactly the opposite direction. It wishes to make the Platonic idea of art—beauty—the immediate and tangible goal for any work of art. . . . Yet, insofar as art remains a system, the system becomes closed; the infinite system becomes a finite system. . . . And this process constitutes the basic precondition of every form of kitsch, but at the same time owes its existence to the specific structure of romanticism (i.e., to the process by which the mundane is raised to the level of the eternal). We can say that Romanticism, without therefore being kitsch itself, is the mother of kitsch and that there are moments when the child becomes so like its mother that one cannot differentiate between them.[17]

In an earlier essay dating from 1933, Broch also spoke of kitsch and romanticism, basing his parallel on their common nostalgic quality. Often, he said, kitsch is nothing else than "an escape into the idyll of history where set conventions are still valid. . . . Kitsch is the simplest and most direct way of soothing this nostalgia."[18] Replacing historical or contemporary reality by clichés, kitsch clearly thrives on some emotional needs that are generally associated with the romantic world view. To a large extent we can see kitsch as a hackneyed form of romanticism.

BAD TASTE, IDEOLOGY, AND HEDONISM

Kitsch appears to be a recent phenomenon even if we identify it simply with bad taste. Although some critics speak of the "universality of kitsch" (theoretically a legitimate assumption), they will never go into specifics beyond, let us say, the baroque period. This is perhaps because it is extremely hazardous to speculate about what bad taste was like in older times. This is also because it may even be that bad taste did not exist in earlier periods or, if it existed, it did not have the means to systematize its conventions and to institutionalize its activities in order to reach a large number of would-be consumers of specifically fake art. This raises the question of the connection of bad taste and the history of modern technology, especially the advent of the machine in producing and reproducing books and other types of works of art.

As a working hypothesis we may consider that bad taste in modern times consists mainly of an ideologically manipulated illusion of taste. That is why mass culture can be described quite adequately in terms of ideology or false consciousness. If true art always contains a finally irreducible element, an element that is constitutive of what we may call "aesthetic autonomy," art that is produced for immediate consumption is clearly and entirely *reducible* to extrinsic causes and motives. To stress this important point it is useful to mention the distinction between genuine art and mass culture proposed by one of the representatives of the Frankfurt School of social and cultural criticism, Leo Lowenthal. A longtime student of the relationships between popular culture and society (as in his book *Literature, Popular Culture, and Society*, 1961), Lowenthal summarizes both his personal position and the cultural philosophy of the Frankfurt School as a whole when he says: "As far as there is any legitimacy to the concept of reductionism, it indeed applies to mass culture. . . . While I totally reject a sociological approach to *literature* which looks at the works of art as mere reflections of society, the reflection theory is exactly the legitimate concept to be applied to mass culture. In classical Marxian terms, mass culture is indeed ideology." And this is so because the significance of the phenomena of mass culture "in no way consists in what they have to say but rather in the extent to which what they say is a generalizable statement about the predispositions and attitudes of those consumers who in large aggregates are accepting the merchandise."[19] If we replace the notion of mass culture by kitsch, this distinction becomes even more convincing. By kitsch in this context we mean simply *false aesthetic consciousness* or, to paraphrase Theodor W. Adorno's definition of kitsch as the "parody of catharsis,"[20] the *parody of aesthetic consciousness*.

During the late 1930s two of the leading members of the Frankfurt School, T. W. Adorno and Max Horkheimer, introduced the notion of the "culture industry" (also referred to as "amusement industry," "entertainment industry," etc.), which they defined from a broader dialectical point of view and analyzed in more detail in their postwar collaborative work *Dialectic of Enlightenment* (first published in 1947).[21] Basically, the culture industry is concerned with supplying the (pseudo) cultural market with products specifically designed to induce *relaxation*. As far back as 1941, Adorno had described the *need* of the masses for distraction or "fun" as both a result of the existing (capitalist) mode of production and, as it were, one of its most characteristic products. Reformulating in a cultural context Marx's famous theory that the mode of production manufactures not only certain commodities but also the need for precisely those commodities, Adorno wrote: "The customers of musical entertainment are themselves objects or, indeed, products of the same mechanism which produces popular music. . . . The power of the process of production extends itself over the time intervals which on the surface appear to be 'free'. . . . The people clamor for what they are going to get anyhow."[22] What is difficult to accept in Adorno's approach is the identification of the "masses" with the "working class" in a conventional Marxian sense. The fact is that, even at the time when the article was written, the concept of mass culture applied to the middle class as well. Today it is perhaps more obvious than three or four decades ago that popular culture—to the extent to which it is kitsch—responds primarily to middle-class psychological needs, which it tries, rather successfully, to generalize to the whole of society in an electronized world that resembles very much McLuhan's "Global Village." This point will be argued later. For the moment we should admit that Adorno's insight into the need for "distraction" is quite accurate if only we broaden the scope of its application and realize that the whole process of production and consumption of mass (pseudo) culture is facilitated by an all-too-human readiness for self-deception. Writes Adorno: "People want to have fun. A fully concentrated and conscious experience of art is possible only to those whose lives do not put such a strain on them that in their spare time they want relief from both boredom and effort simultaneously. The whole sphere of cheap commercial entertainment reflects this dual desire. It induces relaxation because it is patterned and pre-digested."[23]

Certainly, one of the main reasons for the growth of kitsch since the beginning of the nineteenth century, to quote another sociologist of modern culture, Dwight Macdonald, is the fact that "business enterprise found a profitable market in the cultural demands of the newly awakened masses, and the advance technology made possible the cheap production of books, pictures, music, and furniture in sufficient quantities to satisfy the market."[24] But even if the association between kitsch and low cost is often inescapable, we should not overlook the fact that the latter notion is very relative and can therefore become, when used as a unique criterion, dangerously misleading. What is regarded as cheap by a member of the upper-middle class can be prohibitively expensive for somebody less well off. Let us also repeat that sometimes bad taste can enjoy the pos-

session of important financial means for the satisfaction of its ostentatious whims and fancies.

We have, then, to recognize the existence, along with the hum-
bler varieties of kitsch, of a gorgeous kitsch that is the privilege of
the rich. Moreover, even when it is inexpensive, kitsch is often supposed to suggest richness and superfluity: imitation gold or silver
objects and colored-glass jewelry sold in drugstores undoubtedly
have something to do with kitsch. As for actual rich, upperclass
kitsch, the second half of the nineteenth century and then the time
span that has been called *la belle époque* can furnish a great number of examples. Even the kings who happened to reign in that
blessed period were sometimes converts to kitsch, like Ludwig II of
Bavaria, who indulged frenetically in the most luxurious kind of bad
taste. For some writers (for instance, Abraham A. Moles)[25] the real
kitsch has to be looked for precisely in that epoch, our own time
being characterized by the formation of a "neo-kitsch" style, in
keeping with the demands of an affluent consumer society. Even if
we accept such a periodization of kitsch—and I do not see why we
should not—the cheaper contemporary variety has, so to speak, its
traditional roots in the pseudo-aristocratic aesthetic notions of the
rich nineteenth-century bourgeoisie.

The kind of taste that is satisfied by the lower forms of kitsch
ought not be confused with popular taste (although the epithet
"popular" has undergone an important change of meaning during
the last decades, and today's "popular culture" is often pure kitsch).
Throughout the centuries, popular taste found its expression and
natural satisfaction in folk art and poetry, which are in no way aesthetically inferior to the creations of high culture. Folk culture, the
result of a long, organic, and manifold creative-participatory process
is, in spite of its sometimes awkward or naïve appearances, highly
elaborated and refined. What is important—to quote Macdonald
again—is that "Folk Art grew from below," whereas "Mass Culture
is imposed from above. It is fabricated by technicians hired by
business; its audiences are passive consumers, their participation
limited to the choice of buying or not buying. The Lords of *kitsch*, in

short, exploit the cultural needs of the masses in order to make a profit and/or to maintain their class rule—in Communist countries, only the second purpose obtains."[26]

Cheap or expensive, kitsch is sociologically and psychologically the expression of a life style, namely, the life style of the bourgeoisie or the middle class. This style can appeal to members of both the upper and lower classes and, in fact, become the *ideal life style* of the whole society—all the more so when the society grows affluent and more people have more spare time. Insofar as man chooses the ambience that suits his tastes, he can have several distinct types of relations with the objects that make up the decor of his home life. Abraham Moles distinguishes no less than seven modes of behavior in this respect: ascetic, hedonist, aggressive, acquisitive, surrealist, functionalist or cybernetic, and kitsch.[27] And the kitsch mode is absolutely opposed to the ascetic one, combining all others in various proportions. The number of these modes can easily be increased or reduced. But the basic conflict between asceticism and hedonism remains in any ordering of these attitudes. Thus, keeping Moles's classification in mind, it is not difficult to show that, asceticism excepted, all the other categories can be subsumed under hedonism. Aggressiveness, like possessiveness, cannot be dissociated from the pleasure principle. Surrealism is nothing else than an extreme case of enjoyment of quaint, unpredictable combinations, and functionalism (in this context) is just another word for the "comforts of civilization."

To understand the nature of kitsch we should, then, analyze the particular hedonism characteristic of the middle-class mentality. Its primary feature is perhaps that it is a middle-of-the-road hedonism, perfectly illustrated by the "principle of mediocrity" that always obtains in kitsch (this all-pervading mediocrity is easier to notice in the more elaborate and exaggeratedly complicated forms of kitsch). The middle class being an active class, its hedonism is confined to the use of spare time. It is a hedonism of relaxation and, therefore, compensatory in nature. That is why kitsch lends itself to a definition in terms of a systematic attempt to fly from daily reality: in *time* (to a personal past, as indicated by the kitsch cult of the souvenir; to the "idyll of history"; to an adventurous future by means of the clichés of science fiction, etc.); and in *space* (to the most diverse imaginary and exotic lands). At a practical level, the pursuit of relaxation requires that household activities be performed with as little effort and as much fun as possible: this is how the gadget appears (gadgets being produced by a specialized sector of the industry of kitsch objects). Middle-class hedonism is in principle open, unprejudiced, eager for new experience; this openness, unhampered by any critical sense, accounts for the tolerant and sometimes heteroclite character of the world of kitsch. The superficiality of this hedonism can be matched only by its desire for universality and totality, and by its infinite capacity for acquiring beautiful junk.

The fundamental trait of modern middle-class hedonism is perhaps that it stimulates the *desire to consume* to the point that consumption becomes a sort of regulating social ideal. Obviously, consumption and production have always implied each other, but the ethical significance attached to these correlative concepts and activities has varied widely. Traditional civilizations—even those that do not hold labor as such in particularly high esteem—are for diverse reasons inclined to praise the virtues of *saving*, frugality, thrift, etc. (which are nothing but forms of postponing consumption), and will consequently guard against the dangers involved in immoderate consumption (a word that in common language still means primarily "destruction," "waste," "squandering," and that is naturally associated with notions of "luxury," "affluence," and even "decadence"). Although modernity is largely a product of the famous Protestant work ethic (in which Max Weber saw the main cause of capitalism), the dynamics of present-day economics and the whole temporal framework in which social activities are performed encourage a drastic revision, indeed a reversal, of the traditional outlook: consumption is totally vindicated, whereas old temperance, restraint, and saving habits tend to appear as outmoded and touchingly ridiculous relics of the past. More than a mere fulfillment of certain basic needs, consumption has somehow become almost a duty—a way of helping the economic health of the nation—and, beyond mere economics, a way of apprehending and understanding the world.

To better comprehend what underlies today's frenzy of consumption (the "have it now" urge of both cultural and countercultural hedonism) we also have to consider another major characteristic of modernity, namely, its all-pervasive sense of change. The psychological consequences of modernity's increasing pace of change—and in the first place the ensuing axiological relativism—account for a decreasing trust in stability or continuity, without which no ethos of postponement or restraint is possible. In traditional societies, a homogeneous time that perpetually renews itself in a circular movement offers the guarantee that tomorrow will not be substantially different from yesterday or today. Individual anxieties and tragedies are of course possible, and within the framework of an essentially harmonious universe (the Greek Cosmos, for instance, as opposed to Chaos) the accidents and irregularities of chance may provoke untold personal and collective disasters. However, such mishaps do not contradict the belief in the basic unity of existence or the deep sense of continuity derived from respect for tradition. Within the Judeo-Christian eschatological view of history, the importance of tradition is in no way diminished by the implications of the doctrine of salvation. The system of values upon which the Christian ethic is based is among the most stable, and the variegated drama that takes place on the "stage" of this world cannot possibly throw the slightest shadow of doubt upon either the relevance of the past or the certainty of the hereafter.

The Christian ethic is an ethic of postponement *par excellence.* At the dawn of modernity the myth of progress emerged, based on a secularized concept of linear and irreversible time. During its "progressive" phase, modernity managed to preserve some of the older quality of time, and in the first place the sense of *continuity* between the past, the present, and the future. The idea of progress postulates that change has a certain pattern, that it presupposes a certain order that favors a *constant* and *gradual* development from the inferior to the superior. By itself, belief in progress can be an incentive to postponement of consumption. But the alliance between modernity and progress turned out to be only temporary, and in our age the myth of progress appears to have been largely exhausted. It has been replaced by the myth of modernity itself. The future has become almost as unreal and empty as the past. The widespread sense of instability and discontinuity makes instant enjoyment about the only "reasonable" thing to strive for. Hence, the drive toward consumption and the whole paradoxical concept of a "throw-away economy" and, more generally, civilization.

The great psychological discovery on which kitsch is founded lies in the fact that nearly everything directly or indirectly associated with artistic culture can be turned into something fit for immediate "consumption," like any ordinary commodity. It is true that, unlike the ordinary consumer, the art consumer does not use up that which he enjoys. Mentally, however, the modern philistine can behave like a common consumer and, without materially damaging or even touching the original art work, destroy its aesthetic significance (the case of masterpieces, like Mona Lisa, worn out by kitsch will be discussed later). To respond to the "aesthetic" demands of today's compulsive consumer, the culture industry is there to imitate, duplicate, reproduce, and standardize whatever he might enjoy. Uniqueness and even rarity have become anachronous qualities, which are not only out of step with the times but illustrate what an advocate of "cultural consumption" (and a proponent of respectable mid-brow and petit-bourgeois kitsch) calls "the Law of the Inefficiency of Art."[28]

Kitsch, therefore, is "efficient" art, the expendable cultural aspect of today's society, and one of the most direct manifestations of the triumphant aesthetics and ethics of consumerism. Originally, as pointed out before, kitsch emerged as an expression of the taste of the middle class and of its peculiar spare-time hedonism. As a form of ideology (aesthetic false consciousness) kitsch appeared quite spontaneously, and the prevailing Marxist view that it was more or less deliberately introduced by the upper classes to divert the working class or the masses from their revolutionary vocation is fundamentally incorrect. This fallacy does not prevent certain Marxist or para-Marxist critics (Adorno and Horkheimer, for instance) from making a host of extremely perceptive observations with regard to the world of kitsch and its inner dialectic. This, incidentally, is not the first time that a basically erroneous approach has proved intellectually exciting and even fruitful.

If so many students of contemporary "mass culture" have overlooked the middle-class origin and nature of kitsch it may be that, as Jenny Sharp observed in an article published in 1967, this is at the same time the most obvious and the most bizarre characteristic of kitsch. Kitsch, she wrote, "means all those cheap, vulgar, sentimental, tasteless, trashy, pretty, cute objects the vast majority of people in this country like to live with. . . . This pop culture . . . has transcended the barriers of taste and refinement and become absorbed in the archives of the establishment culture. The only page left unturned is the most obvious, in some ways the most bizarre, and therefore overlooked. Kitsch is in fact the taste of the middle classes, which in the present day is the taste of the vast majority of our society."[29]

In the light of the foregoing arguments it becomes clear once again why kitsch as an aesthetic concept cannot be dissociated from modernity and, specifically, from the comparatively recent period that has seen the rapid rise of the middle classes. Kitsch is the direct artistic result of an important ethical mutation for which the peculiar time awareness of the middle classes has been responsible. By and large, kitsch may be viewed as a reaction against the "terror" of change and the meaninglessness of chronological time flowing from an unreal past into an equally unreal future. Under such conditions, spare time—whose quantity is socially increasing—is felt as a strange burden, the burden of emptiness. Kitsch appears as an easy way of "killing time," as a pleasurable escape from the banality of both work and leisure. The fun of kitsch is just the other side of terrible and incomprehensible boredom.

SOME STYLISTIC CONSIDERATIONS

To put some order into an issue so confusingly many-sided, it is helpful to approach the problem of kitsch from three different but complementary angles. To begin, we may consider kitsch as a product of a certain category of "artists," "makers," or "designers" who, addressing themselves to a well-defined audience of average consumers, apply definite sets of rules and communicate varieties of highly predictable messages in stereotyped "aesthetic" packages. From this point of view, kitsch is a *style*, in the sense in which Wedekind spoke of it as the contemporary form of the gothic or baroque or rococo. The second possibility is to take into account the specific kitsch elements that appear in the process of mass production and diffusion of art. Such elements are clearly nonintentional (that is, they are not planned in advance by the producers of kitsch but are rather the fatal consequences of modern technology's intervention in the art world). The third possibility consists of considering kitsch from the vantage point of the consumer who, willing to accept the "aesthetic lie" of kitsch and who, conditioned by the sheer quantity of pseudoart and instant beauty with which he is surrounded, can perceive even genuine works of art as kitsch.

What does the kitsch artist have in mind when he sets out to work? He obviously thinks in the first place of impressing and pleasing the average consumer who is going to buy his products. Aesthetically, then, we may say that the kitsch artist applies—consciously or not—a "principle of mediocrity," which offers him the best guarantee that his works will be favorably received. In the second place, the producer of kitsch must be aware of his public's diversity of interests and desires. This accounts for the basic eclecticism of kitsch as a style. What gives kitsch some kind of stylistic unity in the long run is probably the compatibility of its heterogeneous elements with a certain notion of "hominess." Kitsch is very often the kind of "art" that the average consumer might desire to own and display in his home. Even when displayed elsewhere—waiting rooms, restaurants, etc.—kitsch is meant to suggest some sort of "artistic" intimacy, an atmosphere saturated with "beauty," that kind of beauty one would wish to see one's daily life surrounded with. The characteristics of eclecticism and "hominess" that define kitsch are perceptively described in an article by the English art critic, Roger Fry, first published in 1912 and then collected in his volume *Vision and Design* (1920). Fry does not use the term "kitsch," but the variety of bad taste he is dealing with quite obviously belongs to the category of kitsch. The passage deserves to be quoted in its entirety:

> I take pains to write the succeeding paragraphs in a railway refreshment-room, where I am actually looking at those terribly familiar but fortunately fleeting images which such places afford. And one must remember that public places of this kind merely reflect the average citizen's soul, as expressed in his home.
>
> The space my eye travels over is a small one, but I am appalled at the amount of "art" that it harbours. The window towards which I look is filled in its lower part by stained glass; within a highly elaborate border, designed by someone who knew the conventions of thirteenth-century glass, is a pattern of yellow and purple vine leaves with bunches of grapes, and flitting about among these many small birds. In front is a lace curtain with patterns taken from at least four centuries and as many countries. On the walls, up to a height of four feet, is a covering of lincrusta walton stamped with a complicated pattern in two colours, with sham silver medallions. Above that a moulding but an inch wide, and yet creeping throughout its whole with a degenerate descendant of a Graeco-Roman carved guilloche pattern; this has evidently been cut out of the wood by machine or stamped out of some composition—its nature is so perfectly concealed that it is hard to say which. Above this is a wall-paper in which an effect of eighteenth-century satin brocade is imitated by shaded staining of the paper. Each of the little refreshment-tables has two cloths, one arranged symmetrically with the table, the other a highly ornate printed cotton arranged "artistically" in a diagonal position. In the centre of each table is a large pot in which every beautiful quality in the material and making of pots has been carefully obliterated by

methods each of which implies profound scientific knowledge and great inventive talent. Within each pot is a plant with large dark-green leaves, apparently made of india-rubber. This painful catalogue makes up only a small part of the inventory of the "art" of the restaurant. If I were to go on to tell of the legs of the tables, of the electric-light fittings, of the chairs into the wooden seats of which some tremendous mechanical force has deeply impressed a large distorted anthemion—if I were to tell of all these things, my reader and I might both begin to realize with painful acuteness something of the horrible toil involved in all this display. Display is indeed the end and explanation of it all. Not one of these things has been made because the maker enjoyed the making; not one has been bought because its contemplation would give any one any pleasure, but solely because each of these things is accepted as a symbol of a particular social status. I say their contemplation can give no one pleasure; they are there because their absence would be resented by the average man who regards a large amount of futile display as in some way inseparable from the conditions of that well-to-do life to which he belongs or aspires to belong. If everything were merely clean and serviceable he would proclaim the place bare and uncomfortable.[30]

Fry's catalogue of restaurant art suggests quite aptly what we may term the "stylistic overdetermination" of kitsch. The early twentieth-century refreshment room he describes is literally crammed with objects that fake up stylistic conventions of the most widely different periods, countries, and cultures. The eclecticism of kitsch is often quite clearly a form of aesthetic overkill. Is this dizzying eclecticism simply a matter of "futile display" as Fry believes? And is it true that kitsch "can give no one pleasure"?

The point has been made before that even if kitsch is linked to status-seeking it also has the function—which is psychologically more important—of providing an illusionary escape from the banality and meaninglessness of contemporary day-to-day life. In whatever forms or combinations, kitsch is relaxing and pleasing. The wish-fulfilling element contained in this pleasure stresses its reactive origin, the fear of emptiness that kitsch attempts to assuage. Seen from this viewpoint kitsch is a response to the widespread modern sense of spiritual vacuum: it fills the empty time of leisure with "fun" or "excitement" and it "hallucinates"—if we are allowed to use this verb transitively—empty spaces with an infinitely variegated assortment of "beautiful" appearances.

The stylistic eclecticism of kitsch has another remarkable feature, namely, that of suggesting commercial availability. A kitsch object is attractive not only because it is nice-looking but also because it—or any similar object—can be obtained by anyone willing to buy it. Even the most laborious and expensive varieties of kitsch contain a built-in self-advertisement, an invitation to possession and ready enjoyment. The aesthetic charm of kitsch is transparently commercial.

This feature accounts for the curious semiotic ambiguity of most kitsch objects. Such objects are intended to look both genuine and skillfully fake. The role of this paradoxical fakiness is not too difficult to elucidate. On the one hand, the visible signs of fakiness are devised to dispel the impression of uniqueness or rarity that a perfect fake should create. To be rare would contradict the sense of the commercial availability of kitsch. On the other hand, such a fakiness calls the viewer's attention to certain agreeable qualities of proficiency, imitative skill, versatility and cuteness.

Kitsch's semiotic ambiguity has received little consideration from the analysts of bad taste. Hence, certain widespread errors, such as Gillo Dorfles's views on the kitsch nature of art reproductions. Dorfles contends: "We must regard all reproductions of unique works which were conceived as unrepeatable as equivalent of real forgeries."[31] But the aesthetic falsehood of kitsch should not be confused with that of a forgery. A forgery is meant to be taken for an original. While a forgery illegally exploits the elitist taste for rarity, a kitsch object insists on its antielitist availability. The deceptive character of kitsch does not lie in whatever it may have in common with actual forgery but in its claim to supply its consumers with essentially the same kinds and qualities of beauty as those embodied in unique or rare and inaccessible originals. Kitsch pretends that each one of its potentially innumerable fakes, and fakes of fakes, contains something of the objective aesthetic value of the styles, conventions, and works that it openly counterfeits. Kitsch offers instant beauty, maintaining that there is no substantive difference between itself and original, eternal beauty.

Stylistically, kitsch can also be defined in terms of predictability. Kitsch is, as Harold Rosenberg puts it: "a) art that has established rules; b) art that has a predictable audience, predictable effects, predictable rewards."[32] But literary and artistic conventions change rapidly, and yesterday's successful banality can lose both its appeal and meaning in the eyes of the large audience for which it was devised. This makes for the paradox that older forms of kitsch (as expressions of bad taste) may still be enjoyed, but only by the sophisticated: what was originally meant to be "popular" becomes the amusement of the few. Old kitsch may stimulate the ironical consciousness of the refined or of those who pretend to be refined. This is possibly an explanation of the attempt to redeem some of the outrageously affected and artificial kitsch of *la belle époque* in what is called "camp" in today's America.

Concerning literature, we can mention the interest in older forms of bad writing. Thus, for instance, in his already mentioned essay on "Kitsch," Gilbert Highet professes a high admiration (evidently ironical) for the poetic gems of the nineteenth-century Scottish poet, William McGonagall, whom he considers, quoting from the *Times Literary Supplement*, "the only truly memorable bad poet in our language." Along the same lines is the Wyndham Lewis and Charles Lee anthology, *The Stuffed Owl: An Anthology of Bad Verse* (1930), which limits itself, however, to what its compilers call "good Bad Verse."[33] A more recent example of the same kind of interest is Walther Killy's essay on literary kitsch, supplemented with numerous examples anthologized according to thematic criteria.[34] It is clear that such books are not meant for mass consumption but for the intellectual amusement of a literary elite.

If we think of kitsch as the "style" of bad taste, we arrive at another paradox, much deeper and more puzzling than the one just pointed out, namely, the earlier mentioned possibility of consciously using bad taste (i.e., kitsch) in order to subvert the conventions of a "good taste" that eventually leads to the sclerosis of academicism. Baudelaire, who is rightfully regarded as a precursor of aesthetic avant-gardism, had such a possibility in mind when he wrote in *Fusées* about the intoxicating effect of bad taste, derived from "the aristocratic pleasure of displeasing." Avant-garde movements have often indulged in such kinds of pleasure, satisfying their antiartistic urge by outrageously using kitsch mannerisms both in literature and the arts.[35] Even if we accept Clement Greenberg's view that avant-gardism is radically opposed to kitsch,[36] we have to realize that these two extremes are strongly attracted by one another, and what separates them is sometimes much less striking than what unites them. This is so for two reasons, which have been indicated before in other contexts: (1) the avant-garde is interested in kitsch for aesthetically subversive and ironical purposes, and (2) kitsch may use avant-garde procedures (which are easily transformed into stereotypes) for its aesthetically conformist purposes. The latter situation is another illustration of the old story of the "system" (read kitsch) co-opting its challengers (the avant-garde). The relationship between kitsch and the avant-garde may in a sense be taken as a caricature of the central principle of modernity: Octavio Paz's "tradition against itself." A good example in point is Marcel Duchamp's treatment of Leonardo da Vinci's Mona Lisa, the masterpiece that has probably been the most overworked by kitsch. Everybody knows that some time in 1919, while in New York, Duchamp took a reproduction of the Mona Lisa and, after drawing on moustaches and goatee, entitled it enigmatically "L.H.O.O.Q." (which spelled out loud in French gives the obscenity: "Elle a chaud au cul"). "L.H.O.O.Q." is an example of what Duchamp used to call a "ready-made assisted," as distinct from a straight "ready-made" like the famous urinal that he entered in a 1917 New York art exhibition under the poetic title *Fountain*. Many critics see the artist's aggressive treatment of the Renaissance masterpiece as a humorous case of avant-garde iconoclasm. What Duchamp had in mind, however, was probably different. The Gioconda he abused was not the masterpiece but a *reproduction*, an instance of the modern falsification of tradition. Duchamp would have probably agreed with Adorno's view (expressed in the *Philosophy of Modern Music* and elsewhere) that, in the modern world, tradition has become false, and that there is virtually no tradition that has not been falsified. So Duchamp insulted merely a kitsch object, meant to satisfy a typical form of cultural *Bovarysme*—one of those countless images of the Mona Lisa with which we have been flooded for decades. And I would add that it is not at all certain whether in proceeding as he did, the artist was attacking da Vinci's original painting or whether, on the contrary, he did not try secretly, as I personally believe, to vindicate it. One thing is clear, however; namely that Duchamp resorted to kitsch not only to reject certain crass aesthetic misconceptions and jaded conventions but also to advocate the avant-garde drive toward the abandonment of an aesthetics based on *appearances*, which, in our time, are so easily falsified. But in spite of its efforts, the avant-garde was unable to go beyond appearances and, ironically, certain more advanced representatives of kitsch were not long in realizing that they could profitably use the successful unconventionalities of older avant-garde movements. Duchamp himself was largely kitschified by Andy Warhol.

KITSCH AND CULTURAL INDUSTRIALIZATION

A substantial factor in the "kitschification" of culture—almost all those who have written on the subject agree—is mass diffusion of art through the diverse media: radio, TV, large-scale reproduction, records, cheap magazines and paperbacks sold in supermarkets, etc. This can be so even when the initial elements used (masterpieces of painting or of sculpture, novels turned into film-scripts) are decidedly *not* kitsch.

It is evident that, psychologically, the mass media induce a state of passiveness in the typical onlooker: one simply turns on the TV and is flooded with an indefinite number of technically "predigested" images (which do not require any effort to understand). And, as we shall see, passiveness, combined with superficiality, are important prerequisites of that state of mind that fosters kitsch.

Dorfles sums up the widespread argument that the mass media are almost exclusively designed for a mindless, hedonistic use of spare time: "All trace of a 'rite' in the handing out of cultural and aesthetic nourishment by the mass media . . . has been lost, and this lack of the ritual element has brought about an indifference in the onlooker when he is faced with the different kinds of transmissions and manifestations which are forced upon him."[37]

The media, Macdonald points out, contribute directly to the advent of a perfectly "homogenized culture," as processed and even as "homogenized milk." This homogenization is reflected in the phenomenon that distinctions of age and of intellectual and social status tend to become irrelevant. A largely unified audience has emerged, whose tastes and emotional needs are skillfully manipulated by the technicians of mass culture. This situation has been aptly described by Macdonald as a "merging of the child and grown-up audience," meaning: "(1) infantile regression of the latter, who, unable to cope with the strains and complexities of modern life, escape via *kitsch* (which, in turn, confirms and enhances their infantilism); (2) 'over-stimulation' of the former, who grow up too fast."[38] Let me add that the type of artistic experience provided by the media becomes eventually a norm for all artistic experience in the eyes of the conditioned consumer of our time. Literature is also supposed to fit into that pattern, so that gifted writers, in order not to lose their readers, resort to pop techniques and try to become best-selling authors.

From an antielitist point of view this is a happy thing. A critic like Leslie Fiedler, who has recently become impatient "with all distinctions of kind created on the analogy of class-structured society," is candidly proud of his growing interest in "the kind of books no one has ever congratulated himself on being able to read: books which join together all possible audiences, children and adults, women and men, the sophisticated and the naive.... I am convinced that criticism at the moment can no longer condescend to popular literature...."[39]

To consider the easygoing and overly sentimental world of pop culture free from any association with the class-structured society is naïve, and neither changes the predominantly kitsch nature of pop nor reduces the heavy dependence of pop on the contemporary consumer civilization with its culture industry. This specialized industry not only adapts itself to fluctuating demands but is able to predict and to some extent create new fads: from its point of view, deviance, nonconformism, and radicalism can be readily transformed into marketable items of consumption. The life style of the counterculture has become big business, from records and jeans to psychedelic posters.

The tendency toward massification affects all the arts, but more directly the visual arts. All mechanical reproduction of paintings and sculptures, in quantities limited only by market demand, definitely makes for kitsch. I will not discuss here the degree to which uniqueness accounts for the aesthetic value of a painting or sculpture. Nor will I argue about the imperfect quality of reproductions; one day, we may assume, perfection or near-perfection will be achieved. But even then the problem of the legitimacy of large-scale reproduction will still remain. Kitsch is not, however, the immediate and automatic result of the process of reproduction.

To determine whether an object is kitsch always involves considerations of purpose and context. In theory, there should be nothing kitschy about the use of a reproduction or slide even of the Mona Lisa, in a study of art history. But the same image reproduced on a plate, a table cloth, a towel, or an eyeglass case will be unmistakable kitsch. A number of excellent reproductions of the same painting put beside each other in a shop window will have a kitsch effect because they suggest availability in commercial quantities. The mere consciousness of the industrial multiplication of an art object for purely commercial reasons can kitschify its image.

If we acknowledge that kitsch is the "normal" art of our time, we have to recognize that it is the obligatory starting point of any aesthetic experience. Consider the paradise of kitsch in which most modern children are immersed. In the Disneyland of childhood, aesthetic sensitivity is almost entirely subsumed under the comprehensive category of the *cute*. The infantile taste for cute things by itself has nothing to do with kitsch, because the general "law of aesthetic inadequacy" obviously does not apply to it. However, kitsch readily exploits this taste, and not only in children but also in numerous adults whose understanding of art has not gone too far beyond the level of childhood. If kitsch thrives on aesthetic infantilism, it is only fair to say that it also offers pedagogical possibilities, including the important realization that there is a difference between kitsch or pseudoart and art. Why then should we not accept the paradox proposed by Abraham Moles, namely, that the simplest and most natural way toward "good taste" passes through bad taste? Moles writes specifically:

> The pedagogical function of kitsch has been generally neglected because of the innumerable bad connotations of the term and also because of the instinctive tendency of the writers on this subject to overrate their own aesthetic judgment. In a bourgeois society, and generally in a meritocratic one, the passage through kitsch is the *normal passage* in order to reach the genuine. . . . Kitsch is pleasurable to the members of mass society, and through pleasure, it allows them to attain the level of higher exigencies and to pass from sentimentality to sensation. The relationship between art and kitsch is therefore particularly ambiguous. . . . Kitsch is essentially an aesthetic system of mass communication.[40]

Such a measured approach is somewhat reassuring, especially if we consider it in the context of the dark, Cassandra-like predictions of most students of kitsch.

THE "KITSCH-MAN"

As I have pointed out earlier, the phenomenon of kitsch cannot be adequately understood if the role of the consumer of fake art is disregarded. This requires us to discuss the intricate problem of what has been called the "kitsch-man." We note that authors with widely different backgrounds like Hermann Broch, Ludwig Giesz (a representative of phenomenology), Gillo Dorfles (an aesthetician and art historian), Richard Egenter (a Roman Catholic theologian), and others, have devoted much attention to the concept of the "kitsch-man." A kitsch-man, to put it bluntly, is one who tends to experience as kitsch even nonkitsch works or situations, one who involuntarily makes a parody of aesthetic response. In the tourist's role, for instance, the kitsch man will "kitschify" not only cultural monuments but also landscapes, and especially great sights, such as the Grand Canyon, which are advertised as wonders or freaks of nature. What characterizes the kitsch-man is his inadequately hedonistic idea of what is artistic or beautiful. For reasons that can be analyzed in historical, sociological, and cultural terms, the kitsch-man wants to fill his spare time with maximum excitement (derived from, among other things, "high culture") in exchange for minimum effort. For him the ideal is effortless enjoyment.

The notion of a kitsch-man becomes clear if we think of him not only in aesthetic but also in ethical terms. This combined approach, whatever its theoretical difficulties, is almost unavoidable because the aesthetic attitudes of the kitsch-man—and of the kitsch-artist as well—imply a basic moral ineptitude. Hermann Broch makes a valid point: "The kitsch system requires its followers to 'work beautifully,' while the art system issues the moral order: 'Work well!' Kitsch is the element of evil in the value system of art."[41]

This element of evil can be identified in the fundamental characteristic of kitsch, that of lying (for the equation of kitsch = "aesthetic lie" see Umberto Eco's remarkable essay "La struttura del cattivo gusto").[42] Seen as a lie, a kitsch work implies a close relationship and even a collaboration of sorts between the kitsch-artist and the kitsch-man. The latter wants to be "beautifully" lied to and the former is willing to play the game in exchange for financial gain. The responsibility is clearly shared by both. In this game of illusions and spurious impressions, the liar may end up believing that what he says is the truth. Quite often, the kitsch-artist may have no conscious intention of producing kitsch, although he should realize he is doing so, since he disregards the *inner validity* of his work (Broch's ethical injunction: "Work well!") and seeks only to reach a big consumer market.

The temptation to believe the aesthetic lies of kitsch is a sign of either undeveloped or largely atrophied critical sense. Mental passivity and spiritual laziness characterize the amazingly undemanding lover of kitsch. Theologically, then, Richard Egenter may be right when he identifies kitsch as the sin of "sloth." For the receiver of the artistic message, Egenter thinks, there is almost always

> an opening for sloth and mere pleasure seeking, which becomes dishonest when the pretext of an aesthetic response is maintained. . . . For from both artist and beholder, art . . . demands effort and seriousness; when this is not made, artistic activity becomes a flight from reality. It can become not only a bogus reflection of reality but an opening for the devil. Satan can present himself as an angel of light more strikingly, and much more easily, in an artistic symbol than in a scientific concept.[43]

Let us observe, however, that earnest effort and seriousness by themselves are not guarantees against kitsch (the opposite is frequently true), and waggishness, irony, and self-irony can often have a salutary value. Historically speaking, the modernist reaction against romanticism has more than once taken the extreme form of levity and unseriousness, recasting in a new mold the conception of art as play. Some fine modernist poetry (e.e. cummings is a suggestive example) has resulted precisely from such a stance. At all events, seriousness and effort cannot offer a key to the problem. The fact is that, as always, genuine art does not lend itself to comfortable generalizations.

To speak of kitsch and the devil does not necessarily imply a specialized theological approach. The view that the devil is mainly a symbolic embodiment of mediocrity and even stupidity, widespread in Russian literature since Gogol (and reinforced by writers with such widely different world views as Dostoevsky, Andreev, or Sologub) is suggestively summarized in Nabokov's theory of *poshlust*. As I have pointed out earlier in this chapter, *poshlust* as conceived by Nabokov is a nearly perfect synonym for kitsch. With this terminological equivalence in mind, we can profitably meditate on the following passage in which Nabokov brings together Chichikov, the main character of Gogol's *Dead Souls,* the Devil, and *poshlust*. Nabokov writes:

> Chichikov himself is merely the ill-paid representative of the Devil, a traveling salesman from Hades, "our Mr. Chichikov" as the Satan and Co. firm may be imagined calling their easy-going, healthy-looking but inwardly shivering and rotting agent. The *poshlust* which Chichikov personifies is one of the main attributes of the Devil, in whose existence, let it be added, Gogol believed far more seriously than in that of God. The chink in Chichikov's armor, that rusty chink emitting a faint but dreadful smell (a punctured can of conserved lobster tampered with and forgotten by some meddling fool in the pantry) is the organic aperture in the devil's armor. It is the essential stupidity of *poshlust*. (pp. 73–74)

Nabokov's olfactory parenthesis provides us with one of the closest approximations of what kitsch really smells like—really or ideally, these opposites dialectically coincide here. Rotten conserved lobster is indeed an apt suggestion of the bad odor of bad taste.

In conclusion, there is unfortunately no single definition of kitsch that is entirely satisfactory. However, we can come close to an understanding of the phenomenon by combining (1) the *historico-sociological* approach, in which kitsch, as we use it, is typically modern and as such closely linked to cultural industrialization, commercialism, and increasing leisure in society, and (2) the *aesthetic-moral* approach, in which kitsch is false art, the production on a smaller or larger scale of various forms of "aesthetic lies." A crowd-pleasing art, often devised for mass consumption, kitsch is meant to offer instant satisfaction of the most superficial aesthetic needs or whims of a wide public. Basically, the world of kitsch is a world of aesthetic make-believe and self-deception. As earlier indicated, the dangers of kitsch should not be exaggerated. Offering "duplicates" of almost every known art form, kitsch suggests (sometimes with more accuracy than we would like to believe) the way toward the originals. After all, in today's world no one is safe from kitsch, which appears as a necessary step on the path toward an ever elusive goal of fully authentic aesthetic experience. After seeing many reproduced or fake Rembrandts, a viewer may ultimately be receptive to the experience of coming upon the real painting of a Dutch master. He may finally become aware that art, even when exploited, misunderstood, and misused, does not lose its value and aesthetic truth. In an unexpected manner, this failure of kitsch illustrates reassuringly the old comic motifs of the deceiver who is deceived and the fool who realizes his foolishness and becomes wise.

ON POSTMODERNISM (1986)

A NEW FACE OF MODERNITY

If we accept that there are, as I proposed in the first chapter of this book, two conflicting and interdependent modernities—one socially progressive, rationalistic, competitive, technological; the other culturally critical and self-critical, bent on demystifying the basic values of the first—we are better prepared to understand the often annoying ambivalences and paradoxes linked to the language of modernity. Literary modernism, to take one quick example, is thus both modern and antimodern: modern in its commitment to innovation, in its rejection of the authority of tradition, in its experimentalism; antimodern in its dismissal of the dogma of progress, in its critique of rationality, in its sense that modern civilization has brought about the loss of something precious, the dissolution of a great integrative paradigm, the fragmentation of what once was a mighty unity. To go beyond the all-too-obvious conceptual difficulties raised by the vocabulary of modernity, I have spoken metaphorically of the "faces" of a constitutively double—dual, ambiguous, and duplicitous—modernity.

Hence the new question: Has the notion of postmodernism developed, over the last decade or so, enough distinctive features to make a "cultural physiognomist" regard it as a full-fledged "face of modernity," on a par with modernism, decadence, the avant-garde, or kitsch? Clearly this is a rhetorical question, since the very fact of adding to *Faces of Modernity* this new chapter on postmodernism implies a positive answer. But, on the other hand, this implicit "yes, postmodernism is a new face of modernity" can only remain vague, tentative, and in fact meaningless, until its pros and cons are examined at closer range, properly qualified and modulated. If postmodernism has indeed formed a cultural physiognomy of its own, one should be able to describe it clearly and persuasively, a job that is by no means easy, given the great semantic inflation (or even "hyper-inflation") of the contexts in which the term often appears.

By itself, the increased circulation of the word postmodernism—which nowadays one routinely encounters in the cultural section of newspapers and magazines—proves little if anything. Actually, the more obvious consequence of such loose widespread use has been to enhance the dubious "aura" surrounding postmodernism from early on, an aura that has continued to inspire passionate attacks, not only on the soundness of the concept, but also on the artistic and moral legitimacy of what it purportedly stands for. Gerald Graff has thus denounced literary postmodernism as one of the central myths of the counterculture, intended to authorize an anti-intellectual cele-bration of brute vital energy and an ethos of mindless hedonism.[1] More recently, Charles Newman has assailed the postmodern men-tality even more sweepingly, looking beyond literature into the social and economic factors that account for its destructive appeal.[2]

Polemical sorties of this kind are also a form of (negative) recog-nition and, by a perverse effect, they can contribute to the success of that which they indignantly reject. Popular success, however, does not translate into intellectual credibility. Postmodernism's most powerful enemy has remained the skeptical suspicion with which it is still regarded by a significant segment of the intel-ligentsia. Many fine critics of contemporary literature simply cannot bring themselves to take postmodernism seriously. Typically, they will ignore it, shrug it off, or, as the case may be, make fun of it. Thus, when writing about John Ashbery—a poet who has been so insistently associated with postmodernism—a witty traditionalist like Claude Rawson will try to deflate the notion by suggesting that it is little more than a code for the kind of bizarre childish games that "postpeople" like to play.[3]

But beyond literary criticism, there are increasingly numerous thinkers and scholars in a variety of areas (including philosophy, the history and philosophy of science, and sociology) who believe that modernity has come to an end or is undergoing a deep identity crisis. There is of course little agreement as to what precisely might constitute postmodernism, and even less as to whether the notion itself has any legitimacy. But the mere emergence of this issue—or, better, of this new framework for asking questions about modernity, its modes, and its possible demise—confronts us with a major and puzzling cultural phenomenon. Who, on the basis of the early history of the term *postmodernism,* would have imagined that its career was to go that far?

What we learn from this history is that the early American users of postmodernism, poets such as Randall Jarrell, John Berryman, or, in a more vaticinatory style, Charles Olson, gave the word a certain limited currency in the discussion of the "new poetry" of the late 1940s and the 1950s. Jarrell was perhaps the first American to speak of postmodernism when, in 1946, he characterized the poetry of Robert Lowell as "post- or anti-modernist, and as such certain to be influential."[4] It is quite possible that Jarrell coined the term independently from the British historian Arnold Toynbee, who at about the same time (ventriloquizing through his summarizer, D. C. Somervell)[5] announced to a large reading public a new age of Western history, calling it "Post-Modern" and suggesting that it might be the last.

Toynbee had a great impact on post-World War II intellectual life in the West, but his notion of a postmodern age was not taken up by fellow philosophers of history, nor by other scholars in the social and historical disciplines. Its appeal seemed limited to poets, artists, and literary critics, who often reinterpreted it as applying to the immediate postwar period, ignoring that for Toynbee the beginnings of the postmodern age went back to the mid-1870s. World War II, with its unprecedented savageness and destruction, with its revelation of the brutality at the core of high technological civilization, could appear as the culmination of a demonic modernity, a modernity that had finally been overcome. Thus, some of the more innovative postwar American poets (the aftermath of the war being less somber on this side of the Atlantic than it was in ruined Europe) freed the postmodern notion from the pessimistic anxieties attached to it by Toynbee and hailed the new age as an exalted time in which poetic activity could be defined, according to Charles Olson, as a broadly symbolic "archaeology of morning."[6]

Such an optimistic-apocalyptic interpretation of the term post-modern made it fit to receive a prominent place in the revolutionary rhetoric of the 1960s. Evil modernity was dead and its funeral was a time for wild celebration. The modest prefix "post" became almost overnight a highly honorific modifier in the shibboleth of liberation. The mere fact of "coming after" was an exhilarating privilege, democratically accorded to anybody who wanted to claim it; everything worthwhile started with "post"—post-modern, post-historic, post-human, etc.[7] In the 1960s the fate of postmodernism seemed to have been indissolubly linked to the fate of the counterculture, with its numerous, often contradictory, crosscurrents of anarchism, antinomianism, and a "new gnosis."[8]

Surprisingly, however, postmodernism did not fade away with the radical fervor of that decade. It was in fact during the calmer 1970s and 1980s that postmodernism became a more plausible term in literary and art criticism, and above all in architecture criticism. It was also during these decades that it became acclimatized, to a larger or lesser degree, in other historical-theoretical disciplines, ranging from epistemology to the social sciences. In this process the term, which at the beginning had been used almost exclusively in America, established itself internationally.[9] Furthermore, and this is perhaps more significant, the notion of the postmodern reasserted the initial *philosophical-historical* thrust it had had in Toynbee's periodization.

Before discussing in more detail the artistic aspects of the quarrel between the moderns and the postmoderns, I think that a summary presentation of the main theoretical frameworks in which postmodernism has been (re)conceptualized in recent years might provide us with a useful background. There are two areas in which the concept of postmodernism has appeared more or less insistently since the publication of *Faces of Modernity.* The first is broadly philosophical, including problems of epistemology, the history and philosophy of science, and hermeneutics. The second refers to the notions of modernism and the avant-garde in twentieth-century culture and their possible exhaustion. The analogies among the kinds of questions being asked in the two areas are very interesting, although they do not warrant, I think, any larger hypothesis of a postmodern epistemic structure or cast of mind or *Weltanschauung*. The uses of postmodernism in these two areas do present, however, a "family resemblance" of sorts, and looking at them more closely may help us in our attempt to identify postmodernism, as it were, "physiognomically."

EPISTEMOLOGY AND HERMENEUTICS:
FROM MODERNITY TO POSTMODERNITY

The more comprehensive presentations of the issues of post-modernism sometimes include references to epistemological problems and concepts, such as the crisis of determinism, the place of chance and disorder in natural processes, Heisenberg's principle of indeterminacy, the question of time and particularly irreversible time (whose recognition has displaced the powerful classical clockwork model of the universe), Karl Popper's view of scientific theories in terms of "falsifiability" rather than mere "verifiability," and Thomas Kuhn's "paradigms" and "scientific revolutions." That such ideas can easily be misunderstood and distorted by literary critics and artists goes without saying. Even so, the critics' new interest in theoretical-epistemological issues comes from a real sense that important changes have occurred in the ways science views itself and the legitimacy of its procedures of inference. And this interest is enhanced by a belief that such changes in scientific paradigms cannot be without analogies on the level of artistic consciousness. Significantly, this belief seems to receive recognition or encouragement when a philosopher of science, borrowing the controversial cultural label postmodernism, will speak of a "postmodern science" almost as of a matter of course.[10] But even a more cautious position, like the one taken by Ilya Prigogine and Isabelle Stengers when they elaborate their distinction between a "modern science" and a "new science," can be quite relevant to the larger debate about postmodernism.

To Prigogine and Stengers, authors of *Order out of Chaos*, modern science, enormously creative though it was, showed a bias against two concepts whose full significance has been recognized only by what they call "the new science": irreversible time (the so-called Arrow of Time) and chance. The bias against irreversible time (we recall Einstein's resistance to the introduction of irreversibility in theoretical physics) was mainly due to modern science's effort to discover the eternal laws of matter. For similar reasons chance was viewed negatively, as an obstacle to man's full mastery of the natural laws: chance did not really exist, it was the result of our ignorance, as Laplace implied when he formulated the famous fiction of his omniscient "demon"; chance was ultimately a reflection of the limitations of our intelligence. Characteristically, Einstein said, "God doesn't play dice." Even in modern biology, where the recognition of the role of chance had rendered the theory of natural selection possible, a major figure like Jacques Monod, for example, could not help drawing a philosophically pessimistic conclusion from the existence of randomness. Monod strikes an almost Pascalian note (as Prigogine and Stengers point out) when he writes: "Man knows at last that he is alone in the universe's indifferent immensity out of which he emerged only by chance."[11]

What Prigogine and Stengers set out to do in their book is to show that the new science has actually rebutted the largely negative (and occasionally tragic) views of irreversibility and chance upheld by many modern scientists. Historically, the deterministic mechanical model of the universe and the negative approach to chance contributed to the modern scientific "disenchantment of the world." But now is the time, Prigogine and Stengers believe, to reverse this situation. The new science reappraises the role of irreversibility and chance and promises a full "reenchantment" of the world.

Is this vision overly optimistic or exalted? Be that as it may, Prigogine and Stengers appear to represent a larger trend in today's history and philosophy of science, a trend that consists of accepting that the basic assumptions of scientific theories are in constant need of being discussed, criticized, and reassessed in light of their productivity or creativity. The crisis of the deterministic concept of truth has thus opened new horizons to scientific thought and research. How does order arise from disorder? This is a question that only the new science is capable of addressing fully. Recapitulating the central theme of their book, Prigogine and Stengers write in the concluding chapter: "One of the main sources of fascination in modern science was precisely the feeling that it had discovered eternal laws at the core of nature's transformations and thus had exorcised time and becoming. . . . A new unity is emerging: irreversibility is a source of order at all levels. Irreversibility is the mechanism that brings order out of chaos."[12]

Epistemology as such, even when fully conscious of the historical variations of knowledge, tends to reach beyond history: it normally takes the transhistorical implications or claims of theory seriously. At any rate, its central questions are rarely of a direct historical nature. This may explain why period concepts (such as postmodernism) are seldom used in epistemology. The situation is different in hermeneutics, both in the traditional variety and in the new philosophical hermeneutics, with its deep historical self-consciousness. Acknowledging the great relevance of philosophical hermeneutics to contemporary thought in general, the philosopher Richard Rorty has gone so far as to argue that once traditional epistemology's ahistorical assumptions are proven to have no real "foundations," and therefore to be untenable, epistemology itself has no choice but to become a form of hermeneutics.[13] Whether we accept such a view or not, the notion of hermeneutics in this sense goes back to Nietzsche's critique of both idealism and positivism (we recall his famous dictum that "facts are interpretations") and to Heidegger's radical historicism. The term *hermeneutics* owes its present-day philosophical vogue indirectly to Heidegger and directly to Heidegger's influential disciple, Hans-Georg Gadamer. Neither Heidegger nor Gadamer uses the term *postmodern*, but many of the current philosophical discussions of postmodernity refer to their thought as a source and frequently go back to Nietzsche, whose impact on Heidegger is well known. Little wonder then that, in the United States and elsewhere, Heidegger is occasionally seen as the "first postmodern."[14] To illustrate this position, I will briefly mention the Italian philosopher Gianni Vattimo, who, through his commentaries on Nietzsche and Heidegger, has initiated a lively debate on the "end of modernity" in Italy. Philosophically, according to Vattimo, the end of modernity brings about the emergence of "il pensiero debole" or "weak thought," a typically postmodern mode of reflection that is in direct opposition to "metaphysics" or "strong thought" (a thought that is domineering, imposing, universalistic, atemporal, aggressively self-centered, intolerant in regard to whatever appears to contradict it, etc.).

The strong thought/weak thought opposition, far from being only theoretical, has axiological, practical, and even directly political implications. In a characteristic recent piece (reprinted as the preface to *Al di là del soggetto*), Vattimo makes it clear that a "strong" modern theory of revolution (such as the Marxist one) will always imply some "violent labor of homogenization and universalization"; he stresses that, more generally, "the pretension of having a relation to values that is not governed by memory, nostalgia, supplication, is a demonic pretension."[15] Central to Vattimo's conceptualization of weak thought are the Heideggerian notions of *Andenken* ("recollecting" or "rethinking") and *Verwindung* (different from the more frequent *Uberwindung* or "overcoming" and translatable by such words as "healing," "convalescence," "resignation," or "acceptance"). Another key term is *pietas*, the sign under which the ethics of weak thought will organize itself. The most adequate expression of weak thought is the "right" hermeneutical attitude in which, as Gadamer suggests in *Truth and Methods*, the interpreter practices, as it were, a methodical weakness (made up of attentiveness and compliance to the inner demands of the object of interpretation, respect for its essential fragility, willingness to listen to what it says before questioning it, and renewed efforts not to impose on it one's own "rationality" or convictions).

Of the many aspects of the philosophical discussion of modernity and postmodernity, I will focus here on just one. I have selected it because it has been responsible for an interesting ongoing polemic, which was started in 1980 when Jürgen Habermas, on being awarded the T. W. Adorno prize of the city of Frankfurt, delivered a speech on "Die Moderne: Ein unvollendetes Projekt," translated into English as "Modernity versus Postmodernity." In this speech the neo-Marxist Habermas identifies the notion of postmodernity with the (neo)conservative position of those who believe that modernity has failed and that the utopian impulses it gave rise to should therefore be suppressed. But modernity or the "project of the Enlightenment," Habermas argues from the standpoint of his own emancipatory philosophy, is not a failed project, only an unfinished one. What should be rejected is not modernity, whose critical heritage as reappraised by the Frankfurt School of Adorno, Horkheimer, or Benjamin is still a source of "emulation for the intellectual";[16] what should be rejected is the (neo)conservative ideology of postmodernity.

What actually triggered the polemic was Habermas's attack on French "poststructuralism," defined as a conservative rejection of modernity and its central values of rationality and universality. By suggesting that Michel Foucault and Jacques Derrida are profoundly akin to the group of thinkers known during the Weimar Republic as the *Jungkonservativen* (Young Conservatives),[17] Habermas wanted to stress their common descent not only from Heidegger but ultimately from the most antimodern of modern philosophers, Friedrich Nietzsche.[18] Although not named in the Adorno Prize speech, a third Frenchman, Jean-François Lyotard, was probably the main target of Habermas's criticism.

Both implicitly and explicitly, Lyotard's *La Condition postmoderne* (1979) had challenged Habermas's philosophy of modernity.[19] Explicitly, while using Habermas's approach to knowledge in terms of legitimation, Lyotard had summarily rejected his notion of *Diskurs* or rational consensus, proposing rather fatuously that once modernity disintegrates, the cardinal value of the new postmodern consciousness becomes dissent—dissent as a guiding principle or dissent for the mere sake of dissent. But Lyotard's implicit challenge to Habermas's doctrine of modernity had been the more important one. It took the form of an argument about the lack of credibility of the universalist conceptions, or the great ideological fairy tales, from which the modern project itself had ultimately been derived. Essentially, Lyotard explains in *The Postmodern Condition* and, more recently, in *Le Postmoderne expliqué aux enfants* (1986), there are two kinds of "great stories" (*grands récits*) or "metanarratives" (*métarécits*) that have served to legitimize knowledge in the past or, put differently, to give a convincing answer to the question: What is knowledge ultimately good for? The first kind is mythical (traditional) and the second projective (modern). In traditional cultures, as religious anthropology shows, knowledge is legitimized in reference to the origins, to the primordial time when things came into being. Unlike myths, the metanarratives characteristic of modernity legitimize knowledge in terms not of the past but the future.[20]

What Lyotard's various metanarratives of modernity have in common is the notion of a universal finality. However different, the modern projects are all premised on a finalistic vision of universal history, and in this sense Christianity (as the story of humanity's final redemption from the original Adamic sin) is constitutively modern. All the major "stories of emancipation" of modernity are essentially secularized variations on the Christian paradigm: the Enlightenment metanarrative of progress through knowledge, by which humanity will be emancipated from evil ignorance; the speculative Hegelian story of the emancipation of mind or "Geist" from self-alienation through dialectics; the Marxist story of man's emancipation from exploitation through the revolutionary struggle of the proletariat; and the capitalist story of humanity's emancipation from poverty through the market, that is, through the intervention of Adam Smith's "Invisible Hand," which creates a universal harmony from countless conflicting self-interests.[21] But such modern (ideological) metanarratives have lost their credibility. Universalism has been displaced and the great stories of modernity (which I would call versions of a modern "epistemological theodicy") are disintegrating under our eyes and give way to a multitude of heterogeneous and local "petites histoires," often of a highly paradoxical and paralogical nature. Under such circumstances, Habermas's *Diskurs* can be no more than a lingering illusion.

The meanderings and details of the polemic between Habermas and Lyotard do not interest us here. Its main arguments and counterarguments have been lucidly summarized, from the liberal-pragmatist perspective of a disciple of John Dewey, by Richard Rorty.[22] The purpose of my brief reference to the Habermas/Lyotard/Rorty dispute has been simply to indicate some of the currents of contemporary thought (hermeneutics, neo-Marxism, French "poststructuralism," etc.) in which the concept of postmodernism has figured, positively or negatively, during the last decade or so.

THE SILENCE OF THE AVANT-GARDE

The term postmodernism has enjoyed a more obvious popularity in the discussion of the avant-garde in contemporary art. Typically, the avant-garde, as the experimental cutting edge of modernity, has historically given itself a double task: to destroy and to invent. But negation certainly is the most significant moment in the twofold logic of radical innovation: it is the old, the institutionalized past, the Library and the Museum, that must be effectively rejected, demystified, torn down; the new—unanticipated, radiant, abrupt—will follow by itself.

In postmodernism, it has been observed, it is precisely this purely destructive aspect of the old avant-garde that comes under question. What could justify so much ruthless devastation? Is this the price to be paid for access to the new? But the new, a relative value, not an absolute one, cannot be worth such a steep, exorbitant price. Abandoning the strictures of the avant-garde and opting for a logic of renovation rather than radical innovation, postmodernism has entered into a lively reconstructive dialogue with the old and the past.[23]

Umberto Eco exemplifies this understanding of postmodernism as a reaction to the ultimate "silence" or unavoidable sterility of the avant-garde. Even though he refuses a simply chronological definition of postmodernism (for him the term is rather "an ideal category—or, better still, a *Kunstwollen,* a way of operating"), Eco properly stresses the historical link between the exhaustion of the furiously antitraditional avant-garde and the emergence of the postmodern willingness to *revisit* the past. In his account of how he composed his medieval mystery and freakish best-seller *The Name of the Rose*—an account that may be seen as an ironic postmodern rewriting of "The Philosophy of Composition," Edgar Allan Poe's famous step-by-step logical explanation of how he had conceived his romantic poem "The Raven"—Umberto Eco points out:

> The historic avant-garde . . . tries to settle scores with the past. "Down with moonlight"—a futurist slogan—is a platform typical of every avant-garde; you have only to replace "moonlight" with whatever noun is suitable. The avant-garde destroys, defaces the past: *Les Demoiselles d'Avignon* is a typical avant-garde act. Then the avant-garde goes further, destroys the figure, cancels it, arrives at the abstract, the informal, the white canvas, the slashed canvas, the charred canvas. In architecture and the visual arts, it will be the curtain wall, the building as stele, pure parallelipiped, minimal art; in literature, the destruction of the flow of discourse, the Burroughs-like collage, silence, the white page; in music, the passage from atonality to noise to absolute silence (in this sense, the early Cage is

modern). But the moment comes when the avant-garde (the modern) can go no further. . . . The postmodern reply . . . consists of recognizing that the past, since it cannot really be destroyed, because its destruction leads to silence, must be revisited: but with irony, not innocently.[24]

Eco is aware that this kind of argument (modernism has exhausted all its formal possibilities) had been advanced early on by such theorists of postmodernism as John Barth in his essay "The Literature of Exhaustion" (1967).[25] The new element in Eco's treatment of the problem is his insistence that the postmodernist rediscovery of the past or of the "already said" cannot be innocent and that this lack of innocence must be fully acknowledged. Irony, playfulness, parodic and self-parodic nostalgia are some of the ways of doing so.

But there is a larger moral and aesthetic sense in which postmodernism's loss of innocence goes beyond "the already said" to relate to the darker, savage, unspeakable side of a modernity that culminated in the genocidal policies of Stalin or Hitler. Particularly for the Europeans, the monstrous consequences of modern utopianism (in the Soviet Union) or of countermodern tribalism (in the Third Reich in Germany) cannot and should not be ignored. Thus, many of the artists whom Guy Scarpetta regards as postmodern (Hermann Broch, Samuel Beckett, Milan Kundera, and Pier Paolo Pasolini among them) variously try to come to terms with the debacle of modernity and its tragic legacy. In *L'Impureté*, in which he sets out to to define the essential "impurity" of postmodernist aesthetics, in contrast to the urge for "purity" of the modernists, Scarpetta notes that the old avant-garde often practiced a rhetoric of "the death of art." But this rhetoric was an optimistic one: art was proclaimed (symbolically) dead only as a first step in the avant-garde's thaumaturgic project for resuscitating it in a purer form. The activity of the postmoderns, according to Scarpetta, takes place in a changed, "post-apocalyptic" framework: "The question is to create within the horizon of this death [of art], within the hypothesis that this death is possible—to create even *from this death* (we find the idea already in Adorno: 'The notion of a culture resuscitated after Auschwitz is a pitfall and an absurdity,' which would mean that the only possible culture today is post-apocalyptic). All naiveté, all innocence in this regard would be totally anchronistic."[26]

Ten years ago, in *Faces of Modernity*, I treated postmodernism as a subcategory of the avant-garde, as basically a contemporary avatar of the old avant-garde. This was at a time when the term postmodernism was rarely used outside the United States. My view then was that the more important distinction was that between modernism and the avant-garde and, from a continental standpoint, I was critical of the Anglo-American tendency to collapse it and use the two labels as near-perfect synonyms. I still believe that the opposition between modernism and the avant-garde is defendable analytically in certain (historical) contexts, but on the whole it needs to be revised to accommodate the much sharper recent opposition between modernism (including the avant-garde) and postmodernism. Now that the Europeans, after the Americans, have come to see the avant-garde as an integral part of the modernist project, it is harder to argue that postmodernism is merely an extension of the old avant-garde. Postmodernism is, on the contrary, a departure from it. Would it then be possible to speak of postmodernism as a new "face" in a larger complex of several distinct faces with a strong family resemblance—modernity, in the circumstance, being simply the name of this resemblance?

I thus come to the question with which I started this essay. I think that a positive answer has gained a certain plausibility by now. The term *postmodernism* itself may not be a felicitous verbal coinage, particularly when one is fussy about etymologies: if modern comes from "modo," which in Latin means "just now" or "today," what sense does it make to say that a thing of today is not really of today, nor even of tomorrow, but, quite oddly, of "after-today"? One may also be irritated at the amount of confusion and arbitrariness that went into the making of a category that, as Umberto Eco has complained, is still "bon à tout faire." The fact remains, however, that postmodernism can be employed usefully and even interestingly, as some of the examples examined so far may already have suggested. Postmodernism, as I see it, is not a new name for a new "reality," or "mental structure," or "world view," but a perspective from which one can ask certain questions about modernity in its several incarnations. All period terms, as I have argued elsewhere, are (or should be) modes of historical questioning.[27] Within the lexicon of modernity, postmodernism appears to me as having an even more explicitly interrogative nature than other key terms. Or, to put it differently, among the faces of modernity postmodernism is perhaps the most quizzical: self-skeptical yet curious, unbelieving yet searching, benevolent yet ironic.

THE NOVELTY OF THE PAST:

THE VIEW FROM ARCHITECTURE

Early on in its career as a period term, as we saw, postmodernism was used to describe the cultural present of the Western world, a present that appeared to have distanced itself from the major "modern" currents of thought and imagination, as these had evolved since the Renaissance and the Reformation through the Enlightenment. But Arnold Toynbee's dichotomy between modern rationalism on the one hand, and an anarchic postmodern upsurge of irrationalism starting circa 1875 on the other, remained as misty as it was sweeping. The first American postmoderns were ultimately no less vague in their use of the vast new category. Postmodernism was, at that stage, not only "unfalsifiable" in Popperian terms (an arbitrary and hazy dogma rather than a properly hypothetical construct), but also plainly unfit to deal with questions of historical detail and nuance. A fuzzy all-purpose classifying concept, soon to be bandied around as a battle cry, postmodernism had little discriminating power or heuristic value and stayed that way until the later 1960s.

Among the literary critics who adopted this rather precarious notion, Ihab Hassan was the first to engage in a sustained effort to articulate the criteria of its usage. For Hassan, postmodernism, more than a literary movement, is "a social phenomenon, perhaps even a mutation in Western humanism." He asks: "Can we understand postmodernism in literature without some lineaments of a postmodern society, a Toynbeean postmodernity, or future Foucauldian *épistémè*, of which the literary tendency . . . is but a single, elitist strain?"[28] What is interesting here is that Hassan's question, formulated from an initially literary standpoint, is immediately broadened in a move that goes from the particular (postmodern literature) to the general (a postmodern "episteme" or "discursive formation" in the sense of Michel Foucault). What distinguishes Hassan from earlier literary users of the term is both his superior grasp of philosophical issues and his more lucid perception of the fine points of artistic analogy and contrast between modernism and postmodernism. We may not always agree with his insights into the "postmodern episteme" (which sometimes appear contradictory), we may quarrel with this or that example or formulation, and we may remain skeptical of his playful "paracritical" break-up of the critical text (what he calls his postmodern "politics of the page"), but, on the whole, we cannot help recognizing that his writings, especially since *The Dismemberment of Orpheus* (1971), constitute perhaps the single most impressive attempt to build a philosophical-literary concept of postmodernism in America. With Hassan, in short, postmodernism begins to have a more discernible identity, and it is through him that some Europeans (Lyotard for instance) may have discovered the term.

It was, however, not in connection with literature or philosophy that postmodernism was to receive its first more immediately convincing and influential definitions. As it turned out, the term had to wait for the discussion of trends in contemporary architecture to become intuitively graspable by larger numbers of people. Architecture, the most public of the visual arts, offered a more concrete (if finally no less controversial) basis for testing the claims made by theorists of postmodernism not only in architecture but in other areas as well. Metaphorically speaking, it was architecture that took the issues of postmodernism out of the clouds and down to earth to the realm of the visible.

What is architectural postmodernism? If we describe it as a reaction to modernism (which it obviously is), we must hasten to add that this is not merely a formal reaction but one that engages the whole avant-gardist philosophy underlying the modernist project since the days of the Bauhaus. What is at stake in the conflict is actually much less the modernist legacy as such (we shall soon see why) than the larger statements made by the functional beauty and intransigent purity of forms of architectural modernism: statements about their own necessity and universality, in light of which the legitimacy of all other forms was to be denied once and for all.

At first without making use of the term *postmodernism* (Robert Venturi[29]), later on subsuming in it various directions away from modernism (Charles Jencks,[30] Paolo Portoghesi,[31] and more recently Heinrich Klotz[32]), the supporters of architectural postmodernism have articulated a critique not only of the aesthetics of modernism but, more important, of its ideological assumptions. This critique, I think, should interest any student of contemporary culture. Here I can do no more than outline its main arguments and themes.

Historically, the modernist revolution started as a rejection of the highly ornate architecture that prevailed in Europe in the late nineteenth and early twentieth centuries. The very notion of the ornament was radically contested: as practiced in the so-called la Belle Epoque, the ornament revealed its true parasitic and antifunctional essence. What it symbolized was status-seeking, conspicuous consumption, and display. Decoration and, more generally, expression, the modernists thought, was socially and morally objectionable, intellectually indefensible, and aesthetically corrupt. It was, in a word, what today we would call upper- or middle-class kitsch. To such bad taste and bad faith, modernism opposed its ascetic, utopian, and rationalist aesthetic.

The modernist ideal of geometric and functional purity was clearly ideologically charged and, in this sense, the structures designed by the modernists were to be seen not only as things of beauty but also as anticipations of the radiant, universal city of the future, of the city as a symbol of a finally liberated and nonhierarchic society. The avant-gardist commitment to such a goal required, among other things, a refusal to look backwards to the various architectural traditions, all of which were supposed to carry connotations of authoritarian domination and irrational hierarchy. The old stylistic differences, whether horizontal (among similar communities in different areas or times) or vertical (attributable to class distinctions within the same community), were soon to dissolve anyway, the modernists thought. In short, their approach to urban planning was a radically rationalist *tabula rasa*. Over time, however, to quote Jencks, "the building of New Towns in Britain, or whole new cities like Chandigarh in India and Brasilia in Brazil . . . revealed a recurrent problem evident to architect, planner, and citizen alike: the new creation, however imaginative, was oversimplified and lacked the complexity of life and the continuity with the past that any old, bungled city, with all its faults, possessed."[33]

The postmodernist response to the utopian rigidities of the modernists was to call for a (modern) city with memory. This explains, in architecture and beyond, the emergence of a new historicism. The past began to be insistently revisited, not only as a storehouse of dead or obsolete forms that might be reused within a rationalist context, but also as a "dialogic" space of understanding and self-understanding, a space in which complicated problems had been inventively solved, in which recurrent questions had received diverse creative answers, and in which the challenges of "contradiction" and "complexity" (to use Venturi's favorite terms) had resulted in brilliant technical and aesthetic discoveries. Like other avant-gardes, architectural modernism had artificially "unified" tradition in order to justify its own unrelentingly negative attitude toward it.

The postmoderns have taken the opposite course, namely, that of de-unifying and de-simplifying our image of the past. Fundamentally pluralistic, the historicism of postmodern architecture reinterprets the past in a multiplicity of ways, going from the endearingly playful to the ironically nostalgic, and including such attitudes or moods as humorous irreverence, oblique homage, pious recollection, witty quotation, and paradoxical commentary.

If we accept the view that now modernism has itself become a thing of the past, we should not be surprised that the postmodernists do not treat it any differently (with more hostility or intolerance) than any other things of the past. While criticizing the universalist-utopian claims of modernism, the postmodernist architects are in no way rejecting its formal-stylistic legacy. As a matter of fact, faced with problems of size, capacity, and function encountered earlier in the century by the great modernists, the postmoderns will not hesitate to resort on occasion to some of their technical and aesthetic solutions. It would have been both impossible and unreasonable for them to ignore the modernist methods of construction, as Jencks emphasizes when he points to perhaps the outstanding feature of the postmodern style, double coding as opposed to modernist single coding. Jencks writes: "A Post-Modern building is doubly coded— part Modern and part something else: vernacular, revivalist, local, commercial, metaphorical, or contextual. . . . It is also double coded in the sense that it seeks to speak on two levels at once: to a concerned minority of architects, an elite who recognize the subtle distinctions of a fast-changing language, and to the inhabitants, users, or passersby, who want only to understand to enjoy it."[34]

It is clear even from this very fugitive summary that the broader themes of the modern/postmodern dispute discussed earlier in this chapter are suggestively paralleled in the quarrel of the architects. Thus, in regard to the question of hermeneutics, it is noteworthy that while modernism elaborated its program *more geometrico*, in rationalist and therefore antihermeneutical terms, postmodernism has adopted a more flexible, interpretive, and self-consciously "dialogic" attitude. Thinking of the Italian notion of a "weak thought," to which I briefly referred earlier, we might say that modernism argued from a position of logical certainty and "methodological strength," whereas postmodernism has always been aware of the advantages of a certain "methodological weakness": the "either/or" logic of the former gave way to the "both/and" logic of the latter.

The tall steel-and-glass cylinders and parallelipipeds of modernism, and more generally its "skyscraper-in-the-park" type of aesthetics, emblematized an austere search for purity and antinaturalist abstraction. The postmoderns' reaction has been not against purity as such, but against the apparent monotony and ultimate sterility that was its price. Minimalist repetitiveness gave way to complicated and surprising inventions. For its love of intricate forms and lucid variety, the aesthetic of postmodernism has been persuasively compared with that of sixteenth-century mannerism. In the sixteenth century, Jencks reminds us, "both Raphael and Michelangelo were reacting against the dullness of straightforward, repeated solutions and wanted to enliven the classical language by inventing new tropes or rhetorical figures. In a more recent reaction, the Modernist Ludwig Mies van der Rohe's slogan 'Less is more' was countered by Robert Venturi's answer, 'Less is a bore.'"[35] The enjoyable, deliberately excluded from the austere aesthetics of modernism, has been fully revalued by the postmoderns, not only in architecture or the arts but also in literature (as Umberto Eco, after John Barth, has insisted).[36]

Enjoyment and complexity go together well in postmodernism. Umberto Eco's own *The Name of the Rose* is a good literary case in point. On one level, Eco's novel is an entertaining medieval thriller, which resourcefully employs the schemes of composition of a detective story in an exotic historical setting (a fourteenth-century abbey in Northern Italy). At the same time, on a more sophisticated level, the elaborate unraveling of the mystery uncovers several other codes: one is philosophical (the detective genre being always a potentially metaphysical genre, as it confronts the reader with "the fundamental philosophical question: who is guilty?");[37] another code could be described as cultural (the text of *The Name of the Rose* is full of references and allusions, often of a subtly parodic nature, to countless books and authors, from the Bible to Borges); the third code, which one might call semiotic, uses the mystery as a framework for a sustained meditation on signs and the paradoxes involved in our production and interpretation of signs. The rich orchestration of effects resulting from such multiple coding calls for a reexamination of the classical dichotomy between works designed for popular consumption and avant-garde works (unpopular, experimental, provocative, etc.). One can, Eco writes, "find elements of revolution and contestation in works that lend themselves to facile consumption, and it [is] also possible to realize that . . . certain works, which seem provocative and still enrage the public, do not really contest anything."[38]

The enjoyment offered by postmodern art (architecture included) comes in the form of a broadly defined parodic practice, in which some commentators have discerned a more general characteristic of our cultural times. It has thus been suggested that the new "reconstructive" treatment of the past, parodic or otherwise, shows a marked preference for "double coding" (Jencks and, with different implications, Hutcheon),[39] really for multiple coding or even "overcoding" (Scarpetta).[40] Most frequent among the poetic means by which such multiple coding can be achieved are allusion and allusive commentary, citation, playfully distorted or invented reference, recasting, transposition, deliberate anachronism, the mixing of two or more historical or stylistic modes, etc. Along these lines, the aesthetics of postmodernism has been described as essentially "quotationist" or "citationist," in clear-cut opposition to the "minimalist" avant-gardes, which, as we saw in the case of architecture, banned reference as "impure."

In actuality, of course, the issue of postmodernism in architecture is much more complex and messy than I have made it out to be for purposes of expository convenience and brevity. Even when used by its most vocal proponents, postmodernism is recognized to be a "hybrid," ambiguous concept. Ever since *The Language of Post-Modern Architecture* (1977), Charles Jencks has sought to specify the application of the term, most significantly by introducing the transitional category of "late-modern." The distinction between late-modern and postmodern is defendable on practical grounds, and the way Jencks himself uses it in *Current Architecture* for characterizing differentially the works of a few dozen contemporary architects is certainly acceptable. But, on closer inspection, it reveals a disturbing theoretical vagueness. Simply increasing the number of "variables" to be considered in distinguishing between late-modern and postmodern—Jencks comes up with no less than thirty!—will not decrease this sense of fuzziness.

Jencks may convince us that the Pompidou Centre in Paris, designed by Renzo Piano and Richard Rodgers, is a typically late-modern building, while James Stirling's new Staatsgalerie in Stuttgart is distinctly postmodern. The late-modern style, a mannered exaggeration of modernism that the great modernists of the 1920s would certainly have condemned, achieves its startling effects within a single-minded, single-coded frame of reference. Thus, everything in the design of the Pompidou Centre is subordinated to the explicitly modernist theme of the machine: the search for an isotropic spatial sameness in the interior, the tendency toward a functionalist exoskeleton ("bones," that is, pipes, ducts, and tubes on the outside), the tendency to use technology rhetorically and decoratively (which at least externally doesn't break the modernist interdiction of the ornament), and finally the tendency toward a futuristic-scientific type of fantastic, resulting in the appearance of the building as a "bug-eyed mechanical monster of Science Fiction." Well-illustrated by Stirling's Staatsgalerie, the postmodern style is quite different, with its non-isotropic, unexpectedly varied interior space, with its ironical revival of traditional forms and signs (columns, occasionally painted in *trompe l'oeil*, arches, arcades, etc.), and with its overall tendency toward a new unconstrained, unconventional but clearly intelligible classicism.

As long as we work with a small number of clear-cut examples, the distinction between late-modern and postmodern holds and even has heuristic value. But as soon as the sample gets larger, conceptual difficulties start to appear. To resolve these, Jencks comes up with his thirty variables, a considerable improvement, he thinks, over the five or six variables that most architecture historians utilize to distinguish between styles. But Jencks fails to tell us how many of his thirty variables must be effectively taken into account as a minimum for determining that a specific structure is either late-modern or postmodern. In reality, Jencks himself, when faced with individual cases, seems to use no more than five or six criteria, which he selects as he pleases from the total of thirty—a procedure that is statistically indefensible. It is one thing if, out of five or six "diagnostic criteria," all or most are actually satisfied before making a particular diagnosis. It is a completely different thing if, out of thirty such criteria, only five or six are effectively satisfied—the diagnosis in this case will be extremely unreliable. Thus, while intuitively we may often agree with Jencks's judgments, his introduction of thirty variables is theoretically not very helpful. In an interesting slip, Jencks comes close to recognizing the difficulty of his position, as he explains that his variables are supposed to "bring out the complexity of the situation: the overlap, contradictions, and differences among movements."[41] (Note the position of "overlap" in the sequence.)

By and large, neither Jencks nor other writers on postmodern architecture seem to be aware that postmodernism, like other period terms, can easily generate its own versions of the old "realistic illusion," by virtue of which a mere construct of the mind or model of understanding is perceived as a hard-and-fast reality. If to this we add the temptations of historical teleology, which make us think of the present as a goal of previous developments (and which induce us to read history backwards from the present), we begin to realize how widespread and significant are the fallacies to which the users of postmodernism, or of similar periodizing constructs, are liable.[42] One should therefore insist on the need for a self-conscious and openly hypothetical use of the term, which is rarely the case, either in architecture criticism or elsewhere.

CRITIQUES OF POSTMODERNISM

Thus far I have considered the issues of modernism versus postmodernism mostly from the perspective of the critics of modernism. What I would like to do now is to look at the opposite position. Since the critique of postmodernism cannot be presented here in all its wide-ranging implications, I will concentrate on two more or less typical angles of attack, one "conservative," the other "radical" (and more precisely neo-Marxist). I have placed "conservative" and "radical" in quotation marks to underscore not only that these labels are highly relative, but also that the two attitudes they name, ostensibly antithetical, can on occasion reveal striking similarities.

In saying this, however, I do not wish to imply that the contributions and personalities of the critics I have chosen to exemplify these larger attitudes, Clement Greenberg and Fredric Jameson, are to be equated in any fashion. Greenberg, closely associated with the rise of modernist painting in America (as its major theorist and critic) possesses an unusually broad and rigorous mind. His complex arguments, whether one agrees or disagrees with them, have a taut consistency and a sharp precision that have always been rare qualities in critical writing. Jameson's style of thinking and writing is considerably looser and might be seen as illustrating the serious intellectual problems contemporary Western Marxism is experiencing. What recent Marxism seems to be missing is, most notably, its older methodological integrity and the inner historicist logic that made it recognizable among other modes of social thought. Today's Marxist critics appear ready and even anxious to adopt whatever methods or "antimethods" happen to be intellectually fashionable (from formalism to structuralism to the most esoteric versions of poststructuralism), without caring that such adoptions might result in the bursting of the very Marxist frame of reference they claim to represent. Such theoretical trendiness is more apparent in works by

Jameson that will not be discussed here, but it does have a bearing on his view of modernism versus postmodernism as presented in "Postmodernism and Consumer Society," to which I shall turn momentarily.

One might question the selection of Clement Greenberg to represent the conservative attitude toward postmodernism. After all, wasn't he strongly identified with Marxism at the beginnings of his career? Wasn't he the outspoken Trotskyite editor of *Partisan Review* in the late 1930s? Ideologically on the far left, Greenberg has always been, perhaps even more so than other contributors to the politically radical but culturally modernist *Partisan Review*, an aesthetic "purist" and even a paradoxical "conservative of the avant-garde"—for him the modernist painters had nothing whatsoever to do with artistic innovation or novelty and had all along been, in their commitment to high standards, backward- rather than forward-looking. Over the years, Greenberg's version of modernist conservatism in aesthetics became appealing to the supporters of an increasingly embattled artistic modernism, and today his blunt rejection of postmodernism and his passionate defense of abstract painting coincides, whether he likes it or not, with the cultural policies of the "neoconservatives."

The position of Clement Greenberg in his 1980 lecture entitled *The Notion of the "Post-Modern"* could be summarized in the following terms: modernism in painting has been, since its inception with Manet and the impressionists, a heroic struggle against the encroachment of bad taste or kitsch in the domain of art; postmodernism is only the latest name under which commercial bad taste, masquerading as sophisticated "advancedness," challenges the integrity of art. We recall that early on, in his important essay "Avant-Garde and Kitsch" (1939), Greenberg had already suggested that the incompatibility between the avant-garde (for him synonymous with modernism) and kitsch was largely responsible for the ways in which the avant-garde had evolved. But if we consider Greenberg's other theoretical writings on modernism, particularly his 1966 "Modernist Painting," the model of development of modernism that he proposes is plainly twofold. On the one hand, Greenberg stresses an immanent evolutionary principle, that is, he explains the evolution of modernism in terms of its "inner artistic logic." It is this principle that has compelled successive generations of artists to affirm with increasing force the medium of painting in what is unique to it, namely, its "flatness" or two-dimensionality, as opposed to all other features that painting shares with other arts (the sculptural illusion of three-dimensional space, figuration, color, etc.).[43]

On the other hand, in potential contradiction with his immanentistic view of art history as the unfolding of an inflexible inner logic, Greenberg believes that modernism has been throughout its history nothing more than an endeavor to maintain the high standards of the old masters against the intrusions of commercialism and corrupt market criteria. This second view suggests that modernism has been obliged (by a sort of negative aesthetic-ethical imperative) to withdraw from what an ever-expanding commercial taste had managed to appropriate and then market as "high art," including the modernists' own earlier discoveries. This "reactive" approach is dominant in Greenberg's attack on postmodernism.

In such a "reactive" scheme, modernism "consists in the continuing endeavor to stem the decline of aesthetic standards threatened by the relative democratizing of our culture under industrialism; and the overriding and innermost logic of Modernism is to maintain the levels of the past in the face of an opposition that hadn't been present in the past."[44] The modernists do not really innovate, Greenberg insists, although their aspiration to quality may force them to look new, even outrageously so: "Modernism settled in in painting with Impressionism, and, with that, art for art's sake. For which same sake the successors in Modernism of the Impressionists were forced to forget about truth to nature. They were forced to look even more outrageously new: Cézanne, Gauguin, Seurat, Van Gogh, and all the Modernist painters after them—for the sake of aesthetic value, aesthetic quality, nothing else."[45] Its rigorous and highly demanding quality criteria make modernism the veritable acme of art.

Any deviation from modernism, then, involves a betrayal or corruption of aesthetic standards. Seen from this vantage point, the "postmodern" cannot be much more than a renewed "urge to relax," particularly pervasive after the advent of pop art, with its deleterious effects on the art world. Postmodernism, Greenberg concludes, "is a way, above all, to justify oneself in preferring less demanding art without being called reactionary or retarded (which is the greatest fear of the newfangled philistines of advancedness)."[46]

This type of argument (modernism's self-conscious mission, to exorcise bad taste from the domain of high art, is today as urgent as it ever was) appears in a variety of forms and shapes in the writings of the defenders of modernist purity against the infiltrations of commercialism and fashion. In its stronger versions, this way of arguing invites a direct identification of postmodernism with kitsch or camp, as for instance in Hilton Kramer's sharp attacks on postmodernism.[47]

Whether one stresses Greenberg's notion of an inner artistic logic of development toward greater and greater purity, or the notion of a heroic reaction to a market that conquers and degrades (the second one is not far from Adorno's view of an unyieldingly negative aesthetic avant-garde), one faces the same question: isn't modernism progressively narrowing its formal choices and getting close to the point where its properly creative possibilities might be completely exhausted? And how is modernism to stay alive when the price it has to pay for maintaining its high standards is sheer sterility?

A reasonable way out of the dilemma would certainly not require a rash abandonment of high standards; what it would require, though, is a change of the Manichaean definition of aesthetic quality proposed by Clement Greenberg. Instead of implying that artistic modernity is the scene of a mythical battle between Good Taste and

Bad Taste (High Culture versus Mass Culture, Authentic Beauty versus Kitsch, and so forth), I would take a more relativistic and self-skeptical position in regard to the current aesthetic disputes. Instead of "demonizing" the market and, conversely, "angelizing" the spirit of modernism, I would suggest a more Bakhtinian, "dialogic," "polyphonic," and "carnivalizing" view of things, in which absolute principles would look out of place (too serious, too comically solemn, too arrogant, and, ultimately, too boring).

In their passion for a formalistically conceived purity of standards, the defenders of modernism end up offering little more than a rhetoric of aesthetic conservation or, at best, a conservative version of a typically modernist "great story" of emancipation: the emancipation of art from bad taste. But instead of the earlier and dynamic image of a forward-looking, innovative modernism, what we now get is the image of a paradoxical "backward looking" one (Greenberg's own terms).

Turning to the second, "radical" attitude toward the distinction between modernism and postmodernism, I would note that it is more openly ideological, although as I shall show, it can be as aestheticist as the first. This attitude is pervasive in neo-Marxist circles and it revives the great Marxian story of the inevitable end of capitalism, but with the new twist that capitalism's last days are less apocalyptic and the impending revolution is less clear in shape and meaning than might have appeared to earlier Marxists. A good example of the neo-Marxist views of postmodernism is furnished by Hal Foster's anthology *The Anti-Aesthetic: Essays in Post-Modern Culture* (1983). The contributors to the volume (among them Jürgen Habermas, Kenneth Frampton, Rosalind Krauss, Fredric Jameson, Jean Baudrillard, and Edward Said) seem to share, whatever their particular focus, the general proposition that postmodernism—to be divided into a good, resistant, anticapitalist variety and a bad, reactionary one—is a cultural phenomenon characteristic of "late capitalism." But unlike older orthodox Marxist studies of the "dying culture" of capitalism (one thinks of Christopher Caudwell's rather unsophisticated rejection of modernism in the 1930s), the essays included in *The Anti-Aesthetic* are not wholesale condemnations of either modernism or postmodernism (with the exception of Habermas, whose understanding of postmodernism is entirely negative). The critical arguments found in them are more intricate and more ambivalent, but also more confusing, both theoretically and in relation to particular questions, themes, procedures, or individual examples. Looking at one of these essays, Fredric Jameson's ambitious "Postmodernism and Consumer Society," may give us a more specific idea of the neo-Marxist approach to postmodernism.

Jameson believes that postmodern culture, the result of a veritable social mutation, has lost much of the "subversiveness" (both aesthetic and political) of older modernism. This view implicitly overturns the conclusions of traditional Marxist analyses of modernism (from Caudwell to Lukács), which stressed the socially irresponsible, reactionary, and decadent aestheticism of most high modernists. So far Jameson is close to the para-Marxist line of the Frankfurt School, and particularly that of Adorno, according to whom aesthetic autonomy is the last guarantee that art's "negativity" is safe from bourgeois co-option. But modernist aestheticism, Jameson argues, is more than a tragically ineffectual negation of the culture of capitalism; it is a politically powerful subversion of the false bourgeois values. In explosive combination particularly with the "protofascist" tendencies of some typical modernists (the case of Wyndham Lewis),[48] this aestheticism performs a major critical-political role by showing, beyond the deceptive appearances of liberal democracy and humanism, the monstrously aggressive essence of capitalism. (In *Fables of Aggression*, Jameson states unequivocally that the critique of capitalism found in the works of a Wyndham Lewis, with their aggressive mechanical metaphors, was more convincing and intellectually revealing than anything articulated by the Marxists of the time.)

One can now understand why postmodernism, precisely by being "anti-aesthetic," by blunting the powerful cutting edge of the aesthetic, ends up being less subversive than modernism had been. As a domesticated kind of (anti)modernism, confined to an unavoidably circular "textualism" and refusing to distinguish between the aesthetic and the non-aesthetic, postmodernism cannot help but play, however unwittingly, the part of a "reinforcer of the logic of consumer capitalism."

The postindustrial (and culturally postmodern) society in which we live, Jameson writes, has brought about "new types of consumption; planned obsolescence; the penetration of advertising, television, and the media to a hitherto unparalleled degree throughout society; . . . the growth of the great net of superhighways and the arrival of automobile culture."[49] Postmodernism, in this broad scenario of a social mutation, is the cultural product of "the emergence of this new moment of late, consumer or multinational capitalism. [Postmodernism's] formal features in many ways express the deeper logic of this particular system."[50]

This, however, accounts for only one side of Jameson's ambivalent attitude, for he can show open appreciation for some of the styles invented by artists whom he regards as typically postmodern—John Cage and younger composers such as Philip Glass or Terry Riley in music; John Ashbery and the recent "L=a=n=g=u=a=g=e Poets" in poetry; Thomas Pynchon, William Burroughs, and the French nouveaux romanciers in fiction. Along these lines, when he discusses a piece by the talk poet Bob Perelman ("China"), Jameson comments favorably on the self-conscious, self-reflexive "textuality" of the poem and brings out its correct political orientation (China pointing toward a "third way," a way that exhilaratingly avoids the impasses reached by the two superpowers). Given Jameson's unequivocal praise for both Perelman's craft and politics, one may wonder in what sense postmodernism is really playing into the hands of the detested multinational capitalism. One may also note that Jameson fails to cite any concrete examples of how a postmodernist work of art actually reinforces the logic of late capitalism.

Jameson's ambivalence becomes even more evident, this time in theoretical terms, toward the end of the essay, when he asks himself whether postmodernism is indeed devoid of all subversiveness or social-critical value. The dilemma is stated unambiguously: "We have seen that there is a way in which postmodernism replicates or reproduces—reinforces—the logic of consumer capitalism; the *more significant* [my emphasis] question is whether there is also a way in which it resists that logic. But this question we must leave open."⁵¹

But why? If the question about the critical value of postmodernism is so significant, what could have prevented the author from addressing it, however briefly? All the more so as the editor of the anthology, Hal Foster, had argued in the preface for a distinction between a complacent, essentially reactionary postmodernism and an emancipatory, "resistant" version. (The distinction cannot help recalling crude old dichotomies cherished by Marxist criticism, such as the one between a "reactionary" romanticism, as exemplified by a Coleridge, and a "progressive" romanticism, as exemplified by a Shelley; one may also pause to note that in the current vocabulary of neo-Marxism the opposite of reactionary is "resistant" and very seldom "progressive," suggesting that both the doctrine and the terminology of progress may have lost their appeal to the radical imagination.) So why doesn't Jameson limit the role of reinforcer of the "logic of consumer capitalism" to Foster's bad kind of postmodernism? My own explanation is that even a limited recognition of postmodernism's "resistance" to the spirit of capitalism would have weakened Jameson's neat contrast between modernism and postmodernism and would have cast serious doubts about his central thesis regarding the uniquely exemplary aesthetic subversiveness of modernism.

Be that as it may, I think that the analogies between the "conservative" (Greenbergian) rejection of postmodernism and the "radical" (neo-Marxist) identification of postmodernism with cultural consumerism are more clearly visible now than when I first suggested their existence. From both perspectives modernism emerges as a true hero, whether its heroism was manifested in its aesthetic battle against bourgeois bad taste or in its aesthetic subversion of the capitalist cultural order. Curiously, in both cases there is admiration for modernist aestheticism's negating virtues, ascetic opposition to the corruptions of the art market in the first, unyielding "resistance" to the perverse deceptions of capitalist ideology in the second. In both views postmodernism appears as a "relaxation," whether of artistic standards or of the implicitly political standards of aesthetic criticism.

LITERARY POSTMODERNISM:

THE SHAPING OF A CORPUS

So far I have said very little about the use of postmodernism in specifically literary contexts. Even when such contexts have been mentioned; the emphasis has been either on historical description or, more often, on issues of artistic postmodernism in general (such as the new meaning of the past or the question of postmodern double coding). In the last two sections of this chapter I will focus on literary postmodernism and will try to exemplify the potentially fruitful uses of the category as well as point out its more subtle implications.

A broad-based consensual definition of postmodernism in literature has eluded scholarship and will foreseeably continue to do so. But a certain agreement in regard to postmodernism as a possible framework for discussing contemporary literature seems to have been attained. Along these lines, one notes with some satisfaction that, even if this is not the general rule, the application of the term has become less arbitrary than one might have expected on the basis of its early usage. Over the years a corpus of postmodern writing (or, more accurately, writing that is often referred to as postmodern) has thus emerged. I should add, however, that there is nothing rigid or fixed about this corpus, and that in fact it is wide open to revisions, exclusions, inclusions, and even fundamental challenges. In other words, this corpus—notwithstanding the claims of some promoters of postmodernism—does not qualify as a new canon. I see it simply as the product of a historical-hypothetical perspective from which certain questions about the nature of contemporary writing can be asked.

I would therefore say that the critics who lucidly accept the label of postmodernism do so because they want to be able to deal with questions about the status of "reality" versus "fiction" in today's literary discourses; and those who reject it do so because they believe that these questions have already been satisfactorily answered in the past or that they are unanswerable and should consequently be dismissed as uninteresting, sterile, perhaps even counterproductive. But before dealing at more length with these questions, a few words about the formation of the (hypothetical) corpus of postmodernist writing will be in order.

As we saw, the term *postmodernism* first came into literary use in the United States, where a number of poets of the later 1940s used it to distance themselves from the symbolist kind of modernism represented by T. S. Eliot. Like the early postmoderns, most of those who subsequently joined the antimodernist reaction were aesthetic radicals and often intellectually close to the spirit of the counterculture. The works of these writers constitute the historical nucleus of literary postmodernism. In poetry the corpus of American postmodernist writing would include the Black Mountain poets (Charles Olson, Robert Duncan, Robert Creeley), the Beats (Allen Ginsberg, Jack Kerouac, Laurence Ferlinghetti, Gregory Corso), and the representatives of the San Francisco Renaissance (Gary Snyder) or those of the New York School (John Ashbery, Kenneth Koch). In fiction the names most often quoted are John Barth, Thomas Pynchon, William Gaddis, Robert Coover, John Hawkes, Donald Barthelme, and the "surfictionists" Raymond Federman and Ronald Sukenick.

Certainly the label *postmodernism* would have remained the parochial name of one movement, or perhaps merely one literary mood, in one country, had it not managed to establish a larger meaning with international ramifications. This was achieved through the efforts of the American postmoderns (including their sympathetic critics) to build a more comprehensive frame of reference within which their rejection of modernism could be favorably perceived. Of course most literary movements give themselves a distinguished genealogy of precursors, whose initiatives they claim to have taken to the point of full maturity and self-conscious expression. But this is not without its dangers. The precursors or masters claimed by some of the American postmoderns—important artists such as Borges, Nabokov, and Beckett—ended up occupying central positions in the enlarged postmodernist corpus, from which the very creators of the new movement found themselves displaced. More significantly, the search for precursors has been responsible not only for the rapid extension, both historically and geographically, of the term *postmodernism,* but also for a new understanding of modernism.

Historically, the postmodernist poetics of "indeterminacy" or "undecidability" of meaning came to see itself as the continuation of one direction within modernism, a direction that challenged the prevailing symbolism of modernist poetics. This antisymbolist strain could indeed be more clearly distinguished from the perspective of the poetic anarchism of the American postmodernist poets. Thus, a poetry critic like Marjorie Perloff, starting from her interest in the postmoderns and particularly in John Ashbery and David Antin, could write a copiously exemplified history of poetic indeterminacy from the immediate successors of Baudelaire to the present. Perloff states her thesis unambiguously: "Whereas Baudelaire and Mallarmé point the way to the 'High Modernism' of Yeats and Eliot and Auden, Stevens and Frost and Crane, and their later Symbolist heirs like Lowell and Berryman, it is Rimbaud who strikes the first note of that undecidability we find in Gertrude Stein, in Pound and Williams, as well as in the short prose works of Beckett's later years, an undecidability that has become more marked in the poetry of the last decades."[52]

What is at stake in the conflict between the two poetics, one of symbolism and the other of indeterminacy, is illustrated in convincing detail by Perloff's comparison between two visions of the city, T. S. Eliot's in *The Waste Land* and John Ashbery's in "These Lacustrine Cities."[53] The reshaping of our view of modernism resulting from recent poetry makes it more difficult to speak of a more or less unified poetic modernism or, as often happened in the past, of Eliot *and* Pound in the same breath. The principle of conflict from which postmodernism was supposed to have issued in the 1950s has now been pushed back to the core of the modernist tradition itself. But, at the same time, the novelty of the postwar American postmoderns appears more limited.

The problematic of undecidability, I would argue, is much more acute, and its consequences farther reaching, in prose than in poetry. A certain degree of undecidability of meaning (variously referred to as suggestion, ambiguity, polysemy, or obscurity) has always been a feature of poetry. In prose, however, particularly after the powerful assertion of social and psychological realism in the nineteenth century, there was little room for undecidability of a structural kind (I leave aside the potentially suggestive indeterminacy on the level of style). That is why, in my view, the central questions of postmodernist writing—questions such as: Can literature be other than self-referential, given the present-day radical epistemological doubt and the ways in which this doubt affects the status of representation? Can literature be said to be a "representation of reality" when reality itself turns out to be shot with fiction through and through? In what sense does the construction of reality differ from the construction of mere possibility?—are endowed with more urgency in contemporary prose than in poetry.

Interestingly, the postmodernist problematic appears to have received its clearest and most forceful treatment in the works of two writers who never dreamt of calling themselves postmodern and who were opposed, both ideologically and aesthetically, to almost everything that the early American postmoderns stood for. They are Jorge Luis Borges and Vladimir Nabokov. The differences between the literary temperaments of the two authors are as vast as can be, and there should be no surprise that, for instance, Nabokov thought poorly of Borges, or "Osberg," as he maliciously anagrammatized Borges's name in *Ada*, describing him as a "Spanish writer of pretentious fairy tales and mystico-allegoric anecdotes."[54] But in spite of such differences, Borges and Nabokov shared a profound preoccupation with the question of representation, or more precisely with the question What does representation represent? and with the countless logical contradictions that turn up when one attempts to answer it seriously. Hence, in the works of both, the proliferation of images and actions directly or indirectly linked to the idea of representation: mirrors and copies, reflections and duplications, the unexpected and intricate paradoxes of resemblance, pretending, acting, impersonating, or mimicking, and the various mental predicaments they bring about, in the shape of vicious circles, beggings of the question, and infinite regresses. These are handled in quite dissimilar fashions: in Borges's succinct *ficciones* they function within what I would call a poetics of perplexity; in Nabokov's more expansive and charmingly overwritten novels they are included within a formalist aesthetics of parody, self-parody, and play.

Since James Joyce has also been mentioned among the precursors of postmodernism (particularly for *Finnegans Wake*, as Ihab Hassan has repeatedly stated), it might be useful to compare his literary influence with that of Borges. There is a sense in which, as Christopher Butler has proposed, "the huge over-organization of *Finnegans Wake*" is one pole of a dialectic that governs the postmodern period. On the other hand, though, the overall Joycean model is less important structurally than it is stylistically (for the extensive role of punning, paranomasia, etymological verbal play, etc.). Joyce, Butler observes, "contributes a sense of linguistic texture; but Borges was the first to adopt certain types of narrative handling which are now all too familiar."[55] As Butler underlines, it is Borges's view of the world as a labyrinth of possibilities, of parallel times, of alternative pasts and futures, all of which have equal claims to fictional presentation—a view most intriguingly argued in the story entitled "The Garden of Forking Paths"—that has become one of the major premises of postmodern narrative experimentalism.

The name of another great writer who "problematizes" representation, Samuel Beckett, has also figured in the discussion of postmodernism, alttough Beckett critics as well as proponents of postmodernism (Alan Wilde, for instance)[56] have sometimes protested his inclusion within the corpus of postmodernist writing. Since I regard this corpus as hypothetical, I think that a consideration of Beckett's poetics of impossibility (a poetics that works with impossibility, with the impotence of the word, and with failure;[57] a poetics that states one must write *because* it is impossible to write) could enlarge the postmodern hypothesis by showing that its characteristic "possibilism" also comprises the negation of possibility. Thus, among the "possible worlds" of postmodernism, I would suggest there should be a place for the rigorously "impossible" ones that Beckett sets out to explore.

Once Borges, Nabokov, and Beckett were seen as credible examples of postmodernist writing, the way to the internationalization of the concept was clearly open. The world reputation of the three non-American masters of postmodernism was bound to increase the curiosity for this label and, over time, to enhance its circulation abroad. It may also be true that, on a deeper level, the American conceptualization of the postmodern, nebulous though it was, raised certain questions about literature that were being asked, in different formulations, all over the Western world. At any rate, postmodernism offered a convenient frame for discovering or inventing more or less interesting affinities among a great many contemporary writers.

Today the international corpus of postmodernist writing includes, besides the already mentioned names, writers such as Julio Cortázar, García Márquez, Carlos Fuentes, Cabrera Infante, and perhaps Manuel Puig (in Latin America); Thomas Bernhard, Peter Handke, and Botho Strauss (in Germany and Austria); Italo Calvino and Umberto Eco (in Italy); Alasdair Gray and Christine Brooke-Rose, but also Iris Murdoch, John Fowles, Tom Stoppard, and D. M. Thomas (in Great Britain); Michel Butor, Alain Robbe-Grillet, and Claude Simon (in France); and such outstanding "extra-territorials" as Milan Kundera. What is remarkable about this incomplete list is that it groups authors who rarely resemble each other: their characteristic moods, world views, politics (including antipolitics), and styles may differ widely, and so may their appeal, some of them being highly difficult, esoteric, and recondite, while others write straightforwardly for a large popular readership.

What then justifies grouping them together? The fact, I think, that their works, even when they appear to have little in common, can serve as credible examples of postmodernism. Or, to put it differently, the fact that a critic who would want to consider them together would be likely to come up with a frame of reference closely resembling one or another of the major models of postmodernism. Once such a model is selected or assembled, the works in question will reveal that they do have certain things in common after all. These shared properties, I feel, can be most convincingly brought out on the level of literary conventions (including counter-conventions, ironic or parodic doublings of conventions, etc.). To arrive at a sensitive model of literary postmodernism one should then accept as a working hypothesis that postmodernist texts make a distinctive use of certain conventions, techniques, and recurrent structural and stylistic devices, even though individually their intentions, implications, and aesthetic results may be widely different.

POSTMODERNIST DEVICES AND
THEIR SIGNIFICANCE

To begin with, let me point to what appears to be a more general postmodernist view of convention. Modernism in its avant-garde posture has made us familiar with the device that consists in showing, rather than concealing, the conventions and devices used in constructing a work of art (the Russian Formalists called it by a technical phrase, "the foregrounding of the device"). Brecht's famous "alienation effect" is one classic example. In postmodernism, however, things tend to work differently. The device continues to show itself for the contrivance it is, but in doing so it also states that everything else is a contrivance too and that there simply is no escape from this.* But if everything is of the nature of a device, or simply fiction, the "foregrounding of the device" no longer conveys the sense of novelty, originality, and artistic pride which was associated with it in modernism. We recall Magritte's "realistic" painting of a pipe that includes the inscription "This is not a pipe." Is this an extreme modernist way of calling attention to the painting itself, to its artistic reality, to its imaginative quality? Hardly so. This painting looks rather like a surrealist game, but one in which the expected dream element is strangely absent, one in which we can already identify an anticipation of the postmodernist questioning not only of the "reality" behind the image but also of the "reality," aesthetic or otherwise, of the image itself (Magritte's pipe is unremarkably banal and it does not "suggest" anything).[58] I would propose that what is ultimately foregrounded here is not a convention but conventionality itself, made into an existential puzzle.

ᵃ Against this background, the more obvious postmodernist devices include: a new existential or "ontological" use of narrative perspectivism, different from the mainly psychological one found in modernism (this will be more fully discussed later); duplication and multiplication of beginnings, endings, and narrated actions (one recalls the alternative endings of Fowles's *The French Lieutenant's Woman*); the parodic thematization of the author (the reappearance of the intrusive or manipulative author, but now in a distinctively self-ironic vein); the no less parodic but more puzzling thematization of the reader (the "implied reader" becomes a character, or a series of characters, as in Calvino's *If on a Winter's Night a Traveler*); the treatment on an equal footing of fact and fiction, reality and myth, truth and lying, original and imitation, as a means to emphasize undecidability; self-referentiality and "metafiction" as means to dramatize inescapable circularity (as in Borges's "Circular Ruins" and "Tlön, Uqbar, Orbis Tertius"); extreme versions of the "unreliable narrator," sometimes used, paradoxically, for purposes of a rigorous construction (the "perfect crime" that Nabokov recounts in *Despair* in the voice of a self-confessed but also self-deluded mythomaniac). Other examples of such structural conventions could be easily added. Stylistically, aside from the special, often parodic uses of the great traditional rhetorical devices, one might note a marked preference for such unconventional figures as deliberate anachronism, tautology, and palinode or retraction, which often play an extensive and even structural role.

To go beyond a mere listing of such devices, to bring into focus their intricate historical affinities, connections, and mutual reinforcements, one needs to formulate a larger comparative hypothesis. The three students of postmodernism I want to discuss now, D. W. Fokkema, Brian McHale, and Elrud Ibsch, do not hesitate to advance such a hypothesis. Furthermore, the way they construct the category *postmodernism* is particularly interesting to me since it illustrates, by a number of convincing literary examples, what I have described earlier as a major shift in contemporary thought from epistemology to hermeneutics.

D. W. Fokkema sees the "poetical device of hypothesis" as the outstanding feature of modernist prose.[59] Proust, for instance, or rather his narrator and double, Marcel, when he cannot know enough about a character, will resort to abundant and intricate hypothesizing, to the great intellectual delight of the reader of *A la recherche du temps perdu;* or, in the words of Jacques Rivière, as quoted by Fokkema, he will fill the gaps in his knowledge with hypotheses ("il les peuplera de ses hypothèses"). Fokkema writes: "The major convention of modernism with regard to the composition of literary texts is the selection of hypothetical constructions expressing uncertainty and provisionality."[60] He then proceeds to illustrate this central convention in works by Gide, Larbaud, Thomas Mann, Ter Braak, and others.

To such expansive "modernist hypotheses" the postmodern writers (Borges, Barthelme, and Robbe-Grillet among them) oppose, according to Fokkema, their "impossibilities" and a pervasive sense of radical, unsurpassable uncertainty, a sort of epistemological nihilism, as I would call it. In the postmodernist view, there simply is no "reality" that might validate such hypotheses, even under ideal conditions. The modernist play of hypothesis and counterhypothesis, with its particular dramatic tensions and anticipations, anxieties and joys, has lost its basis. "Reality" being nothing but a composite of construals and fictions, Fokkema argues that the postmodernists can no longer write from hypothesis; they will write, as it were, from impossibility.

Acknowledging the importance of Fokkema's choice of an epistemological point of view, Brian McHale changes the terms of his distinction. Instead of opposing "epistemological doubt" (a catalyst for the modernist imagination of hypothesis) to a postmodern epistemological impossibilism, McHale prefers to speak of an "epistemological dominant" in the case of modernist fiction and an "ontological dominant" in the case of postmodernism. Before examining McHale's central argument, some quick terminological clarification is needed.

The notion of "dominant" comes from Roman Jakobson. Literary evolution, according to Jakobson, could be seen as a shift from one period's primary or dominant system of poetic norms to a new one, which will be dominant in the next period. Summarizing the position of the Russian Formalists, of whom he was one of the most prominent, Jakobson notes that what was secondary in the old period becomes primary in the new one and, symmetrically, what was essential in the old hierarchy of conventions becomes subsidiary or optional in the new hierarchy. It is noteworthy that in adopting the Jakobsonian concept of dominant, McHale frees it from its originally "monolithic" implications. Like the "strategic" notion of period, the notion of dominant can make no claims to being unique. There is not one but many possible theories of modernism and postmodernism, defined by the strategic objectives of those who articulate them. Likewise, one can conceive of many dominants in one period, depending on one's point of view, on what one wishes to study, and on the purposes of such study. The way McHale uses the word "ontology" may confuse those who are more familiar with the language of German metaphysics (including Heidegger) than with the language of post-Wittgensteinian analytical philosophy. To dispel potential misunderstandings, McHale explains that his "ontology" comes "from the use of the term in poetics, above all by Roman Ingarden . . . and by Thomas Pavel and others who have adapted terms from modal logic ('possible worlds') to the description of fictional worlds. . . . For a working definition, let me cite Pavel: an ontology is 'a theoretical description of a universe.'"[61]

And now to McHale's argument. He starts out by formulating two theses, whose claimed validity is limited to "an historical poetics of twentieth century fiction." The first thesis: "The dominant of Modernist writing is *epistemological*. That is, Modernist writing is designed to raise such questions as: what is there to be known? who knows it? how do they know it and with what degree of certainty? how is knowledge transmitted from one knower to another and with what degree of reliability? etc."[62] The second thesis reads: "The dominant of Postmodernist writing is *ontological*. That is, Postmodernist writing is designed to raise such questions as: what is a world? what kinds of world are there, how are they constituted, and how do they differ? . . . what is the mode of existence of a text, and what is the mode of existence of the world (or worlds) it projects? etc."[63] To explain the passage from one dominant to another McHale resorts to an immanent model of change: when the inner logic of modernist questioning is pushed to the extreme, it brings about postmodernist questioning and vice versa. McHale writes: "Push epistemological questions far enough and they 'tip over' into ontological questions— the progression is not linear and one-way, but circular and reversible."[64]

To support his theses, McHale discusses works by William Faulkner, Samuel Beckett, Alain Robbe-Grillet, Carlos Fuentes, Vladimir Nabokov, and Robert Coover and tries to show that the modernism/postmodernism distinction may be profitably employed in dealing with the *oeuvre* of one writer, and sometimes with a single work. Thus, for instance, Robbe-Grillet's *The Jealousy* would exemplify the epistemological (modernist) dominant, while the same author's *In the Labyrinth* would be characteristically ontological or postmodern; as for William Faulkner's *Absalom, Absalom!* it is a largely modernist novel, but with intriguing postmodern elements. In the concluding part of his paper, McHale returns to the idea that the two dominants are reversible and writes: "The crossover from Modernist to Postmodernist poetics *is not irreversible*, not a gate that swings one way only. . . . It is possible to 'retreat' from Postmodernism to Modernism, or indeed to vacillate between the two."[65]

All through his essay McHale appears to be reluctant to acknowledge that irreversibility (without which no properly historical research or thought is possible) may have anything to do with the modern/postmodern duality. This is surprising, given McHale's declaration that his work is a study in historical poetics. The questions left out in his account are of the type: Is modernism (whatever model of modernism we choose) a distinct moment in an irreversible sequence or, as some contemporary "textualist" critics have maintained, an essential urge of all (authentic) literature at all times? And: Is postmodernism (whatever model of postmodernism we choose) a distinct moment in such a sequence or a recurrent possibility given within the inner logic of a transhistorical modernism? *

A certain lingering structuralist bias against historical irreversibility prevents McHale from entertaining such questions, even though a historicist answer would not have been incompatible with the general thrust of his remarks. I have no difficulty accepting his view that the postmodernists have, among others, the option to return to modernist types of epistemological questioning or to vacillate between the epistemological and the ontological dominant. But is not the very availability of such an option the result of a historical process? Did earlier modernists, before the ontological dominant was fully articulated, have a similar choice? A Faulkner in *Absalom, Absalom!*, which McHale analyzes with subtlety, may well have been confronted with ontological puzzles (as indeed were a long line of novelists starting perhaps with Cervantes), but can we really say that he was in a position to choose between an epistemological alternative and an ontological one? Such a choice, I would argue, can emerge only from an irreversible historical cultural development. At the time when Faulkner wrote *Absalom, Absalom!* the postmodernist option was not really available to him. But McHale is right that a Beckett or a Robbe-Grillet can freely switch back and forth between modernism and postmodernism.

The "possible worlds" or "ontological" dominant of postmodern fiction is not without its own version of "impossibilism." This is what Elrud Ibsch attempts to illustrate in her essay "From Hypothesis to *Korrektur*,"[66] by way of a contrastive analysis of Robert Musil's *Der Mann ohne Eigenschaften* (1930–43) and Thomas Bernhard's *Korrektur* (1975). In Ibsch's view, Ulrich, or "the man without qualities," the hero of Musil's great novel, is a modernist embodiment of Nietzsche's perspectivist epistemology, an epistemology, we recall, that opposes with equal force the idealistic and the materialistic theories of knowledge in their modern forms. Musil "novelizes," as it were, the philosophical and cultural aporias of modernity that Nietzsche brought into focus. Thus, Musil's hero, a highly paradoxical and incisive "raisonneur," is constantly confronted with a host of characters in ambiguous moral, political, legal, and linguistic situations, which incite him to endless critical and self-critical hypothesizing. Through Ulrich, Musil furnishes one of the most fascinating examples of modernist use of the "poetic device of hypothesis," to repeat Fokkema's phrase. In contrast with Ulrich, the hero of Thomas Bernhard's *Correction*, the intriguingly Wittgensteinian Roithammer, is intent on demystifying hypothesis, on showing the inherent imprecision, shabbiness, and weakness of hypothetical thought. Ibsch's argument is one about a historical "mutation of hypothesis into refutation: the presentation of various tentative points of view in Musil, which question the dogmatic fixation of one perspective, is replaced by an unrelenting attempt at refutation in Bernhardt."[67] Thus Ulrich's epistemological skepticism and creative use of conjecture gives way, in Bernhard's Roithammer, to a pathos of "correction," correction of correction, and so forth, until the hero's final suicide or (self)correction out of existence.

Going beyond Ibsch's analysis of this particular novel, it would be interesting to consider the extent to which other postmodernist writers make use not only of refutation or correction, but more generally of figures and devices that belong, I would suggest, under the larger category of palinode. The Greek etymological meaning of the word "palinode" (i.e., taking back what one has said in an "ode" or song of praise) has long been extended to comprise any explicit withdrawal of a statement (be it a recantation, an admission of having been mistaken, of having been a dupe, or a recognition of having lied from whatever motive, serious or playful). Could we speak of a certain direction within postmodernism, whose outstanding characteristic would be the insistent use of a rhetoric of palinode or retraction, a rhetoric that earlier modes of writing had used only marginally? This question cannot be answered here. But a quick example of how such a rhetoric functions in the works of a major contemporary writer might establish its relevance. *

I am thinking of Beckett's narrative strategy, as it interrelates with the stylistic, textual, and intertextual patterns of his prose, in his famous trilogy of the 1950s (*Molloy, Malone Dies,* and *The Unnamable*). The question of palinode starts to dominate the reader's horizon of expectations early on. As one of the commentators of the trilogy, Brian T. Fitch, points out, the attentive reader soon learns that "each turn of phrase could annul all the sentences that preceded it. . . . Qualifications and revisions intervene ceaselessly; what was just said is immediately contradicted and then repeated again, and so on."[68] The sense of unsolvable uncertainty is constantly reinforced by the narrator's hesitations and self-conscious inconsistencies (blamed, among others, on amnesia, confusion, and inability to separate "fact" from "fiction"). Typically, the Beckettian narrator will tell the reader: "For I cannot stoop, neither can I kneel, because of my infirmity, and if I ever stoop, forgetting who I am, or kneel, make no mistake, it will not be me, but another."[69] Or, even more teasingly: "This woman has never spoken to me, *to the best of my knowledge* [my emphasis]. If I have said anything to the contrary I was mistaken. If I say anything to the contrary again I shall be mistaken again. Unless I am mistaken now."[70] On the level of the structure of the whole trilogy, the technique of creating (existential) puzzles takes the form of larger successive revisionary moves or retroactive disclaimers. In the first novel the narrative voice, however indeterminate, seems to be Molloy's (or, later, that of Molloy's double, Jacques Moran). But the narrative voice of the second novel, Malone's, suggests that the first novel had in fact been written by Malone himself, so that Molloy and Moran are nothing but the products of Malone's odd imagination. In the third novel this revision is itself revised and Malone's existence becomes as doubtful as that of Molloy and Moran. As for the uncertain, nameless, floundering narrative voice of *The Unnamable*, the reader is at a loss to say whether it is one broken voice or several. Retraction is still the main technique, but who is retracting what is impossible to determine.

CONCLUSION

At the end of this essay, in which I have tried to argue in favor of a historical-hypothetical concept of postmodernism, the reasons why I have eschewed a conventional definition of such a concept should be stressed again, in the form of a more general summation. "All concepts in which an entire process is semiotically concentrated elude definition," Nietzsche once observed, adding: "Only that which has no history is definable."[71] In his succinct statement

of method in *The Protestant Ethic and the Spirit of Capitalism,* Max
Weber repeats the Nietzschean thesis about the undefinability of
historical categories, but goes further to specify why, when, and
how such categories, though undefined, can be legitimately used.
In regard to his own "somewhat pretentious" phrase "the *spirit* of
capitalism," Weber notes that it can only have an understandable
meaning if it refers to "a complex of elements associated in historical
reality which we unite into a conceptual whole." It is emphatically
we who select the elements and construct (or put together, or make
up) this whole, as Weber insists in a key passage, which deserves to
be quoted at length:

> An historical concept . . . cannot be defined according to the for-
> mula *genus proximus, differentia specifica,* but it must be gradually
> put together out of the individual parts which are taken from histor-
> ical reality to make it up. . . . We must, in other words, work out in
> the course of the discussion, as its most important result, the best
> conceptual formulation of what we understand by the spirit of cap-
> italism, that is the best from the point of view which interests us
> here. This point of view . . . is, further, by no means the only
> possible one from which the historical phenomena we are investigat-
> ing can be analysed. Other standpoints would, for this as for every
> historical phenomenon, yield other characteristics as the essential
> ones. . . . This is a necessary result of the nature of historical con-
> cepts which attempt for their methodological purposes not to grasp
> historical reality in abstract general formulae, but in concrete genet-
> ic sets of relations which are inevitably of a specifically unique and
> individual character.[72]

The importance of point of view and methodological purpose is
paramount. As I made clear at several junctures in the course of this
essay, my account of postmodernism has set itself three larger goals:
(1) to indicate the areas and the main ways in which postmodernism
has been conceptualized from the 1940s to the 1980s; (2) to bring out
the hypothetical nature of the term, which should be seen as an
explanatory and operational construct (significantly, the adoption or
rejection of postmodernism involves a reconceptualization of other
major period constructs, such as modernism and the avant-garde);

and (3) to suggest, from a metatheoretical vantage point, the basic requirements that a good theory of postmodernism should fulfill. Among these requirements I have given particular attention to hypothetical self-consciousness (especially rare in historical studies, which are traditionally predisposed to the "realistic" and "teleological" fallacies), specificity of application, and, in the last two sections of this chapter, postmodernism's ability to produce insights that are new, exciting, and, if not really testable, arguable (also in the sense of worth arguing).

My own theory or, better, understanding of postmodernism remains largely metaphorical and can best be stated in terms of the physiognomical "family resemblances" to which I have referred earlier. Postmodernism is a face of modernity. It reveals some striking likenesses with modernism (whose name it continues to carry within its own), particularly in its opposition to the principle of authority, an opposition that now extends to both the utopian reason and the utopian unreason that some modernists worshiped. Postmodernism's refined eclecticism, its questioning of unity, and its valuation of the part against the whole in this fin de siècle may remind one of the "decadent euphoria" of the 1880s. But the popular code that it conspicuously uses can also make postmodernism look very much like kitsch or camp, with which its adversaries deliberately identify it. And finally, postmodernism can on occasion bear the resemblance of a twin to the avant-garde, especially to its nonminimalist versions (from the metaphysical school of De Chirico to the surrealists). We perceive these varied faces as related because of their common association with a larger modernity and with its spirit. Were it not for this larger modernity, the partial similarities and the expressive differences among these faces would melt away and become meaningless. We would no longer be attracted to compare and contrast them. We may then assume that as long as we compare and contrast them, modernity survives, at least as the name of a cultural family resemblance in which, for better or for worse, we continue to recognize ourselves.

NOTES

THE IDEA OF MODERNITY

1. Mircea Eliade, *The Myth of the Eternal Return*, trans. from the French by Willard R. Trask (New York: Pantheon Books, 1965). For a broad discussion of various ideas of time, from the "dream" time of primitive man to the "irresistibly passing time" of modern man, see also J. B. Priestley, *Man and Time* (Garden City, New York: Doubleday, 1964), pp. 136–89.

2. *Thesaurus Linguae Latinae* (Leipzig: Teubner, 1966), vol. VIII, p. 1211.

3. Ernst Robert Curtius, *European Literature and the Latin Middle Ages*, trans. from the German by Willard R. Trask (New York: Harper & Row, 1963), pp. 251, 254.

4. For a detailed discussion of this question, and more generally of medieval time categories, see Walter Freund, *Modernus und andere Zeitbegriffe des Mittelalters* (Köln: Böhlau Verlag, 1957), pp. 4 ff. For an account of later medieval uses of *modernus* versus *antiquus*, see *Antiqui und Moderni: Traditionsbewusstsein und Fortschrittsbewusstsein in späten Mittelalter*, ed. Albert Zimmermann (Berlin, New York: Walter de Gruyter, 1974), and especially the contributions of Wilfried Hartmann, Elisabeth Gössmann, and Günter Wolf; also, Elisabeth Gössmann, *Antiqui und Moderni: Eine geschichtliche Standortbestimmung* (Munich: Schöningh, 1974). The overall traditionalism of the Middle Ages and the prevailing medieval disregard of *historical time*, made up of unique, unrepeatable moments, go against the deep sense of historicity implied by Christianity's philosophy of time. The paradoxical view of the Middle Ages' rejection of the original Christian notion of time has been convincingly argued by Denis de Rougemont in *Man's Western Quest*, trans. Montgomery Belgion (New York: Harper, 1957). To the revolutionary challenge of Christian time, Denis de Rougemont writes, "the Middle Ages resisted by going back to cyclical conceptions and by a sharp limitation upon the size of the past and the future: the effect of the kind of congelation of time which this entailed was *the elimination of all becoming*" (p. 95). According to de Rougemont, "the Middle Ages were the 'Eastern' period of Europe," because of their "growing propensity... to substitute tradition, mystical allegory, and legend for the *facts* which only Scripture, very little read at the time, showed to be historical. All this strengthens my view that the Middle Ages,

far from standing for some vague 'golden age of Christianity'—as the Romantics were the first to allege and has been repeated *ad nauseam* ever since—were much rather, generally speaking, a long defensive reaction against the revolutionary ferment introduced into the world by the Gospel" (p. 90).

5. Curtius, op. cit., p. 119.

6. John of Salisbury, *The Metalogicon*, trans. with Introd. and Notes by Daniel D. McGarry (Gloucester, Mass.: Peter Smith, 1971), p. 167. The Latin original reads: ". . . Fruitur tamen aetas nostra beneficio praecedentis, et saepe plura novit, non suo quidem praecedens ingenio, sed innitens viribus alienis, et opulenta doctrina Patrum. Dicebat Bernardus Carnotensis nos esse quasi nanos, gigantium humeris incidentes, ut possimus plura eis et remotiora videre, non utique proprii visus acumine, aut eminentia corporis, sed quia in altum subvenimur et extollimur magnitudine gigantea." (*Metalogicus*, III, 4, C, in Migne, *Patrologia Latina*, vol. 199, col. 900).

7. For an interpretation of Bernard's simile, see Edouard Jeauneau, "'Nani gigantum humeris incidentes': Essai d'interprétation de Bernard de Chartres," *Vivarium* V, 2 (November 1967):79–99. On the circulation of Bernard's figure in the twelfth century (Peter of Blois, Alexander Neckham), see J. de Ghellinck, "Nani et gigantes," *Archivum Latinitatis medii aevi* 18 (1945):25–29. Very useful references for later treatments of this topos are: Foster E. Guyer, "The Dwarf on Giant's Shoulders," in *Modern Language Notes* (June 1930):398–402; George Sarton, "Standing on the Shoulders of Giants," *Isis*, no. 67, XXIV, I (Dec. 1935):107–109, and the answer to Sarton's note by Raymond Klibansky, "Standing on the Shoulders of Giants," *Isis*, no. 71, XXVI, I (Dec. 1936):147–49. For a more recent discussion of the theme of dwarfs and giants, see Robert K. Merton, *On the Shoulders of Giants: A Shandean Postscript* (New York: The Free Press, 1965). This is, as Catherine Drinker Bowen characterizes it in the foreword, a "brilliant, crazy, riotous Shandean Postscript, . . . a romp, a frolick, a frisk, a ball—an impossible mad excursion into scholarship and round about and out again . . ." (p. VII).

8. E. J. Trenchmann, trans., *The Essays of Montaigne* (London: Oxford University Press, 1927), vol. 2, p. 545. The quotation reads in the original: "Nos opinions s'entent les unes sur les autres. La première sert de tige . . . à la seconde, la seconde à la tierce. Nous eschellons ainsi de degré en degré. Et advient de là que le plus haut monté a souvent plus d'honneur que de merite; car il n'est monté que d'un grain sur les espaules du penultime." In Montaigne, *Oeuvres complètes*, textes établis par A. Thibaudet et Maurice Rat (Paris: Gallimard, Bibliothèque de la Pléiade, 1962), p. 1046.

9. Robert Burton, *The Anatomy of Melancholy* (London: Dent, Everyman's Library, 1964), p. 25.

10. Quoted in L. T. More, *Isaac Newton* (New York: Charles Scribner's Sons, 1934), pp. 176–77.

11. Blaise Pascal, *Thoughts, Letters, and Opuscules*, trans. O. W. Wight (Boston: Houghton, Mifflin and Co., 1882), p. 544.

12. Ibid., p. 548. Here is the original: "C'est de cette façon que l'on peut aujourd'hui prendre d'autres sentiments et des nouvelles opinions sans mépris et sans ingratitude, puisque les premières connaissances qu'ils nous ont données ont servi de degrés aux nôtres, et que dans ces avantages nous leurs sommes redevables de l'ascendent que nous avons sur eux; parce que, s'étant élevés jusqu'à un certain degré où ils nous on portés, le moindre effort nous fait monter plus haut, et avec moins de peine et moins de gloire nous nous trouvons au-dessus d'eux. C'est de là que nous pouvons découvrir des choses qu'il leur était impossible d'apercevoir. Notre vue a plus d'étendue, et, quoiqu'ils connussent aussi bien que nous tout ce qu'ils pouvaient remarquer de la nature, ils n'en connaissaient pas tant néanmoins, et nous voyons plus qu'eux." In Pascal, *Oeuvres complètes*, texte établi et annoté par Jacques Chevalier (Paris: Gallimard, Bibliothèque de la Pléiade, 1954), p. 532.

13. See J. B. Priestley, op. cit., p. 38. Also, L. Thorndike, "Invention of the Mechanical Clock about 1271 A.D.," *Speculum* 16 (1941):242–43. About the distinction between old and new forms of time consciousness in the late Middle Ages, with special reference to the impact of new, mechanical methods of measuring time, see Jean Leclercq, "Zeiterfahrung und Zeitbegriff in Spätmittelalter," in *Antiqui und Moderni*, ed. Zimmermann, pp. 1–20. A remarkable article on two conflicting medieval notions of time—religious time versus commercial time—is Jacques Le Goff's "Au Moyen Age: Temps de l'Eglise et temps du marchand," *Annales—Economies, Sociétés, Civilisations* 15 (1960):417–33.

14. Ricardo Quinones, *The Renaissance Discovery of Time* (Cambridge, Mass.: Harvard University Press, 1972), p. 7.

15. Ibid., p. 11.

16. Theodor E. Mommsen, "Petrarch's Conception of the 'Dark Ages,'" *Speculum* XVII, 2 (April 1942):241.

17. *Africa*, IX, 451–57. Quoted after Mommsen, op. cit., p. 240. Here is the original:

> ... Michi degere vitam
> Impositum varia rerum turbante procella.
> At tibi fortassis, si—quod mens sperat et optat—
> Es post me victura diu, meliora supersunt

Secula: non omnes veniet Letheus in annos
Iste sopor. Poterunt discussis forte tenebris
Ad purum priscumque iubar remeare nepotes.

Cf. *Edizione nazionale delle opere di Francesco Petrarca* (Florence: G. C.
Sansoni, 1926), vol. 1, p. 278.

18. Francis Bacon, *The Advancement of Learning*, ed. W. A. Wright
(Oxford: Clarendon Press, 1900), p. 38. Thomas Hobbes made use of the
same paradox in the "Conclusion" of his *Leviathan* (1651): "Though I reverence those men of Ancient Time, that either have written Truth
perspicuously, or set us in a better way to find it out ourselves; yet to
Antiquity itself I think nothing due: For if we will reverence the Age, the
Present is the Oldest." (*Hobbes' Leviathan*, reprinted from the Edition of
1651, Oxford: Clarendon Press, 1947, p. 556). By Swift's time such a view
had become almost a cliché. So the author of the *Battle of the Books* (1704)
could write, making fun of the whole argument (especially as it was applied
to literary matters): "Here a solitary *Antient*, squeezed up among a whole
shelf of *Moderns*, offered fairly to dispute the Case, and to prove by manifest Reasons, that the Priority was due to them, from long Possession, and
in regard to their Prudence, and seemed very much to wonder, how the
Antients could pretend to insist upon their Antiquity, when it was so plain
(if they went to that) that the Moderns were much the more Antient of the
two." (Swift, *A Tale of a Tub*, Oxford: Clarendon Press, 1920, p. 227).

19. *The Works of Francis Bacon*, ed. J. Spedding et al. (Boston: Tag-
gard and Thompson, 1868), vol. VIII, p. 26.

20. Ibid., p. 116.

21. For Fontenelle's use of Bacon's paradox, see his "Digression..." in
Oeuvres (Paris: 1742), vol. IV, pp. 191–92. The old Augustinian comparison
between the development of mankind and that of an individual man is used
to fit the Enlightenment doctrine of infinite progress. Thus, the moderns
are older than the ancients but they will never become actually old because
humanity as such (unlike the transitory individuals that it is made of) can
preserve the advantages of adulthood indefinitely. Fontenelle writes: "Ainsi
cet Homme qui a vécu depuis le commencement du monde jusqu'à présent, a eu son enfance, où il ne s'est occupé que des besoins les plus
pressants de la vie, sa jeunesse où il a assés bien réussi aux choses de
l'imagination, telles que la Poësie et l'Eloquence, et où même il a com-
mencé à raisonner, mais avec moins de solidité que de feu. Il est maintenant dans l'âge de virilité...." But, adds Fontenelle, "cet Homme-là n'aura
point de vieillesse." Although Bacon's maxim had been used in France as
early as the time of Descartes, it was still regarded as strikingly paradoxical
by Fontenelle's contemporary, the Jesuit *Père* Dominique Bouhours. In his

La manière de bien penser dans les ouvrages de l'esprit (1687), Bouhours quotes Bacon: "Pour moi, je suis un peu de l'avis du Chancelier Bacon, qui croit que l'antiquité des siècles est la jeunesse du monde, et qu'à bien compter nous sommes proprement les anciens." But then he notes: "Je ne sçay... si la pensée de Bacon n'est point trop subtile...." (*La manière de bien penser*..., ed. 1715, Brighton: Sussex Reprints, 1971, pp. 138–39).

22. Foster E. Guyer, "'C'est nous qui sommes les anciens'," in *Modern Language Notes* XXXVI, 5 (May 1921):260.

23. Augustine in fact was a consistent adversary of the "progressivist" and optimistic theologians of the time (Eusebius of Cesarea and his followers), and his conception of history was definitely pessimistic (he spoke of his age as "malignant," "evil," etc.). For a treatment of Augustine's antiprogressive philosophy of history, see Theodor E. Mommsen, "St. Augustine and the Christian Idea of Progress," *Journal of the History of Ideas*, vol. XII (1951):346–74.

24. A discussion of this dialogue and of the theme of the origins of the *Querelle*, in Giacinto Margiotta, *Le origini italiane de la Querelle des Anciens et des Modernes* (Rome: Studium, 1953). For the reference to Bruni, see pp. 34 ff.

25. Curtius, op. cit., p. 254.

26. H. R. Jauss's study was published as an introduction to the facsimile edition of Charles Perrault's *Parallèle des Anciens et des Modernes en ce qui regarde les arts et les sciences* (Munich: Eidos, 1964), pp. 8–64.

27. Perrault, op. cit. (see Note 26), p. 322.

28. Ibid., p. 308.

29. "A Digression in the Modern Kind," in *A Tale of a Tub* (Oxford: Clarendon Press, 1920), p. 129.

30. Perrault, op. cit., p. 296.

31. Pascal, op. cit., pp. 545–46.

32. Boileau, *The Art of Poetry*, ed. Albert S. Cook, Engl. trans. by Soame (New York: Stechert, 1926), pp. 195–96.

The French text:

> C'est donc bien vainement que nos auteurs déçus,
> Bannissant de leurs vers ces ornements reçus,
> Pensent faire agir Dieu, ses saints et ses prophètes,
> Comme ces dieux éclos du cerveau des poètes;
> Mettent à chaque pas le lecteur en enfer;
> N'offrent rien qu'Astaroth, Belzébuth, Lucifer.
> De la foi d'un chrétien les mystères terribles
> D'ornements égayés ne sont point susceptibles....

33. Quoted from H. Rigault, *Histoire de la Querelle des Anciens et des*

Modernes, facsimile edition of the 1859 printing (New York: Burt Franklin, 1965), p. 89. Rigault notes the resemblance between Desmarets's view of the Bible as an unsurpassable model of poetic beauty and the basic assumption of Chateaubriand's *Genius of Christianity.* But he does not fail to stress also the difference. Commenting on Desmarets's *Délices de l'esprit* (1658), Rigault writes: "Qu'a fait Desmarets de cette idée féconde? Un livre curieux en certains passages, mais à cela près illisible. M. de Chateaubriand en a fait le *Génie du Christianisme.* Singulière fortune des idées qui portent dans leurs sein de tels ouvrages, et qui attendent des siècles entiers un grand écrivain pour les faire éclore!" (pp. 88–89).

34. Richard Hurd, *Letters on Chivalry and Romance,* facsimile edition of the 1762 printing (New York: Garland, 1971), p. 57.

35. Ibid., p. 56.

36. Ibid., p. 55.

37. In fact, the section devoted to "ideal Beauty" in Stendhal's *Histoire . . .* had been written as early as 1814. Striking and clear-cut as it may seem today, Stendhal's early distinction between *le beau idéal antique* and *le beau idéal moderne* (see his *Oeuvres complétes,* ed. Georges Eudes [Paris: Larrive, 1953], vol. 3, *Histoire de la peinture en Italie,* Books IV through VI, pp. 155–241), was more original in formulation than in substance, coming after the numerous terminological and typological oppositions proposed in England, Germany, and even in France, where Madame de Staël's *De l'Allemagne* had introduced the aesthetic opposition *classique/romantique* in 1813. What Stendhal understood by modern beauty was, after all, in keeping with the broad historical meaning of "modernity" or romanticism that had emerged from the late stages of the Quarrel between the Ancients and the Moderns. As an example, we may recall that Stendhal offers a quotation from Tasso's late sixteenth-century *Gerusalemme liberata* to illustrate the distinction between modern beauty, as embodied in poetry, and ancient beauty (p. 216). Also, stressing the importance of love—more specifically romantic love—in shaping the modern ideal of beauty, Stendhal predictably brings in the medieval institution of chivalry.

What is actually new in his approach, leaving aside his consistent polemical historicism in explaining ancient and modern beauty through such factors as the climate, the system of laws, and the theory of temperaments, is his emphasis on certain values of modern *civilization,* as summarized in the suggestive contrast he establishes between Paris, the modern metropolis *par excellence,* and ancient Athens. Stendhal writes:

> Le soleil est un peu pâle en France; on y a beaucoup d'esprit, on est porté à mettre de la recherche dans l'expression des passions. . . . Pour les choses de sentiment, c'est peut-être à Paris que se trouvent les juges les plus délicats;

mais il surnage toujours un peu de froideur. C'est donc à Paris qu'on a le
mieux peint l'amor délicat, qu'on a le mieux fait sentir l'influence d'un mot,
d'un coup d'oeil, d'un regard.... Dans Athènes l'on ne cherchait pas tant de
nuances, tant de délicatesse. La beauté physique obtenait un culte partout où
elle se recontrait. Ces gens-là n'allèrent-ils pas jusqu'à s'imaginer que les âmes
qui habitaient de beaux corps s'en détachaient avec plus de répugnance que
celles qui étaient cachées sous des formes vulgaires?... Mais aussi le culte de la
beauté n'était que physique, l'amour n'allait pas plus loin... (pp. 226–27).

What are, according to Stendhal, the main features of the modern ideal
of beauty? The writer lists them in what seems a rather capricious order:

1. Un esprit extrêmement vif.
2. Beaucoup de grâces dans les traits.
3. L'oeil étincelant, non pas du feu sombre des passions, mais du feu de la
   saillie. L'expression la plus vive des mouvements de l'âme est dans l'oeil,
   qui échappe à la sculpture. Les yeux modernes seraient donc fort grands.
4. Beaucoup de gaieté.
5. Un fonds de sensibilité.
6. Une taille svelte, et surtout l'air agile de la jeunesse (p. 219).

To these qualities we must add "elegance" (p. 229) and a "noble" appearance (p. 223). Might not this concept of beauty be mistaken for a belated
expression of eighteenth-century rococo taste? Stendhal's aesthetic views
are actually more complex and interesting. Even as early as his *History of
Painting in Italy* he makes a strong point that *freedom* and *originality* are
indispensable to art. No submission to any set of rules, principles, or directions can lead to true artistic success. A genuine artist obeys only his own
individuality and resists the temptation to imitate other artists, ancient or
modern. What emerges as the central quality of modern beauty is, then, a
certain sense of refined psychological complexity, which has little to do with
the frivolousness of the rococo style. But to develop fully his theory of
modernity Stendhal seems to have needed the term *romanticisme*, which
he adopted in 1823 from the Italian *romanticismo*, and by which he designated modernity in a sense both more precise and fluid than in *Histoire....*

38. Stendhal, *Oeuvres complètes*, ed. Georges Eudes (Paris: Larrive,
1954), vol. XVI, p. 27. The text in French:

Le *romanticisme* est l'art de présenter aux peuples les oeuvres littéraires qui,
dans l'état actuel de leur habitudes et de leurs croyances, sont susceptibles de
leur donner le plus de plaisir possible.
Le *classicisme*, au contraire, leur présente la littérature qui donnait le plus
grand plaisir possible à leurs arrière-grands-pères.... Imiter aujourd'hui
Sophocle et Euripide, et prétendre que ces imitations ne feront pas bailler le
français du dix-neuvième siècle, c'est du classicisme.

39. Ibid., p. 227.

40. Ibid., p. 28.

41. Inhibiting imagination, habit diminishes man's capacity for aesthetic pleasure. Stendhal puts this very clearly: "... L'habitude exerce un pouvoir despotique sur l'imagination des hommes même les plus éclairés, et, par leur imagination, sur les plaisirs que les arts peuvent leur donner." Ibid., p. 54.

42. An extensive study of "modernity" as a concept is Hans Robert Jauss's "Literarische Tradition und gegenwärtiges Bewusstsein der Modernität—Wortgeschichtliche Betrachtungen," in Aspekte der Modernität, ed. Hans Steffen (Göttingen: Vandenhoeck & Ruprecht, 1965), pp. 150–97. The analysis of "modernity" from a terminological point of view forms the object of a large part of Adrian Marino's book Modern, modernism, modernitate (Bucharest: Editura Univers, 1970). More recently, Marino has addressed himself to the question of modernity in a learned article, "Modernisme et modernité, quelques précisions sémantiques," published in Neohelicon 3–4 (1974):307–18.

43. The passage is from a letter to William Cole, dated 22 February 1782. "There is a report," Horace Walpole writes, "that proof of some part of Chatterton's forgery is to be produced from an accomplice.... I have scarce seen a person who is not persuaded, that the *fashion* of the poems was Chatterton's own, though he might have found some old stuff to work upon ... ; but now that the poems have been so much examined, nobody (that has an ear) can get over the *modernity* [my italics] of the modulation, and the recent cast of the ideas and phraseology.... Still the boy remains a prodigy ... and still it will be inexplicable how he found time or materials for operating such miracles." In The Yale Edition of Horace Walpole's Correspondence, ed. W. S. Lewis (New Haven: Yale University Press, 1937), vol. II, pp. 305–306.

44. Émile Littré, Dictionnaire de la langue française (Paris: Gallimard-Hachette, 1957), vol. 5, p. 315.

45. Paul Robert, Dictionnaire alphabétique et analogique de la langue française (Paris, 1959), vol. IV, p. 607. The quotation from Chateaubriand reads in the original: "La vulgarité, la modernité de la douane et du passeport, contrastaient avec l'orage, la porte gothique, le son du cor et le bruit du torrent." For the context in which the passage occurs, see Chateaubriand, Memoires d'outre-tombe, ed. Edmond Biré (Paris: Garnier, n.d.), vol. VI, pp. 25–26.

46. Quoted from Peter Demetz, Marx, Engels and the Poets (Chicago: The University of Chicago Press, 1967), pp. 167, 169.

47. Théophile Gautier, Souvenirs de théâtre, d'art et de critique (Paris:

Charpentier, 1883), p. 203. The article from which the quotation is taken was published in *L'Evénement* (August 8, 1848).

48. When not otherwise indicated, Baudelaire is quoted in English translation from *Baudelaire As a Literary Critic*, Selected Essays, Intro. and Trans. by Lois Boe Hylsop and Francis E. Hylsop (University Park, Penn.: The Pennsylvania State University Press, 1964). The previous quotation is from p. 40.

49. Ibid. The passage in the original reads:

... Ainsi, comme il y a eu autant d'idéals qu'il y a eu pour les peuples de façons de comprendre la morale, l'amour, la religion, etc., le romantisme ne consistera pas dans une exécution parfaite, mais dans une conception analogue à la morale du siècle.... Il faut donc, avant tout, connaître les aspects de la nature et les situations de l'homme, que les artistes du passé ont dédaignés ou n'ont pas connu. Qui dit romantisme dit art moderne,—c'est-à-dire intimité, spiritualité, couleur, aspiration vers l'infini, exprimées par tous les moyens que contiennent les arts.

In Baudelaire, *Oeuvres complètes*, texte établi et annoté par Y.-G. Le Dantec, éd. révisée par Claude Pichois (Paris: Gallimard, Bibliothèque de la Pléiade, 1961), p. 879.

50. Ibid., p. 41.

51. Ibid., pp. 296-97. The text in French:

La modernité, c'est le transitoire, le fugitif, le contingent, la moitié de l'art, dont l'autre moitié est l'éternel et l'immuable.... Cet élément transitoire, fugitif, dont les métamorphoses sont si fréquentes, vous n'avez pas le droit de le mépriser ou de vous en passer. En le supprimant, vous tombez forcément dans le vide d'une beauté abstraite et indéfinissable, comme celle de l'unique femme avant le premier péché.... En un mot, pour que toute *modernité* soit digne de devenir antiquité, il faut que la beauté mystérieuse que la vie humaine y met involontairement en ait été extraite.... Malheur à celui qui étudie dans l'antique autre chose que l'art pur, la logique, la méthode générale! Pour s'y trop plonger, il perd la mémoire du présent; il abdique la valeur et les privilèges fournis par la circonstance; car presque toute notre originalité vient de l'estampille que le *temps* imprime à nos sensations.

In Baudelaire, op. cit., pp. 1163-65.

52. Paul de Man, "Literary History and Literary Modernity," in *Blindness and Insight* (New York: Oxford University Press, 1971), pp. 142-65.

53. Ibid., p. 147.

54. Ibid., pp. 151-52.

55. Ibid., p. 162.

56. Ibid., p. 161.

57. Ibid., p. 164.
58. Baudelaire, *Oeuvres complètes,* ed. cit., p. 1277.
59. Ibid., p. 1255.
60. Ibid.
61. Ibid., p. 951.
62. *Poems of Baudelaire,* trans. Roy Campbell (New York: Pantheon Books, 1959). The text in French:

> Viens-tu du ciel profond ou sors-tu de l'abîme,
> O Beauté? ton regard, infernal et divin,
> Verse confusément le bienfait et le crime,
> Et l'on peut pour cela te comparer au vin.
>
> . . . .
>
> Tu marches sur les morts, Beauté, dont tu te moques;
> De tes bijoux l'Horreur n'est pas le moins charmant,
> Et le Meurtre, parmi tes plus chères breloques,
> Sur ton ventre orgueilleux danse amoureusement.
>
> L'éphèmere ébloui vole vers toi, chandelle,
> Crépite, flambe et dit: Bénissons ce flambeau!

Oeuvres complètes, p. 23.
63. See "Since It Is a Question of Realism," in *Baudelaire As a Literary Critic,* pp. 85-88. For the text in French, "Puisque réalisme il y a," *Oeuvres complètes,* pp. 634-37.
64. Ibid., pp. 92-94. The passage in French is from the Crépet edition:

> De tous les documents que j'ai lus est résultée pour moi la conviction que les États-Unis ne furent pour Poe qu'une vaste prison qu'il parcourait avec l'agitation fiévreuse d'un être fait pour respirer dans un monde plus aromal,— qu'une grande barbarie éclairée au gaz,—et que sa vie intérieure, spirituelle... n'était qu'un effort perpétuel pour échapper à l'influence de cette atmosphère antipathique. Impitoyable dictature que celle de l'opinion dans les sociétés démocratiques.... On dirait que de l'amour impie de la liberté est née une tyrannie nouvelle, la tyrannie des bêtes, ou zoocratie, qui par son insensibilité féroce ressemble à l'idole de Jaggernaut.... Le temps et l'argent ont là-bas une valeur si grande! L'activité matérielle, exagerée jusque'aux proportions d'une manie nationale, laisse dans les esprits bien peu de place pour les choses qui ne sont pas de la terre. Poe, qui... professait que le grand malheur de son pays était de n'avoir pas d'aristocratie de race, attendu, disait'il, que chez un peuple sans aristocratie le culte du Beau ne peut que se corrompre, s'amoindrir et disparaître,—qui accusait chez ses concitoyens, jusque dans leur luxe emphatique et coûteux, tous les symptômes du mauvais goût caractéristique des parvenus,—qui considérait le Progrès, la grande idée moderne, comme une extase de gobe-mouches.... Poe était là-bas un cerveau singulièrement solitaire.

In Charles Baudelaire, *Oeuvres complètes*, ed. Jacques Crépet (Paris: Conard, 1932), vol. VI, "Edgar Poe, sa vie et ses oeuvres," pp. VIII–IX, X–XI.

65. Ibid., p. 125. The original reads in the Crépet edition: "Pour toute intelligence du vieux monde, un État politique a un centre de mouvement qui est son cerveau et son soleil, des souvenirs anciens et glorieux, de longues annales poétiques et militaires, une aristocratie... mais *Cela*! cette cohue de vendeurs et d'acheteurs, ce sans-nom, ce monstre sans tête, ce déporté derrière l'Océan, un État!" In Baudelaire, *Oeuvres complètes* (Conard, 1933), vol. VII, "Notes nouvelles sur Edgar Poe," p. XIII.

66. Ibid., p. 119.

67. Ibid., p. 298. The text in French: "Passez en revue, analysez tout ce qui est naturel, toutes les actions et les désirs du pur homme naturel, vous ne trouverez rien que d'affreux. Tout ce qui est beau et noble est le résultat de la raison et du calcul. Le crime, dont l'animal humain a puisé le goût dans le ventre de sa mère, est originellement naturel. La vertu, au contraire, est *artificielle*, surnaturelle.... Le mal se fait sans effort, *naturellement*, par fatalité; le bien est toujours le produit d'un art." In Baudelaire, *Oeuvres complètes*, p. 1183.

68. *Oeuvres complètes*, p. 1256.

69. In a famous letter to Fernand Desnoyers dating from late 1853 or early 1854, Baudelaire writes: "... Vous savez bien que je suis incapable de m'attendrir sur les végétaux, et que mon âme est rebelle à cette singulière religion nouvelle, qui aura toujours, ce me semble, pour tout être *spirituel*, je ne sais quoi de *shocking*. Je ne croirai jamais que *l'âme des Dieux habite dans les plantes*, et, quand même elle y habiterait, je m'en soucierais médiocrement et considérerais la mienne comme d'un bien plus haut prix que celle des légumes sanctifiées. J'ai même toujours pensé qu'il y avait dans la Nature, florissante et rajeunie, quelque chose d'impudent et d'affligeant." In Baudelaire, *Correspondance*, ed. by Claude Pichois (Paris: Gallimard, Bibliothèque de la Pléiade, 1973), Vol. I, p. 248. For Baudelaire's attitude toward nature, see F. W. Leakey's book *Baudelaire and Nature* (Manchester: Manchester Univ. Press, 1969).

70. *Oeuvres complètes*, p. 890.

71. Renato Poggioli, "Technology and the Avant-Garde," in *The Theory of the Avant-Garde*, trans. Gerald Fitzgerald (New York: Harper & Row, Icon Editions, 1971), pp. 131–47.

72. Octavio Paz, *Children of the Mire*, trans. Rachel Phillips (Cambridge, Mass.: Harvard University Press, 1974), p. 23.

73. Ibid., pp. 45–46.

74. Thomas Molnar, *Utopia, the Perennial Heresy* (New York: Sheed and Ward, 1967).

75. Ernst Bloch, *A Philosophy of the Future*, trans. John Cumming

(New York: Herder and Herder, 1970), p. 91. Here is the whole passage: "Of course there is Schiller's dictum with its idealism, its resignation: 'Only that which has never come to pass never grows old.' But when applied to the *utopicum* and what that postulates, its truth relies solely upon a utopian interpolation—the adverbial 'not yet.' Then, *cum grano salis* (seasoned with the salt of historically exact understanding, the understanding of latency), the saying is just: 'Only that which has never yet come to pass never grows old.'"

76. Jurgen Habermas, "Ernst Bloch—A Marxist Romantic," *Salmagundi* 10–11 (Fall 1969–Winter 1970):313.

77. Paz, op. cit., pp. 27–28.

78. See *The Correspondence of Jonathan Swift*, ed. Harold Williams (Oxford: Clarendon Press, 1965), vol. 5, pp. 58–59. The complete sentence in Swift's letter to Alexander Pope (June 1734) reads: "I wish you would give order against the corruption of English by those Scribblers who send us over their trash in Prose and Verse, with abominable Curtailings and quaint Modernisms." The letter was first published in 1734.

79. In "A Digression on Madness," Swift writes in connection with his "most ingenious Friend, Mr. W-tt-n" that "his Brain has undergone an unlucky Shake; which even his Brother *Modernists* themselves, like Ungrates, do whisper so loud, that it reaches up to the very Garret I am now writing in." *A Tale of a Tub*, ed. cit., p. 169.

80. In "The Revolt Against Positivism in Recent European Literary Scholarship," René Wellek points out that "Factualism most nearly triumphed in France just after the first World War: The heavily documented thèse; the wide ramifications of a well-organized school of comparative literature, inspired by Fernand Baldensperger; the successes of scholars who furnished extremely elaborate editions of French classics; the theories of Daniel Mornet, who demanded an 'integral' literary history of minor and even minimal authors—all these are symptoms that France tried to catch up with the purely historical scholarship of the nineteenth century." In René Wellek, *Concepts of Criticism* (New Haven: Yale University Press, 1963), p. 261.

81. For a comprehensive study of Darío's pronouncements on *modernismo*, see Allen W. Phillips, "Rubén Darío y sus juicios sobre el modernismo," *Revista Iberoamericana* 24 (1959):41–64. For an overall history of the term *modernismo* in Hispanic criticism, see Max Henríquez Ureña, *Breve historia del modernismo*, 2d ed. (Mexico: Fondo de Cultura Económica, 1962), pp. 158–72. Also, Ned J. Davison, *The Concept of Modernism in Hispanic Criticism* (Boulder, Colorado: Pruett Press, 1966). Darío is quoted after Henríquez Ureña, p. 158.

82. Henríquez Ureña, op. cit., p. 159.
83. Ibid., p. 160.
84. Ibid.
85. Ibid., p. 163.
86. Ibid., p. 161.
87. Ibid., p. 168.
88. Ibid., p. 169.
89. Quoted after Davison, op. cit., p. 6.
90. Cf. Davison, op. cit., pp. 41–48.
91. Pedro Salinas, "El problema del modernismo en España, o un conflicto entre dos espíritus," in Homero Castillo, ed., *Estudios críticos sobre el modernismo* (Madrid: Editorial Gredos, 1968), p. 24.
92. Salinas, op. cit., p. 28.
93. Juan Ramón Jiménez, *El Modernismo: Notas de un curso*, ed. Ricardo Gullón, and Eugenio Fernández Méndez (Madrid: Aguilar, 1962).
94. Ricardo Gullón, *Direcciones del Modernismo*, 2d ed. (Madrid: Editorial Gredos, 1971).
95. Isaac Goldberg, "The 'Modernista' Renovation," in *Studies in Spanish American Literature* (New York: Brentano's, 1920), pp. 1–3.
96. Federico de Onís, "Sobre el concepto del Modernismo" (1949), in his *España en América: Estudios, ensayos y discursos sobre temas españoles e hispanoamericanos*, 2d ed. (San Juan: Universidad de Puerto Rico, 1968), p. 177.
97. Ibid., p. 183.
98. Cf. Gullón, op. cit., p. 26.
99. Federico de Onís, *Antología de la poesía española e hispanoamericana (1882–1932)* (New York: Las Americas, 1961), p. XVIII.
100. Federico de Onís, "Martí y el Modernismo" in *España en América*, p. 625.
101. The bibliography of the controversy is huge. A good introduction to the problem and personalities involved is *Roman Catholic Modernism*, ed. and intr. by Bernard M. G. Reardon (Stanford, Calif.: Stanford University Press, 1970).
102. Poggioli, op. cit., pp. 216–18.
103. Joseph T. Shipley, *Dictionary of World Literary Terms* (Boston: The Writer, 1970), p. 156.
104. Laura Riding and Robert Graves, *A Survey of Modernist Poetry* (London: Heinemann, 1929), p. 156.
105. Ibid., p. 9.
106. Ibid.
107. Ibid., p. 11.

108. Ibid., p. 155.

109. Ibid., p. 156.

110. Ibid., p. 157.

111. Ibid., p. 158.

112. Ibid., p. 156.

113. René Wellek and Austin Warren, *Theory of Literature*, 3d ed. (New York: Harcourt, 1956), pp. 262 ff. ". . . A period is not a type or a class but a time section defined by a system of norms embedded in the historical process and irremovable from it. . . . An individual work of art is not an instance in a class, but a part which, together with all the other works, makes up the concept of the period. It thus modifies the concept of the whole" (p. 265). However, established period terms have been and will continue to be used to designate artistic or psychological types, detached from historical context.

114. G. R. Hocke, *Manierismus in der Literatur. Sprach-Alchimie und esoterische Kombinationskunst* (Hamburg: Rowohlt, 1969).

115. Stephen Spender, *The Struggle of the Modern* (London: Hamilton, 1963), pp. 71–72.

116. Ibid., p. 77.

117. Lionel Trilling, *Beyond Culture* (New York: The Viking Press, 1961), pp. 3–30.

118. Ibid., pp. 15–16.

119. Interestingly, the distinction between "modern" and "contemporary" has been very popular in Soviet and post-World War II East European criticism. The whole discussion about "contemporariness" (within the framework of the theory of socialist realism, of which it is a constitutive part) is a way of rejecting the ideologically harmful concepts of "modernity" and "modernism," both of them considered aspects of bourgeois decadence.

THE IDEA OF THE AVANT-GARDE

1. There are comparatively few contributions concerning the term and the concept "avant-garde," although the word appears, misleadingly, in quite a number of recent titles. I will limit myself to a single example, namely, John Weightman's *The Concept of the Avant-Garde*, subtitled *Explorations in Modernism* (La Salle, Illinois: Library Press, 1973). In fact, this volume is simply a collection of articles and reviews dealing with French literature, mostly twentieth century. The concept of the avant-garde is treated in only one essay (pp. 13–38) and even there the approach is extremely general. Let me say that the book as such is very interesting, and full of witty and stimulating views, but this does not mean that after reading

it one has a clearer idea of what the concept of the avant-garde actually represents. These brief remarks are obviously not meant as a critique of Weightman's book; what I am objecting to is only its misleading title. And even this abuse is not without interest: it points out that the term "avant-garde" has become, a few decades after being introduced into English, a fashionable word.

One of the most extensive and well-informed terminological essays on the avant-garde is Adrian Marino's "Avangarda," in his *Dictionar de idei literare* (Bucharest: Editura Eminescu, 1973), pp. 177–224. See also "Antiliteratura," ibid., pp. 100–59.

Other major contributions are referred to in the course of the chapter.

2. Renato Poggioli, *The Theory of the Avant-Garde*, p. 8.

3. Donald Drew Egbert, "The Idea of 'Avant-garde' in Art and Politics," *American Historical Review* 73 (1967):339–66. This article has been assimilated into the comprehensive study *Social Radicalism and the Arts—Western Europe* (New York: Knopf, 1970). See also my article "Avant-Garde: Some Terminological Considerations," *Yearbook of Comparative and General Literature* 23 (1974):67–78.

4. Etienne Pasquier, *Oeuvres choisies*, ed. Léon Feugère (Paris: Firmin Didot, 1849), vol. 2, p. 21.

Ce fut une belle guerre que l'ont entreprit lors contre l'ignorance, dont j'attribue *l'avant-garde* [my italics] à Scève, Bèze et Pelletier; ou si le voulez autrement, ce furent les avant-coureurs des autres poëtes. Après se mirent sur les rangs Pierre de Ronsard, Vendômais, et Joachim du Bellay, Angevin, tous deux gentilhommes extraits de très-nobles races. Ces deux rencontrèrent heureusement, mais principalement Ronsard, de manière que sous leurs enseignes plusieurs se firent enrôler.

5. Ibid., vol. 1, pp. 234–49.

6. Ibid., vol. 2, p. 69.

7. Ibid., p. 72.

8. Ibid., p. 73.

9. Robert Estivals, Jean-Charles Gaudy, Gabrielle Vergez, *L'Avant-Garde* (Paris: Bibliothèque Nationale, 1968), pp. 22–24. This book is a bibliographical and sociological study of all the French periodicals carrying the word "avant-garde" in their title, from 1794–1967.

10. *Opinions littéraires, philosophiques et industrielles* (Paris: Galérie de Bossange Père, 1825). "L'Artiste, le Savant et l'Industriel. Dialogue" appears as the Conclusion of the volume, pp. 331 ff. In *Oeuvres de Saint-Simon et d'Enfantin*, Réimpression photomécanique de l'édition de 1865–79 (Aalen: Otto Zeller, 1964), Rodrigues's dialogue is published, under its author's name, in volume XXXIX of the general collection (volume X of

Saint-Simon's works), pp. 201–58. For the passage in which the word *avant-garde* occurs, see pp. 210–11.

11. *Oeuvres de Claude-Henri de Saint-Simon* (Paris: Editions Anthropos, 1966), VI, 422. (The sixth volume of the Anthropos edition collects Saint-Simon's writings not included in *Oeuvres de Saint-Simon et d'Enfantin*.)

12. *Oeuvres de Saint-Simon et d'Enfantin*, XXXIX, (X), pp. 137–38. The passage in French reads:

... dans cette grande entreprise, les artistes, les hommes à imagination ouvriront la marche: ils ôteront au passé l'âge d'or pour en enrichir les générations futures; ils passionnéront la société pour l'accroissement de son bien-être, en lui présentant la tableau de prospérités nouvelles, en faisant sentir que tous les membres de la société participeront bientôt à des jouissances qui, jusqu'à ce jour, ont été l'apanage d'une classe peu nombreuse; ils chanteront les bienfaits de la civilisation, et ils mettront en oeuvre, pour atteindre leur but, tous les moyens des beaux arts, l'éloquence, la poésie, la peinture, la musique, en un mot, ils développeront la partie poétique du nouveau système.

13. See note 10. Here is the original:

C'est nous, artistes, qui vous servirons d'*avant-garde* [my italics]; la puissance des arts est en effet la plus immédiate et la plus rapide. Nous avons des armes de toute espèce: quand nous voulons répandre des idées neuves parmi les hommes, nous les inscrivons sur le marbre ou sur la toile; nous les popularisons par la poésie et le chant; nous employons tour-à-tour la lyre ou le galoubet, l'ode ou la chanson, l'histoire ou le roman; la scène dramatique nous est ouverte, et c'est là surtout que nous exerçons une influence électrique et victorieuse. Nous nous adressons à l'imagination et aux sentiments de l'homme: nous devrons donc exercer toujours l'action la plus vive et la plus décisive; et si aujourd'hui notre rôle paraît nul ou au moins très secondaire, c'est qu'il manquait aux arts ce qui est essentiel à leur énergie et à leur succès, une impulsion commune et une idée générale.

14. *Shelley's Critical Prose*, ed. Bruce R. McElderry, Jr. (Lincoln: University of Nebraska Press, 1967), p. 13.

15. Poggioli, *The Theory of the Avant-garde*, p. 9.

16. D. Laverdant, *De la mission de l'art et du rôle des artistes* (Salon de 1845) (Paris: Aux Bureaux de la Phalange, 1845), p. 4.

17. *Social Radicalism*, p. 135.

18. Ibid., p. 134.

19. Stéphane Mallarmé, *Oeuvres complètes* (Paris: Gallimard, Bibliothèque de la Pléiade, 1970), p. 870. Mallarmé says: "L'attitude du poëte

dans une époque comme celle-ci, où il est en grève devant la société est de mettre de côté tous les moyens viciés qui peuvent s'offrir à lui."

20. *Trésor de la langue française* (Paris: Éditions du Centre National de la Recherche Scientifique, 1974), vol. 3, p. 1056. "Les encyclopédistes, Diderot en tête, les physiocrats, Turgot en tête, les philosophes, Voltaire en tête, les utopistes, Rousseau en tête, ce sont les quatre légions sacrées. L'immense avance de l'humanité vers la lumière leur est due. Ce sont les quatre avant-gardes du genre humain allant aux quatre points cardinaux du progrès, Diderot vers le beau, Turgot vers l'utile, Voltaire vers le vrai, Rousseau vers le juste."

21. Honoré de Balzac, *Oeuvres complètes* (Paris: Club de l'honnête homme, 1956), *La Comédie humaine*, tome 11, p. 561. "Nous venons après Robespierre et Saint-Just, c'est pour mieux faire."

22. Ibid. "Tout conspire pour nous. Ainsi tous ceux qui plaignent les peuples, qui *braillent* sur la question des prolétaires et des salaires, qui font des ouvrages contre les Jésuites, qui s'occupent de l'amélioration de n'importe quoi... les Communistes, les Humanitaires, les philanthropes... vous comprenez, tous ces gens-là sont notre *avant-garde* [italics mine]. Pendant que nous amassons de la poudre, ils tressent la mèche à laquelle l'étincelle d'une circonstance mettra le feu."

23. "Nous le voyons nous mêmes, le zèle d'avant-garde, l'ardeur de l'escarmouche a emporté l'abbé de Pons, et lui, d'ordinaire poli, il a des gros mots." Sainte-Beuve, *Causeries du Lundi* (Paris: Garnier, n.d.), vol. XIII, p. 152.

24. "Il prétendait que, dans ces matières de poésie et de belles-lettres, le monde fût affranchi des jugements d'autorité et même de la tradition, exactement comme il était en matière de philosophie depuis Descartes." Ibid., p. 153.

25. Charles Baudelaire, *My Heart Laid Bare*, trans. Norman Cameron (London: Weidenfeld & Nicolson, 1950), pp. 188–89. The text in French: "De l'amour, de la prédilection des Français pour les métaphores militaires. Toute métaphore ici porte des moustaches. Littérature militante. Rester sur la brèche. Porter haut le drapeau.... A ajouter aux métaphores militaires: Les poètes de combat. Les littérateurs d'avant-garde. Ces habitudes de métaphores militaires dénotent des esprits, non pas militants, mais faits pour la discipline, c'est-à-dire pour la conformité; des esprits nés domestiques, des esprits belges, qui ne peuvent penser qu'en société." In Charles Baudelaire, *Oeuvres complètes*, Pléiade, p. 1285.

26. Hans Magnus Enzensberger, "The Aporias of the Avant-Garde," in *Issues in Contemporary Literary Criticism*, ed. Gregory T. Polletta (Boston:

Little, Brown and Co., 1973), p. 745. English translation by John Simon.
27. Arthur Rimbaud, *Complete Works, Selected Letters* (French-English), trans. Wallace Fowlie (Chicago: The University of Chicago Press, 1966), p. 308.
28. Poggioli, op. cit., pp. 11–12.
29. Ibid., pp. XVI–XVII.
30. To be in the avant-garde is certainly to play a leading role, and this is a matter of pride. Avant-garde and megalomania often go together. This specific association has been discussed by Robert Estivals in *La philosophie de l'histoire de la culture dans l'avant-garde culturelle parisienne depuis 1945* (Paris: Guy Leprat, 1962). The author, whose approach is basically Marxist, describes the post-World War II Parisian avant-garde as a "petty bourgeois" phenomenon, characterized by what he calls "egocentric megalomania." This attitude is traced in the writings of some representatives of the avant-garde, and extensively analyzed in the case of the Romanian Isidore Isou, who founded the so-called "Lettrisme." In *L'Avant-garde* (see note 2), the first symptoms of that megalomania which characterizes today's intellectual avant-garde are discovered as far back as 1847, in the program of a magazine entitled *L'Avant-garde agricole.* "Ce phénomène s'était annoncé dès 1847: on voit alors naître une avant-garde dans le secteur de l'économie agricole: elle a perdu toute référence d'ordre politique. La psychologie de son créateur est intéressante à suivre, dans la mesure où elle se révèle mégalomane et égocentrique.... Qu'il s'agisse de trouver un nouveau système agricole ou une nouvelle théorie picturale, l'homme est seul on en petit groupe. Seul l'individu innove pour incarner l'avant-garde" (p. 73).
31. *Social Radicalism*, p. 123.
32. V. I. Lenin, 'The Re-Organization of the Party' and 'Party Organization and Party Literature,' trans. from the Russian (London: IMG Publications, n.d.), p. 17.
33. In connection with Lukács's attitude toward the avant-garde and the use of the term in German, see the comprehensive and well-informed article by Ulrich Weisstein, "Le terme et le concept d'avant-garde en Allemagne," in *Revue de l'Université de Bruxelles*, 1975/1, pp. 10–37. Lukács distinguishes between the false, "decadent" *Avantgardismus* and a genuine, politically conscious, literary avant-garde. This distinction occurs in the essay "Es geht um den Realismus" (1938). Summarizing Lukács's position, Weisstein writes:

Lukács... discerne trois tendences fondamentales dans la littérature contemporaine (en d'autres termes la littérature bourgeoise décadente): 1) ce qu'il appelle la "*teils offen antirealistische, teils pseudorealistische Literatur der*

Verteidigung und Apologetik des bestehenden Systems", 2) la littérature *"der sogenannten Avantgarde"* et 3) les écrits *"der bedeutendsten Realisten dieser Periode"*. Pour ce qui est du deuxième groupe—qu'il oppose par la suite à l'avant-garde littéraire authentique, c'est-à-dire éclairée politiquement—il le conçoit comme s'étendant du naturalisme au surréalisme et définit son trait dominant comme *"eine immer stärkere Entfernung vom Realismus."* (p. 32)

As concerns Lukács's sketch of the genuine avant-garde—extending from Cervantes to Balzac, Tolstoy and Thomas Mann—we cannot but agree with Weisstein's comment: "Ici l'auteur prend la signification esthétique de *l'avant-garde*, pour ainsi dire, à rebours, dans la mesure où il applique précisément ce terme à des écrivains dont les méthodes romanesques—voire, dans certains cas, la Weltanschauung—sont franchement conservatrices" (p. 33).

34. Apollinaire's article was published in *L'Intransigeant* (February 7, 1912). Collected in G. Apollinaire, *Chroniques d'art (1902-1918)*, textes réunis, avec préface et notes, par L. C. Breunig (Paris: Gallimard, 1960), pp. 212–13.

35. Poggioli, op. cit., p. 5.

36. Eugène Ionesco, *Notes and Counter-Notes*, trans. Donald Watson (London: J. Calder, 1964), pp. 40–41. For the text in the original see: E. Ionesco, *Notes et contre-notes* (Paris: Gallimard, 1962), p. 27.

37. Roland Barthes, *Critical Essays*, trans. Richard Howard (Evanston: Northwestern University Press, 1972), p. 67. For the French text see: R. Barthes, *Essais critiques* (Paris: Editions du Seuil, 1964), p. 80.

38. See *Issues in Contemporary Literary Criticism*, pp. 734–53.

39. *The Collected Essays of Leslie Fiedler* (New York: Stein and Day, 1971), vol. II, pp. 454–61.

40. From "The Idea of the Modern," in *Literary Modernism*, ed. Irving Howe (Greenwich, Conn.: Fawcett Publications, 1967), p. 24. "The Idea of the Modern" was reprinted under the title "The Culture of Modernism" in Irving Howe, *The Decline of the New* (New York: Harcourt, Brace and World, 1970), pp. 3–33. *Literary Modernism* includes some essays dealing with the avant-garde, such as "Advance-guard Writing in America: 1900–1950" by Paul Goodman (pp. 124–43) or "The Fate of the Avant-garde" by Richard Chase (pp. 144–57). In these essays, however, the term avant-garde is simply a synonym for modernism.

41. Leonard B. Meyer, *Music, the Arts, and Ideas: Patterns and Predictions in Twentieth-Century Culture* (Chicago: University of Chicago Press, 1967), p. 169.

42. Angelo Guglielmi, *Avanguardia e sperimentalismo* (Milan: Feltrinelli, 1964), p. 56.

43. José Ortega y Gasset, *The Dehumanization of Art,* trans. Helene Weyl (Princeton: Princeton University Press, 1968), p. 11.

44. L. Althusser, *For Marx,* trans. Ben Brewster (London: Allen Lane, 1969), pp. 229–30.

45. The problem of humanism is further discussed in Althusser's polemic against the British Marxist John Lewis: L. Althusser, *Réponse à John Lewis* (Paris: Maspero, 1973).

46. The problem of the decline of ideology came up in the 1950s. One of the first to elaborate on the subject was Raymond Aron in his challenging book *The Opium of the Intellectuals,* pub. in French, 1955; Engl. trans. by Terence Kilmartin (Garden City, New York: Doubleday, 1957). In 1960, Daniel Bell published *The End of Ideology* (Glencoe, Ill.: Free Press, 1960). The debate continued through the 1960s and, notwithstanding the criticisms brought against it, the hypothesis of the waning of ideology did not collapse. For a more detailed account, see: Chaim I. Waxman, ed., *The End of Ideology Debate* (New York: Funk & Wagnalls, 1969), and Mostafa Rejai, ed., *Decline of Ideology?* (Chicago: Aldine-Atherton, 1971).

47. Guglielmi, p. 79.

48. Ibid., p. 80.

49. Ibid., p. 81. Marxism is taken here in a broadly philosophical sense, "... con le sue premesse antimetafisiche (anche se non sempre rispettate), con la sua sensibilità per il dato storico immediato, ... con la sua estrema elasticità di fronte alla emersione di ogni nuova situazione (e l'unico sistema concettuale in cui l'incoerenza si pone come virtù)...."

50. See *Yearbook of Comparative and General Literature* 22 (1973):42–50. For a broader presentation of anarchist aesthetics, see André Reszler, *L'Esthétique anarchiste* (Paris: Presses Universitaires de France, 1973).

51. Michel Foucault, *Les Mots et les choses* (Paris: Gallimard, 1966). For the problem of the death of man see chs. IX ("L'Homme et ses doubles") and X ("Les Sciences humaines").

52. Gilles Deleuze and Félix Guattari, *L'Anti-Oedipe: Capitalisme et schizophrénie* (Paris: Editions de Minuit, 1971).

53. Poggioli, *The Theory of the Avant-Garde,* p. 178.

54. Fiedler, II, 404.

55. Meyer, p. 72.

56. More recently, the term "*postmodernismo*" has been used to designate the whole of the interbellum period in the Hispanic world. Octavio Corvalán explains in the preface to his book *El postmodernismo: La literatura hispano-americana entre dos guerras mundiales* (New York: Las Américas, 1961): "Como lo aclara el subtítulo, la denominación 'postmoder-

nismo' abarca el período cuyos límites históricos son las dos guerras mundiales. Claro está que las primeras manifestaciones de una estética nueva aparecen algunos años antes de 1914 y muchas características de lo que llamamos postmodernismo se prolongan más allá de 1939" (p. 7). "En suma," Corvalán writes, "llamo postmodernismo a lo que Federico de Onís separaba en dos momentos consecutivos, 'post' y 'ultra' modernismo" (p. 8). *El postmodernismo* as such is nothing but a rather conventional textbook of interbellum Latin American literary history with clearly stated didactic purposes. The concept of *"postmodernismo"* stands for very much that in Anglo-American criticism would be considered as undisputedly "modernist."

57. F. Kermode, "The Modern," in *Modern Essays* (London: Collins, Fontana Books, 1971), pp. 39–70. Comparing "neo-modernism" to "paleo-modernism," Kermode writes:

... the theoretical bases of neo-modernism in so far as they show themselves in relation to form, chance, humour, are not "revolutionary." They are marginal developments of older modernism. It can be added that disparagement and nihilist rejection of the past are founded partly on ignorance and partly on a development of the earlier modernist doctrine which spoke of retrieving rather than abolishing tradition, just as the abolition of form is a programme founded on the paleo-modernist programme to give form a new researched look. A certain extremism is characteristic of both phases. Early modernism tended towards fascism, later modernism towards anarchism.... The anti-humanism—if Mr. Connoly will allow the expression—the anti-humanism of early modernism (anti-intellectualist, authoritarian, eugenicist) gives way to the anti-humanism (hipsterish, free-sexed, anti-intellectualist) of later modernism. As to the past, history continues to be the means by which we recognize what is new as well as what is not. What subverts form is "an effort essentially formal"; and the sense of standing at an end of time, which is so often invoked as an explanation of difference, is in fact evidence of similarity. (pp. 60–61)

All the characteristics that Kermode attributed in the mid-1960s to "later modernism" are found in the standard descriptions of postmodernism. Kermode is right when he says that later modernism is not truly "revolutionary" with regard to older modernism. However, the proponents of postmodernism also are right if we recognize that modernity is a "tradition against itself" and that the idea (or the illusion) of revolution is its deep motive power. That is why the term postmodernism, stressing rupture rather than continuity, came to be eventually preferred.

58. Cf. *A Study of History* (London: Oxford University Press, 1954), vol. IX, pp. 182 ff.

59. Ibid., p. 235. See also vol. I (London: Oxford University Press, 1934), p. 1, n. 2, where Toynbee argues that a new age (not yet named) in Western history opens around 1875; the same idea is elaborated on in vol. I, p. 171.

60. Ibid., IX, p. 185.

61. Ibid., p. 189.

62. Ibid., VIII, p. 338.

63. Ibid.

64. *The Collected Essays of Leslie Fiedler*, vol. II, pp. 379–400.

65. "Mass Society and Postmodern Fiction," *Partisan Review* 26 (1959):420–36. Reprinted in Irving Howe, *The Decline of the New*, ed. cit., pp. 190–207.

66. Howe, *The Decline of the New*, pp. 196–97.

67. Ibid., p. 198.

68. Ibid., p. 255.

69. Ibid., p. 258.

70. Harry Levin, *Refractions* (New York: Oxford University Press, 1966), p. 271. For the use of "post-modern" see also p. 277.

71. Levin, *Grounds for Comparison* (Cambridge, Mass.: Harvard University Press, 1972), p. 15.

72. Fiedler, op. cit., vol. II, p. 461. Interested in semantics as I am, I cannot help noticing the resentment the name 'Modern' evokes in this quotation.

73. Ibid., pp. 462–63.

74. "POSTmodernISM: A Paracritical Bibliography," *New Literary History* 3 (1971):5–30. Reprinted in Ihab Hassan, *Paracriticisms: Seven Speculations of the Times* (Urbana: University of Illinois Press, 1975), pp. 39–59.

75. Robert Langbaum, review of *The Theory of the Avant-Garde* by Renato Poggioli, in *Boundary* 2, I, 1, Fall 1972, p. 234.

76. John Cage, *Silence* (Middletown, Conn.: Wesleyan University Press, 1961), p. 10.

77. *Against Interpretation*, ed. cit., pp. 13–23. Commenting on the movie *Last Year at Marienbad* and on the fact that it had been "consciously designed . . . to accommodate a multiplicity of equally plausible interpretations," Susan Sontag writes characteristically: "But the temptation to interpret should be resisted. What matters in *Marienbad* is the pure, untranslatable, sensuous immediacy of some of its images . . ." (p. 19).

78. Gérard Genette, *Figures* I (Paris: Editions du Seuil, 1966), p. 206.

79. Meyer, p. 72.

80. Ibid., pp. 93, 102.

THE IDEA OF DECADENCE

1. For a discussion of Plato's attitude toward primitivism (including his view of the mythical Golden Age), see A. O. Lovejoy and George Boas, *Primitivism and Related Ideas in Antiquity* (New York: Octagon Books, 1965), pp. 155–68.

2. B. A. Van Groningen, *In the Grip of the Past: Essay on an Aspect of Greek Thought* (Leiden: E. J. Brill, 1953). In the conclusion of the book, the author quotes an illuminating passage from Plutarch: "The foolish overlook and neglect past blessings through their thoughts being ever intent on the future; but the wise make the past clearly present to them through memory" (p. 121).

3. Henri-Charles Puech, "Gnosis and Time," in *Man and Time: Papers from the Eranos Yearbooks*, Joseph Campbell, ed. (New York: Pantheon Books, Bollingen Series, 1957), p. 43.

4. Ibid., pp. 47–48.

5. Koenraad W. Swart, *The Sense of Decadence in Nineteenth-Century France* (The Hague: Nijhoff, 1964), p. 19.

6. Vladimir Jankélévitch, "La Décadence," *Revue de Métaphysique et de Morale* 55, 4 (October–December 1950):339.

7. For a convincing treatment of the question of Nisard's influence on Bourget and then of the influence of Bourget on Nietzsche, see: J. Kamerbeek, "'Style de Décadence'," *Revue de littérature comparée* 39, 2 (April–June 1965):268–86.

8. From Montesquieu, *Cahiers (1716–1755)*, quoted after W. Krauss and Hans Kortum, eds., *Antike and Moderne in der Literaturdiskussion des 18. Jahrhunderts* (Berlin: Akademie Verlag, 1966), p. 253. Here is the passage in French: "Mais, comme dans les empires, rien n'approche plus de la décadence qu'une grande prospérité, aussi, dans notre république littéraire, il est à craindre que la prospérité ne mène à la décadence."

9. Madame de Staël, *De la littérature considerée dans ses rapports avec les institutions sociales*, Paul van Tieghem, ed. (Geneva: Droz, 1959), vol. I, p. 124. "On a prétendu que la décadence des arts, des lettres et des empires devoit arriver, nécessairement, après un certain degré de splendeur. Cette idée manque de justesse; les arts ont un terme, je le crois, au-delà duquel ils ne s'élèvent pas; mais ils peuvent se maintenir à la hauteur à laquelle ils sont parvenus; et dans toutes les conoissances susceptibles de progression, la nature morale tend à se perfectionner."

10. Ibid.

11. Ibid., pp. 127–30. "La décadence des empires n'est pas plus dans l'ordre naturel que celle des lettres et des lumières.... La civilisation de

l'Europe, l'établissement de la religion chrétienne, les découvertes des sciences... ont... détruit d'anciennes causes de barbarie. Ainsi donc la décadence des nations, et par conséquent celle des lettres, est maintenant beaucoup moins à craindre."

12. D. Nisard, *Études de moeurs et de critique sur les poètes latins de la décadence*, 5th ed., 2 vols. (Paris: Hachette, 1888), I:IX. "J'expose une théorie développée sur les caractères communs des poésies en décadence.... Je tâche d'expliquer par quelles nécessités successives et insensibles l'esprit humain arrive à ce singulier état d'épuisement, où les imaginations les plus riches ne peuvent plus rien pour la vraie poésie, et n'ont plus que la force de détruire avec scandale les langues."

13. D. Nisard, *Essais sur l'école romantique* (Paris: Calman-Lévy, 1891), pp. 245, 248. "Quand nous disons qu'il [Victor Hugo] a été novateur, ce n'est pas un éloge que nous lui donnons. En France, pays de littérature essentiellement pratique et sensée, un écrivain qui n'a que de l'imagination, fût-elle de l'espèce la plus rare, ne peut être un grand écrivain.... Chez lui... l'imagination tient lieu de tout; l'imagination seule conçoit et exécute: c'est une reine qui gouverne sans contrôle.... La raison n'a aucune place dans ses ouvrages. Point d'idées pratiques ou applicables, rien ou presque rien de la vie réelle; nulle philosophie, nulle morale...."

14. Ibid., p. 267.

15. Ibid., p. 352.

16. K. W. Swart, op. cit., p. XI.

17. E. Renan, *Cahiers de jeunesse* (1845–1846) (Paris: Calman-Lévy, 1906), p. 112. "Ces époques de décadence sont fortes en critique, souvent même plus fortes que les grands siècles."

18. Ibid., p. 105. "En un sens, la critique est supérieure à la composition.... Jusqu'ici la critique s'est tenue humblement en servante *et pedis sequa*; peut-être serait-il temps qu'elle se comprît, et s'exaltât elle-même au-dessus de ceux qu'elle juge. Ainsi, ce siècle est peu composant en fait de fictions originales classiques; est-il inférieur? Non, car il est plus philosophe."

19. Ibid., p. 383. "Fait curieux de l'histoire littéraire que la vraie fureur qui s'est emparée du goût de notre temps pour les littératures non classiques. Non qu'on ne porte quelque intérêt aux littératures grecques, latines, françaises, mais c'est surtout aux époques anté-classiques et postclassiques qu'on les cultive. Cela seul a vogue.... Tout l'intérêt s'attache à ce qu'on appelle les origines et les décadences."

20. Théophile Gautier, *Portraits et souvenirs littéraires* (Paris: Charpentier, 1881), p. 171. I have used the English translation of the famous passage

found in G. L. Van Roosbroeck, *The Legend of the Decadents* (New York: Institut des Etudes Françaises, Columbia University, 1927), pp. 8–9.

21. Ch. Baudelaire, *Oeuvres complètes*, Pléiade, p. 1525. "Ne semble-t-il pas au lecteur comme à moi, que la langue de la dernière décadence latine—suprême soupir d'une personne robuste, déjà transformée et préparée pour la vie spirituelle,—est singulièrement propre à exprimer la passion telle que l'a comprise et sentie le monde poétique moderne?"

22. Ibid., p. 889. "... un ouvrier beaucoup plus adroit qu'inventif, un travailleur beaucoup plus correct que créateur.... C'est un compositeur de décadence.... M. Hugo était naturellement académicien avant que de naître...."

23. Ibid., p. 1099. "Est-ce par une fatalité des décadences qu'aujourd'hui chaque art manifeste l'envie d'empiéter sur l'art voisin, et que les peintres introduisent des gammes musicales dans la peinture, les sculpteurs, de la couleur dans la sculpture, les littérateurs, des moyens plastiques dans la littérature, et d'autres artistes, ceux dont nous avons à nous occuper aujourd'hui, une sorte de philosophie encyclopédique dans l'art plastique lui-même?"

24. Ibid., p. 1211.

25. Ibid., p. 1214. "Aucun musicien n'excelle, comme Wagner, à *peindre* l'espace et la profondeur.... Il semble parfois, en écoutant cette musique ardente et despotique, qu'on retrouve peintes sur le fond des ténèbres, déchiré par la rêverie, les vertigineuses conceptions de l'opium."

26. E. Delacroix, *Journal*, ed. André Joubin (Paris: Plon, 1932), vol. 2, p. 439 (Entry dated 9 April 1856): "Le fond de mon idée était la nécessité d'être de son temps.... De là le ridicule de tenter de remonter le courant et de faire de l'archaisme. Racine paraît raffiné déjà en comparaison de Corneille: mais combien on a raffiné depuis Racine.... Nos modernes ne peignent plus seulement les sentiments, ils décrivent l'extérieur, ils analysent tout."

27. Ibid., p. 443 (Entry dated 16 April 1856): "Du besoin de raffinement dans les temps de décadence. Les plus grands esprits ne peuvent s'y soustraire.... Les Anglais, les Germaniques nous ont toujours poussés dans cette route. Shakespeare est très raffiné. En peignant avec une grande profondeur des sentiments que les anciens négligeaient ou ne connaissaient même pas, il découvrit tout un petit monde de sentiments qui sont chez tous les hommes de tous les temps à l'état confus...."

28. Edmond et Jules de Goncourt, *Journal*, texte intégral établi et an-

noté par Robert Ricatte (Paris: Fasquelle and Flammarion, 1956), vol. 6, p. 207. "Depuis que l'humanité va, son progrès, ses acquisitions sont toutes de sensibilité. Elle se nervosifie, s'hystérise, chaque jour. Et quant à cette activité,... savez-vous si ce n'est pas d'elle que découle la mélancolie moderne? Savez-vous si la tristesse de ce siècle-ci ne vient pas du surmenage, de son mouvement, de son prodigieux effort, de son travail enragé, de ses forces cérébrales tendues à se rompre, de son excès de production dans tous les sens?"

29. Émile Zola, *Mes haines* (Paris: Charpentier-Fasquelle, 1913), pp. 57–58. "Nous sommes malades, cela est bien certain, malades de progrès.... Cette victoire des nerfs sur le sang a décidé de nos moeurs, de notre littérature, de notre époque toute entière." And Zola goes on to characterize contemporary literature: "Etudiez notre littérature contemporaine, vous verrez en elle tous les effets de la névrose qui agite notre siècle; elle est le produit direct de nos inquiétudes, de nos recherches âpres, de nos paniques, de ce malaise général qu'éprouvent nos sociétés aveugles en face d'un avenir inconnu."

30. Goncourt, *Journal*, vol. 5., p. 159. "Nous, nous trois, avec deux ou trois autres, sommes des malades.... Nous ne sommes pas des décadents, nous sommes des primitifs.... Non, encore non, mais des particuliers bizarres, indéfinis, exaltés."

31. Paul Bourget, *Essais de psychologie contemporaine* (Paris: Lemerre, 1893), p. 28.

32. See J. Kamerbeek, " 'Style de Décadence'," *Revue de littérature comparée* 39, 2 (Avril-Juin 1965): 268–86. Kamerbeek compares Bourget's emphasis on the cult of *detail* as a characteristic of "decadent style" with the similar treatment of the question in Nisard. Although there is no proof that Bourget had read Nisard, the author of the article speculates about the possibility that Bourget knew of Nisard through Barbey d'Aurevilly. Barbey d'Aurevilly was an admirer of Ernest Hello, a conservative like himself, who in *L'Homme* (1872) offered his own definition of "style de décadence," quite close to that of Nisard. Kamerbeek makes a point about the sympathy with which Nisard was regarded in right-wing circles in France. Charles Maurras, the leader of the *Action française*, also was an admirer of Nisard, with whom he shared the idea that romanticism and decadence should be equated.

33. Quoted from *Le Siècle littéraire* (1876) after Jacques Lethève, "Le thème de la décadence dans les lettres françaises à la fin du XIXe siècle," *Revue d'Histoire Littéraire de la France* LXIII (1963):51. Bourget wrote: "Nous acceptons... ce terrible mot de *décadence*.... C'est la décadence, mais vigoureuse: moins accomplie dans ses oeuvres, elle l'emporte sur les

époques organiques par l'intensité des génies. Les créations plus heurtées, plus violentes, manifestent des artistes plus hardis, et l'audace est une vertu qui enlève malgré nous la sympathie."

34. Bourget, p. 24.

35. Ibid.

36. Ibid., p. 28.

37. Ibid., p. 29.

38. J.-K. Huysmans, À Rebours, vol. VII of Oeuvres complètes (Paris: Les Éditions G. Crès et Co., 1928), p. 134.

39. Ibid., p. 142.

40. A. E. Carter, The Idea of Decadence in French Literature (Toronto: University of Toronto Press, 1958), p. 20.

41. Huysmans, p. 287.

42. Ibid., p. 303. "En effet, la décadence d'une littérature, irréparablement atteinte dans son organisme, affaiblie par l'âge des idées, épuisée par les excès de la syntaxe, sensible seulement aux curiosités qui enfièvrent les malades et cependant pressée de tout exprimer à son déclin, archarnée à vouloir réparer toutes les omissions de jouissance, à léguer les plus subtils souvenirs de douleur, à son lit de mort, s'était incarnée en Mallarmé, de la façon la plus consommée et la plus exquise."

43. Ibid., p. XXI.

44. See Oscar Wilde, Intentions and the Soul of Man under Socialism, ed. Robert Ross (London: Dawsons of Pall Mall, 1969).

45. The "decadent" forgery of Gabriel Vicaire and Henri Beauclair appeared as Les Déliquescences, poèmes décadents d'Adoré Floupette (Paris: "Byzance," chez L. Vanné, 1885). For a discussion of this book see Noël Richard, À l'aube du symbolisme: hydropathes, fumistes, décadents (Paris: Nizet, 1961), Part III, "Une mystification décadente," pp. 174–268. See also in the Appendix of Richard's study, the critical edition of the Preface to Les Déliquescences, pp. 270–315.

46. Quoted from Noël Richard, Le Mouvement décadent: dandys, esthètes et quintessents (Paris: Nizet, 1968), p. 24. "Se dissimuler l'état de décadence ou nous sommes arrivés serait le comble de l'insenséisme. Religion, moeurs, justice, tout décade.... La société se désagrège sous l'action corrosive d'une civilisation déliquescente.... Nous vouons cette feuille aux innovations tuantes, aux audaces stupéfiantes, aux incohérences à trente-six atmosphères dans la limite la plus reculée de leur compatibilité avec ces conventions archaiques étiquettées du nom de morale publique. Nous serons les vedettes d'une littérature idéale.... En un mot, nous serons les mahdis clamant éternellement le dogme élixirisé, le verbe quintessencié du décadisme triomphant."

47. Ibid., p. 25. "Les Anciens étaient de leur temps. Nous voulons être du nôtre. Vapeur et électricité sont les deux agents indispensables de la vie moderne. Nous devons avoir une langue et une littérature en harmonie avec les progrès de la science. N'est-ce pas notre droit? Et c'est ce qu'on appelle la décadence?—Décadence, soit. Nous acceptons le mot. Nous sommes des *Décadents*, puisque cette décadence n'est que la marche ascensionelle d l'humanité vers des idéals reputés inaccessibles."

48. Ibid., p. 173. "*Décadisme* est un mot de génie, une trouvaille amusante et qui restera dans l'histoire littéraire; ce barbarisme est une miraculeuse ensigne. Il est court, commode, 'à la main,' *handy*, éloigne précisement l'idée abaissante de décadence, sonne littéraire sans pédanterie, enfin fait balle et fera trou. . . ."

49. Quoted from André Billy, *L'époque 1900 (1885–1905)* (Paris: Tallandier, 1951), pp. 422–23.

50. To realize fully the extent to which these words were used and abused, let me cite the account of a recent study of the decadent movement in France. "Le terme décadent," Noël Richard writes, "est un mot à succès, employé à tort et à travers par les publicistes de la décennie 1881–1891. Si quelqu'un tue sa maîtresse, on le proclame décadent. Des anarchistes lancent-ils des bombes? Ce sont des décadents montés en graine. Je ne sais quel plaisantin demanda un jour dans un restaurant 'du cresson au décadent'." *Le Mouvement décadent*, p. 256.

51. Friedrich Nietzsche, *The Birth of Tragedy and the Case of Wagner*, trans. Walter Kaufmann (New York: Vintage Books, 1967), p. 155. The text in German, quoted after *Nietzsche Werk*, Kritische Gesamtausgabe, herausgegeben von Giorgio Colli und Mazzino Montinari (Berlin: Walter de Gruyter, 1969), part VI, vol. 3, pp. 3–4. "Was mich am tiefsten beschäftigt hat, das ist in der That das Problem der décadence,—ich habe Gründe dazu gehabt. 'Gut und Böse' ist nur eine Spielart jenes Problems. Hat man sich für die Abzeichen des Niedergangs ein Auge gemacht, so versteht man auch die Moral,—man versteht, was sich unter ihren heiligsten Namen und Werthformeln versteckt: das *verarmte* Leben, der Wille zum Ende, die grosse Müdigkeit. Moral *verneint* das Leben. . . ."

52. Ibid., pp. 155–156. For the German text, Ibid., p. 4. "Wagner gehört bloss zu meinen Krankheiten. Nicht dass ich gegen diese Krankheit undankbar sein möchte. Wenn ich mit dieser Schrift den Satz aufrecht halte, dass Wagner *schädlich* ist, so will ich nicht weniger aufrecht halten, wem er trotzdem unentbehrlich ist—dem Philosophen. Sonst kann man vielleicht ohne Wagner auskommen: dem Philosophen aber steht es nicht frei, Wagners zu entrathen. Er hat das schlechte Gewissen seiner Zeit zu sein,—dazu muss er deren bestes Wissen haben. . . . Ich verstehe es voll-

kommen, wenn heut ein Musiker sagt 'ich hasse Wagner, aber ich halte keine andre Musik mehr aus'. Ich würde aber auch einen Philosophen verstehn, der erklärte: 'Wagner *resümirt* die Modernität. Es hilft nichts, man muss erst Wagnerianer sein. . . .'"

53. F. Nietzsche, *On the Genealogy of Morals and Ecce Homo*, trans. W. Kaufmann. (New York: Vintage Books, 1969), p. 222. For the German text, Ibid., p. 262. "Das Glück meines Daseins, seine Einzigkeit vielleicht, liegt in seinem Verhängniss: ich bin, um es in Räthselform auszudrücken, als mein Vater bereits gestorben, als meine Mutter lebe ich noch und werde alt. Diese doppelte Herkunft, gleichsam aus der obersten und der untersten Sprosse an der Leiter des Lebens, décadent zugleich und *Anfang*—dies, wenn irgend Etwas, erklärt jene Neutralität, jene Freiheit von Partei im Verhältniss zum Gesammtprobleme des Lebens, die mich vielleicht auszeichnet. Ich habe für die Zeichen von Aufgang und Niedergang eine feinere Witterung als je ein Mensch gehabt hat, ich bin der Lehrer par excellence hierfür,—ich kenne Beides, ich bin Beides."

54. Ibid., p. 223. For the German text, Ibid., p. 263. "Mitten in Martern, die ein ununterbrochner dreitägiger Gehirn-Schmerz sammt mühseligem Schleimerbrechen mit sich bringt,—besass ich eine Dialektiker-Klarheit par excellence und dachte Dinge sehr kaltblütig durch, zu denen ich in gesünderen Verhältnissen nicht Kletterer, nicht raffinirt, nicht *kalt* genug bin. Meine Leser wissen vielleicht, in wie fern ich Dialektik als Décadence-Symptom betrachte, zum Beispiel im allerberühmtesten Fall: im Fall des Sokrates."

55. Ibid. For the German text, Ibid., pp. 263–64. "Eine lange, allzulange Reihe von Jahren bedeutet bei mir Genesung,—sie bedeutet leider auch zugleich Rückfall, Verfall, Periodik einer Art décadence. Brauche ich, nach alledem, zu sagen, dass ich in Fragen der décadence *erfahren* bin? Ich habe sie vorwärts und rückwärts buchstabirt. . . . Von der Kranken-Optik aus nach gesünderen Begriffen und Werthen, und wiederum umgekehrt aus der Fülle und Selbstgewissheit des *reichen* Lebens hinuntersehn in die heimliche Arbeit des Décadence-Instinkts—das war meine längste Übung, meine eigentliche Erfahrung, wenn irgend worin wurde ich darin Meister. Ich habe es jetzt in der Hand, ich habe die Hand dafür, *Perspektiven umzustellen:* erster Grund, weshalb für mich allein vielleicht eine 'Umwerthung der Werthe' überhaupt möglich ist.—"

56. *The Birth of Tragedy*, p. 164. For the German text, Ibid., p. 15. "Ein typischer décadent, der sich nothwendig in seinem verderbten Geschmack fühlt, der mit ihm einen höheren Geschmack in Anspruch nimmt, der seine Verderbniss als Gesetz, als Fortschritt, als Erfüllung in Geltung zu bringen weiss."

57. F. Nietzsche, *The Gay Science*, trans. W. Kaufmann (New York: Vintage, 1974), p. 96. For the German text, ed. cit. (Berlin, 1973), part V, vol. 2, p. 69. "Der Abergläubische ist, im Vergleich mit dem Religiösen, immer viel mehr 'Person', als dieser, und eine abergläubische Gesellschaft wird eine solche sein, in der es schon viele Individuen und Lust am Individuellen giebt."

58. It might be interesting here to make a few remarks about the term and concept of *ressentiment*, so important to Nietzsche's critique of Christianity, whose triumph over ancient paganism he interpreted as a successful "revolt of the slaves." (Cf. *On the Genealogy of Morals*, Section I, 10, 11, 13, 14, 16; Section II, 11, 17, etc.) But *ressentiment*, through and beyond Christianity proper, is linked to the whole problem of modernity and decadence. Such modern doctrines or trends as socialism, anarchism, and nihilism—nihilism being the main characteristic of modernity in Nietzsche's eyes—are specifically defined in terms of *ressentiment*. In *The Will to Power*, trans. W. Kaufmann and R. J. Hollingdale (New York: Vintage Books, 1968), Nietzsche writes:

> In other cases, the underprivileged man seeks reason not in his "guilt" (as the Christian does), but in society: the socialist, the anarchist, the nihilist—in as much as they find their existence something of which someone must be *guilty*—they are still the closest relations of the Christian, who also believes he can better endure his sense of sickness and ill-constitutedness by finding someone whom he can make responsible for it. The instinct of revenge and *ressentiment* appears here in both cases as a means of enduring, as the instinct of self-preservation: just as is the preference for altruistic theory and practice.

Nietzsche identifies the representatives of *ressentiment* in contemporary Europe as "those pessimists... who make it their mission to sanctify their filth under the name 'indignation'" (ibid., p. 402). The "instinct of decline" and *ressentiment* are clearly related in another passage from the same book, and it is interesting to note that Nietzsche's prototypes for decadence in the arts, Victor Hugo and Richard Wagner, are mentioned in this context:

> The bearers of the instincts of decline (or *ressentiment*, discontent, the drive to destroy, anarchism, and nihilism), including the slave instincts, the instincts of cowardice, cunning, and *canaille* in those orders that have been kept down, mingle with the blood of all classes: two or three generations later... everything has become mob.... The privileged themselves actually succumb to it, ... the "geniuses" above all: they become heralds of those feelings with which one moves the masses—the note of sympathy, even reverence, for all that has lived a life of suffering, lowliness, contempt, persecution, sounds above all other notes (types: Victor Hugo and Richard Wagner) (ibid., p. 461).

As in the case of *décadence* and *décadent*, Nietzsche takes the word *ressentiment* directly from the French. This is another instance of Nietzsche's preference for the lucidity and flexibility of French psychological and moral notions as opposed to the metaphysical fuzziness of corresponding German terms. The importance of the concept of *ressentiment* in Nietzsche's thought and, on a larger plane, in the phenomenology and sociology of moral judgments has been brilliantly demonstrated by Max Scheler in his essay "Das Ressentiment im Aufbau der Moralen" (1915). In the "Prefatory Remarks" to the essay, Scheler notes:

> We do not use the word *"ressentiment"* because of a special predilection for the French language, but because we did not succeed in translating it into German. Moreover, Nietzsche has made it a *terminus technicus*. In the natural meaning of the French word I detect two elements. First of all, *ressentiment* is the repeated experiencing and reliving of a particular emotional response or reaction against someone else. The continual reliving of the emotion sinks it more deeply into the center of the personality, but concomitantly removes it from the person's zone of action and expression. It is not a mere intellectual recollection of the emotion and of the events to which it "responded"—it is a re-experiencing of the emotion itself, a renewal of the original feeling. Secondly, the word implies that the quality of this emotion is negative, i.e., that it contains a movement of hostility. Perhaps the German word *"Groll"* (rancor) comes closest to the essential meaning of the term. "Rancor" is just suppressed wrath, independent of the ego's activity, which moves obscurely through the mind (Max Scheler, *Ressentiment,* ed. with an Introd. by Lewis A. Coser, trans. William W. Holdheim [New York: Schocken Books, 1972], p. 39).

It is noteworthy that in the 1840s, a few decades before Nietzsche, Kierkegaard described modernity in terms that clearly anticipated Nietzsche's concept of *ressentiment*. This explains why, in 1914, when translating Kierkegaard's essay on the *Present Age* (1846), under the title *Kritik der Gegenwart,* Theodor Haecker felt free to use *"ressentiment"* for the Danish word for "envy." (See Kierkegaard, *Kritik der Gegenwart,* trans. Theodor Haecker [Basel: Hess, 1946], pp. 29ff.) The English translator of Kierkegaard's essay, Alexander Dru, followed Haecker's suggestion and used the word *"ressentiment,"* explaining the term, not so familiar to English readers, in a footnote in which Max Scheler is quoted. (See Kierkegaard, *The Present Age and Two Minor Ethico-Religious Treatises,* trans. Alexander Dru and Walter Lowrie [London: Oxford University Press, 1940], pp. 23–24.)

Speaking of the "present age" as a passionless, reflective age, dominated by "envy," abstract thought, and a general levelling tendency, Kierkegaard writes (in Dru's translation): "No one, for example, wishes to bring about the downfall of the eminent, but if distinction could be shown to be purely fictitious then everyone would be prepared to admire it. . . . In an age which is very reflective and passionless *envy is the negative unifying principle*" (p. 21). And a few pages later, Kierkegaard goes on to say: "The further it is carried the more clearly does the envy of reflection become moral *ressentiment.* Just as air in a sealed space develops poison, so the imprisonment of reflection develops *ressentiment* if it is not ventilated by action or incident of any kind. In reflection the state of strain . . . results in the neutralization of all the higher powers, and all that is low and despicable comes to the fore, its very impudence giving the spurious effect of strength, while protected by its very baseness it escapes attracting the attention of *ressentiment*" (pp. 23–24).

Kierkegaard's critique of modernity, as expounded directly in his *Present Age* and in the pamphlet series *The Instant*, and indirectly in his various pseudonymous works—especially *Either/Or, Stages on Life's Road, Repetition, Concluding Unscientific Postscript to the "Philosophical Fragments"*—is not examined in this book. The reason is that such an analysis would have carried us too far from our line of research, which is essentially terminological, into the realms of theology, ontology, metaphysics, and social criticism in the broadest sense. For those interested in the more philosophical aspects of the rejection of modernity during the nineteenth century, I would recommend Karl Löwith's magnificent book *From Hegel to Nietzsche: The Revolution in Nineteenth-Century Thought*, trans. from the German by David E. Green (New York: Holt, Rinehart and Winston, 1964). Written mainly during the 1930s and first published in Switzerland in 1941, *From Hegel to Nietzsche* is concerned with the impact of Hegel's philosophy, and mainly with the reactions against Hegel's attempt to reconcile reason and reality, as summarized in his famous statement from the preface to the *Philosophy of Right (Rechtsphilosophie):* "Whatever is rational is real; and whatever is real is rational." Kierkegaard, like Marx, Stirner, and Nietzsche, is among those who are responsible for laying the "philosophical basis" of what Löwith calls the "radical criticism of the existing order" (or, in the terms of the present study, *modernity*). For Kierkegaard's critique of the "rationality" of his age, see especially Chapter III, "The Dissolution of Hegel's Mediations in the Exclusive Choices of Marx and Kierkegaard," pp. 137–74.

59. Ibid., p. 99. For the text in German, Ibid., p. 73. "China ist das Beispiel eines Landes, wo die Unzufriedenheit im Grossen und die Fähigkeit der Verwandelung seit vielen Jahrhunderten ausgestorben ist; und die Socialisten und Staats-Götzendiener Europa's könnten es mit ihren Maass-

regeln zur Verbesserung und Sicherung des Lebens auch in Europa leicht zu chinesischen Zuständen und einem chinesischen 'Glücke' bringen, vorausgesetzt, dass sie hier zuerst jene kränklichere, zartere, weiblichere, einstweilen noch überreichlich vorhandene Unzufriedenheit und Romantik ausrotten könnten. Europa ist ein Kranker, der seiner Unheilbarkeit und ewigen Verwandelung seines Leidens den höchsten Dank schuldig ist; diese beständigen neuen Lagen, diese ebenso beständigen neuen Gefahren, Schmerzen und Auskunftsmittel haben zuletzt eine intellectuale Reizbarkeit erzeugt, welche beinahe so viel, als Genie, und jedenfalls die Mutter alles Genie's ist."

60. F. Nietzsche, *The Will to Power*, trans. W. Kaufmann (New York: Vintage, 1968), pp. 25–26.

61. Ibid., p. 29. For the text in German, ed. cit. (Berlin, 1974), part VIII, vol. 3, p. 42. "*Gesundheit* und *Krankheit* sind nichts wesentlich Verschiedenes. . . . Man muss nicht distinkte Principien, oder Entitäten daraus machen, die sich um den lebenden Organismus streiten und aus ihm ihren Kampfplatz machen. Das ist altes Zeug und Geschwätz, das zu nichts mehr taugt."

62. Ibid., pp. 26–27. For the text in German, Ibid., p. 326. "Man verwechselt Ursache und Wirkung: man versteht die décadence nicht als physiologisch und sieht in ihren Folgen die eigentliche Ursache des Sich-schlecht-befindens
—dahin gehört die ganze religiöse Moral"

63. Hans Vaihinger, *The Philosophy of 'As If'*, trans. C. K. Ogden, 2d ed. (New York: Harcourt, Brace & Co., 1934), pp. 341–62.

64. Ibid., p. 345.

65. Ibid., p. 357.

66. Ibid., p. 362.

67. Georg Simmel, *The Conflict of Modern Culture and Other Essays*, trans. K. Peter Etzkorn (New York: Teachers College Press, 1968), p. 15.

68. Walter Kaufmann, *Nietzsche: Philosopher, Psychologist, Antichrist* (Princeton, New Jersey: Princeton University Press, 1968), p. 73.

69. *The Birth of Tragedy*, p. 170. For the text in German, ed. cit., part VI, vol. 3, p. 21. "—Womit kennzeichnet sich jede *litterarische* décadence? Damit, dass das Leben nicht mehr im Ganzen wohnt. Das Wort wird souverain und springt aus dem Satz hinaus, der Satz greift über und verdunkelt den Sinn der Seite, die Seite gewinnt Leben auf Unkosten des Ganzen—das Ganze ist kein Ganzes mehr. Aber das ist das Gleichniss für jeden Stil der décadence: jedes Mal Anarchie der Atome, Disgregation des Willens. . . ."

70. Kaufmann, p. 75. "The elusive quality of this style, which is so

characteristic of Nietzsche's way of thinking and writing, might be called *monadologic* to crystallize the tendency of each aphorism to be self-sufficient while yet throwing light on almost every other aphorism. We are confronted with a 'pluralistic universe' in which each aphorism is itself a microcosm."

71. W. D. Williams, *Nietzsche and the French: A Study of the Influence of Nietzsche's French Reading on His Thought and Writing* (Oxford: Blackwell, 1952). See esp. chapter 9, "Culture and Decadence," pp. 153 ff.

72. *The Portable Nietzsche*, selected and trans. by W. Kaufmann (New York: The Viking Press, 1968), pp. 553–54. For the text in German, ed. cit., VI, 3, pp. 145–46. "*Goethe*—kein deutsches Ereigniss, sondern ein europäisches: ein grossartiger Versuch, das achtzehnte Jahrhundert zu überwinden durch eine Rückkehr zur Natur, durch ein *Hinauf*kommen zur Natürlichkeit der Renaissance, eine Art Selbstüberwindung von Seiten dieses Jahrhunderts.—Er trug dessen stärkste Instinkte in sich: die Gefühlsamkeit, die Natur-Idolatrie, das Antihistorische, das Idealistische, das Unreale und Revolutionäre (—letzteres ist nur eine Form des Unrealen). Er nahm die Historie, die Naturwissenschaft, die Antike, insgleichen Spinoza zu Hülfe, vor Allem die praktische Thätigkeit; er umstellte sich mit lauter geschlossenen Horizonten; er löste sich nicht vom Leben ab, er stellte sich hinein; er war nicht verzagt und nahm so viel als möglich auf sich, über sich, in sich. Was er wollte, das war *Totalität.*... Goethe war, inmitten eines unreal gesinnten Zeitalters, ein überzeugter Realist: er sagte Ja zu Allem, was ihm hierin verwandt war,—er hatte kein grösseres Erlebniss als jenes ens realissimum, genannt Napoleon.

Ein solcher freigewordner Geist steht mit einem freudigen und vertrauenden Fatalismus mitten im All, im *Glauben*, dass nur das Einzelne verwerflich ist, dass im Ganzen sich Alles erlöst und bejaht—*er verneint nicht mehr*... Aber ein solcher Glaube der höchste aller möglichen Glauben: ich habe ihn auf den Namen des *Dionysos* getauft.—"

73. Ibid., p. 555. For the text in German, Ibid., p. 146. "Ist nicht das neunzehnte Jahrhundert, zumal in seinem Ausgange, bloss ein verstärktes *verrohtes* achtzehntes Jahrhundert, das heisst ein *décadence*—Jahrhundert?"

74. Ibid., pp. 669–70. For the text in German, Ibid., p. 423. "Jede Kunst, jede Philosophie darf als Heil- und Hülfsmittel des wachsenden oder des niedergehenden Lebens angesehen werden: sie setzen immer Leiden und Leidende voraus. Aber es giebt zweierlei Leidende, einmal die an der *Überfülle* des Lebens Leidenden, welche eine dionysische Kunst wollen und ebenso eine tragische Einsicht und Aussicht auf das Leben—und sodann die an der *Verarmung* des Lebens Leidenden, die Ruhe, Stille,

glattes Meer *oder* aber den Rausch, den Krampf, die Betäubung von Kunst und Philosophie verlangen. Die Rache am Leben selbst—die wollüstigste Art Rausch für solche Verarmte!"

75. Ibid., pp. 667–68. For the text in German, Ibid., pp. 421–22. "Die Musik kommt von allen Künsten . . . als die letzte aller Pflanzen zum Vorschein, vielleicht weil sie die innerlichste ist und, folglich, am spätesten anlangt,—im Herbst und Abblühen der jedes Mal zu ihr gehörenden Cultur. . . . Erst Mozart gab dem Zeitalter Ludwig des Vierzehnten und der Kunst Racine's und Claude Lorrain's in *klingendem* Golde heraus; erst in Beethoven's und Rossini's Musik sang sich das achtzehnte Jahrhundert aus. . . . Jede wahrhafte, jede originale Musik ist Schwanengesang."

76. *The Birth of Tragedy*, p. 25. (This remark appears in the 1886 "Attempt At Self-Criticism," written for a new edition of *The Birth of Tragedy*.)

77. Ibid., p. 157. For the text in German, ed. cit., VI, 3, pp. 7–8. "Diese Musik scheint mir vollkommen. Sie kommt leicht, biegsam, mit Höflichkeit daher. Sie ist liebenswürdig, sie *schwitzt* nicht. . . . Diese Musik ist böse, raffinirt, fatalistisch: sie bleibt dabei populär—sie hat das Raffinement einer Rasse, nicht eines Einzelnen. Sie ist reich. Sie ist präcis. Sie baut, organisirt, wird fertig: damit macht sie den Gegensatz zum Polypen in der Musik, zur 'unendlichen Melodie'. Hat man je schmerzhaftere tragische Accente auf der Bühne gehört? Und wie werden dieselben erreicht! Ohne Grimasse! Ohne Falschmünzerei! Ohne die *Lüge* des grossen Stils!"

78. Ibid., p. 173. For the text in German, Ibid., p. 25. "Wagner's Musik ist niemals wahr. Aber *man hält sie dafür. . . .*"

79. Ibid., pp. 172–73. For the text in German, Ibid., p. 24. "Wagner war *nicht* Musiker von Instinkt. Dies bewies er damit, dass er alle Gesetzlichkeit und, bestimmter geredet, allen Stil in der Musik preisgab, um aus ihr zu machen, was er nöthig hatte, eine Theater-Rhetorik, ein Mittel des Ausdrucks, der Gebärden-Verstärkung, der Suggestion, des Psychologisch-Pittoresken. . . . Er ist der Victor Hugo der Musik als Sprache. Immer vorausgesetzt, dass man zuerst gelten lässt, Musik *dürfe* unter Umständen nicht Musik, sondern Sprache, sondern Werkzeug, sondern ancilla dramaturgica sein. Wagner's Musik, nicht vom Theater-Geschmacke, einem sehr toleranten Geschmacke, in Schutz genommen, ist einfach schlechte Musik, die schlechteste überhaupt, die vielleicht gemacht worden ist."

80. Ibid., p. 179. For the text in German, Ibid., pp. 31–32. "Victor Hugo und Richard Wagner—sie bedeuten Ein und Dasselbe: dass in Niedergangs-Culturen, dass überall, wo den Massen die Entscheidung in

die Hände fällt, die Echtheit überflüssig, nachtheilig, zurücksetzend wird. Nur der Schauspieler weckt noch die *grosse* Begeisterung."
   81. Ibid., p. 183. For text in German, Ibid., p. 36. "Das Theater ist eine Form der Demolatrie in Sachen des Geschmacks, das Theater ist ein Massen-Aufstand, ein Plebiscit *gegen* den guten Geschmack . . . *Dies eben beweist der Fall Wagner*: er gewann die Menge,—er verdarb den Geschmack, er verdarb selbst für die Oper unsren Geschmack!—"
   82. José Ortega y Gasset, *The Modern Theme*, trans. James Cleugh (New York: W. W. Norton, 1933), pp. 67–69.
   83. Karl Mannheim, *Ideology and Utopia*, trans. Louis Wirth and Edward Shils (New York: Harcourt, Harvest Books), p. 310.
   84. *Marxism and Art*, ed. Maynard Solomon (New York: Vintage, 1974), p. 256.
   85. *Marx and Engels on Literature and Art, A Selection of Writings*, ed. Lee Baxandall and Stefan Morawski (St. Louis: Telos Press, 1973), p. 135.
   86. *Marxism and Art*, p. 64.
   87. *Radical Perspectives in the Arts*, ed. Lee Baxandall (Baltimore: Penguin, 1972), "Symposium on the Question of Decadence," p. 228.
   88. *Marxism and Art*, pp. 68–69.
   89. *Great Soviet Encyclopedia*, a translation of the third edition (New York: Macmillan, 1975), vol. 8, pp. 65–66.
   90. G. V. Plekhanov, *Art and Social Life* (London: Lawrence and Wishart, 1953), p. 193.
   91. Ibid., pp. 223, 226.
   92. Ibid., p. 204.
   93. Ibid., p. 222.
   94. Ibid.
   95. Ibid., pp. 222–23.
   96. Christopher Caudwell, *Studies and Further Studies in a Dying Culture* (New York and London: Monthly Review Press, 1971), part 2, p. 107.
   97. Ibid., part 1, p. 47.
   98. Ernst Fischer, *Art Against Ideology*, trans. Anna Bostock (London: Allen Lane, 1969), p. 156.
   99. Ibid., p. 157. For the text of Adolf Hitler's speech inaugurating the "Great Exhibition of German Art in 1937," see *Die Kunst im Dritten Reich* (Munich), I, 7–8 (July–August 1937), pp. 47–61. Excerpts from this speech, translated into English by Ilse Falk, are reproduced in Herschel B. Chipp, ed., *Theories of Modern Art* (Berkeley: University of California Press, 1968), pp. 474–83. Hitler not only established a clear-cut parallelism between Germany's general "decline" (economical, political) and the "degenerate art" of modernism but went on to reject the whole idea of modernity in

art, which he explicitly blamed on Judaism. "Modern," used in connection with art, was no less anathema to Hitler than it was to Stalin's ideologues. With regard to the notion of modernity itself, the following passage from Hitler's speech is of interest:

Art, on the one hand, was defined as nothing but an international communal experience, thus killing altogether any understanding of its integral relationship with an ethnic group. On the other hand, the relationship to time is stressed, that is: There was no longer any art of peoples or even of races, but only an art of the times. . . . Therefore today no German or French or Japanese or Chinese art exists, but plainly and simply a "modern art." Consequently, art . . . is the expression of a certain vintage which is characterized by the word "modern". . . . One day Impressionism, then Futurism, Cubism, maybe even Dadaism, etc. A further result is that even for the most insane and inane monstrosities thousands of catchwords to label them will have to be found, and have indeed been found. . . . Until the moment when National-Socialism took power, there existed in Germany a so-called "modern art". . . . National-Socialism, however, wants again a German Art, and this shall and will be of eternal value (Chipp, p. 476).

Certain striking similarities between Nazi and Zhdanovist aesthetics, as well as certain no less obvious differences have long been noted; both reject "decadent" or "sick" "modern art," but, as André Reszler notes in his recent essay, *Le marxisme devant la culture* (Paris: Presses Universitaires de France, 1975), p. 58, the Nazi aesthetic was never transformed into an officially codified cultural program. Reszler writes: "Esthétique idéologique par excellence, l'esthétique nazie soumet la création artistique à des normes d'essence politique; contrairement à d'autres esthétiques transformées en programme culturel d'un parti totalitaire, elle n'a jamais été formellement codifiée."

100. Ibid., p. 160.

101. This article was first published in English, in *Studies in Philosophy and Social Science*, vol. 9 (1941). The quotation is from pp. 318–19. A German version of the essay, under the title "Spengler nach dem Untergang" was reprinted in T. W. Adorno, *Prismen: Kulturkritik und Gesellschaft* (Frankfurt/Main: Suhrkamp, 1955), pp. 43–67.

102. Ibid., p. 325.

103. See *The Philosophy of Modern Music*, trans. Anne G. Mitchell and Wesley V. Blomster (New York: The Seabury Press, 1973), pp. 7 ff. In our time, Adorno thinks, it is impossible to compose *true* music (that is, music free from "false musical consciousness") in any kind of traditional style. All tradition that is used for creative purposes becomes Kitsch. Adorno writes (p. 10):

It is not only that the ears of the public are so flooded with light music that any other form of musical expression strikes them as "classical"—an arbitrary category existing only as a contrast to the other. And it is not only that the perceptive faculty has been so dulled by the omnipresent hit tune that the concentration necessary for responsible listening has become permeated by traces of recollection of this musical rubbish, and thereby impossible. Rather, sacrosanct traditional music has come to resemble commercial mass production in the character of its performances and in its role in the life of the listener and its substance has not escaped this influence. Music is inextricably bound up with what Clement Greenberg called the division of all art into kitsch and the avant-garde, and this kitsch—with its dictate of profit over culture—has long since conquered the social sphere. Therefore, considerations concerning the revelation of truth in aesthetic objectivity make reference only to the avant-garde, which is cut off from official culture.

104. *Negative Dialectics*, trans. E. B. Ashton (New York: The Seabury Press, 1973), p. 3.

105. *Decadence* is plainly opposed to manipulative and anti-intellectual "Mass culture" in *The Philosophy of Modern Music*. See esp. pp. 13–14, and pp. 112 ff. Music, Adorno thinks, "is not threatened, as the reactionaries claim, by its decadent, individualistic, and asocial character. It is actually too little threatened by those factors" (112). And he goes on to say that "decadent" or "avant-garde" functionless music has an important (critical) function to perform. "As long as an art, which is constituted according to the categories of mass production, contributes to this ideology, . . . that other functionless art has its own function" (p. 113).

106. Riccardo Scrivano, *Il decadentismo e la critica: Storia e Antologia della critica* (Florence: "La nuova Italia," 1963), p. 7. For a presentation of the post-World War II development of the idea of *decadentismo*, with special emphasis on the Marxist approach, see Adriano Seroni, *Il decadentismo* (Palermo: Palumbo, 1964), pp. 56–74.

107. Benedetto Croce, *La poesia* (Bari: Laterza, 1946), p. 51.

108. B. Croce, *Storia d'Europa nel secolo XIX* (Bari: Laterza, 1948), p. 50.

109. Nisard is quoted approvingly in Croce's study on the concept of the baroque ("il barocco"), published as an introduction to his *Storia dell' età barocca in Italia*, 5th ed. (Bari: Laterza, 1967). Significantly, Croce establishes a very close relationship between the idea of the baroque and the idea of decadence: "È noto che il barocco è stato studiato soprattutto nei cosidetti artisti e poeti di decadenza, e particolarmente in quelli della letteratura romana . . . , i quali porsero materia a un bel libro del Nisard" (p. 34).

110. For Croce's view of *decadenza*, see *Storia dell'età barocca* pp. 42–52.
111. B. Croce, *Nuovi saggi di estetica*, 3rd ed. (Bari: Laterza, 1948), pp. 261–80.
112. *Storia dell'età barocca*, p. 33.
113. Ibid., p. 34.
114. Ibid., p. 35.
115. Cf. "Letteratura narrativa della nuova Italia," and especially "Tendenze europeizzanti della nuova letteratura italiana," in Luigi Russo's *Ritratti i disegni storici* (Bari: Laterza, 1946), pp. 199–205.
116. Walter Binni, *La poetica del decadentismo* (Florence: Sansoni, 1961), p. 19.
117. Ibid., p. 20.
118. Ibid.
119. Ibid., p. 21.
120. Norberto Bobbio, *La filosofia del decadentismo* (Torino: Chiantore, 1944). *The Philosophy of Decadentism*, trans. David Moore (Oxford: Blackwell, 1948).
121. For Francesco Flora's later view of *decadentismo*, apart from various studies dealing with poetry (in which he establishes continuities but also distinctions between the poetics of decadentism and *ermetismo*), see especially his synthesis "Il decadentismo" in *Questioni e correnti di storia letteraria*, vol. 3 of the series *Problemi ed orientamenti critici di lingua e di letteratura italiana*, ed. A. Momigliano (Milan: Marzorati, 1949), pp. 760–810. On a European plane, Flora thinks, artists and thinkers like Oscar Wilde, W. B. Yeats, A. Symons (England), Wagner, Nietzsche, Gerhart Hauptmann, S. George, Thomas Mann, and the expressionists (Germany), Dostoevsky and in certain respects Tolstoy (Russia), are among those who exemplify various aspects of *decandentismo* (pp. 791–92).
122. Elio Gioanola, *Il decadentismo* (Roma: Editrice Studium, 1972). Gioanola operates with a very broad concept of *decadentismo*, a concept that, according to him, accounts decisively for "the artistic experiences of our time." He argues, therefore, against the restrictive use of *decadentismo* in connection with *fin de siècle* aestheticism only: "In reality, aestheticism is only one branch of the great decadent plant, and one of the less fruitful, although one of the most visible." This branch was among the first to dry up (p. 8). Consistent with this broad terminological option, Gioanola discusses within the context of *decadentismo* such poetic movements as symbolism, *crepuscolarismo*, futurism, expressionsism, surrealism, *ermetismo*. As we might expect, writers like Joyce, D. H. Lawrence, Robert Musil, André

Gide, Cesare Pavese, Thomas Mann, etc., that is, authors that are almost automatically associated with modernism, are frequently cited.

123. The role of Gramsci within the framework of Italian Marxist criticism, with special reference to the questions raised by the notion of *decadentismo*, is discussed in Adriano Seroni, *Il decadentismo*, pp. 58 ff.

124. Arcangelo Leone de Castris, *Decadentismo e realismo* (Bari: Adriatica, 1959), pp. 15 ff. In his book on *Italo Svevo* (Pisa: Nistri-Lischi, 1959), the concept of decadentism is specifically applied to the work of Svevo. See esp. pp. 27–38.

125. Carlo Salinari, *Miti e coscienza del decadentismo italiano*, 4th ed. (Milan: Feltrinelli, 1969), pp. 9–10. The decadentist "consciousness of crisis" is analyzed in the novels of Luigi Pirandello ("La coscienza della crisi," pp. 249–84).

KITSCH

1. Frank Wedekind, *Gesammelte Werke* (Munich: Georg Müller, 1924), vol. 9, p. 210.

2. Harold Rosenberg, *The Tradition of the New*, 2d ed. (New York: McGraw-Hill, 1965), p. 268.

3. Alexis de Toqueville, *Democracy in America*, trans. Henry Reeve (New York: Schocken Books, 1961), vol. II, pp. 59–60.

4. Ibid., pp. 60–61.

5. T. W. Adorno, "Veblen's Attack on Culture," *Studies in Philosophy and Social Science* 9 (1941):401.

6. In his much discussed "Alchemy of the Word" Rimbaud declared: "I liked stupid paintings, door panels, stage sets, back-drops for acrobats, signs, popular engravings, old-fashioned literature, church Latin, erotic books with bad spelling, novels of our grandmothers, fairy tales, little books from childhood, old operas, ridiculous refrains, naïve rhythms." (*Complete Works*, trans. Wallace Fowlie [Chicago: The University of Chicago Press, 1970], p. 193).

7. Susan Sontag, *Against Interpretation* (New York: Dell, 1969), p. 293.

8. Hilton Kramer, "New Art of the 70's in Chicago: Visual Bluster and Camp Sensibility," *New York Times*, 14 July 1974, Section 2, p. 19.

9. See "Hermann Broch e il problema del 'kitsch'," in *Le idee correnti* (Florence: Vallecchi, 1968), pp. 47 ff.

10. Ibid., p. 48.

11. Ramón Gómez de la Serna, *Lo cursi y otros ensayos* (Buenos Aires: Editorial Sudamericana, 1943), pp. 7–54.

12. Ludwig Giesz, *Phänomenologie des Kitsches* (Heidelberg: Rothe,

1960), p. 21. For a discussion of these and other assumptions regarding the origin of *kitsch* and its diverse shades of meaning, see Manfred Durzak's essay "Der Kitsch—seine verschiedenen Aspekte" in *Der Deutschunterricht,* 19, 1967, 1, pp. 95–97; also, Jochen Schulte-Sasse, *Die Kritik an der Trivialliteratur seit der Aufklärung* (Munich: Fink Verlag, 1971), pp. 136–38. For a general bibliography of scholarship on kitsch, see H. Schüling, *Zur Geschichte der ästhetischen Wertung: Bibliographie der Abhandlungen über den Kitsch* (Giessen, 1971).

13. Gilbert Highet, "Kitsch," in *A Clerk of Oxenford* (New York: Oxford University Press, 1954), p. 211.

14. This distinction was worked out in Germany, in the late 1940s, and elaborated upon by, among others, H. E. Holthusen in "Uber den sauren Kitsch," in his *Ja und Nein* (Munich: Piper Verlag, 1954), pp. 240–48.

15. *Democracy in America,* II, pp. 70–71.

16. Ibid., p. 72.

17. Hermann Broch, "Notes on the Problem of Kitsch," in *Kitsch, the World of Bad Taste,* ed. Gillo Dorfles (New York: Universe Books, 1969), p. 62.

18. Ibid., p. 73.

19. Intervention at the Symposium "The Comparative Method: Sociology and the Study of Literature," published in the *Yearbook of Comparative and General Literature* 23 (1974):18.

20. T. W. Adorno, *Ästhetische Theorie* (Frankfurt/Main: Suhrkamp, 1970), pp. 355 ff.

21. Cf. "Kulturindustrie, Aufklärung als Massenbetrug," in Max Horkheimer and Theodor W. Adorno, *Dialektik der Aufklärung* (Frankfurt/Main: Fischer Verlag, 1969), pp. 128–76. John Cumming has translated the book into English as *Dialectic of Enlightenment* (New York: Herder and Herder, 1972). For an overall historical view of the Frankfurt School see Martin Jay's comprehensive and perceptive book *The Dialectical Imagination: A History of the Frankfurt School and the Institute of Social Research, 1923–1950* (London: Heinemann Educational Books, 1973). Especially relevant to the question of mass culture is chapter 6 of the book, "Aesthetic Theory and the Critique of Mass Culture," pp. 173–218.

22. Adorno, "On Popular Music," *Studies in Philosophy and Social Science* 9 (1941):38. Similar ideas are developed by Horkheimer in the essay "Art and Mass Culture," originally published in the same issue of *Studies.* Horkheimer insists on the specifically *false* content of popular art: "The opposition of individual and society, and of private and social existence, which gave seriousness to the pastime of art, has become obsolete. The so-called entertainments, which have taken over the heritage of art, are

today nothing but popular tonics, like swimming or football. Popularity no longer has anything to do with the specific content or the truth of artistic productions. In the democratic countries, the final decision no longer rests with the educated but with the amusement industry. . . . For the totalitarian countries, the final decision rests with the managers of direct and indirect propaganda, which by its nature is indifferent to truth. Competition of artists in the free market, a competition in which success was determined by the educated, has become a race for the favor of the powers-that-be. . . ." Quoted from M. Horkheimer, *Critical Theory*, trans. M. J. O'Connell (New York: Herder and Herder, 1972), pp. 289-90.

23. "On Popular Music," ibid.

24. Dwight Macdonald, "A Theory of Mass Culture," in *Mass Culture*, ed. Bernard Rosenberg and David Manning White (New York: Free Press, 1964), p. 66. This essay, originally published in *Diogenes* (Summer 1953), was revised and enlarged as "Masscult and Midcult"—see *Against the American Grain* (New York: Random House, 1962), pp. 3-79. I still prefer the earlier version for its directness and greater impact.

25. Abraham A. Moles, *Le kitsch: l'art du bonheur* (Paris: Mame, 1971).

26. Macdonald, p. 60.

27. Moles, pp. 29-36.

28. Alvin Toffler, *The Culture Consumers: A Study of Art and Affluence in America* (New York: St. Martin's Press, 1964), pp. 163 ff. The author, whose approach may be summarized in the observation that "what is good for General Motors may conceivably be good for art" (p. 108), establishes a direct relationship between cultural consumption, the quality of cultural products consumed, and affluence. Taken in quantitative terms alone, cultural consumption in the United States is an index not only of wealth but also, according to the author, of cultural progress (the author accepts the notion of a "cultural explosion"). From his rather crude economic perspective, Toffler rejects the elitist view that standards of taste have steadily deteriorated with the rise of mass culture, and argues that "High Culture" has never been more prosperous than in our time. Of course, he is unaware that High Culture can be exploited by kitsch exactly as popular culture is, and that both are nowadays regulated to a large extent by the laws of mass production and mass diffusion.

29. Jenny Sharp, "It's New, It's Different, It's Been Here All the Time," in *Ark 41 (The Journal of the Royal College of Art,* London), 1967, pp. 24-25.

30. Roger Fry, *Vision and Design* (London: Chatto and Windus, 1920), pp. 44-45.

31. Dorfles, p. 31.

32. Rosenberg, p. 266.

33. *The Stuffed Owl* (London: Dent, 1930) is mainly concerned with such examples of bad poetry as can be found in eminent poets. The authors explain in the preface: "There is bad Bad Verse and good Bad Verse. . . . Good Bad Verse is grammatical, it is constructed according to the Rubrics, its rhythms, rimes, and meters are impeccable. . . . Good Bad Verse has an eerie, supernal beauty comparable in its accidents with the beauty of Good Verse. . . . Good Bad Verse . . . is devilish pleasing" (pp. VIII–X). Although the authors do not use the term kitsch, what they provide the reader with is distinguished poetic kitsch, defined in the first place by bathos and by "that windy splurging and bombinating which makes Victor Hugo's minor rhetoric so comic and terrible" (XIII). Other characteristics of "good Bad Verse" are "all those things connoted by poverty of imagination, sentimentality, banality, the prosaic, the *style pompier* and what Mr. Polly called 'rockcockyo'; anaemia, obstipation, or constipation of the poetic faculty; inability to hold the key of inspiration . . ." (XIII). As an example of what the authors consider "good Bad Verse"—a beautiful instance of romantic kitsch—we may quote Wordsworth's sonnet, which lends its title to the whole anthology:

The Stuffed Owl

(This is taken from the account given by Miss Jewsbury of the pleasure she derived, when long confined to bed by sickness, from the inanimate object on which this sonnet turns.—W. W.)

> While Anna's peers and early playmates tread,
> In freedom, mountain-turf and river's marge;
> Or float with music in the festal barge;
> Rein the proud steed, or through the dance are led;
> Her doom it is to press a weary bed—
> Till oft her guardian Angel, to some charge
> More urgent called, will stretch his wings at large,
> And friends too rarely prop the languid head.
> Yet, helped by Genius—untired Comforter,
> The presence even of a stuffed Owl for her
> Can cheat the time; sending her fancy out
> To ivied castles and to moonlight skies,
> Though he can neither stir a plume, nor shout;
> Nor veil, with restless film, his staring eyes.

34. Walther Killy, *Deutscher Kitsch. Ein Versuch mit Beispielen* (Göttingen: Vandenhoeck & Ruprecht, 1962).

35. For a more detailed discussion of the deliberate use of kitsch by the avant-garde, see the "Conclusion" of Dorfles's *Kitsch*, pp. 291 ff.; see also

Haroldo de Campos, "Vanguarda e kitsch" in *A arte no horizonte do provável*, 2d ed. (São Paulo: Editôra Perspectiva, 1972), pp. 193–201.

36. Greenberg's "Avant-garde and Kitsch," originally published in *Partisan Review* VI, 5 (Fall 1939), is collected in his *Art and Culture* (Boston: Beacon Press, 1965), pp. 3–21.

37. Dorfles, p. 30.

38. Macdonald, p. 66.

39. *The Collected Essays of Leslie Fiedler* (New York: Stein and Day, 1971), vol. II, p. 404.

40. Moles, p. 74.

41. Dorfles, p. 63.

42. Umberto Eco, in *Apocalittici e Integrati* (Milan: Bompiani, 1965), pp. 67–132.

43. Richard Egenter, *The Desecration of Christ*, Engl. version of *Kitsch und Christenleben* (Chicago: Franciscan Herald Press, 1967), p. 75. The theme of the "diabolical character" of religious kitsch is not new. Speaking on behalf of Roman Catholic orthodoxy and attributing the main cause of the modern decadence of religious art to the movement of the Reformation, Alexandre Cingria wrote in his book *La Décadence de l'art sacré* (Lausanne: Les Cahiers Vaudois, 1917): "Venons-en à un autre moyen d'action du diable: je veux parler du mensonge. Il existe un certain art vraiment diabolique qui singe la beauté. Cet art attire les suffrages de presque tout le public, par un certain joli, des apparences poétiques, un poli matériel qui cache aux yeux peu sensibles, peu exercés, peu attentifs, paresseux, une absence complète de vie, d'intelligence et de beauté" (p. 45). Although he does not use the term kitsch, Cingria is the author of probably the first book-length study on the subject. His notion of "decadence" is perfectly synonymous with kitsch, and the reasons for the decay of religious art as he sees them (moral reasons, such as boredom, laziness, lying, and historical reasons, such as the Reformation, the French Revolution and the rise of secularism, romanticism, and industrialism) lead to the inescapable conclusion that what he calls "decadence" is a specifically *modern* phenomenon. The relationship between modernity and kitsch is confirmed once again. Cingria's book was reprinted in 1930 with a preface by Paul Claudel (Paris: L'Art Catholique).

ON POSTMODERNISM (1986)

1. See Gerald Graff, "The Myth of the Postmodern Breakthrough," in *Literature Against Itself* (Chicago: University of Chicago Press, 1979), pp. 31–62.

2. See Charles Newman, *The Post-Modern Aura: The Act of Fiction in an Age of Inflation*, with a preface by Gerald Graff (Evanston: Northwestern University Press, 1985).

3. Claude Rawson's recent review article on John Ashbery, "A Poet in the Postmodern Playground," appeared in *Times Literary Supplement*, July 4, 1986, p. 724.

4. Jarrell's review of *Lord Weary's Castle* by Lowell, originally published in 1946, was reprinted in Randall Jarrell, *Poetry and the Age* (New York: Knopf, 1953). The quotation is from p. 216. In his *Postmodern American Poetry* (Urbana: University of Illinois Press, 1980), Jerome Mazzaro stresses that Jarrell was the first user "of the term postmodern in regard to American poetry" and notes that two years later, in 1948, "John Berryman used the same term . . . citing Jarrell as its source" (p. viii).

5. Somervell's abridgement of vols. 1–6 of Arnold Toynbee's *A Study of History* was published in 1946 by Oxford University Press. I have used the Dell edition (New York: Dell, 1965). The "Post-Modern Age" appears to be the fourth major period of Western history, after Western I ('Dark Ages'), Western II ('Middle Ages'), and Western III ('Modern'), 1475–1875 (p. 57).

6. Charles Olson, *Additional Prose*, ed. George F. Butterick (Bolinas: Four Seasons Foundation, 1974), p. 40. The whole passage reads: "I am an archaeologist of morning. And the writing acts which I find bear upon the present job are (I) from Homer back, not forward; and (II) from Melville on, particularly himself, Dostoevsky, Rimbaud, and Lawrence. These are the modern men who projected what we are and what we are in, who broke the spell. They put the men forward into the post-modern, the post-humanist, the post-historic, the going live present, the 'Beautiful Thing.'"

7. For a more extensive list of the "post" vocabulary, drawn from one representative critic, Leslie Fiedler, see p. 137 in the text.

8. For a critical presentation of the "new gnosticism" and other characteristic currents of thought of the 1960s, see Ihab Hassan, *Paracriticisms: Seven Meditations of the Times* (Urbana: University of Illinois Press, 1975).

9. For a detailed history of the term postmodernism in its earlier phases, see Michael Köhler, "'Postmodernismus': ein begriffshistorischer Überblick," *Amerikastudien* 22, no. 1 (1977): 8–17. A more recent and more comprehensive cultural-historical synthesis in Ihab Hassan's "Postface 1982: Toward a Concept of Postmodernism," in *The Dismemberment of Orpheus*, 2d ed. (Madison: University of Wisconsin Press, 1982), pp. 259–71. The most complete survey of the terminological career of postmodernism to date is Hans Bertens, "The Postmodern Weltanschauung and Its Relation with Modernism," in *Approaching Postmodernism*, ed. Douwe W.

Fokkema and Hans Bertens (Amsterdam and Philadelphia: John Benjamins, 1986), pp. 9–51.

10. Stephen Toulmin, "The Construal of Reality: Criticism in Modern and Postmodern Science," in *The Politics of Interpretation*, ed. W. J. T. Mitchell (Chicago: University of Chicago Press, 1983), pp. 99–117.

11. Ilya Prigogine and Isabelle Stengers, *Order Out of Chaos: Man's New Dialogue with Nature*, with a foreword by Alvin Toffler (New York: Bantam Books, 1984). For the Monod quotation and comments on its significance, see pp. 3–4 and 84.

12. Ibid., p. 292.

13. See Richard Rorty, *Philosophy and the Mirror of Nature* (Princeton: Princeton University Press, 1979), especially chapter 7, "From Epistemology to Hermeneutics," pp. 315–56.

14. In this country the view that postmodernism goes back to Heidegger is upheld by William V. Spanos and Richard Palmer. See particularly *Martin Heidegger and the Question of Literature: Toward a Postmodern Literary Hermeneutics*, ed. William V. Spanos (Bloomington: Indiana University Press, 1979). The essay contributed to that volume by Richard Palmer, "The Postmodernity of Heidegger," pp. 71–92, can be taken as programmatic for this approach to the question of postmodernism.

15. I quote from the English translation of Vattimo's "Bottle, Net, Truth, Revolution, Terrorism, Philosophy," *Denver Quarterly* 16, no. 4 (Winter 1982): 26–27. For Vattimo's major statements on philosophical postmodernism, see his *Al di là del sogetto: Nietzsche, Heidegger e l'ermeneutica* (Milan: Feltrinelli, 1981), and *La fine de la modernità: Nichilismo ed ermeneutica nella cultura postmoderna* (Milan: Garzanti, 1985). The debate on "weak thought" was started by *Il pensiero debole*, ed. Gianni Vattimo and Pier Aldo Rovatti (Milan: Garzanti, 1983). For a useful discussion of postmodernism in Italy, see Stefano Rosso, "Postmodern Italy: Notes on the 'Crisis of Reason,' 'Weak Thought,' and *The Name of the Rose*," in *Exploring Postmodernism*, ed. Matei Calinescu and D. W. Fokkema (Amsterdam and Philadelphia: John Benjamins, forthcoming).

16. Jürgen Habermas, "Modernity versus Postmodernity," *New German Critique* 22 (Winter 1981): 14.

17. Ibid., p. 13.

18. See Jürgen Habermas, "Questions and Counterquestions," in *Habermas on Modernity*, ed. Richard Bernstein (Cambridge, Mass.: MIT Press, 1985), p. 196 and p. 229, n. 6. Habermas explains that in comparing Foucault and Derrida to the "Young Conservatives" of the Weimar Republic (Arnold Gehelen, Martin Heidegger, Carl Schmitt, and Ernst Jünger), he wanted to stress "that they all take from Nietzsche the radical

gesture of a break with modernity and a revolutionary renewal of premodern energies, most often reaching back to archaic times. Like any comparison, it has its weaknesses, but in the German context it does illuminate intellectual affinities that, notwithstanding the political contrary positions, stem from the authority of Nietzsche" (p. 229). In another essay, "The French Path to Postmodernity: Bataille between Eroticism and General Economics," *New German Critique* 33 (Fall 1984): 79–102, Habermas points again to Nietzsche as being at the origin of a certain discourse on modernity, a discourse initiated in France by Georges Bataille. Their common descent from Nietzsche may explain the surprising links between two otherwise extremely different thinkers such as Bataille and Heidegger. Both of them, Habermas writes, are "concerned to break out of the prison of modernity, out of an Occidental rationalism that has been victorious on the scale of world history. Both want to overcome subjectivism. . . . So much do both thinkers agree on this project that what Foucault says about Bataille's idea of transgression might as well be said of the later Heidegger's concept of transcendence, etc." (pp. 80–81).

19. Jean-François Lyotard, *The Postmodern Condition: A Report on Knowledge*, trans. Geoff Bennington and Brian Massumi (Minneapolis: University of Minnesota Press, 1984); originally published as *La Condition postmoderne* (Paris: Minuit, 1979).

20. Ibid., pp. 18–37. See also Jean-François Lyotard, *Le Postmoderne expliqué aux enfants* (Paris: Galilée, 1986), pp. 37–42 and 45–64.

21. Lyotard, *Le Postmoderne*, p. 47.

22. Richard Rorty, "Habermas and Lyotard on Postmodernity," in *Habermas on Modernity* (see note 18), pp. 161–76. For a Habermasian perspective on the debate, see Peter Dews's introduction to his edition of Jürgen Habermas, *Autonomy and Solidarity: Interviews* (London: Verso, 1986), pp. 1–35. Lyotard is seen here as a typical representative of French poststructuralism under the influence of Nietzsche. Another German neo-Marxist account of the Habermas-Lyotard dispute on modernity and postmodernity is found in Albrecht Wellmer, "On the Dialectic of Modernism and Postmodernism," *Praxis International* 4, no. 4 (January 1985): 337–61.

23. The question of the two strategies of the new—innovation and renovation—is the central theme of the essays included in *Innovation/Renovation: New Perspectives in the Humanities*, ed. Ihab and Sally Hassan (Madison: University of Wisconsin Press, 1983). See particularly Ihab Hassan, "Ideas of Cultural Change," pp. 15–46. For the rediscovery of the past from a perspective that I have called "dialogic pluralism," see my "From the One to the Many: Pluralism in Today's Thought," pp. 263–88.

24. Umberto Eco, *Postscript to "The Name of the Rose"* (in Italian), trans. William Weaver (New York: Harcourt Brace Jovanovich, 1984), pp. 66–67.

25. See John Barth, *The Literature of Exhaustion and the Literature of Replenishment* (Northridge, Calif.: Lord John's Press, 1982).

26. Guy Scarpetta, *L'Impureté* (Paris: Grasset, 1985), p. 42.

27. See my "Postmodernism and Some Paradoxes of Periodization," in *Approaching Postmodernism* (see note 9), p. 249.

28. Ihab Hassan, *The Dismemberment of Orpheus* (see note 9), p. 266.

29. Robert Venturi, *Complexity and Contradiction in Architecture*, 2d ed. (New York: Museum of Modern Art, 1977); and, with Denise Scott Brown and Steven Izenour, *Learning from Las Vegas* (Cambridge, Mass.: MIT Press, 1972).

30. Charles Jencks, *The Language of Post-Modern Architecture* (New York: Rizzoli, 1977); *Late-Modern Architecture* (New York: Rizzoli: 1980); *Post-Modern Classicism: The New Synthesis* (London: Academy Editions, 1980); and, with a contribution by William Chaitkin, *Current Architecture* (London: Academy Editions, 1982).

31. Paolo Portoghesi et al., *The Presence of the Past: First International Exhibition of Architecture—Venice Biennale 1980* (London: Academy Editions, 1980); Portoghesi, *After Modern Architecture* (in Italian), trans. Meg Shore (New York: Rizzoli, 1982); and Portoghesi, *Postmodern, the Architecture of the Post-Industrial Society* (in Italian), trans. Ellen Schapiro (New York: Rizzoli, 1983).

32. Heinrich Klotz, *Postmodern Visions* (New York: Abeville Press, 1985.

33. Jencks, *Current Architecture* (see note 30), p. 158.

34. Ibid., p. 111.

35. Ibid., p. 12.

36. Umberto Eco, *Postscript to "The Name of the Rose"* (see note 24), p. 71.

37. Ibid., p. 54.

38. Ibid., p. 64.

39. Linda Hutcheon, *A Theory of Parody: The Teachings of Twentieth-Century Art Forms* (New York and London: Methuen, 1985). This book discusses the question of postmodernism in terms of intertextual parodic double coding. For a more detailed discussion of Hutcheon's theory of parody, see my review article, "Parody and Intertextuality," forthcoming in *Semiotica*.

40. Guy Scarpetta (see note 26) opposes the postmodernist "overcoding" to the minimalist coding characteristic of certain avant-gardes. But his

opposition is not as trenchant as it might seem, since he observes that the postmodern liberation from the strictures of the avant-garde is not achieved through "rejection, reaction, but through prolongation, extension, exasperation, overcoding—not by negating what avant-gardism had introduced but by absorbing it into less minimalist postmodern procedures" (p. 187).

41. Jencks, *Current Architecture* (see note 30), p. 16.

42. For the "realistic" (or, as I called it, "theatrical") fallacy in the use of postmodernism, see my "Postmodernism: The Mimetic and Theatrical Fallacies," in *Exploring Postmodernism* (see note 15). For a more general discussion of the "realistic illusion" in the social sciences, see Raymond Boudon, *La place du désordre* (Paris: Presses Universitaires de France, 1984), pp. 229–38.

43. Clement Greenberg, "Modernist Painting," in *The New Art: A Critical Anthology*, ed. Gregory Battcock (New York: Dutton, 1966), pp. 100–110.

44. Clement Greenberg, *The Notion of 'Post-Modern'*, offered as the Fourth Sir William Dobell Memorial Lecture at the University of Sydney in 1980 (Sydney: Bloxham and Chambers, 1980), p. 12.

45. Ibid., p. 11.

46. Ibid., p. 14.

47. Hilton Kramer, "Postmodern Art and Culture in the 1980's," *New Criterion* 1, no. 1 (1982): 36–42. As the editor of *The New Criterion*, Kramer has made the defense of modernism and the blanket rejection of postmodernism into the general policy of this journal.

48. Fredric Jameson, *Fables of Aggression: Wyndham Lewis, the Modernist as Fascist* (Berkeley: University of California Press, 1979). For a more extended discussion of Jameson's position on the politics of modernism, see my essay "Modernism and Ideology," in *Modernism: Challenges and Perspectives*, ed. Monique Chefdor, Ricardo Quinones, and Albert Wachtel (Urbana: University of Illinois Press, 1986), pp. 79–94.

49. Fredric Jameson, "Postmodernism and Consumer Society," in *The Anti-Aesthetic: Essays on Postmodern Culture*, ed. Hal Foster (Port Townsend, Wash.: Bay Press, 1983), pp. 124–25.

50. Ibid., p. 125.

51. Ibid. In a more recent piece, "The Politics of Theory: Ideological Positions in the Postmodernism Debate," *New German Critique* 33 (Fall 1984): 53–65, Jameson discusses and grades with ideological pluses and minuses the approaches to postmodernism of, among others, Jencks, Lyotard, Habermas, and Hilton Kramer. He appears to suggest that postmodernism is distinguished from modernism by its "populism," by its incorporation of elements of mass or popular culture "to the point where

many of our older critical and evaluative categories (founded precisely on the radical differentiation of modernist and mass culture) no longer seem functional"; but he concludes that, if this is indeed the case, "then it seems at least possible that what wears the mask and makes the gestures of 'populism' in the various postmodernist apologias and manifestoes is in reality a mere reflex and a symptom of a (to be sure momentous) cultural mutation, in which what used to be stigmatized as mass or commercial culture is now received into the precincts of an enlarged cultural realm" (p. 65)—which is a reassertion of the older ambivalent but ultimately negative position.

52. Marjorie Perloff, *The Poetics of Indeterminacy: Rimbaud to Cage* (Princeton: Princeton University Press, 1981), p. 4.

53. Ibid., "Unreal Cities," pp. 3–44.

54. Vladimir Nabokov, *Ada* (New York: McGraw-Hill, 1969), pp. 262–63.

55. Christopher Butler, *After the Wake: An Essay on the Contemporary Avant-Garde* (Oxford: Clarendon Press, 1980), p. 39. For an excellent theoretical discussion of the concept of postmodernism in relation to fiction and metafiction (and "surfiction"), see Christine Brooke-Rose's *A Rhetoric of the Unreal* (Cambridge: Cambridge University Press, 1981), particularly the chapter "Eximplosions," pp. 339–63.

56. In *Horizons of Assent: Modernism, Postmodernism, and the Ironic Imagination* (Baltimore: Johns Hopkins University Press, 1981), Alan Wilde, while explicitly excluding Beckett from postmodernism, never considers either Borges or Nabokov within the context of postmodern irony, taking his examples almost exclusively from Anglo-American writers. Based on Wilde's examples one might conclude that modernism is a largely English affair (E. M. Forster and Christopher Isherwood appear as typical modernists) and postmodernism a largely American one.

57. The Beckettian "aesthetics of failure," an apparently paradoxical notion, has been insightfully discussed by, among others, Hugh Kenner in *Samuel Beckett* (Berkeley: University of California Press, 1968). Commenting on an important statement made by Beckett in 1957 ("The more Joyce knew the more he could. He's tending toward omniscience and omnipotence as an artist. I'm working with impotence, ignorance. I don't think impotence has been exploited in the past."), Kenner proposes an enlightening metaphoric opposition between the type of the "acrobat" (who skillfully exploits ability) and the "clown" (who skillfully exploits inability). The clown, Kenner points out, thematizes "his own inability to walk a tightrope. . . . He does not *imitate* the acrobat; it is plain that he could not; he offers us, directly, his personal incapacity, an intricate art form" (pp. 33–34).

58. Some typically postmodern paradoxes (of the infinite regress kind) have been read into Magritte's painting by Michel Foucault, in his witty commentary entitled *This Is Not a Pipe*, trans. James Harkness (Berkeley: University of California Press, 1982). Looking at Magritte's canvas, Foucault writes that scarcely has one decided " 'this is a pipe,' before he must correct himself and stutter, 'This is not a pipe, but the drawing of a pipe,' 'This is not a pipe, but a sentence saying that this is not a pipe,' 'In the sentence "this is not a pipe," *this* is not a pipe: the painting, written sentence, drawing of a pipe—all this is not a pipe' " (p. 30).

59. See D. W. Fokkema, *Literary History, Modernism, and Postmodernism* (Amsterdam: John Benjamins, 1984), and "The Semantic and Syntactic Organization of Postmodernist Texts," in *Approaching Postmodernism* (see note 9), pp. 81–98.

60. Fokkema, *Literary History*, p. 14.

61. Brian McHale, "Change of Dominant from Modernist to Postmodernist Writing," in *Approaching Postmodernism* (see note 9), p. 75.

62. Ibid., p. 58.

63. Ibid., p. 60.

64. Ibid.

65. Ibid., p. 74.

66. Elrud Ibsch, "From Hypothesis to *Korrektur:* Refutation as a Component of Postmodernist Discourse," in *Approaching Postmodernism* (see note 9), pp. 119–33.

67. Ibid., p. 122.

68. Brian T. Fitch, *Dimensions, structures, textualité dans la trilogie de Beckett* (Paris: Lettres Modernes—Minard, 1977), p. 92.

69. Samuel Beckett, *Molloy*, trans. Patrick Bowles and author (New York: Grove Press, 1955), p. 48.

70. Samuel Beckett, *The Unnamable*, trans. author (New York: Grove Press, 1958), p. 79.

71. Friedrich Nietzsche, *"On the Genealogy of Morals" and "Ecce Homo,"* trans. Walter Kaufmann and R. J. Hollingdale (New York: Vintage, 1969), p. 80.

72. Max Weber, *The Protestant Ethic and the Spirit of Capitalism*, trans. Talcott Parsons (London: Unwin, 1985), pp. 47–48.

SELECTED CRITICAL BIBLIOGRAPHY

MODERNITY/MODERNISM

Ackroyd, Peter. *Notes for a New Culture: An Essay on Modernism.* New York: Barnes and Noble, 1976.

Adorno, Theodor W. *Philosophy of Modern Music* (in German). Translated by G. Mitchell and Wesley V. Blomster. New York: Seabury Press, 1973.

Anderson, Robert Roland. *Spanish American Modernism: A Selected Bibliography.* Tucson: University of Arizona Press, 1970.

Aron, Raymond. *Progress and Disillusion: The Dialectics of Modern Society.* New York: Praeger, 1968.

Baron, H. "The 'Querelle' of the Ancients and the Moderns as a Problem for Renaissance Scholarship." *Journal of the History of Ideas* 20 (1959): 3–22.

Barzun, Jacques. *Classic, Romantic, and Modern.* 2d rev. ed. Boston: Little, Brown, 1961.

Baudouin, Charles. *The Myth of Modernity.* Translated by Bernard Miall. London: Allen and Unwin, 1950.

Baudrillard, Jean. "Modernité." *Encyclopaedia Universalis,* vol. 11, pp. 139–41. Paris: Encyclopaedia Universalis, 1974.

Beebe, Maurice. "Introduction: What Modernism Was." *From Modernism to Post-Modernism.* Issue of *Journal of Modern Literature* 3, no. 5 (July 1974): 1065–84.

Bell, Daniel. *The Cultural Contradictions of Capitalism.* New York: Basic Books, 1976.

Berger, Peter L., Brigitte Berger, and Hansfried Kellner. *The Homeless Mind: Modernization and Consciousness.* New York: Vintage Books, 1974.

Berger, Peter L. *Facing Up to Modernity.* New York: Basic Books, 1977.
_____. *The Heretical Imperative.* Garden City, N.Y.: Anchor Press/Doubleday, 1979.

Bergonzi, Bernard, ed. *Innovations: Essays on Art and Ideas.* London: Macmillan, 1968.

Berman, Marshall. *All That Is Solid Melts into Air: The Experience of Modernity.* New York: Simon and Schuster, 1982.

Bloch, Ernst. *A Philosophy of the Future* (in German). Translated by John Cumming. New York: Herder and Herder, 1970.

Bradbury, Malcolm, and James McFarlane, eds. *Modernism: 1890–1930*. New York: Penguin Books, 1976.

Buck, August. "Aus der Vorgeschichte der 'Querelle des Anciens et des Modernes' in Mittelalter und Renaissance." *Die humanistische Tradition in der Romania*, pp. 75–91. Bad Homburg: Gehlen, 1968.

————. *Die "Querelle des Anciens et des Modernes" im italienischen Selbstverständnis der Renaissance und des Barocks*. Wiesbaden: F. Steiner, 1973.

Bury, J. B. *The Idea of Progress: An Inquiry into Its Origin and Growth*. Introduction by Charles A. Beard. New York: Dover Publications, 1955.

Calinescu, Matei. "Hermeneutics or Poetics." *Journal of Religion* 59, 1 (1979): 1–17.

————. "Marxism as a Work of Art: Poststructuralist Readings of Marx in France." *Stanford French Review* 3, no. 1 (1979): 123–35.

————. "Literature and Politics." In J. P. Barricelli and J. Gibaldi, eds., *Interrelations of Literature*, pp. 123–50. New York: M.L.A., 1982.

————. "The 'End of Man' in Twentieth-Century Thought." In Saul Friedländer, Leo Marx, Gerald Holton, Eugene Skolnikoff, eds., *Visions of Apocalypse: End or Rebirth?* pp. 171–96. New York: Holmes and Meier, 1985.

————. "Modernism and Ideology." In Monique Chefdor, Ricardo Quinones, and Albert Wachtel, eds., *Modernism: Challenges and Perspectives*, pp. 79–94. Urbana: University of Illinois Press, 1986.

Castillo, Homero, ed. *Estudios críticos sobre el modernismo*. Madrid: Editorial Gredos, 1968.

Chefdor, Monique, Ricardo Quinones, and Albert Wachtel, eds. *Modernism: Challenges and Perspectives*. Urbana: University of Illinois Press, 1986.

Chenu, M.-D. "Notes de lexicographie philosophique médiévale: Antiqui, moderni." *Revue des sciences philosophiques et théologiques* 17 (1928): 82–94.

Chiari, Joseph. *The Aesthetics of Modernism*. London: Vision Press, 1970.

Cohn, Norman. *The Pursuit of the Millennium: Revolutionary Millennarians and Mystical Anarchists of the Middle Ages*. Rev. and expanded ed. London: Maurice Temple Smith, 1970.

Connolly, Cyril. *The Modern Movement*. London: André Deutsch, Hamish Hamilton, 1965.

Cronin, Anthony. *A Question of Modernity*. London: Secker and Warburg, 1966.

Curtius, Ernst Robert. *European Literature and the Latin Middle Ages* (in German). Translated by Willard R. Trask. New York: Harper and Row, 1963.

Davis, Alistair. *An Annotated Critical Bibliography of Modernism*. Totowa, N.J.: Barnes and Noble, 1982.

Davison, Ned. J. *The Concept of Modernism in Hispanic Criticism*. Boulder, Co.: Pruett Press, 1966.

Décaudin, Michel, and Georges Raillard, eds. *La Modernité*. Special issue of *Cahiers du 20e siècle*, no. 5. Paris: Klincksieck, 1975.

Edelstein, Ludvig. *The Idea of Progress in Classical Antiquity*. Baltimore: Johns Hopkins University Press, 1967.

Eliade, Mircea. *The Myth of the Eternal Return* (in French). Translated by Willard R. Trask. New York: Pantheon Books, 1965.

Ellmann, Richard, and Charles Feidelson, Jr., eds. *The Modern Tradition: Backgrounds of Modern Literature*. New York: Oxford University Press, 1965.

Freund, Walter. *Modernus und andere Zeitbegriffe des Mittelalters*. Köln: Böhlau Verlag, 1957.

Faulkner, Peter. *Modernism*. London: Methuen, 1977.

Frye, Northrop. *The Modern Century*. Toronto: Oxford University Press, 1967. (Esp. chap. 2, "Improved Binoculars," pp. 50–86.)

Gablik, Suzi. *Has Modernism Failed?* New York: Thames and Hudson, 1984.

Ghellinck, J. de. "Nani et gigantes." *Archivum Latinitatis medii aevi* 18 (1945): 25–29.

Gilson, Etienne. "Le Moyen Age comme 'saeculum modernum.'" In *Concetto, storia, miti e immagini del Medio Evo*, edited by Vittore Branca. Florence: Sansoni, 1973.

Goldberg, Isaac. "The 'Modernista' Renovation." *Studies in Spanish American Literature*, pp. 1–3. New York: Brentano's, 1920.

Gössmann, Elisabeth. *Antiqui und Moderni im Mittelalter: Eine geschichtliche Standortbestimmung*. Munich: Schöningh, 1974.

Greenberg, Clement. *Art and Culture*. Boston: Beacon Press, 1965.

―――. "Modernist Painting." In Gregory Battcock, ed., *The New Art: A Critical Anthology*, pp. 100–110. New York: Dutton, 1966.

Gullón, Ricardo. *Direcciones del Modernismo*. 2d ed. Madrid: Editorial Gredos, 1971.

Guyer, Foster E. "'C'est nous qui sommes les anciens.'" *Modern Language Notes* 36 (1921): 257–64.

―――. "The Dwarf on the Giant's Shoulders." *Modern Language Notes* 45 (1930): 398–402.

Habermas, Jürgen. "Ernst Bloch—A Marxist Romantic." *Salmagundi* 10–11 (Fall 1969–Winter 1970): 311–25.

Habermas on Modernity. Edited by Richard Bernstein. Cambridge, Mass.: MIT Press, 1985.

Henríquez Ureña, Max. *Breve historia del modernismo*. 2d ed. Mexico: Fondo de Cultura Económica, 1962.

Howe, Irving, ed. *Literary Modernism*. Greenwich, Conn.: Fawcett Publications, 1967.

———. *The Decline of the New*. New York: Harcourt, Brace and World, 1970.

Jauss, H. R. Introduction to the facsimile edition of Charles Perrault's *Parallèle des Anciens et des Modernes en ce qui regarde les arts et les sciences*, pp. 8–64. Munich: Eidos, 1964.

Jeauneau, Edouard. "Nani gigantum humeris incidentes: Essai d'interprétation de Bernard des Chartres." *Vivarium* 5, no. 2 (November 1967): 79–99.

Jiménez, Juan Ramón. *El Modernismo: Notas de un curso*. Edited by Ricardo Gullón and Eugenio Fernández Méndez. Madrid: Aguilar, 1962.

Karl, Frederick. *Modern and Modernism: The Sovereignty of the Artist, 1885–1925*. New York: Atheneum, 1985.

Kenner, Hugh. *The Pound Era*. Berkeley and Los Angeles: University of California Press, 1971.

Kermode, Frank. *Modern Essays*. London: Collins, Fontana Books, 1971.

Kiely, Robert, ed. *Modernism Reconsidered*. Cambridge, Mass.: Harvard University Press, 1983.

Klibansky, Raymond. "Standing on the Shoulders of Giants." *Isis* 26 (1936): 147–49.

Kolakowski, Leszek. "Modernity on Endless Trial." *Encounter* 66 (March 1986): 8–12.

Krauss, Werner, and Hans Kortum, eds. *Antike und Moderne in der Literaturdiskussion des 18. Jahrhunderts*. Berlin: Akademie Verlag, 1966.

Krutch, Joseph Wood. *The Modern Temper*. New York: Harcourt, Brace and Co., 1929.

———. *"Modernism" in Modern Drama: A Definition and an Estimate*. Ithaca: Cornell University Press, 1953.

Landes, David S. *Revolution in Time: Clocks and the Making of the Modern World*. Cambridge, Mass.: Harvard University Press, 1983.

Leclercq, Jean. "Experience and Interpretation of Time in the Early Middle Ages." *Studies in Medieval Culture* 5 (1975). 9–19.

Lefebvre, Henri. *Introduction à la modernité: préludes*. Paris: Editions de Minuit, 1962.

Le Goff, Jacques. "Au Moyen Age: Temps de l'Eglise et temps du marchand." *Annales: Economies, Sociétés, Civilisations* 15 (1960): 417–33.

Levenson, Michael H. *A Genealogy of Modernism: A Study of English Literary Doctrine, 1908–1922*. New York: Cambridge University Press, 1984.

Levin, Harry. *Memories of the Moderns*. New York: New Directions, 1980.

Lodge, David. *The Modes of Modern Writing: Metaphor, Metonymy and the Typology of Modern Literature*. Ithaca: Cornell University Press, 1977.

Lukács, Georg. *Realism in Our Time* (in German). Preface by George Steiner. Translated by John and Necke Mander. New York: Harper and Row, 1964.

Man, Paul de. *Blindness and Insight*. New York: Oxford University Press, 1971.

Margiotta, Giacinto. *Le origini italiane de la Querelle des Anciens et des Modernes*. Rome: Studium, 1953.

Marino, Adrian. *Modern, modernism, modernitate*. Bucharest: Editura Univers, 1970.

––––––. "Modernisme et modernité, quelques précisions sémantiques." *Neohelicon* 2, 3–4 (1974): 307–18.

Merton, Robert K. *On the Shoulders of Giants: A Shandean Postscript*. New York: Free Press, 1965.

Michaud-Quantin, Pierre, with M. Lemoine. *Etudes sur le vocabulaire philosophique du Moyen Age*. Rome: Edizioni dell'Ateneo, 1971.

Molnar, Thomas. *Utopia, the Perennial Heresy*. New York: Sheed and Ward, 1967.

Mommsen, Theodor E. "Petrarch's Conception of the 'Dark Ages.'" *Speculum* 17 (1942): 226–42.

––––––. "St. Augustine and the Christian Idea of Progress." *Journal of the History of Ideas* 12 (1951): 346–74.

Muir, Edwin. *We Moderns: Enigmas and Guesses*. New York: Knopf, 1920.

Nisbet, Robert. *History of the Idea of Progress*. New York: Basic Books, 1980.

Onís, Federico de. *Antología de la poesia española e hispanoamericana (1882–1932)*. New York: Las Américas, 1961.

––––––. "Sobre el concepto del Modernismo" and "Martí y el Modernismo." *España en América: Estudios, ensayos y discursos sobre temas españoles e hispanoamericanos,* pp. 179–85 and 622–31. 2d ed. San Juan: Universidad de Puerto Rico, 1968.

Ortega y Gasset, José. *The Dehumanization of Art* (in Spanish). Translated by Helene Weyl. Princeton: Princeton University Press, 1968.

———. *The Modern Theme* (in Spanish). Translated by James Cleugh. New York: W. W. Norton, 1933.

Papaioannou, Kostas. "Modernité et histoire." *Preuves* 207 (May 1968): 32–37.

Paz, Octavio. *Children of the Mire* (in Spanish). Translated by Rachel Phillips. Cambridge Mass.: Harvard University Press, 1974.

Philipps, Allen W. "Rubén Darío y sus juicios sobre el modernismo." *Revista Iberoamericana* 24 (1959): 41–64.

Pollard, Sidney. *The Idea of Progress: History and Society.* Baltimore: Penguin Books, 1971.

Priestley, J. B. *Man and Time.* Garden City, N.Y.: Doubleday, 1964.

Quinones, Ricardo. *The Renaissance Discovery of Time.* Cambridge, Mass.: Harvard University Press, 1972.

———. *Mapping Literary Modernism: Time and Development.* Princeton: Princeton University Press, 1985.

Ransom, John Crowe. "The Future of Poetry." *The Fugitive* 3 (February 1924): 2–4.

Ratté, John. "Modernism in the Christian Church." *Dictionary of the History of Ideas,* pp. 418–27. New York: Charles Scribner's Sons, 1973.

Read, Herbert E. *Form in Modern Poetry.* London: Vision Press, 1948.

———. *The Philosophy of Modern Art.* London: Faber and Faber, 1952.

Reardon, Bernard M. G. *Roman Catholic Modernism.* Stanford: Stanford University Press, 1970.

Reszler, André. *Le marxisme devant la culture.* Paris: Presses Universitaires de France, 1975.

Riding, Laura, and Robert Graves. *A Survey of Modernist Poetry.* London: Heinemann, 1929.

Rigault, H. *Histoire de la Querelle des Anciens et des Modernes.* Facsimile edition of the 1859 printing. New York: Burt Franklin, 1965.

Rougemont, Denis de. *Man's Western Quest* (in French). Translated by Montgomery Belgion. New York: Harper and Row, 1975.

Sarton, George. "Standing on the Shoulders of Giants." *Isis* 24 (1935–36): 107–9.

Scott, Nathan A. *The Broken Center.* New Haven: Yale University Press, 1966.

Sorel, Georges. *The Illusions of Progress* (in French). Translated by John and Charlotte Stanley. Berkeley and Los Angeles: University of California Press, 1969.

Spears, Monroe K. *Dionysus and the City: Modernism in Twentieth-Century Poetry.* New York: Oxford University Press, 1970. (Esp. "The Modern and the Past," pp. 3–34.)

Spender, Stephen. *The Struggle of the Modern.* London: Hamish Hamilton, 1963.

Steffen, Hans, ed. *Aspekte der Modernität.* Göttingen: Vandenhoeck and Ruprecht, 1965.

Thorndike, Lynn. "Invention of the Mechanical Clock about 1271 A.D." *Speculum* 16 (1941): 242–43.

Toulmin, Stephen, and Goodfield, June. *The Discovery of Time.* New York: Harper and Row, 1967.

Trilling, Lionel. *Beyond Culture.* New York: Viking Press, 1961.

———. *Mind in the Modern World.* New York: Viking Press, 1973.

Wellek, René. *A History of Modern Criticism: 1750–1950.* New Haven: Yale University Press, 1955–86. 6 vols.

———. *Concepts of Criticism.* New Haven: Yale University Press, 1963.

———. *Discriminations: Further Concepts of Criticism.* New Haven: Yale University Press, 1970.

Wellek, René, and Austin Warren. *Theory of Literature.* 3d ed. New York: Harcourt, Brace and Co., 1959.

Williet, Jean. "Baudelaire et le mythe du progrès." *Revue des sciences humaines,* fasc. 125–28 (1967): 417–31.

Wolff, Ph. "Le temps et sa mesure au moyen âge." *Annales: Economies, Sociétés, Civilisations* 17 (1962): 1141–45.

Zilsel, Edgar. "The Genesis of the Concept of Scientific Progress." *Journal of the History of Ideas* 6 (1945): 325–49.

Zimmermann, Albert, ed. *Antiqui und Moderni: Traditionsbewusstsein und Fortschrittsbewusstsein in späten Millelalter.* Berlin and New York: Walter de Gruyter, 1974.

AVANT-GARDE

Ackerman, James S. "The Demise of the Avant-Garde: Notes on the Sociology of Recent American Art." *Comparative Studies in Society and History* 11, no. 4 (October 1969): 371–84.

Barbato, Andrea, et al. *Avanguardia e neo-avanguardia.* Introduction by Giansiro Ferrata. Milan: Sugar, 1966.

Barthes, Roland. "Whose Theatre? Whose Avant-Garde?" (in French). In

Critical Essays, translated by Richard Howard. Evanston, Ill.: Northwestern University Press, 1972.

Bergman, Pär. *'Modernolatria' et 'Simultaneità.' Recherches sur deux tendences dans l'avant-garde littéraire en Italie et en France à la veille de la première guerre mondiale.* Uppsala: Svenska Bokförlaget/Bonniers, 1962.

Büger, Peter. *The Theory of the Avant-Garde.* Translated by Michael Shaw, foreword by Jochen Schulte Sasse. Minneapolis: University of Minnesota Press, 1984. Originally published as *Theorie der Avantagarde* (Frankfurt am Main: Suhrkamp, 1974).

Butler, Christopher. *After the Wake: An Essay on the Contemporary Avant-Garde.* Oxford: Clarendon Press, 1980.

Cage, John. *Silence.* Middletown, Conn.: Wesleyan University Press, 1961.

Calvesi, Maurizio. *Le due avanguardie: dal Futurismo alla Pop Art.* Milan: Lerici, 1966.

Chiarini, Paolo. *L'Avanguardia e la poetica del realismo.* Bari: Laterza, 1961.

Corvalán, Octavio. *El postmodernismo: La literatura hispano-americana entre dos guerras mundiales.* New York: Las Américas, 1961.

Egbert, Donald Drew. "The Idea of 'Avant-Garde' in Art and Politics." *American Historical Review* 73 (1967): 339–66.

————. *Social Radicalism and the Arts—Western Europe.* New York: Knopf, 1970.

Enzensberger, Hans Magnus. "The Aporias of the Avant-Garde" (in German). Translated by John Simon. In *Issues in Contemporary Literary Criticism,* edited by Gregory T. Polletta. Boston: Little, Brown, 1973.

Estivals, Robert. *La philosophie de l'histoire de la culture dans l'avant-garde culturelle parisienne depuis 1945.* Paris: Guy Leprat, 1962.

Estivals, Robert, Jean-Charles Gaudy, and Gabrielle Vergez. *L'Avant-Garde: Etude historique et sociologique des publications périodiques ayant pour titre "L'avant-garde".* Paris: Bibliothèque Nationale, 1968.

Gilman, Richard. "The Idea of the Avant-Garde." *Partisan Review* 39, no. 3 (1972): 382–96.

Gómez de la Serna, Ramón. *Ismos.* Madrid: Biblioteca Nueva, 1931.

Guglielmo, Angelo. *Avanguardia e sperimentalismo.* Milan: Feltrinelli, 1964.

Holthusen, Hans Egon. *Avantgardismus und die Zukunft der modernen Kunst.* Munich: Piper, 1964.

————, et al. *Avantgarde—Geschichte und Krise einer Idee. Gestalt und Gedanke,* no. 11. Munich: R. Oldenburg, 1966.

Hughes, Robert. *The Shock of the New.* New York: Knopf, 1981.

Jannini, Pasquale Aniel. *Le avanguardie letterarie nell'idea critica di Guillaume Apollinaire.* Rome: Bulzoni, 1971.

Kramer, Hilton. *The Age of the Avant-Garde.* New York: Farrar, Straus and Giroux, 1973.

Marino, Adrian. "Avangarda" and "Antiliteratura." In *Dictionar de idei literare,* pp. 177–224 and 100–159. Bucharest: Editura Eminescu, 1973.

Meyer, Leonard B. *Music, the Arts, and Ideas: Patterns and Predictions in Twentieth-Century Culture.* Chicago: University of Chicago Press, 1967.

Micheli, Mario de. *Le avanguardie artistiche del Novecento.* Milan: Feltrinelli, 1966.

Noszlopy, George T. "The Embourgeoisement of Avant-Garde Art." *Diogenes* 67 (Fall 1969): 83–190.

Plebe, A., T. Chiaretti, and V. Saltini. "Avanguradia e marxismo." *Angelus Novus* 3 (Spring 1965): 1–21.

Poggioli, Renato. *The Theory of the Avant-Garde* (in Italian). Translated by Gerald Fitzgerald. Cambridge, Mass.: Harvard University Press, 1968.

Raffa, Pietro. *Avanguardia e realismo.* Milan: Rizzoli, 1967.

Reszler, André. *L'Esthétique anarchiste.* Paris: Presses Universitaries de France, 1973.

Rosenberg, Harold. *The Anxious Object: Art Today and Its Audience.* New York: Horizon Press, 1964.

————. *The De-definition of Art.* New York: Collier Books, 1972.

————. *Discovering the Present.* Chicago: University of Chicago Press, 1973.

Russell, Charles. *Poets, Prophets, and Revolutionaries: The Literary Avant-Garde from Rimbaud through Postmodernism.* New York: Oxford University Press, 1985.

Sainz de Robles, Federico Carlos. "Vanguardismo." In *Ensayo de un Diccionario de la literatura,* vol. 1: *Términos, Conceptos, "Ismos" Literarios,* pp. 1192–93. Madrid: Aguilar, 1965.

Sanguineti, Edoardo. "Sopra l'avanguardia." *Il Verri* 8, no. 11 (December 1963): 15–19.

————. "Pour une avant-garde révolutionnaire." *Tel Quel* 29 (1967): 76–95.

————. "Sociologie de l'avant-garde." Followed by discussion of the paper by Robert Escarpit, Alphons Silbermann, Lucien Goldmann. In *Littérature et société: Problèmes de méthodologie en sociologie de la littérature,* pp. 11–29. Brussels: Editions de l'Institut de Sociologie de l'Université Libre de Bruxelles, 1967.

Shattuck, Roger. *The Banquet Years: The Origins of the Avant-Garde in France, 1885 to World War I*. Rev. ed. New York: Vintage Books, 1968.

Szabolcsi, Miklós. "Avant-Garde, Neo-Avant-Garde, Modernism: Questions and Suggestions." *New Literary History* 3 (1971–72): 49–70.

————. "L'avant-garde littéraire et artistique comme phénomène international." *Proceedings of the Vth Congress of the International Comparative Literature Association*, pp. 315–34. Amsterdam: Swets and Zeitlinger, 1969.

Torre, Guillermo de. *Historia de las literaturas de vanguardia*. 3 vols. Madrid: Ediciones Guadarrama, 1965, 1971. (First published as *Literaturas europeas de vanguardia*. Madrid: Caro Raggio, 1925.)

Volpe, Galvano della. "Sul concetto di 'avanguardia.'" *Critica del gusto*, pp. 159–60. 3d ed. Milan: Feltrinelli, 1966.

Weightman, John. *The Concept of the Avant-Garde*. La Salle, Ill.: Library Press, 1973.

Weisstein, Ulrich. "Le terme et le concept d'avant-garde en Allemagne." *Revue de l'Université de Bruxelles* 1 (1975): 10–37.

Weisgerber, Jean, ed. *Les Avant-gardes littéraires au XXe siècle. I. Histoire. II. Théorie*. Vols. 4 and 5 of *A Comparative History of Literatures in European Languages*. Sponsored by the International Comparative Literature Association. Budapest: Akadémiai Kiadó, 1984.

DECADENCE

Adorno, Theodor W. "Spengler Today." *Studies in Philosophy and Social Science* 9 (1941): 305–25.

Anceschi, Luciano. *Le poetiche del Novecento in Italia*. Milan: Marzorati, 1962.

Annoni, Carlo. *Il Decadentismo*. Brescia: La Scuola, 1982.

Aspects du décadentisme européen. Special issue of *Revue des sciences humaines*, no. 153 (1974).

Bernhart, Ingeborg. "*Décadence* und *Style décadent*." *Neohelicon* 2, nos. 3–4 (1974): 193–218.

Billy, André. *L'époque 1900 (1885–1905)*. Paris: Tallandier, 1951.

Binni, Walter. *La poetica del decadentismo*. Florence: Sansoni, 1961.

Bobbio, Norberto. *The Philosophy of Decadentism*. Translated by David Moore. Oxford: Blackwell, 1948. Originally published as *La filosofia del decadentismo* (Torino: Chiantore, 1944).

Bourget, Paul. *Essais de psychologie contemporaine*. Paris: Lemerre, 1893.

Buckley, Jerome Hamilton. *The Triumph of Time: A Study of the Victorian*

Concepts of Time, History, Progress, and Decadence. Cambridge, Mass.: Harvard University Press, 1966.

Carter, A. E. *The Idea of Decadence in French Literature, 1830–1900*. Toronto: University of Toronto Press, 1958.

Caudwell, Christopher. *Studies and Further Studies in a Dying Culture*. Introduction by Sol Yurick. New York and London: Monthly Review Press, 1971.

Cioran, E. M. *A Short History of Decay*. Translated by Richard Howard. Oxford: Blackwell, 1975. Originally published as *Précis de décomposition* (1949).

Croce, Benedetto. "Aesthetics." *Encyclopaedia Britannica*, 1929 edition.

————. *La poesia*. Bari: Laterza, 1946.

————. *Storia d'Europa nel secolo XIX*. Bari: Laterza, 1948.

————. *Storia dell'età barocca in Italia*. 5th ed. Bari: Laterza, 1967.

Curtius, Ernst Robert. "Entstehung und Wandlungen des Dekadenzproblems in Frankreich." *Internationale Monatsschrift für Wissenschaft, Kunst und Technik* 15 (1921): 147–66.

"Decadence." *Great Soviet Encyclopedia*, vol. 8, pp. 65–66. 3d ed. (English translation). New York: Macmillan, 1975.

Dowling, Linda C. *Aestheticism and Decadence: A Selective Annotated Bibliography*. New York: Garland, 1977.

Farmer, Albert J. *Le mouvement esthétique et 'décadent' en Angleterre (1873–1900)*. Paris: Champion, 1931.

Fischer, Ernst. "The Problem of Decadence." In *Art Against Ideology* (in German), translated by Anna Bostock, pp. 135–62. London: Allen Lane, Penguin Press, 1969.

Fletcher, Ian, ed. *Decadence in the 1890's*. London: E. Arnold, 1979.

Flora, Francesco. *Dal Romanticismo al Futurismo*. Rev. ed. Milan: Mondadori, 1925.

————. "Il Decadentismo." In *Problemi ed orientamenti critici di lingua e di letteratura italiana*, edited by Attilio Momigliano, vol. 3: *Questioni e correnti di storia letteraria*, pp. 761–810. Milan: Marzorati, 1949.

Frye, Northrop. "*The Decline of the West* by Oswald Spengler." *Daedalus* 103 (1974): 1–14.

Gabetti, Giuseppe. "Il Decadentismo." In *Dizionario letterario Bompiani delle opere e dei personaggi*, vol. 1: *Movimenti spirituali*, pp. 57–60. Milan: Bompiani, 1949.

Garaudy, Roger. *Literature of the Graveyard: Jean-Paul Sartre, François Mauriac, André Malraux, Arthur Koestler*. Translated by Joseph M. Bernstein. New York: International Publishers, 1948. Originally published as *Une littérature de fossoyeurs* (Paris, 1947).

Gilman, Richard. *Decadence: The Strange Life of an Epithet.* New York: Farrar, Straus and Giroux, 1979.

Ghidetti, Enrico, comp. *Il decadentismo.* Roma: Editori Riuniti, 1976.

Gioanola, Elio. *Il decadentismo.* Roma: Studium, 1972.

Gourmont, Remy de. *Decadence and Other Essays on the Culture of Ideas.* Translated by W. A. Bradley. New York: Harcourt, Brace and Co., 1921. Originally published as *La culture des idées*) (Paris: Mercure de France, 1900).

Huszar, George de. "Nietzsche's Theory of Decadence and the Transvaluation of All Values." *Journal of the History of Ideas* 6 (1945): 259–72.

Jankélévitch, Vladimir. "La Décadence." *Revue de méthaphysique et de morale* 55 (1950): 337–69.

Kahn, Gustave. *Symbolistes et décadents.* Paris: Vanier, 1902.

Kamerbeek, Jan. "'Style de décadence': Généalogie d'une formule." *Revue de littérature comparée* 39 (1965): 268–86.

Koppen, Erwin. *Dekadenter Wagnerismus: Studien zur europäischen Literatur des Fin de siècle.* Berlin and New York: Walter de Gruyter, 1973.

Kunne-Ibsch, Elrud. *Die Stellung Nietzsches in der Entwicklung der modernen Literaturwissenschaft.* Tübingen: Niemeyer, 1972. (Esp. chap. 8, "Die Begriffe 'Romantik,' 'Dekadenz,' 'Barock' und 'Klassik,'" pp. 166–237.)

Leone de Castris, Arcangelo. *Decadentismo e realismo.* Bari: Adriatica, 1959.

———. *Italo Svevo.* Pisa: Nistri-Lischi, 1959.

———. *Il decadentismo italiano.* Bari: De Donato, 1974.

Lethève, Jacques. "Le thème de la décadence dans les lettres françaises à la fin du XIX-e siècle." *Revue d'histoire littéraire de la France* 63 (1963): 46–61.

Marzot, Giulio. *Il decadentismo italiano.* Bologna: Cappelli, 1970.

Michaud, Guy. *Message poétique du symbolisme.* Paris: Nizet, 1961.

Momigliano, Attilio. "Intorno al decadentismo." *Storia della letteratura italiana*, pp. 584–615. Milan: Principato, 1947.

Nisard, Désiré. *Etudes de moeurs et de critique sur les poètes latins de la décadence.* 5th ed. Paris: Hachette, 1888.

———. *Essais sur l'école romantique.* Paris: Calman-Lévy, 1891.

Plekhanov, G. V. *Art and Social Life.* London: Lawrence and Wishart, 1953.

Petrini, Domenico. *Dal Barocco al Decadentismo.* Florence: Le Monnier, 1957.

Pierrot, Jean. *The Decadent Imagination, 1880–1900* (in French). Translated by Derek Coltman. Chicago: University of Chicago Press, 1981.

Poggioli, Renato. "*Qualis Artifex Pereo!* or Barbarism and Decadence." *Harvard Library Bulletin* 13 (1959): 135–59.

Pouilliart, Raymond. "Paul Bourget et l'esprit de la décadence." *Les lettres romanes* 5 (1951): 199–229.

Praz, Mario. *The Romantic Agony.* Translated by Angus Davidson. London: Oxford University Press, 1933. Originally published as *La carne, la morte e il diavolo nella letteratura romantica.*

————. *Il patto col serpente,* Milan: Mondadori, 1972.

Raynaud, Ernest. *La mêlée symboliste (1870–1910): Portraits et souvenirs.* Paris: La Renaissance du livre, 1920.

Reed, John R. *Decadent Style.* Athens: Ohio University Press, 1985.

Richard, Noël. *A l'aube du symbolisme: Hydropathes, fumistes et décadents.* Paris: Nizet, 1968.

————. *Le mouvement decadent: Dandys, esthètes et décadents.* Paris: Nizet, 1968.

Roda, Vittorio. *Decadentismo morale e decadentismo estetico.* Bologna: R. Pàtron, 1966.

Rudler, Madeleine. *Parnassiens, symbolistes et décadents.* Paris: Messein, 1938.

Ruprecht, Erich, and Bänsch, Dieter, eds. *Literarische Manifeste der Jahrhundertwende 1890–1910.* Stuttgart: J. B. Metzler, 1970. (See "Neue Romantik/'Fin de siècle' und 'Décadence,'" pp. 270–320.)

Russo, Luigi. *I Narratori (1850–1950).* New ed. Milan: Principato, 1950.

————. "La letteratura del decadentismo." In *Compendio storico della letteratura italiana,* pp. 713–37. Messina and Florence: D'Anna, 1961

Salinari, Carlo. *Miti e coscienza del decadentismo italiano.* 4th ed. Milan: Feltrinelli, 1969.

Sartre, Jean-Paul, et al. "Symposium on the Question of Decadence." In *Radical Perspectives in the Arts,* edited by Lee Baxandall, pp. 225–39. Baltimore: Penguin Books, 1972. Originally published as "Entretiens à Prague sur la notion de décadence" (*La Nouvelle critique* 6/7 [1964]: 71–84).

Schorske, Carl. E. *Fin de siècle Vienna: Politics and Culture.* New York: Knopf, 1980.

Scrivano, Riccardo. *Il decadentismo e la critica: Storia e antologia della critica.* Florence: La Nuova Italia, 1963.

Seroni, Adriano. *Il decadentismo.* Palermo: Palumbo, 1964.

Smith, James M. "Concepts of Decadence in Nineteenth-Century French Literature." *Studies in Philology* 50 (1953): 640–51.

Spengler, Oswald. *The Decline of the West.* New York: Knopf, 1950.

Swart, Koenraad W. *The Sense of Decadence in Nineteenth-Century France.* The Hague: Nijhoff, 1964.

Sydow, Eckart von. *Die Kultur der Dekadenz.* Dresden: Sibyllen-Verlag, 1922.

Thornton, R. K. R. *The Decadent Dilemma.* London: E. Arnold, 1983.

Van Bever, Pierre. "Signification du "Décadentisme.'" *Revue des langues vivantes* 34 (1968): 366–72.

Van Roosbroeck, G. L. *The Legend of the Decadents.* New York: Columbia University, Institut des Etudes Françaises, 1927.

Williams, W. D. *Nietzsche and the French: A Study of the Influence of Nietzsche's French Reading on His Thought.* Oxford: Blackwell, 1952.

Zhdanov, A. A. *Essays on Literature, Philosophy, and Music.* New York: International Publishers, 1950.

KITSCH

Adorno, Theodor W. "On Popular Music." *Studies in Philosophy and Social Science* 9 (1941): 17–48.

———. "Veblen's Attack on Culture." *Studies in Philosophy and Social Science* 9 (1941): 389–413.

———. *Ästhetische Theorie.* Frankfurt am Main: Suhrkamp, 1970.

Argan, Giulio Carlo, ed. *Il Revival.* Milano: G. Mazzotta, 1974.

Baldacci, Luigi. "Hermann Broch e il problema del 'kitsch.'" In *Le idee correnti,* pp. 47–51. Florence: Vallecchi, 1968.

Benjamin, Walter. "Traumkitsch." *Angelus Novus.* In *Ausgewählte Schriften,* vol. 2, pp. 158–60. Frankfurt am Main: Suhrkamp, 1966.

Brantlinger, Patrick. *Bread and Circuses: Theories of Mass Culture and Social Decay.* Ithaca: Cornell University Press, 1983.

Broch, Hermann. "Einige Bemerkungen zum Problem Kitsches" and "Der Kitsch." In *Gesammelte Werke,* vol. 6: *Dichten und Erkennen* (Essays, 1), pp. 295–309 and 342–48. Zürich: Rhein, 1955.

Brown, Curtis F. *Star-Spangled Kitsch.* New York: Universe Books, 1975.

Campos, Haroldo de. "Vanguarda e kitsch." In *A arte no horizonte do provável,* pp. 193–201. 2d ed. São Paulo: Editôra Perspectiva, 1972.

Celebonović, Aleksa. *Some Call It Kitsch.* New York: H. N. Abrams, 1974.

Cingria, Alexandre. *La Décadence de l'art sacré.* Lausanne: Les Cahiers Vaudois, 1917.

Deschner, Karlheinz. *Kitsch, Konvention und Kunst.* Frankfurt am Main: Ullstein, 1980.

Dorfles, Gillo. *Kitsch: The World of Bad Taste.* New York: Universe Books,

1969. New Italian edition, *Il kitsch: Antologia del cattivo gusto.* Milan: Mazzotta, 1972.

Durzak, Manfred. "Der Kitsch—seine verschiedenen Aspekte." *Der Deutschunterricht* 19, no. 1 (1967): 93–120.

Eco, Umberto. "La struttura del cattivo gusto." In *Apocalittici e Integrati,* pp. 67–132. Milan: Bompiani, 1965.

Egenter, Richard. *The Desecration of Christ.* Chicago: Franciscan Herald Press, 1967. Originally published as *Kitsch und Christenleben.*

Fetzer, Günther. *Wertungsprobleme in der Trivialliteraturforschung.* Munich: Fink, 1980.

Fry, Roger. "Art and Socialism." In *Vision and Design,* pp. 36–55. London: Chatto and Windus, 1920.

———. *Art and Commerce.* London: Hogarth Press, 1926.

Gans, Herbert J. *Popular Culture and High Culture: An Analysis and Evaluation of Taste.* New York: Basic Books, 1974.

Giesz, Ludwig. *Phänomenologie des Kitsches.* Heidelberg: Rothe, 1960. 2d ed. Munich: Fink, 1971.

Gómez de la Serna, Ramón. "Lo cursi." In *Lo cursi y otros ensayos,* pp. 7–54. Buenos Aires: Editorial Sudamericana, 1943.

Greenberg, Clement. "Avant-Garde and Kitsch." In *Art and Culture,* pp. 3–21. Boston: Beacon Press, 1965. Originally published in *Partisan Review* 6, no. 5 (Fall 1939).

Grimm, Reinhold, and Jost Hermand, eds. *Popularität und Trivialität: Fourth Wisconsin Workshop.* Frankfurt am Main: Athenäum, 1974.

Haden-Guest, Anthony. *The Paradise Program: Travels through Muzak, Hilton, Coca-Cola, Texaco, Walt Disney, and Other World Empires.* New York: Morrow, 1973.

Hermann, Wolfgang. "Der allein ausziehende Held: Zur Problematik literarischer Wertung am Beispiel des Abenteur-und Wildwestromans." *Deutsche Vierteljahrsschrift für Literaturwissenschaft und Geistesgeschichte* 46 (1972): 320–58.

Highet, Gilbert. "Kitsch." In *A Clerk of Oxenford,* pp. 210–19. New York: Oxford University Press, 1954.

Holthusen, Hans Egon. "Über den sauren Kitsch." In *Ja und Nein,* pp. 240–48. Munich: Piper, 1954.

Horkheimer, Max. "Art and Mass Culture." In *Critical Theory,* pp. 273–90. Reprinted from *Studies in Philosophy and Social Science* 9 (1941). New York: Herder and Herder, 1972.

Horkheimer, Max, and T. W. Adorno. *Dialectic of Enlightenment* (in German). Translated by John Cumming. New York: Herder and Herder, 1972.

Jacobs, Norman, ed. *Culture for the Millions?* Princeton, N.J.: Van Nostrand, 1961.

Killy, Walter. *Deutscher Kitsch: Ein Versuch mit Beispielen.* Göttingen: Vandenhoeck and Ruprecht, 1962.

Kramer, Hilton. "New Art of the 70's in Chicago: Visual Bluster and Camp Sensibility." *New York Times,* 14 July 1974, sec. 2, p. 19.

La Motte-Haber, Helga de, ed. *Das Triviale in Literatur, Musik und Bildender Kunst.* Frankfurt am Main: Klostermann, 1972.

Lewis, Wyndham, and Charles Lee, eds. *The Stuffed Owl: An Anthology of Bad Verse.* London: Dent, 1930.

Lowenthal, Leo. *Literature, Popular Culture, and Society.* Englewood Cliffs, N.J.: Pacific Books, 1961.

————. Intervention at the Symposium "The Comparative Method: Sociology and the Study of Literature." *Yearbook of Comparative and General Literature* 23 (1974): 13–18.

Macdonald, Dwight. "A Theory of Mass Culture." In *Mass Culture,* edited by Bernard Rosenberg and D. M. White, pp. 59–73. New York: Free Press, 1964. Originally published in *Diogenes* (Summer 1953): 1–17.

————. "Masscult and Midcult." In *Against the American Grain,* pp. 3–79. New York: Random House, 1962.

Moles, Abraham A. *Le kitsch: l'art du bonheur.* Paris: Mame, 1971.

Morin, Edgar. *L'Esprit du temps.* Paris: Grasset, 1962.

Nabokov, Vladimir. *Nikolai Gogol.* Norfolk, Conn.: New Directions, 1944. (For the definition of *poshlust,* see pp. 63–74.)

Osta, Jean d'. *Encyclopédie du kitsch.* Brussels: P. de Méyère, 1972.

Pignatari, Décio. "Comunicação e cultura de massas" and "Kitsch e repertorio." In *Informação, Linguagem, Comunicação.* São Paulo: Editôra Perspectiva, 1969.

Praz, Mario. "Il Kitsch" and "Kitschmuseum: un romanzo stile liberty." In *Il Patto col serpente,* pp. 483–87 and 488–505. Milan: Mondadori, 1972.

Ridless, Robin. *Ideology and Art: Theories of Mass Culture from Walter Benjamin to Umberto Eco.* New York: Peter Lang, 1984.

Rissover, Frederick, and David C. Birch. *Mass Media and the Popular Arts.* New York: McGraw-Hill, 1971.

Rosenberg, Bernard, and David Manning White, eds. *Mass Culture: The Popular Arts in America.* 1957. Reprint. Glencoe, Ill.: Free Press, 1964.

————. *Mass Culture Revisited.* New York: Van Nostrand and Reinhold, 1971.

Rosenberg, Harold. "Pop Culture: Kitsch Criticism." In *The Tradition of the New,* pp. 259–68. 2d ed. New York: McGraw-Hill, 1965.

Russell, John, and Suzi Gablik, eds. *Pop Art Redefined.* London: Thames and Hudson, 1969.

Schulte-Sasse, Jochen. *Die Kritik an der Trivialliteratur seit der Aufklä-rung: Studien zur Geschichte des modernen Kitschbergriffs.* Munich: Fink, 1971.

Schüling, H. *Zur Geschichte der ästhetischen Wertung: Bibliographie der Abhandlungen über den Kitsch.* Giessen, 1971.

Sontag, Susan. "Notes on Camp." In *Against Interpretation,* pp. 277–93. New York: Dell, Laurel Edition, 1969.

Sternberg, Jacques, comp. *Kitsch* (translated from French). New York: St. Martin's Press, 1972.

Suares, Jean-Claude. "Designer's Guide to Schlock, Camp & Kitsch—and the Taste of Things to Come." *Print* (January–February 1975): 25–35.

Ueding, Gert. *Glanzvolles Elend: Versuch über Kitsch und Kolportage.* Frankfurt am Main: Suhrkamp, 1973.

Wedekind, Frank. "Kitsch." Notes for an unfinished play. In *Gesammelte Werke,* vol. 9, pp. 207ff. Munich: Georg Müller, 1924.

Wellek, René. "The Comparative Method: Sociology and the Study of Literature." *Yearbook of Comparative and General Literature* 23 (1974): 18–20.

POSTMODERNISM

Allen, Donald, and George F. Butterick, eds. *The Postmoderns: The New American Poetry Revisited.* New York: Grove Press, 1982.

Altieri, Charles. "From Symbolist Thought to Immanence: The Ground of Postmodern American Poetics." *Boundary 2* 1 (1972–73): 605–41.

———. "Postmodernism: A Question of Definition." *Par Rapport* 2 (1979): 605–41.

Antin, David. "Modernism and Postmodernism: Approaching the Present in American Poetry." *Boundary 2* 1 (1972–73): 98–132.

Barth, John. *The Literature of Exhaustion and the Literature of Replenish-ment.* Northridge, Calif.: Lord John's Press, 1982.

Benamou, Michel, and Charles Caramello. *Performance in Postmodern Culture.* Madison, Wisc.: Coda Press, 1977.

Brooke-Rose, Christine. *A Rhetoric of the Unreal.* Cambridge: Cambridge University Press, 1981.

Calinescu, Matei. "Ways of Looking at Fiction." In *Romanticism, Modern-ism, Postmodernism,* edited by Harry R. Garvin, pp. 155–70. Special issue of *Bucknell Review*, vol. 25, no. 2 (1980). Lewisburg, Pa.: Bucknell University Press, 1980.

————. "From the One to the Many: Pluralism in Today's Thought." In *Innovation/Renovation*, edited by Ihab and Sally Hassan, pp. 263–89. Madison: University of Wisconsin Press, 1983.

————. "Postmodernism and Some Paradoxes of Periodization." In *Approaching Postmodernism*, edited by Douwe W. Fokkema and Hans Bertens, pp. 239–54. Amsterdam and Philadelphia: John Benjamins, 1986.

————. "Postmodernism: The Mimetic and Theatrical Fallacies." In *Exploring Postmodernism*, edited by M. Calinescu and D. W. Fokkema. Amsterdam and Philadelphia: John Benjamins (forthcoming).

Calinescu, Matei, and Douwe W. Fokkema, eds. *Exploring Postmodernism*. Amsterdam and Philadelphia: John Benjamins (forthcoming).

Caramello, Charles. *Silverless Mirrors: Book, Self, and Postmodern American Fiction*. Tallahassee: University Presses of Florida, 1983.

Eco, Umberto. *Postscript to "The Name of the Rose"* (in Italian). Translated by William Weaver. New York: Harcourt Brace Jovanovich, 1984.

Federman, Raymond, ed. *Surfiction: Fiction Now and Tomorrow*. 2d ed. Chicago: Swallow Press, 1981.

Fiedler, Leslie. *The Collected Essays of Leslie Fiedler*. New York: Stein and Day, 1971.

Fokkema, Douwe W. *Literary History, Modernism, and Postmodernism*. Amsterdam and Philadelphia: John Benjamins, 1984.

Fokkema, Douwe W., and Hans Bertens, eds. *Approaching Postmodernism*. Amsterdam and Philadelphia: John Benjamins, 1986.

Foster, Hal. *The Anti-Aesthetic: Essays on Postmodern Culture*. Port Townsend, Wash.: Bay Press, 1983.

Garvin, Harry R., ed. *Romanticism, Modernism, Postmodernism*. Special issue of *Bucknell Review*, vol. 25, no. 2 (1980). Lewisburg, Pa.: Bucknell University Press, 1980.

Graff, Gerald. *Literature Against Itself*. Chicago: University of Chicago Press, 1979.

Greenberg, Clement. *The Notion of 'Post-Modern'*. Fourth Sir William Dobell Memorial Lecture, University of Sydney, 1980. Sydney: Bloxham and Chambers, 1980.

Habermas, Jürgen. "Modernity versus Postmodernity." *New German Critique* 22 (Winter 1981): 3–14.

————. "Questions and Counterquestions." In *Habermas on Modernity*, edited by Richard Bernstein. Cambridge, Mass.: MIT Press, 1985.

Hassan, Ihab. *Paracriticisms: Seven Speculations of the Times*. Urbana: University of Illinois Press, 1975.

————. *The Right Promethean Fire*. Urbana: University of Illinois Press, 1980.

————. *The Dismemberment of Orpheus: Toward a Postmodern Literature*. 2d ed. Madison: University of Wisconsin Press, 1982.

————. *The Postmodern Turn: Essays in Postmodern Theory and Culture*. Columbus: Ohio State University Press, 1987.

Hassan, Ihab, and Sally Hassan, eds. *Innovation/Renovation: New Perspectives in the Humanities*. Madison: University of Wisconsin Press, 1983.

Hoesterey, Ingeborg. "Die Moderne am Ende? Zu den ästhetischen Positionen von Jürgen Habermas und Clement Greenberg." *Zeitschrift für ästhetik und allgemeine Kunstwissenschaft* 29, no. 1 (1984): 19–32.

Hutcheon, Linda. *A Theory of Parody: The Teachings of Twentieth-Century Art Forms*. New York and London: Methuen, 1985.

Huyssen, Andreas. *After the Great Divide: Modernism, Mass Culture, Postmodernism*. Bloomington and Indianapolis: Indiana University Press, 1986.

Jameson, Fredric. "Postmodernism and Consumer Society." In *The Anti-Aesthetic*, edited by Hal Foster, pp. 111–25. Port Townsend, Wash.: Bay Press, 1983.

Jencks, Charles. *The Language of Post-Modern Architecture*. New York: Rizzoli, 1977.

————. *Late-Modern Architecture*. New York: Rizzoli, 1980.

————. *Post-Modern Classicism: The New Synthesis*. London: Academy Editions, 1980.

————. *Current Architecture*. London: Academy Editions, 1982.

Klinkowitz, Jerome. *Literary Disruptions: The Making of a Post-Contemporary American Fiction*. 2d ed. Urbana: University of Illinois Press, 1980.

Klinkowitz, Jerome, and James Knowlton. *Peter Handke and the Postmodernist Transformation*. Columbia: University of Missouri Press, 1983.

Köhler, Michael. "'Postmodernismus': ein begriffshistorischer Überblick." *Amerikastudien* 22, no. 1 (1977): 8–17.

Levin, Harry. "What Was Modernism?" In *Refractions*, pp. 271–95. New York: Oxford University Press, 1966.

Lodge, David. "Modernism, Antimodernism, Postmodernism." In *Working with Structuralism*, pp. 3–16. London: Routledge and Kegan Paul, 1981.

Lyotard, Jean-François. *The Postmodern Condition: Report on Knowledge*.

Translated by Geoff Bennington and Brian Massumi. Minneapolis: University of Minnesota Press, 1984. Originally published as *La Condition postmoderne: Rapport sur le savoir* (Paris: Minuit, 1979).

―――. *Le Postmoderne expliqué aux enfants.* Paris: Galilée, 1986.

Mazzaro, Jerome. *Postmodern American Poetry.* Urbana: University of Illinois Press, 1980.

Modernity and Postmodernity. Special issue of *New German Critique* 33 (Fall 1984).

Morrissette, Bruce. "Post-Modern Generative Fiction." *Critical Inquiry* 2 (1975): 253–62.

Newman, Charles. *The Post-Modern Aura: The Act of Fiction in an Age of Inflation.* Evanston, Ill.: Northwestern University Press, 1985.

Perloff, Marjorie. *The Poetics of Indeterminacy: Rimbaud to Cage.* Princeton: Princeton University Press, 1981.

―――. *The Dance of the Intellect: Studies in the Poetry of the Pound Tradition.* Cambridge: Cambridge University Press, 1985.

Portoghesi, Paolo, et al., eds. *The Presence of the Past: First International Exhibition of Architecture—Venice Biennale 1980.* London: Academy Editions, 1980.

―――. *After Modern Architecture* (in Italian). Translated by Meg Shore. New York: Rizzoli, 1982.

―――. *Postmodern, the Architecture of the Post-industrial Society* (in Italian). Translated by Ellen Schapiro. New York: Rizzoli, 1983.

Rorty, Richard. "Habermas and Lyotard on Postmodernity." In *Habermas on Modernity,* edited by Richard Bernstein, pp. 161–76. Cambridge, Mass.: MIT Press, 1985.

Scarpetta, Guy. *L'Impureté.* Paris: Grasset, 1985.

Spanos, William V. "The Detective at the Boundary: Some Notes on the Postmodern Literary Imagination." *Boundary 2* 1 (1972–73): 147–68.

―――. "De-Struction and the Question of Postmodernist Literature: Toward a Definition." *Par Rapport* 2 (1979): 107–22.

―――, ed. *Martin Heidegger and the Question of Literature: Toward a Postmodern Literary Hermeneutics.* Bloomington: Indiana University Press, 1979.

Steiner, George. "In a Post-Culture." In *Extraterritorial: Papers on Literature and the Language Revolution,* pp. 155–71. New York: Atheneum, 1971.

Toulmin, Stephen. "The Construal of Reality: Criticism in Modern and Postmodern Science." In *The Politics of Interpretation,* edited by W. J. T. Mitchell, pp. 99–117. Chicago: University of Chicago Press, 1983.

Vattimo, Gianni. *La fine de la modernità: Nichilismo ed ermeneutica nella cultura postmoderna*. Milan: Garzanti, 1985.

Venturi, Robert. *Complexity and Contradiction in Architecture*. 2d ed. New York: Museum of Modern Art, 1977.

Venturi, Robert, with Denise Scott Brown and Steven Izenour. *Learning from Las Vegas*. Cambridge, Mass.: MIT Press, 1972.

Wilde, Alan. *Horizons of Assent: Modernism, Postmodernism, and the Ironic Imagination*. Baltimore: Johns Hopkins University Press, 1981.

Zavarzadeh, Mas'ud. *The Mythopoeic Reality: The Postwar American Non-fiction Novel*. Urbana: University of Illinois Press, 1976.

INDEX

THE AUTHOR

Matei Calinescu is Professor of Comparative Literature, English, and West European Studies at Indiana University, Bloomington. His books and articles include studies on modernism, postmodernism, and the relations between literature, religion, and politics. A volume entitled *Exploring Postmodernism,* which he has coedited with D. W. Fokkema, is forthcoming, and among his current projects is a book-length study of Mircea Eliade's fiction.